Veröffentlichungen zum Verfahrensrecht
Band 50

herausgegeben von
Rolf Stürner und Gerhard Walter

GW00546312

Neil Andrews

The Modern Civil Process

Judicial and Alternative Forms
of Dispute Resolution in England

Mohr Siebeck

Neil Andrews, born 1959; studied law at Oxford University; currently a member of the Law Faculty of Cambridge University, Bencher of Middle Temple in London and barrister.

ISBN 978-3-16-149532-8
ISSN 0722-7574 (Veröffentlichungen zum Verfahrensrecht)

The Deutsche Nationalbibliothek lists this publication in the Deutsche Nationalbibliographie; detailed bibliographic data is available in the internet at *http://dnb.d-nb.de*.

© 2008 by Mohr Siebeck, P. O. Box 2040, D-72010 Tübingen.

The book was set by Computersatz Staiger in Rottenburg/N., printed by Gulde-Druck in Tübingen on non-aging paper and bound by Buchbinderei Held in Rottenburg.

Printed in Germany.

For Tony Jolowicz

Professor Emeritus of Comparative Law,
University of Cambridge, Fellow of Trinity College,
Cambridge, QC

Dr hc (National University of Mexico), LL D (hc)
(University of Buckingham), Honorary Bencher of Gray's Inn,
Chevalier de la Légion d'Honneur (France)

And for Elizabeth, Sam, Hannah and Ruby

Foreword by Lord Mustill*

The opportunity to offer some words of welcome to this excellent book is not to be missed. Its virtues are plain at first sight. Foremost among them is accessibility. For anyone in search of information about English procedural law and practice the first problem is to know where to look, since the pathways are often hard to find. Fortunately, the present work makes this task altogether less demanding, for it is clearly and logically laid out, so much so that it would be possible to navigate by reference to the table of contents alone, without recourse to the index. In this particular field, however, it is not enough simply to locate the materials, for they must then be understood, usually an unappealing task given that the sources and commentaries on English procedural law tend, with a few honourable exceptions, to vary between the desiccated and the penitential. The present work is such an exception, for its free and open style make it easy, and indeed pleasurable, to read, and students who are called on to study it will have much to be thankful for.

At the other extreme, the book provides the researcher and professional with a gateway to a fund of cosmopolitan sources, drawn from the author's extensive learning and research. Whilst the text is mercifully free from citations even a glance at the foot of almost every page is enough to show that there are whole strata of resources ready to be mined.

Most importantly, this breadth of perspective has enabled the author to position the book where it is most needed; that is, at the confluence of national systems of civil justice, where steps towards procedural harmonisation are currently under way. This is a much more difficult undertaking than the kindred process for substantive laws. The reason is essentially cultural. Where the task is to approximate the content of positive legal rules the two essentials are a desire to make it work, and the maturity to recognise that this will require the professional to cast aside some of the learning which he or she has painstakingly acquired and subsequently honed by long experience. The process can sometimes be painful, but patience will usually prevail.

---

* Fellow of the British Academy; LL D (Cantab); leading commercial arbitrator; distinguished author on arbitration; formerly a Lord of Appeal in Ordinary, House of Lords, London.

With procedural law the position is not the same, for reasons which are essentially cultural, and deeply engrained. Here, those involved are not so much engaged in comparing statutes and lists of rules as trying to find common ground between contrasting methods of approaching, resolving and articulating conflicts in the real world. Anyone who attempts this task must accept that these methods are a reflection of the general cultural environment into which the individual has been immersed throughout his or her lifetime, and that they may unconsciously be carried over into the specialist world of the law.

This can foster a tenacious devotion to a particular form of national procedural regime, where even the most open-minded of lawyers may assume that their own system is best, simply because it accords with their own intellectual make-up. For this, the best remedy is information about other systems; information which is clear, free from nationalistic bias, and of sufficient calibre to acquaint the reader not only with the rules prescribed but also with at least a part of the reasons why they take the shape which they do. So informed, the professional is in a much better position to form a balanced and unprejudiced judgment on where compromises can best be made. This function the present work admirably performs.

There is something in this book for everyone. I am glad to wish it the success which it deserves.

Acknowledgements

The themes of this book are introduced in chapter one. I have tried to write an accessible and relatively succinct account of a subject which is notoriously technical, fast-moving, multi-layered, and inter-connected. If I have succeeded, I hope that this book will be useful to lawyers in all jurisdictions and at all levels who are interested in discovering the main patterns and methods of English civil justice. The text is based upon materials available to me (with reasonable diligence) at the end of July 2007.

Here I would like to express my gratitude to various people and bodies.

Colin Turpin and Jillaine Seymour kindly took over my College duties during my sabbatical leave in the first nine months of 2007. Peter Zawada in the Squire Law Library was a tower of strength. The University of Cambridge and Clare College provided me with the free-time and space to complete this project. Natalie Moore helped me with the editing of the text. She did a superb job.

Professor Dr iur Rolf Stürner kindly introduced me to the publishers (see n 2 chapter 1 for my long association with him). In placing these English materials and developments before an international readership, I am delighted to have received the encouragement of this famous scholar and the support of this distinguished publishing house. I am grateful to Lord Mustill for his generous foreword.

Tony Jolowicz, to whom I respectfully dedicate this book, will require no introduction to this international readership. In the early 1980s, he introduced me to 'civil justice' and to the remarkable world of comparative procedural studies. I am sorry that this appears too late to coincide with his eightieth birthday. I wish him, Poppy, his wife, and their family, much happiness.

21 August, 2007   N.H.A.
Cambridge

Contents

Part I

The New Landscape of Civil Justice

Chapter 1

'Courts of Last Resort':
The Decline of Public Adjudication[1]

Contents

(1) Foreign Interest in English Systems of Dispute Resolution

Lawyers in many countries have told me that they are interested in the modern   **1.01**
and dynamic Common Law system of civil procedure and dispute resolution.[2]
This interest reflects the commercial importance of English law and, of course,
the economic domination of the United States of America.

In fact English law is sandwiched between civil law Europe and the distinc-   **1.02**
tive Common Law system of the USA.[3] The main aim of this work is to show

---

[1] Citation: unless otherwise stated, the place of publication of books referred to in this work is London.

[2] Professor Dr iur Rolf Stürner encouraged me to publish this work in Germany. I have had the pleasure to collaborate with him since 2000, when we were members of the working group on the American Law Institute/UNIDROIT's *Principles of Transnational Civil Procedure* (on line at: http://www.unidroit.org/english/principles/civilprocedure/main.htm); also published as *ALI/UNIDROIT: Principles of Transnational Civil Procedure* (Cambridge UP, 2006); the working group's membership was as follows: Neil Andrews, Clare College, Cambridge, UK; Professor Frédérique Ferrand, Lyon, France; Professor Pierre Lalive, University of Geneva and practice as an arbitrator, Switzerland; Professor Masanori Kawano, Nagoya University, Japan; Madame Justice Aida Kemelmajer de Carlucci, Supreme Court, Mendoza, Argentina; Professor Geoffrey Hazard, USA; Professor Ronald Nhlapo, formerly of the Law Commission, South Africa; Professor Dr iur Rolf Stürner, University of Freiburg, Germany. The two General Reporters for the UNIDROIT project were Professors Hazard and Stürner; the two reporters for the ALI project were Professors Hazard (Hastings College of the Law, San Francisco) and Taruffo (University of Pavia, Italy).

[3] For references to US literature, see **[A] on the decline of adjudication**: Oscar Chase, *Law, Culture, and Ritual: Disputing Systems in Cross-Cultural Context* (New York UP, 2005), ch 6; M Galanter, 'The Vanishing Trial ... in Federal and State Courts' (2004) 1 J

how English law has adapted (and needs to continue to adapt) to offer an attractive and modern system of civil justice. But this book is not confined to court litigation. Arbitration and mediation are also examined, as well as out-of-court settlement by private agreement, see chapters 10 to 12.

(2) The English Civil Procedural Code ('CPR')

1.03   English civil procedure is governed by the new procedural code, the Civil Procedure Rules (1998) ('the CPR'). Parts II and V of this book (chapters 2 to 9, and 14) examine that system. The new code has changed the culture of English court-based litigation. English civil procedure has moved from an antagonistic style to a more co-operative ethos. Lawyers have adapted to the judicial expectation that they should no longer pursue their clients' interests in a relentless and aggressive manner.

Empirical Legal Studies 451; J Resnik, 'For Owen M Fiss: Some Reflections on the Triumph and Death of Adjudication' (2003) 58 Miami U L Rev 173; J Resnik 'Whither and Whether Adjudication' (2006) 86 Boston ULRev 1101, 1123 ff; J Resnik, 'Uncovering, Discovering and Disclosing How the Public Dimensions of Court-Based Processes are at Risk' (2006) 81 Chicago-Kent LR 521 and J Resnik and DE Curtis, 'From "Rites" to "Rights" of Audience: The Utilities and Contingencies of the Public's Role in Court Business' in A Masson and K O'Connor (eds), *Representation of Justice* (Brussels, 2007); A Miller, 'The Pre-trial Rush to Judgment: Are the "Litigation Explosion", "Liability Crisis", and Efficiency Cliches Eroding our Day in Court and Jury Commitments?'(2003) 78 NYULRev 982; [B] **on the rise of ADR and settlement**: O Fiss, 'Against Settlement' (1984) Yale LJ 1073 (for references to the debate which this engendered in the US, O Fiss and J Resnik, *Adjudication and Its Alternatives* (Foundation Press, New York, 2003) 481, 488); M Galanter and M Cahill, 'Most Cases Settle: Judicial Promotion and Regulation of Settlements' (1994) 46 Stanford L Rev 1329; DR Hensler, 'Out Courts, Ourselves: How the ADR Movement is Reshaping our Legal System' (2003) 108 Penn State L Rev 165; Judith Resnik, 'Many Doors? Closing Doors? Alternative Dispute Resolution and Adjudication' (1995) 10 Ohio State Journal on Dispute Resolution 211; Steve Subrin, 'A Traditionalist Looks at Mediation' (2003) 3 Nevada LJ 196; and other US literature cited in and O Fiss and J Resnik, *Adjudication and Its Alternatives* (Foundation Press, New York, 2003), ch 4, notably p 495 and O Chase, *The Rise of ADR in Cultural Context, in Law,Culture, and Ritual: Disputing Systems in Cross-Cultural Context* (NYU Press, 2005), ch 6; [C] **general introductions**: G Hazard and M Taruffo, *American Civil Procedure* (Yale UP, 1993); Oscar Chase, *The Rise of ADR in Cultural Context, in Law, Culture, and Ritual: Disputing Systems in Cross-Cultural Context* (New York Univ Press, 2005); J Resnik, *Processes of the Law* (Foundation Press, New York, 2004); S Subrin and M Woo, *Litigating in America* (Aspen, New York, 2006); [D] **comparative discussion**: Oscar Chase, Helen Hershkoff, Linda Silberman, Vincenzo Varano, Yasuhei Taniguchi, Adrian Zuckerman, *Civil Procedure in Comparative Context* (Thomson West, 2007); John H Langbein, 'Cultural Chauvinism in Comparative Law' (1997) 5 Cardozo J of Int & Comp L 41.

The central tenets of the new code are set out in Part One of the CPR, 'The   **1.04**
Overriding Objective' (for the text see **2.14**). One tenet is 'proportionality'.
This is a broad concept. It regulates allocation of actions to suitable levels of
court (**2.15, 3.04, 3.13**). It also determines the intensity with which proceedings are structured and prepared. A related tenet is the need for focus: the parties and court, especially through case management (**3.14 ff**), should concentrate on the heart of the dispute rather than side issues. A third tenet is avoidance of delay: for this purpose, court-fixed timetables and trial dates are the
main instruments (**3.14**).

In many fields of dispute, parties and their lawyers must now comply with   **1.05**
pre-action protocols (see further **3.01 ff, 6.07**). These regulate preparation of a
case before commencement of formal proceedings (**3.04**). The main function
of these protocols is to assist the parties to settle the case. The rules contained
in the protocols are largely self-executing and require the disputants to co-
operate. The courts become involved in the pre-action phase of litigation only
retrospectively, once proceedings have begun. The judges are then prepared to
criticise parties who have failed to comply with the pre-action protocol. The
courts have a wide discretion to adjust costs orders to reflect this criticism
(**3.02**).

There has been a significant reduction in litigation before the ordinary   **1.06**
courts, especially in the High Court. During the last three decades of the twentieth century, too much court traffic had clogged up the litigation system. But
this crisis has now disappeared. Waiting times for hearings are now much
shorter, or have even disappeared (**2.22**).

Business and other civil disputes arising in England can now be processed   **1.07**
or resolved within four distinct but complementary general 'systems' or zones
of civil justice: pure settlement negotiations (without the intervention of a third
party 'neutral'); mediated settlement; arbitration; court proceedings. Of these
the first three are the great pillars of 'alternative civil justice'. Settlement, mediation and arbitration are examined in Part III, at chapters 10 to 12.

Not all of this is new. Arbitration has a long history in England. Settlement   **1.08**
has always been the most common method of terminating a dispute. So what is
new?

(3) The Rise of Mediation in England

In the author's opinion, the most significant change is recognition of media-   **1.09**
tion's potential as a means of achieving settlement. Three waves of change are
discernible.

First, the private market of dispute resolution in England has embraced me-   **1.10**
diation in civil and commercial matters (see chapter 11). The expense of court

litigation has been a powerful factor (see **2.23**). In response, a new profession of private mediators has arisen, many of these being former practitioners or judges. But not all mediators are legally qualified, nor of course need they be. Some mediators who are lawyers operate only part-time, the rest of their professional energy being devoted to clients. English solicitors, but especially barristers, have been learning new tricks, or rather a new art. Furthermore, a new literature has emerged (see the bibliography at **11.65**).

1.11   The second major change is that the English courts have shown impressive enthusiasm for mediation. English law has no system of 'mandatory mediation': it does not require parties to court proceedings first to mediate before permitting judicial examination of the case (**11.36** to **11.39**). Nor do English judges directly engage in mediation sessions. Nor can an English court issue a positive order backed by a direct sanction that parties must mediate. But the courts are prepared to induce mediation indirectly: by staying court proceedings so that the opportunity for mediation is created; and by making adverse costs orders if a party unreasonably rejects a suggestion to attempt mediation (a 'stay' is an order prohibiting further activity in the action; this bar remains effective until lifted by the court: see **11.31**, **11.38**).[4] The opposing party can make such a suggestion either before or after commencement of formal proceedings. Or the court can itself suggest a pause (a 'stay', as just explained) for out-of-court mediation, sometimes even without one of the parties requesting this. These forms of judicial influence are explained at **11.31** ff.

1.12   Thirdly, it has become recognised that settlement can take place at several occasions and as a result of different factors or procedural stimuli. It might occur before proceedings, especially under the influence of pre-action protocols (see further **6.07**). Or settlement might be the result of mediation. Mediation can take place before or during formal proceedings, or even after judgment, while an appeal is pending. Furthermore, settlement might be achieved following adherence to a dispute resolution clause. Such a clause normally requires the parties to a transaction to endeavour 'in good faith' to resolve their dispute by proceeding through these stages (**11.46**): negotiation, mediation, and finally adjudication (the last either by arbitration or a judge).

---

[4] CPR 3.1(2)(f).

(4) Reasons for the Rise of 'ADR'
(Alternative Dispute Resolution)

The rise of mediation, consolidation of a settlement culture, and in general the   **1.13**
emphasis now placed upon ADR, are exciting and interesting developments.
The 'public route' to judgment has become a matter of 'last resort' in England.
Why has there been this change of emphasis?

One explanation is economic. The wider public, even large companies and   **1.14**
government departments, no longer wish to spend large sums on litigation.
Commercial or other complex litigation requires expensive legal representation. Even preparation for possible litigation can consume large sums.[5] This
sense of dissatisfaction amongst potential litigants has grown in recent years.
But it can hardly occasion surprise. The Civil Procedure Rules (1998), although
excellent in many respects, did not alter the system of remuneration for lawyers. The financial background is well known. Law firms require revenue. Litigation is a source of fees. Individual lawyers have 'billing targets'. Billing clients by the hour naturally leads to the search for more 'billable' hours in preparation for trial (**2.23; 9.03; 11.19; 13.28**).

Furthermore, the economic malaise is not just a private aversion to high   **1.15**
costs. Government also needs to practise economy. The court system can become a major drain on public resources. Consider the range of expenditure: on
construction and maintenance of court buildings, information technology
systems, the salaries and pensions of judges and court-staff, and expenditure
on 'legal aid'. Since the Access to Justice Act 1999, this last category of expenditure has been 'capped'.

There are also non-economic factors affecting a disputant's decision to en-   **1.16**
ter settlement negotiations, or to attend a mediation session, or to pursue arbitration. He might wish to avoid the uncertainty, delay, and publicity of court
litigation (**13.13**). There is also the remoteness of the court system: by electing
to go to court, the parties have decided to hand the matter over to lawyers and
to the judicial system. By contrast, disputants can retain greater control if they
keep their dispute close to their organisation, conducting private settlement
negotiations, perhaps permitting a mediator to intervene.

---

[5] In a complex commercial dispute, one party recently spent £1M ensuring that it could
comply with the Technology and Construction Court's pre-action protocol for 'construction and engineering disputes' (personal communication); in April 2007 a new version of
this pre-action protocol was adopted; as the CPR site states: 'The Pre-Action Protocol for
Construction and Engineering Disputes has been revised and reissued following consultation to address issues relating to the time and cost of complying with the protocol.' For the
text of the April 2007 version, see http://www.dca.gov.uk/civil/procrules_fin/contents/front
matter/notes44_advance.htm.

1.17   These private choices, whether economic or otherwise, are supported and channelled by Government and judicial activity. The new premise is that court litigation must be regarded as a matter of 'last resort' in England. The civil justice system (embracing its four main forms, settlement, mediation, arbitration, and court litigation, see **1.07**) is a complex relationship between private interest and public policy; it involves interplay between private mechanisms and public facilities; and it requires contact and co-operation between private agents and public servants.

(5) Sceptical Voices

1.18   But there are sceptical voices. The three main anxieties concerning 'the flight to private justice' are: (i) secrecy (ii) the private status of the 'neutral' (no longer a public judge holding tenure, but a hired mediator), and (iii) the fear of one-sided or unfair settlement agreements. These concerns are considered in chapters 10 and 11 but will be introduced here.

Secrecy

1.19   The traditional aim of litigation before the courts has been to enable unequal parties (as they nearly always are) to enjoy 'equality of arms' in a public forum before an independent and impartial tribunal.[6] Through that public process, wrongdoing can be exposed; rights can be vindicated or newly recognised; people can vent their complaints and frustration, or direct their lawyers to express this sense of grievance. Ironically, at the time when many disputes have gone underground, English court judgments have become more accessible. Nowadays these judgments can be read on 'laptops', perhaps on hilltops, from China to Peru. Such is the miracle of electronic access.[7] By contrast, confidential settlement arrangements or the secret processes of mediation and arbitration bar public access.

1.20   Because of the high level of settlement, civil trial has always been a relatively rare event within the Common Law system. But now there is the fear that the stream of reasoned judgments will virtually dry up. In the author's opinion, this fear is misplaced.

---

[6] On these, and other aspects of European human rights law in this field, **2.11**.

[7] eg, using the (free) cornucopia of English and other legal materials at: http://www.bailii.org/

Private Mediators

English mediation is currently a private activity. There is no central or official   **1.21**
regulation. Admittedly, mediators can become 'accredited'. This involves
training by private mediation organisations. It is doubtful whether this laissez-
faire system will long escape interference from national or European authorities.

Inequality and Unfairness

Settlements, spontaneous or mediated, might not achieve a fair adjustment of   **1.22**
the partics' interests. One party's greater economic power or superior knowledge might have shaped the outcome. Adjudication might have corrected such
inequality.

(6) Aspects of Continuity

Although court litigation has declined, it has not collapsed. Court litigation   **1.23**
will retain an important place in the English civil justice system (**13.19** ff).
Commercial arbitration in London also remains strong (on this see chapter
12). Chapter 13 considers the 'global market-place' for dispute resolution.
English law continues to make an important contribution to transnational litigation.

Part II

Court Proceedings

Chapter 2

The Framework of English Civil Litigation

Contents

(1) Introduction[1]

This chapter contains an overview of litigation under the Civil Procedure Rules **2.01** (the 'CPR'), the English code of civil procedure.[2] We begin, in section (2) of this chapter, with a brief description of the English system of courts, lawyers, and its general legal methods. Sections (3) to (5) explain the main aspects of the English system of civil procedure and evidence, and provide brief assess-

---

[1] Civil Procedure Rules (1998): accessible at: http://www.justice.gov.uk/civil/procrules_fin/menus/rules.htm.

Other literature: Lord Woolf, *Access to Justice: Interim Report* (Stationery Office, June 1995); *Access to Justice: Final Report* (Stationery Office, July 1996); *Blackstone's Civil Practice* (Oxford UP); *Civil Procedure* ('the White Book') (regular new editions); *Civil Court Practice* ('the Green Book') (regular new editions); Neil Andrews, *English Civil Procedure* (Oxford UP, 2003); *Halsbury's Laws of England* (4th edn, 2001 re-issue), *Practice and Procedure*, vol 37, (by Master John Leslie, QBD); Sir Jack Jacob, *The Fabric of English Civil Justice* (1987) (a classic distillation of the pre-CPR system, presented as the Hamlyn Lectures for 1986); JA Jolowicz, *On Civil Procedure* (Cambridge UP, 2000) (including comparative themes); AAS Zuckerman and Ross Cranston (eds), *The Reform of Civil Procedure* (Oxford UP, 1995); *Zuckerman on Civil Procedure* (2nd edn, 2006); AAS Zuckerman (ed), *Civil Justice in Crisis: Comparative Perspectives of Civil Procedure* (Oxford UP, 1999); see also R Cranston, *How Law Works: The Machinery and Impact of Civil Justice* (Oxford UP, 2006), esp ch 5.

[2] Note on Abbreviations: CCR (County Court Rules; sch 2 to the Civil Procedure Rules accommodates the survivors; again the intention is that they should be phased out); *CPR* (Civil Procedure Rules, effective from 26 April, 1999, enacted SI 1998/3132, but with many later amendments); *PD* eg PD (3) 4.1 (Practice Directions appended to the Civil Procedure Rules; the relevant 'Part' of those rules is given in round brackets and the relevant paragraph is then indicated); *RSC* (Rules of the Supreme Court; some of these survive in sch 1 to the Civil Procedure Rules, but the intention is to phase them out).

ment of these changes. Section (6) charts the main phases of court proceedings, including the important pre-action phase.

(2) General Aspects of English Courts and the Legal Professions

2.02   This sub-section is intended to delineate the essential features of this system.
There is a very useful description of the court system in each year's issue of *Judicial Statistics*[3] and in specialist works.[4]

Civil Courts

2.03   The two civil courts of first instance are the county courts and the High Court.[5]
Small claims and actions for moderate amounts must be commenced in the
county courts (see **3.05**). These are located in many cities and towns.[6] Actions
for larger sums proceed to the High Court, which sits in the main provincial
cities and in London (for monetary and other criteria governing allocation to
the different first instance courts, see **3.05**). There is no longer a right to appeal
from a first instance decision (**8.12**). Instead, permission to appeal must be obtained from the first instance court or from the relevant appellate court. In this
way, appeals are controlled. The Court of Appeal hears appeals from judgments made by High Court judges. Final appeal to the House of Lords occurs
in relatively few actions each year (see also **2.08**).

2.04   The Ministry of Justice and the Secretary of State for Justice have overall responsibility for the administration of justice in civil and criminal matters.[7]
Judges are appointed by the Judicial Appointments Commission[8] from the ranks

---

[3] The latest issue, the 2005 report as revised in August 2006, is available at: http://www.
official-documents.gov.uk/document/cm69/6903/6903.pdf.

[4] Full accounts: C Elliott and F Quinn, *English Legal System* (7th edn, 2006); G Slapper
and D Kelly, *The English Legal System* (8th edn, 2006).

[5] *http://www.hmcourts-service.gov.uk/* and http://www.direct.gov.uk/en/Gtgl1/Guide
ToGovernment/Judiciary/DG_4003285.

[6] http://www.hmcourts-service.gov.uk/HMCSCourtFinder/.

[7] http://www.justice.gov.uk/.

[8] For discussion of judicial appointments in England, and in many other jurisdictions, K
Malleson and PH Russell (eds), *Appointing Judges in an Age of Judicial Power: Critical Per-
spectives from around the World* (University of Toronto Press, 2006); on the position in
England, ibid ch 2, by K Malleson; see also: *http://www.judicialappointments.gov.uk/* ('...
It does so on merit, through fair and open competition, from the widest range of eligible
candidates'); for details of their background, P Darbishire, 'Where do English and Welsh
Judges Come From?' [2007] CLJ 365.

of practising solicitors or barristers.[9] Traditionally, High Court judges have been former barristers.[10] The distinctive feature of the English judiciary is that appointments are made only after a lawyer has gained extensive experience of practice as a solicitor or barrister. In other words, England has no 'career judiciary'. Judges sitting in the county court are known as 'district judges' (or 'deputy district judges'), or 'circuit judges', or 'recorders (civil)'.[11] The High Court is composed of three 'divisions': the Chancery Division, Family Division, and the Queen's Bench Division. Judges sitting in the High Court are: full High Court judges ('puisne' judges), who are decorated as 'Knights' or 'Dames', for example, Sir Gavin Lightman and Dame Mary Arden (now a Lady Justice of Appeal); or Deputy High Court judges (part-time, drawn from the ranks of senior practitioners); Masters;[12] or circuit judges.[13] Until the sartorial revolution of January 2008, the greatest challenge facing High Court judges was to work out what to wear in court on different days during the course of the judicial calendar.[14]

---

[9] http://www.judiciary.gov.uk/about_judiciary/index.htm.

[10] The highest promotion, thus far, of a former solicitor is Sir Lawrence Collins, a celebrated legal author, and now a member of the Court of Appeal.

[11] http://www.judiciary.gov.uk/about_judiciary/index.htm.

[12] Either in the Queen's Bench Division, or the Chancery Division; QBD Masters deal with pre-trial business, apart from in the Commercial Court where High Court judges conduct both pre-trial and trial hearings (see **3.16**); Masters lack jurisdiction to issue injunctions: see also **4.07**.

[13] On these various categories of judge: http://www.judiciary.gov.uk/about_judiciary/index.htm.

[14] ibid, 'High Court judges' dress depends on the division in which they sit, the type of case they are trying and the time of year. On Red Letter days – which include the Sovereign's birthday, the State Opening of Parliament and some Saints' days – all judges wear the scarlet robe for the appropriate season. A short wig is worn in all cases. Queen's Bench judges have five sets of robes. When trying civil cases in the winter, they wear a black robe faced with fur, a black scarf and girdle and a scarlet tippet. In summer, dress includes a violet robe faced with silk, a black scarf and girdle and a scarlet tippet. When dealing with criminal cases in the winter, judges wear the scarlet robe of the ceremonial dress but without the scarlet cloth and fur mantle. The costume also includes a black scarf and girdle and a scarlet casting-hood or tippet. For criminal business in the summer, a similar scarlet robe is worn but with silk rather than fur facings. Chancery judges have one set of scarlet and ermine robes and one of black silk. Other items include a scarf, a mantle, a hood, black cap, a tippet, white gloves, knee breeches and steel buckled shoes – most of these only worn on ceremonial occasions. In the Chancery and Family divisions, judges wear a court coat and waistcoat with bands and a skirt or trousers beneath a black silk gown and a short wig. Court dress is not worn in chambers. When sitting in the Criminal Division of the Court of Appeal, High Court judges wear a black silk gown and a short wig.' *All of this will now change* (Lord Chief Justice's Press Release July 2007, announcing changes effective from 1 January 2008): '**Civil and Family Jurisdiction:** Judges will no longer wear wigs, wing collars and bands when sitting in open court in civil and family proceedings. The Circuit Bench, in accordance with their current wish, will continue to wear the same gown. All other judges will wear a new, simple, gown which is in the course of design. **Advocates:** It is expected that advocates will adopt a similar dress code to that of the judge. Thus there will be no change to what is worn by the Bar in criminal proceedings but in civil proceedings wigs, wing collars and bands will no longer be worn.'

There are separate parts of the Chancery and Queen's Bench Division. For example, the Commercial Court (**3.16** ff) is part of the Queen's Bench Division and the Patents Court is part of the Chancery Division.

English Lawyers: Solicitors and Barristers

2.05   Practising lawyers in England and Wales are either solicitors or barristers (for comment on changes in the balance of power between branches of the legal profession, **13.15** and **13.16**). At the time of writing, there are important proposals before Parliament concerning the re-organisation of legal practices.[15] Solicitors are enrolled as members of the Law Society for England and Wales.[16] Barristers are members of an Inn of Court. These are ancient societies located near the courts in central London. There are four: Middle Temple, Inner Temple, Lincoln's Inn, and Gray's Inn. The Bar Council is the regulatory and representative body for barristers in England and Wales.[17] Its responsibilities include hearing complaints against barristers.

2.06   English lawyers must hold a university degree, not necessarily in law (indeed, roughly a half of trainee solicitors recruited by the large City firms of solicitors in London are non-law graduates). If a person wishes to qualify as a solicitor, it is necessary to obtain a degree and to pass examinations in the following 'Foundation Subjects': Constitutional and Administrative Law, Contract Law, Criminal Law, Trusts and Equity, Land Law, Tort Law, and European Union Law. These subjects form part of a recognised law degree. In the case of a non-law graduate, these seven subjects can be taken as a post-graduate course at certain recognised institutions. Qualification as a solicitor requires two more years under a 'training contract' (formerly known as 'articles'). Qualification as a barrister is subject to the same requirements just mentioned except, in lieu of a two year 'training contract', a pupil barrister must serve a year of 'pupillage' in Chambers (or under the Government lawyers' scheme). This year involves supervision by one or more 'pupil master' barristers.

2.07   Most advocates appearing before the High Court, the Court of Appeal, or House of Lords, are barristers. But it is possible for a solicitor to gain a special right of audience in these superior courts. He can then call himself a 'solicitor-advocate'. Barristers are normally not consulted directly by a client, but following a request to his or her Chambers by a solicitor (known as the 'instruct-

---

[15] The Legal Services Act 2007; for comment, K Underwood, 'The Legal Services Bill-Death by Regulation?' (2007) 26 CJQ 124.

[16] http://www.lawsociety.org.uk/home.law.

[17] http://www.barcouncil.org.uk/.

ing solicitor'). For example, in important litigation before the Commercial Court, the client will have a direct contractual relationship with a firm of solicitors. The solicitor agrees a fee for the barrister's services. This will be paid from monies supplied by the client. The barrister owes a duty of care and other professional responsibilities to the client. Conduct of most hearings, including trial and appeal, will be by a barrister, or sometimes one or more junior barristers, led by Queen's Counsel ('QC'). A QC is a senior barrister of proven distinction. The Queen's Counsel Selection Panel and the Secretary of State for Justice administer the system of promoting barristers to become a QC (a process known as 'taking silk').[18] Barristers also assist in the case's preparation for trial, and provide advice on points of evidence, law, and general tactics (however, some solicitors now tend to prepare most of the preliminary documents in preparation for litigation).

(3) Sources of Law

English law is now heavily influenced by statutes. These include secondary legislation (especially, 'statutory instruments', see **2.09**). European 'Regulations' have the force of primary legislation.[19] As for 'Precedent Decisions',[20] the 'Common Law' is an expression often used to denote the body of generally binding court decisions. Some parts of English law rest largely on precedent decisions. For example, many contractual doctrines are wholly the product of the precedent system. Judicial interpretation of statutory rules (by the High Court or superior appellate courts) can also furnish binding law (for example, see **6.18** n 67 and **6.19** n 70). Only the High Court (including decisions by Deputy High Court judges, see **2.04**) and higher appellate courts: the Court of Appeal, House of Lords (see also **8.13**), and the Privy Council have power to establish precedent decisions.[21] A new UK Supreme Court will soon be intro-

2.08

---

[18] 'Silk' being the superior material of a QC's courtroom gown. See www.qcapplications.org.uk.

[19] eg, the (revised) 'Brussels Convention': Council Regulation 44/2001 of 22 December 2001 on 'jurisdiction and the recognition and enforcement of judgments in civil and commercial matters'.

[20] The leading English study is R Cross and J Harris, *Precedent in English Law* (4th edn, 1991, Clarendon Press: Oxford).

[21] For details of these courts, C Elliott and F Quinn, *English Legal System* (7th edn, 2006); G Slapper and D Kelly, *The English Legal System* (8th edn, 2006), and *Judicial Statistics*: (*http://www.official-documents.gov.uk/document/cm69/6903/6903.pdf*); for an example of a Deputy High Court judge's decision establishing a precedent, *Cattley v Pollard* [2006] EWHC 3130 (Ch); [2007] 3 WLR 317 on which ch 3 nn 59, 85; the binding quality of a Deputy High Court judge's decision on county courts was noted in *Howard De Walden Estates Ltd v Les Aggio* [2007] EWCA Civ 499 at [86] ff; problems can arise because of (i)

duced.[22] There is a hierarchy of precedents within that pyramid of courts. Thus decisions of the House of Lords are binding on all lower courts, including the Court of Appeal. Decisions of the Court of Appeal are not binding on the House of Lords, which is superior in this curial hierarchy. A Court of Appeal decision is binding not only on the lower courts (such as the High Court or county courts) but also on the Court of Appeal itself. Certain exceptions exist to this last proposition. A decision of the High Court is neither binding on the Court of Appeal nor on the House of Lords, but it is binding on the county courts.[23] However, long-standing precedents at any level within this hierarchy, from the High Court upwards, can acquire considerable force if they express fundamental principle, or at least hallowed doctrine. For these reasons, the system of precedent remains a corner-stone of English law.

2.09   The main sources of civil procedure are: statutory instruments (notably the Civil Procedure Rules)[24]; practice directions; judicial decisions; official 'Guides' to practice within certain parts of the High Court (see **2.12**);[25] and juristic writing.[26] These will now be explained.

Civil Procedure Rules

2.10   The CPR is by far the largest source of procedural rules. Until April 1999 there were two sets of rules, the RSC ('Rules of the Supreme Court'[27]) dealing with matters in the High Court and Court of Appeal, and the CCR ('County Court

---

the length of some modern common law judgments and (ii) (unless a single composite judgment is given) confusing lack of unanimity of multi-judge courts, eg *Sempra Metals Ltd v Inland Revenue Commissioners* [2007] UKHL 34; [2007] 3 WLR 354 cited at **12.43** n 100 (the judgments total c 45,000 words and 241 paragraphs; there are subtle differences of analysis between the five judges).

[22] The creation of a Supreme Court under the Constitutional Reform Act 2005 will strengthen the tendency for the highest echelon of judges to devote a high percentage of their time to public law, human rights, and constitutional matters, rather than private law and commercial disputes. It is easily predicted that media attention to these high-profile cases will distract attention from the important business of providing adjudication of matters relevant to commerce: I am grateful to Professor Shetreet, Hebrew University, Jerusalem, for observations on this topic: seminar University of Cambridge, 2006.

[23] *Howard De Walden Estates Ltd v Les Aggio* [2007] EWCA Civ 499 at [86] ff.

[24] SI 1998/3132, with subsequent amendments (enacted under the parent statute, Civil Procedure Act 1997); for detailed account of these sources: Neil Andrews, *English Civil Procedure* (Oxford UP, 2003), 1.01 to 1.38.

[25] eg for the Chancery Division (2005), for the Queen's Bench (January 2007) (both accessible on-line). The Admiralty and Commercial Court Guide (7th edn, 2006) is available at http://www.hmcourts-service.gov.uk/publications/guidance/admiralcomm/index.htm

[26] Sir Jack Jacob, *The Fabric of English Civil Justice* (1987) 50 ff.

[27] 'Supreme Court' in this context denoted the High Court and Court of Appeal, both created under the Supreme Court of Judicature Acts 1873, 1875.

Rules').[28] But since April 26, 1999 there has been a composite set of rules, the CPR, applicable to the High Court, county courts, and to the Court of Appeal.[29] These rules have been drafted by the Rule Committee, which replaced the former separate rules committees responsible for the RSC and CCR (see also **13.06**).[30] The three Heads of Divisions of the High Court (see **2.04**) have an inherent power to issue practice directions governing matters of procedure. This power is now largely regulated by legislation.[31]

Judicial Decisions Concerning Procedure: English and European Case Law

This source of procedural law concerns the case law of the High Court and   **2.11**
higher appellate courts.[32] Judges in these courts apply the rules authoritatively and develop new principles or doctrines. The creativity of these courts must be admired.[33] Many decisions in the field of civil procedure since the introduction of the CPR (1998) have provided guidance or commentary upon the rules.[34] European case law is also important:[35] notably the European Court of Justice's

---

[28] On the history of the RSC, M Dockray (1997) 113 LQR 120, 123–4, notably nn 32–33.

[29] CPR 2.1 defines the scope of the new rules.

[30] ss 2–4, Civil Procedure Act 1997, the full title of the committee is 'the Civil Procedure Rule Committee'.

[31] s 5, Civil Procedure Act 1997; the Practice Directions are also accessible at: http://www.justice.gov.uk/civil/procrules_fin/menus/rules.htm.

[32] Sir Jack Jacob, *The Fabric of English Justice* (1987), 57 ff.

[33] For an appreciation of eight fundamental judicial innovations in civil procedure, Neil Andrews, 'Development in English Civil Procedure' (1997) ZZPInt 2, 7 ff.

[34] Case law illuminating the new process includes: *Biguzzi v Rank Leisure Plc* [1999] 1 WLR 1926, CA (range of court's disciplinary powers, see **2.17**, **3.13**); *Swain v Hillman* [2001] 1 All ER 91, 92, CA (summary judgment, see **5.20**); *Daniels v Walker* [2000] 1 WLR 1382 CA (discussion of 'single, joint experts' see **7.13**); *Marcan Shipping (London) Ltd v Kefelas* [2007] EWCA Civ 463; [2007] 1 WLR 1864 (automatic application of sanctions for breach of 'unless' orders, see **2.21**).

[35] There are two European courts: (1) the European Court of Justice (Luxembourg), concerning EU law and the Brussels Jurisdiction Regulation (Council Regulation 44/2001 of 22 December 2001 on 'jurisdiction and the recognition and enforcement of judgments in civil and commercial matters'; on which, *Dicey, Morris, and Collins on the Conflict of Laws* (14th edn, 2006) and A Briggs and P Rees, *Civil Jurisdiction and Judgments* (4th edn, 2005); and for the author's summary, Neil Andrews, *Judicial Co-operation: Recent Progress* (Nomos Verlagsgesellschaft, Baden-Baden, 2001); as for the 'Lugano' Convention, applicable to Switzerland, Norway, and Iceland, a new text has been agreed, and is likely to take effect in 2009; (2) the European Court of Human Rights (Strasbourg), especially concerning the European Convention on Human Rights (1953) (Cmd 8969, UK Stationery Office); for examples of the English courts revising Common Law doctrine to ensure compliance with European Union or European Human Rights law, see *C plc v P* [2007] EWCA Civ 493; [2007] 3 WLR 437,

application of the 'Brussels' system of jurisdictional rules;[36] and the European Court of Human Rights' jurisprudence concerning the 'fair hearing' rights under Article 6(1) of the European Convention on Human Rights.[37] Article 6(1)

cited at **6.26** n 106, and *Sempra Metals Ltd v Inland Revenue Commissioners* [2007] UKHL 34; [2007] 3 WLR 354 cited at **12.43** n 100.

[36] Recent problematic decisions concerning the latter system are: (1) *Gasser GmbH v MISAT Srl (Case C-116/02)* [2003] ECR I-14693 (a court (2) of a Member State on which exclusive jurisdiction has been conferred pursuant to article 23 of the 2001 Regulation, must even so stay its proceedings pending resolution of the question of jurisdiction by a court (1) of another Member State if court (1) was first seised of the dispute; 'a court second seised whose jurisdiction has been claimed under an agreement conferring jurisdiction must nevertheless stay proceedings until the court first seised has declared that it has no jurisdiction') and (2) *Turner v Grovit (Case C-159/02)* [2004] ECR I – 3565 (a court of a Member State may not issue an injunction to restrain a party from commencing or prosecuting proceedings in another Member State which has jurisdiction under the Regulation, on the ground that those proceedings have been commenced in bad faith in order to intimidate the opponent and so constituted, under English procedural principles, an abuse of process; generally on abuse of process, Neil Andrews, *English Civil Procedure* (Oxford UP, 2003) ch 16); (3) *Owusu v Jackson (Case C-281/02)* [2005] QB 801, ECJ (the Jurisdiction regulation, and the earlier Brussels Convention (1968), 'preclude a court of a [Member State] from declining the jurisdiction conferred on it by Article 2 of that convention on the ground that a court of a non-[Member State] would be a more appropriate forum for the trial of the action even if the jurisdiction of no other [Member State] is in issue or the proceedings have no connecting factors to any other [Member State]; English court's stay of English proceedings not compatible with 2001 Regulation because English principles of *forum non conveniens* inconsistent with Regulation's rules for allocation of jurisdiction to English court; Art 2 of 2001 Regulation conferring jurisdiction on English court by reason of first defendant's domicile in England; ECJ stating also that English court's inability to apply its *forum non conveniens* doctrine includes situation where allegedly more suitable or convenient non-English jurisdiction is in a non-[Member State]; the jurisdictional wrangle in this case lasted nearly four years, from May 2001 until March 2005); (4) *West Tankers Inc v RAS Riunione Adriatica di Sicurta SpA* [2007] UKHL 4 (whether English anti-suit injunction to enforce an arbitration clause is compatible with the same European jurisdiction rules; question referred to the European Court of Justice, Luxembourg: 'Is it consistent with EC Regulation 44/2001 for a court of a Member State to make an order to restrain a person from commencing or continuing proceedings in another Member State on the ground that such proceedings are in breach of an arbitration agreement?') see also **12.21**; on cases (1) and (2) in this series, see the author's 'Abuse of Process and Obstructive Tactics under the Brussels Jurisdictional System: Unresolved problems for the European Authorities' (2005) European Community Private L Rev 8–15 (this journal is also entitled Zeitschrift fürGemeinschaftsprivatrecht and Revue de droit privé international); for further comment and for additional references on cases (1) and (2) see CJS Knight [2007] CLJ 288, citing the extensive English literature and B Steinbrück (2007) 26 CJQ 358; on case (3) B Steinbrück, ibid.

[37] Article 6(1) of the European Convention on Human Rights (1950), and Sch 1 to the Human Rights Act 1998; for textbook analysis of Article 6(1), JM Jacob, *Civil Justice in the Age of Human Rights* (Aldershot, 2007); L Mulcahy, *Human Rights and Civil Practice* (2001), chaps 10–12; R Clayton and H Tomlinson, *The Law of Human Rights* (Oxford UP, 2000), 2 vols; and 2001 supplement), ch 11; S Grocz, J Beatson and P Duffy, *Human Rights: The 1998 Act and the European Convention* (2000), paras C 6–01 ff; A Lester and D Pannick, *Human Rights Law and Practice* (1999) at section 4.6; A Le Sueur, 'Access to Justice in the United Kingdom' [2000] EHRLR 457 (a perceptive overview); on the Convention's historical back-

creates five guarantees: (i) access to justice (a right which although not explicitly stated in the text of Article 6(1) has been implied by the European Court of Human Rights);[38] (ii) 'a fair hearing'; this includes:[39] (a) the right to be present at an adversarial hearing; (b) the right to equality of arms; (c) the right to fair presentation of the evidence; (d) the right to cross examine; (e) the right to a reasoned judgment (see notes to **7.09**); (iii) 'a public hearing'; this includes public pronouncement of judgment (see also **8.03**); (iv) 'a hearing within a reasonable time';[40] and (v) 'a hearing before an independent and impartial tribunal established by law.'[41]

---

ground, Brian Simpson, *Human Rights and the End of Empire: Britain and the Genesis of the European Convention* (Oxford UP, 2001); for a review of Art 6(1), *Brown v Stott* [2003] 1 AC 681, PC, especially Lords Bingham and Steyn.

[38] *Golder v UK* (1975) 1 EHRR 524, ECtHR, para 35.

[39] R Clayton and H Tomlinson, *The Law of Human Rights* (Oxford UP, 2000), para 11.201.

[40] eg, the extraordinarily bold, and successful, complaint against the English judicial process, brought under the European Convention on Human Rights, by the ex-prisoner, convicted double-agent, disgraced English civil servant, George Blake (invoking, the provision, 'In the determination of his civil rights and obligations ..., everyone is entitled to a ... hearing within a reasonable time by [a] ... tribunal ... ", Art 6(1): *Blake v The United Kingdom* – *68890/01* [2006] ECHR 805 (26 September 2006) (Strasbourg) (there had been English civil proceedings, culminating in the House of Lords' decision in *Att-Gen v Blake* [2001] 1 AC 268, to prevent Blake's publisher sending Blake a royalty cheque; memoirs composed in breach of Blake's life-long duty to obtain official permission for publication; novel points of law; *held* by European Court of Human Rights, breach of human right enjoyed by spy, resident of Moscow; at [40] 'The period to be taken into consideration began therefore on 24 May 1991 (when the writ was filed) and ended on 27 July 2000 (with the delivery of the judgment of the House of Lords). It thus lasted 9 years and 2 months for three levels of jurisdiction'; violation of Blake's right to determination of civil rights and obligations 'within a reasonable time'; award against UK of 5,000 Euros as damages, and 2,000 Euros as legal expenses).

[41] Neil Andrews, *English Civil Procedure* (Oxford UP, 2003) 4.02 ff (judicial indpendence), 4.28 ff (impartiality); a judge should recuse himself for apparent bias when circumstances would lead 'a fair-minded and informed observer to conclude that there was a real possibility ... that the tribunal was biased': a test established in *Porter v Magill* [2001] UKHL; [2002] 2 AC 357, at [102], [103], (following Lord Phillips MR in *Re Medicaments and Related Class of Goods (No 2)* [2000] EWCA Civ 350; [2001] 1 WLR 700, CA, at [85]; and as explained in *Lawal v Northern Spirit* [2003] UKHL 35, [2004] 1 All ER 187 [2003] IC 856, at [14] by Lord Steyn, adding at [22], 'What the public was content to accept many years ago is not necessarily acceptable in the world of today. The indispensable requirement of public confidence in the administration of justice requires higher standards today than was the case even a decade or two ago. The informed observer of today can perhaps "be expected to be aware of the legal traditions and culture of this jurisdiction" as was said in *Taylor and Another v Lawrence* [2003] QB 528, per Lord Woolf CJ, at pp 548–549, at paras 61–64. But he may not be wholly uncritical of this culture'); this test is illustrated by *AWG Group Ltd v Morrison* [2006] EWCA Civ 6; [2006] 1 All ER 967 (High Court judge well-acquainted with one of witnesses over period of 30 years; judge's connection would lead to perception of bias even if proposed witness no longer called; 6 month trial in prospect; despite procedural inconvenience, new judge to be chosen to conduct the trial) and *Howell v Lees Mil-*

Other Sources of Procedural Law

2.12   There are various specialist 'Guides' to practice, composed by the relevant courts, notably: The Chancery Guide, Admiralty and Commercial Court Guide, the Queen's Bench Division Guide.[42] Specialised learned works enjoy 'persuasive' authority.[43]

(4) The Civil Procedure Rules 1998 ('CPR')[44]

Innovation under the CPR

2.13   The CPR is 'a new procedural code'.[45] It took effect on April 26, 1999. Lord Woolf's, in his two reports of 1995 and 1996, identified five aims: (1) to speed up civil justice, (2) to render civil procedure more accessible to ordinary people, (3) to simplify the language of civil procedure, (4) to promote swift settlement, (5) to make litigation more efficient and less costly by avoiding excessive and disproportionate resort to procedural devices.[46]

---

lais [2007] EWCA Civ 720 (High Court judge not accepted for position within a national law firm; members of law firm party to subsequent proceedings before that judge on an unrelated matter); see also *Drury v BBC* [2007] EWCA Civ 605 (out of a sense of abundant caution, Lord Justice recusing himself because of earlier judicial contact with one of the parties); for comment on these recent decisions, L Flannery (2007) NLJ 1097 and (2006) NLJ 278. In *Steadman-Byrne v Amjad* [2007] EWCA Civ 625 a district judge was held to have formed, and articulated, a premature disinclination to accept the other side's evidence.

[42]   Accessible on-line at http://www.justice.gov.uk/civil/procrules_fin/menus/court_gui des.htm. The Admiralty and Commercial Court Guide (7th edn, 2006) is available at http:// www.hmcourts-service.gov.uk/publications/guidance/admiralcomm/index.htm

[43]   eg *Cross and Tapper on Evidence* (11th edn, 2007) (eg, the citation at **11.54** n 97); the various writings of Sir Lawrence Collins, LL D, FBA, now a Lord Justice of Appeal, (per Bingham LJ *Re Harrods (Buenos Aires) Ltd* [1992] Ch 72, 103, CA, a 'very considerable authority'), notably *Dicey, Morris and Collins on the Conflict of Laws* (14th edn, 2006); Spencer Bower, Turner and Handley, *The Doctrine of Res Judicata* (3rd edn, 1996); *Arlidge, Eady and Smith on Contempt* (3rd edn, 2005) ('the leading textbook on contempt', per Jacob J in *Adam Phones Ltd v Goldschmidt* [1999] 4 All ER 486, 494).

[44]   Detailed account: Neil Andrews, *English Civil Procedure* (Oxford UP, 2003), ch 2.

[45]   So described in CPR 1.1(1).

[46]   Lord Woolf, *Access to Justice, Interim Report* (1995) and *Access to Justice, Final Report* (1996) available on line at: *http://www.dca.gov.uk/civil/reportfr.htm*. Responses to these reports include: S Flanders, 'Case Management: Failure in America? Success in England and Wales?' (1998) 17 CJQ 308; M Zander, 'The Government's Plans on Civil Justice' (1998) 61 MLR 383–389 and 'The Woolf Report: Forwards or Backwards for the New Lord Chancellor?' (1997) 16 CJQ 208; AAS Zuckerman and R Cranston (eds), *Reform of Civil Procedure: Essays on 'Access to Justice'* (Oxford UP, 1995) (essays by various authors); AAS Zuckerman, 'The Woolf Report on Access to Justice', ZZPInt 2 (1997), 31 ff; see also R Cranston, *How Law Works: The Machinery and Impact of Civil Justice* (Oxford UP, 2006) (Oxford UP, 2006), ch 5.

A novel feature of the code is that it contains an opening statement of gen- **2.14** eral procedural aims.[47] 'The Overriding Objective' is defined in CPR (1998) 1.1, as follows:[48]

(1) 'These Rules are a new procedural code with the overriding objective of dealing with cases justly.
(2) Dealing with cases justly includes, so far as is practicable –
    (a) ensuring that the parties are on an equal footing;
    (b) saving expense;
    (c) dealing with the case in ways which are proportionate – (i) to the amount of money involved; (ii) to the importance of the case; (iii) to the complexity of the issues; (iv) to the financial position of each party;
    (d) ensuring that it is dealt with expeditiously and fairly;
    (e) allotting to it an appropriate share[49] of the court's resources, while taking into account the need to allot resources to other cases.'[50]

The main change introduced by the CPR code was to confer extensive manage- **2.15** rial powers upon the courts (see **2.18** below).[51] Other important changes introduced by the CPR, or accompanying the modern wave of reform, are:[52] tripartite re-structuring of first instance jurisdiction into small claims, fast-track and multi-track litigation (see **3.04**);[53] consolidation of the conditional fee agreement system (see **9.19** ff); the rise of pre-action protocols (see **6.07**); permitting settlement ('Part 36') offers to be made not just by defendants but also by claimants and potential claimants (see **10.25**); introduction of 'single joint experts' (see **7.10**); the capacity of a defendant to seek summary judgment against the claimant (see **5.18**); a general judicial power to order pre-action disclosure of documents (see **6.12**); introduction of a general judicial power during proceedings to order disclosure of documents from non-parties (see **6.16**).

---

[47] The technique was also used in the Arbitration Act 1996, s 1 (which preceded the CPR drafting); generally on the 1996 Act see ch 12 s 1, 1996 Act states: 'The provisions of [Part 1 of the Act] are founded on the following principles, and shall be construed accordingly – (a) the object of arbitration is to obtain the fair resolution of disputes by an impartial tribunal without unnecessary delay or expense; (b) the parties should be free to agree how their disputes are resolved, subject only to such safeguards as are necessary in the public interest; (c) in matters covered by [Part 1 of the Act] the court should not intervene except as provided by [Part 1].'

[48] For CPR Part 1's pervasiveness, see, eg, the index at Neil Andrews, *English Civil Procedure* (Oxford UP, 2003), p 1067, at 'Overriding Objective'.

[49] eg, in the context of interim injunctions, see **5.13**.

[50] There are related provisions: CPR (1998) 1.2: 'The court must seek to give effect to the overriding objective when it (a) exercises any power given to it by the Rules; or (b) interprets any rule'; CPR (1998) 1.3: 'The parties are required to help the court to further the overriding objective.'

[51] CPR 1.4(2), 3.1.

[52] Neil Andrews, *English Civil Procedure* (Oxford UP, 2003), generally, on these developments, see also *Zuckerman on Civil Procedure* (2006).

[53] Respectively, CPR Parts 27 to 29.

Time Rules

2.16 Under the CPR system, the parties can no longer relax 'time' rules or directions. The court and the procedural rules now intensely regulate the progress and timetabling of the action.[54] In general, delay is now less of a problem in the English civil courts (see also **2.22** below). Admittedly, resolution of novel points of law can sometimes take too long, because of delays in exhausting the tiers of appeal.[55]

Case Management under the CPR

2.17 Until the enactment of the CPR, English procedure was premised on the so-called 'adversarial principle', or 'the principle of party control'. The parties and their lawyers controlled the pre-trial progress of the litigation. After the CPR there is much less scope for the parties to control the case's development. This is because the courts have been granted extensive 'case management' powers and duties (generally, see **3.13** ff). In an early decision under the CPR system, Lord Woolf commented on such powers:

> '... judges have to be trusted to exercise the wide discretions which they have fairly and justly in all the circumstances ... When judges seek to do that, it is important that the [Court of Appeal] should not interfere unless judges can be shown to have exercised their powers in some way which contravenes the relevant principles.'[56]

2.18 The CPR contains two lists of extensive and varied managerial responsibilities for the time-tabling, preparation, possible settlement, and general co-ordina-

---

[54] CPR 3.8(3); cf non-mandatory time provisions, CPR 2.11, eg, the period for service of claim form: *Thomas v The Home Office* [2006] EWCA Civ 1355; [2007] 1 WLR 230; noted J Sorabi [2007] CJQ 168.

[55] *Blake v The United Kingdom – 68890/01* [2006] ECHR 805 (26 September, 2006) (Strasbourg); English proceedings, culminating in the House of Lords' decision in *Att-Gen v Blake* [2001] 1 AC 268, to prevent Blake's publisher sending Blake a royalty cheque; memoirs composed in breach of Blake's life-long duty to obtain official permission for publication; novel points of law; *held* by European Court of Human Rights, breach of human right enjoyed by spy, resident of Moscow; at [40] 'The period to be taken into consideration began therefore on 24 May 1991 (when the writ was filed) and ended on 27 July 2000 (with the delivery of the judgment of the House of Lords). It thus lasted 9 years and 2 months for three levels of jurisdiction'; violation of Blake's right to determination of civil rights and obligations 'within a reasonable time'; award against UK of 5,000 Euros as damages and 2,000 Euros as legal expenses.

[56] *Biguzzi v Rank Leisure plc* [1999] 1 WLR 1926, 1934 F, CA, per Lord Woolf MR; on the new system from the perspective of the traditional adversarial principle, Neil Andrews, 'A New Civil Procedural Code for England: Party-Control "Going, Going, Gone"' (2000) 19 CJQ 19; Neil Andrews, *English Civil Procedure* (Oxford UP, 2003), 13.12 to 13.41; 14.04 to 14.45; 15.65 to 15.72; D Piggott, 'Relief from Sanctions ...' (2005) CJQ 103.

tion of civil proceedings. These are listed at **3.16**. Because the court's role is 'active', judges do not have to wait to be called upon by a party to exercise these powers.[57]

The court's role is not confined to issuing pre-trial directions and achieving a   **2.19** procedural spirit of co-operation. The court can also threaten and correct, and to an extent punish. The three main sanctions for breach of a procedural requirement are: adverse costs orders (see **9.09** to **9.12**);[58] staying the proceedings (a 'stay' is an order prohibiting further activity in the action; this bar remains effective until lifted by the court: see **11.31, 11.38**);[59] striking out part or all of the claim or defence (see **5.23**).[60] Breach of a judicial order or injunction, for example a freezing injunction (see **4.03**),[61] can involve contempt of court (see **8.35**). The court's procedural order can be expressed as a so-called 'unless' order (such an order specifies the sanction which will take effect if the order is not obeyed). A common example of such a sanction will be an order stating that that the claim or defence will be struck out or dismissed unless the relevant party complies by a specified date. The Court of Appeal has made clear that, in the event of disobedience, the sanction mentioned in an 'unless' order takes effect automatically, that is, there is no need for the innocent party to apply to the court to 'activate' the sanction.[62] Instead, it is incumbent upon the party subject to this sanction to apply to the court for relief from the sanction. The only other possibility is that, exceptionally, the court itself will take the initiative to investigate whether there should be such relief.

(5) The CPR System 'Ten Years On'

The 'Woolf reforms' contained in the CPR (1998) profoundly modified the re-   **2.20** lationship between the court and the parties. Lord Woolf recognised the need, especially in cases of high monetary value and complexity, for the courts to become intensely involved in the pre-trial development of the issues and in

---

[57] CPR 1.4(2) setting out a dozen forms of 'active case management'; CPR 3.1(2) presenting 13 forms of 'general management'; see also the general provisions relating to case management: CPR Parts 26(general), 28 (fast-track), 29 (multi-track) and parallel PD (26), (28), (29).

[58] CPR 3.8(2).

[59] CPR 3.1(2)(f).

[60] CPR 3.4(2)(c).

[61] Generally on protective provisional relief, see chapter 4.

[62] *Marcan Shipping (London) Ltd v Kefelas* [2007] EWCA Civ 463; [2007] 1 WLR 1864; see [33] to [36] for a lucid distillation of principles; see also [14], [28] to [30]; the court considered CPR 3.1(3) power to issue an 'unless', that is, conditional order; and CPR 3.8(1) (sanctions take effect automatically); and CPR 3.9 (relief from sanctions); and CPR 3.5 (innocent party's right to file for judgment with costs if opponent's whole defence or claim is struck out automatically for non-compliance with an 'unless' order); the court noted authorities before and after the CPR.

preparation for trial. Timetabling and a pervasive striving for focus and proportionality are central features of the new procedural activism. This has
meant that litigation lawyers have had to accommodate a greater degree of judicial scrutiny and interference with a case's preparation.

Procedural Discipline

2.21   Professor Adrian Zuckerman (University of Oxford) has contended that the
English courts have not been consistent and tough enough in exercising their
powers of case management under the new CPR system.[63] In particular, he
maintains that they have shown undue clemency towards procedural default.
In his view, the courts are wrong to relieve parties and their lawyers from failure to comply efficiently with the procedural framework and specific orders
administered during case management. Against this it might be suggested that
it is important to apply the principle of 'procedural equity'.[64] 'Procedural non-
compliance' cannot be treated as uniformly reprehensible. Examples of procedural default vary greatly in their intrinsic importance. They also cause, or
have the potential to cause, different degrees of 'collateral' impact, that is, disturbing the 'case flow' of other litigation in the same 'list' of actions. For example, the courts have sensibly refrained from making draconian orders where
parties have slightly delayed in making disclosure of expert reports or witness
statements, provided this delay can be acceptably explained.[65] Furthermore,

---

[63] AAS Zuckerman in M Andenas, Neil Andrews, R Nazzini (eds), *The Future of Transnational Commercial Litigation: English Responses to the ALI/UNIDROIT Draft Principles and Rules of Transnational Civil Procedure* (British Institute of Comparative and International Law, London, 2006) ch 12; and in N Trocker and V Varano (eds), *The Reforms
of Civil Procedure in Comparative Perspective* (2005) 143 ff, and *Zuckerman on Civil
Procedure* (2nd edn, 2006) ch 10, esp at 10.139 and 10.164 ff; D Piggott, 'Relief from Sanctions ...' (2005) CJQ 103.

[64] Neil Andrews, *English Civil Procedure* (Oxford UP, 2003) 6.66 ff; recent examples,
Keen Phillips (A Firm) v Field [2006] EWCA Civ 1524; [2007] 1 WLR 686 at [18] (this decision was considered in *Marcan Shipping (London) Ltd v Kefelas* [2007] EWCA Civ 463;
[2007] 1 WLR 1864 at [32] and [33]); *Estate Acquisition and Development Ltd v Wiltshire*
[2006] EWCA Civ 533; [2006] CP Rep 32; *Horton v Sadler* [2006] UKHL 27; [2006] 2
WLR 1346; *Baldock v Webster* [2004] EWCA Civ 1869; [2006] QB 315; but there are limits, eg, *Olafsson v Gissurarson* [2006] EWHC 3162 (QB); [2007] 1 All ER 88 (invalid service
in Iceland could not be cured under CPR 3.10).

[65] *Meredith v Colleys Vacation Services* Ltd [2001] EWCA Civ 1456; [2002] CP 10; *RC
Residuals Ltd v Linton Fuel Oils Ltd* [2002] EWCA Civ 11; [2002] 1 WLR 2782; N Madge
in L Blom-Cooper (ed), *Experts in Civil Courts* (Oxford UP, 2006) 4.34 ff; cf, in a slightly
different context, *Calden v Nunn* [2003] EWCA Civ 200 (where the trial window would be
missed and the application for permission to adduce the report of a party-appointed expert
was unacceptably late); and for refusal to make a disproportionate order in respect of late
disclosure of a witness report, *Halabi v Fieldmore Holdings Ltd* (Ch D 11 May 2006, All
England Reporter); a party in trivial and innocent default was also exonerated in *Keen Phil-*

litigants in person require special consideration[66] (see also discussion of 'procedural equity' in the context of summary judgment, at **5.21**).

Decline of Litigation

One of the ironies of the post-CPR era is that the crowds of litigants waiting **2.22** for 'judge-time' have diminished, although the rules furnish the judges with extensive means of crowd control (see also **10.08, 13.12**). Against the background of these changes during the last ten years, it would have become ludicrous for the judges to create a culture of 'zero tolerance'. If the crowds return, judges might need to apply a stronger regime of procedural discipline. But nowadays there are fewer mainstream civil cases. This explains why litigation departments in English law firms have re-styled themselves as 'dispute resolution' service providers and why so many barristers have become accredited mediators (generally on mediation, see chapter 11).

Costs

It is apparent that the greatest source of complexity under the CPR system is **2.23** 'costs' (generally, see chapter 9). This is a bewilderingly knotty topic. New provisions have been grafted onto the stem of well-settled principle. Litigation on costs issues has grown. Discretion has removed the keen edge from hallowed principle, such as the hitherto dominant rule that the losing party must pay all of the other side's recoverable costs (**9.06**). The overall picture is that the English costs rules are over-detailed. They are also ineffective to control the tendency of cases to be priced out of the reach of individuals and businesses. It is still very expensive to litigate in England.[67] Admittedly, lawyers are subject to procedural constraints and can even be ordered to pay costs in person under the system of 'wasted costs' (see **9.18**). They must provide their clients with

---

lips (A Firm) v Field [2006] EWCA Civ 1524; [2007] 1 WLR 686 at [18] (this decision was considered in *Marcan Shipping (London) Ltd v Kefelas* [2007] EWCA Civ 463; [2007] 1 WLR 1864 at [32] and [33]).

[66] *Hougie v Hewitt* (Ch D Lawtel 27 September 2006) (relief from striking out for breach of an 'unless order'; litigant in person's default mitigated by depression).

[67] For Brooke LJ's severe comments on the costs claimed by counsel in conducting a one day hearing in an appeal, see *Traefi v Russell* [2005] EWCA Civ 901 at [97] ff; in a complex commercial dispute, one party recently spent £1M ensuring that it could comply with the Technology and Construction Court's pre-action protocol for 'construction and engineering disputes' (personal communication, 2007) and for an example of the Court of Appeal rejecting an exorbitant claim for costs, see the *Henry Boot* case [2005] 3 All ER 932, CA, at [87] to [90] (where the size of the claim was described as 'breathtaking').

costs estimates.[68] But the basic system of remuneration remains payment by
the hour. Charging rates are high. The sum to be paid as costs can be very
large, both absolutely and in relation to the value of the substantive claim.[69]
However, the amount in fact recovered from the defeated defendant will be
significantly less than the overall payment,[70] unless the claimant receives an
order for 'indemnity costs'.[71] Businesses have responded by finding cheaper
and more satisfactory ways of dealing with disputes. This explains the consolidation of settlement by various means, the remarkable rise of commercial
mediation, and the retrenching of commercial arbitration (see chapters 10 to
12 on these three topics).

Access to Justice and Conditional Fee Agreements

2.24 Access to justice has improved, despite the endemic problem of expense. The
conditional fee agreement system enables ordinary people to have their claims
financed by entrepreneurial lawyers (see **9.19** ff).[72] The risk of liability to pay
the defendant's costs, if the case is lost, can be covered by 'after-the-event' legal expenses insurance ('ATE' insurance, see **9.21**). But the result is that the
overall cost of litigation has increased. This is because the two sets of legal
costs now produce a larger sum. This increase is caused by the addition of a

---

[68] *Garbutt v Edwards* [2005] EWCA Civ 1206; [2006] 1 WLR 2907; costs estimates
must also be disclosed to the opponent at various stages and the court will have regard to
these when determining costs awards: *Tribe v Southdown Gliding Club Ltd* [2007] EWHC
90080 (Costs), considering *Leigh v Michelin Type Co plc* [2003] EWCA Civ 1766; [2004] 1
WLR 846; A Zuckerman in 'Lord Woolf's Access to Justice ...' (1996) 59 MLR 773 has argued that the only way of reducing the expense of English civil litigation is to introduce a
general system of fixed fees which reflect a claim's value, as in Germany, on which, he notes
D Leipold, 'Limiting Costs for Better Access to Justice – the German Experience' in AAS
Zuckerman and R Cranston (eds), *The Reform of Civil Procedure: Essays on 'Access to
Justice'* (1995); on fixed costs, A Cannon, 'Designing Cost Policies to Provide Sufficient Access to Lower Courts' (2002) 21 CJQ 198, 219. However, possible counter-arguments to
wholesale adoption of fixed costs are (i) inflexible bureaucratic influence upon the civil
justice system; (ii) unrealistic depression of lawyers' rates; (iii) weakening legal recruitment
and retention; (iv) those who can pay more will pay more, because this is merely a cap on
recoverable costs.
[69] eg, *Daniels v Commissioner for Police for the Metropolis* [2005] EWCA Civ 1312;
[2006] CP Rep 9, at [32], [35].
[70] For many decades there has been a discrepancy between legal fees actually incurred
and the level of recoverable costs; as noted nearly fifty years ago by RE Megarry, *Lawyer
and Litigant* (1962) 199–201.
[71] On which see **9.12**; **10.26**.
[72] See also MJ Cook, *Cook on Costs* (2007); M Harvey, *Guide to Conditional Fee Agreements* (2nd edn, 2006); Neil Andrews, *English Civil Procedure* (Oxford UP, 2003) ch 35; for
an Italian scholar's study of the English system, A De Luca, *L'Accesso alla Giustizia in Inghilterra: fra Stato e Mercato* (Torino, 2007).

percentage bonus for the sponsoring lawyers (reckoned as a percentage of his ordinary fee) and the cost of the ATE insurance premium.

(6) Stages in a Case's Development

The stages to be discussed here are: (i) the pre-action phase; (ii) commence-   2.25
ment and pleadings; (iii) party preparation of factual evidence, expert evidence, and exchange of documents between the parties ('disclosure', formerly
known as 'discovery'); (iv) trial; (v) appeal; (vi) enforcement. 'Pre-trial applications', including 'case management' hearings, can take place at stages (ii) and
(iii). Protective relief, for example, 'freezing injunctions', (on which see chapter
4), can be sought at stage (i), or at later stages.

Pre-Action Phase[73]

The 'pre-action phase' covers the period from when the relevant ground of   2.26
complaint or contested issue arose until that matter produces formal civil proceedings. When the period of prescription (or 'limitation of actions', on which
3.09) is generous, pre-litigation phase will not be short (for example, six years
for ordinary contractual claims, or even twelve years if the contract is contained in a formal 'deed').[74] Perhaps no other subject so vividly reflects the
scope for national difference than the fixing of periods of prescription.[75]

The CPR (1998) system introduced an important set of 'pre-action proto-   2.27
cols' (see also **3.01, 6.07, 11.09**). These prescribe 'obligations' which the prospective parties and their legal representatives must satisfy before commencing

---

[73] See the author's 'general report' (examining nearly 20 jurisdictions) on this topic for
the world congress on procedural law in Brazil (2007) Neil Andrews in A Pellegrini Grino-
ver and P Calmon (eds), *Direito Processual Comparado* (Editora Forense, Rio de Janeiro,
2007) 201–241.

[74] Also known as a 'covenant'; a deed is a formal written contract, signed by the covenantor, who makes the promise, witnessed by a third party, and 'delivered', normally by
face-to-face transfer, to the covenantee; for the formalities of a deed, s 1(2)(3) Law of Property (Miscellaneous Provisions) Act 1989; GH Treitel, *The Law of Contract* (12th edn,
2007) 5–008; *Bolton MBC v Torkington* [2004] Ch 66, CA.

[75] For comparative discussion, R Zimmermann, *Comparative Foundations of a European Law of Set-off and Prescription* (Cambridge UP, 2002); in England the subject of limitation of actions, based largely on case law interpretation of the Limitation Act 1980, is so
fast-moving and abstruse that Parliament seems to have despaired of reforming it; the nature of possible legislative reform remains controversial: Neil Andrews, *English Civil Procedure* (Oxford UP, 2003) ch 12; *Zuckerman on Civil Procedure* (2006) 24.4 ff; A McGee,
Limitation Periods (2006); Law Commission's discussion, *Limitation of Actions* (Law Com
No 270, HC 23, 2001; and L Com CP No 151, 1998); on which, Neil Andrews [1998] CLJ
588; R James (2003) 22 CJQ 41.

formal proceedings. One of the aims of this system is that each side should
know the strengths of his opponent's case. It is also hoped that settlement will
be promoted by efficient exchange of information.[76] For example, a person
who alleges that he was the victim of medical negligence can gain access to
hospital or medical records under this system of pre-action protocols.

2.28   The 'Practice Direction on Protocols' states:[77] 'In all cases not covered by
any approved protocol, the court will [also] expect the parties ... to act reasonably in exchanging information and documents relevant to the claim and
generally in trying to avoid the necessity for the start of proceedings.' If the
dispute does proceed to a formal action, the court has power to sanction a
person's failure to comply. This will involve the court issuing an appropriately adverse costs order.

Other Pre-Action Processes

2.29   Various rules or judicial powers regulate preservation of, or access to, potential evidence and information before formal commencement of proceedings.
The reader is referred to **6.12** for details.

Commencement and Pleadings

2.30   Proceedings begin once the claimant issues a claim form (see **3.05**). This requires a positive act by the claimant, who must notify the relevant court of his
wish to instigate proceedings. Not surprisingly, despite the efforts of procedural draftsmen to achieve absolute precision, the moment when the procedural 'starter's gun' has been fired is often disputed.[78] The date when pro-

---

[76] In *Carlson v Townsend* [2001] 3 All ER 663, CA, at [24], [28], [31], Brooke LJ, '[These
protocols] are guides to good litigation and pre-litigation practice, drafted and agreed by
those who know all about the difference between good and bad practice.' And Judge LJ said
in *Ford v GKR Construction Ltd* [2000] 1 WLR 802, 807, CA: 'Civil litigation is now developing a system designed to enable the parties involved to know where they stand in reality
at the earliest possible stage, and at the lowest practicable cost, so that they may make informed decisions about their prospects and the sensible conduct of their cases.'

[77] At 4.1.

[78] The time of commencement of civil proceedings is when the court enters the date on
the claim form, CPR 7.2(2); however, for limitation purposes, the date can be earlier: when
the claim form was received in the court office: PD (7) 5.1; thus in *St Helens MBC v Barnes*
[2006] EWCA Civ 1372; [2007] 1 WLR 879 (noted J Sorabi [2007] CJQ 166) the Court of
Appeal held that a claim was 'brought' when a claimant's request for the issue of a claim
form was delivered to the correct court office during its opening hours on the day before the
expiry of the limitation period, even though the claim was not issued by the court office until four days later, by which date it was out of time.

ceedings are 'commenced' or 'brought' or become 'definitively pending' varies between legal systems. This date is important for determining at least two important procedural issues: whether the plaintiff's attempt to bring proceedings is in fact 'out of time' for the purpose of the limitation or prescription rules; and whether the present proceedings are to be accorded priority under a regime of *lis alibi pendens* (for example, under the Brussels jurisdictional regime).[79] But it is unnecessary to investigate this matter further. What is significant for us is that the process of court proceedings has an officially defined beginning. Before that point, any dispute or disagreement is not subject to formal proceedings.

Each party to English civil proceedings must produce a sworn 'statement of case' (formerly known as 'pleadings', see **3.08**). This must set out the main aspects of the claim or defence. There is no need to include in a 'statement of case' any detailed evidence or details of legal argument. The claimant should also specify the relief he is seeking, such as the remedies of a debt claim, damages, injunction, or a declaration. **2.31**

Party Preparation of Factual Evidence

The decision to call particular factual witnesses and to use particular documents lies with the parties. The claimant bears the burden of proof. For example, he must show that the defendant breached his contract, or failed to exercise reasonable care, or committed some other legal wrong. The defendant bears the burden of proof on points of defence, for example that the claimant failed to act reasonably in order to 'mitigate' his loss.[80] The 'standard of proof', that is, level or quantum of proof in civil cases, is that the court must be satisfied that the relevant matter has been substantiated 'on the balance of probabilities'. This contrasts with the higher standard of proof in criminal cases, which is 'beyond reasonable doubt'. However, the more serious the alleged civil wrong, the more the court will tend to require cogent proof that the allegation is sound. The civil courts have emphasised this need for more exacting **2.32**

---

[79] (EC) No 44/2001 of 22 December 2000 on 'jurisdiction and the recognition and enforcement of judgments in civil and commercial matters': [2001] OJ L 12/1; see, eg, *Gasser GmbH v MISAT Srl (Case C-116/02)* [2003] ECR I-14693; on this and related cases see n 36 above.

[80] A qualification exists where the claimant seeks damages for expenditure wasted as a result of the defendant's breach of contract; the claim will succeed unless the *defendant* shows that the claimant had entered a loss-making contract, that is, one which would have resulted in economic loss to the claimant even if there had been no breach of contract (*CCC Films (London) Ltd v Impact Quadrant Films Ltd* [1985] QB 16, Hutchison J; approved in *Dataliner Ltd v Vehicle Builders and Repairers Association The Independent* 30 August 1995, CA); see, in the context of the defence of self-defence, the *Ashley* case [2007] 1 WLR 398, CA.

proof where the case concerns allegations of assaults upon children or fraud claims.[81]

2.33   English 'evidence collection' and 'preparation' are controlled by the parties, subject only to case management directions. Thus the court does not compel the parties to produce particular witnesses or documents. The parties also select the particular expert(s) for the case (on the system of experts, besides **2.35** below, see chapter 7). The Common Law system presupposes that the impartial court will determine the victor in a factual dispute by listening to rival presentations of evidence (see also **8.03; 8.05; 8.07**). Under the CPR system, the court retains this 'responsive' and 'reactive' role. But the modern civil judge is required to control the proceedings to ensure that the case is not unduly prolonged, nor unreasonably complicated, nor unfairly tilted in favour of a stronger party (this last aim is known as the 'equality of arms' principle or 'procedural equality', see also **2.11**). We shall see (at **8.07**) that the court has power to restrict the number of witnesses at trial. This power should not be used heavy-handedly. The trial judge can also place limits on the time devoted at trial to examining witnesses.

2.34   Each party must normally produce a witness statement in respect of each factual witness, including the party's own intended factual evidence. No witness can be heard unless such a statement has been made and exchanged before trial. The judge will be expected to have read the witness statements before trial. Each party is competent to give evidence as a 'factual witness', that is evidence of what he or she saw or heard. This must take the form of a witness statement. At trial this evidence can be supplemented by oral examination (see **2.39** and **2.40** below).

Expert Evidence

2.35   This topic is the subject of chapter 7. The court can restrict use of experts. It can require the parties to agree upon the nomination of a 'single, joint expert'. However, in more complex cases, the traditional system of 'party-appointed' witnesses continues to apply. This permits the parties to select their own 'rival' experts.

---

[81] Lord Nicholls said in *Re H (Minors) (Sexual Abuse: Standard of Proof)* [1996] AC 563, 586, HL: '... the criminal standard does not apply in civil cases, although the more serious the allegation or the greater its inherent improbability, the more the civil judge will require persuasion: When assessing the probabilities the court will have in mind as a factor ... that the more serious the allegation the less likely it is that the event occurred and, hence, the stronger should be the evidence before the court concludes that the allegation is established on the balance of probability. Fraud is usually less likely than negligence. Deliberate physical injury is usually less likely than accidental physical injury ... Built into the preponderance of probability standard is a generous degree of flexibility in respect of the seriousness of the allegation.'

Disclosure of Documents: Main Framework[82]

Both the system of pre-*action* disclosure (see **2.27** above) and pre-*trial* dis-   **2.36**
closure are intended to enable each side of the contest to gain access to relevant
information which might otherwise be known only to one side. Chapter 6 (especially at **6.21**) examines the system of disclosure in greater detail. Reciprocal
disclosure achieves equality of access to information, facilitates better settlement of disputes, and avoids 'trial by ambush' (where a party is unable to respond properly to a surprise revelation at the final hearing).

After proceedings have begun each party must prepare a list of documents on   **2.37**
which he will rely, or which might assist the other party.[83] A party is obliged both
to provide a list of documents ('disclosure') and to allow inspection of these by the
other side.[84] Such information is not yet evidence: it only becomes evidence if it is
'adduced' by one party for the purpose of a trial or other 'hearing'. 'Standard disclosure' concerns:[85] documents on which party A will rely; or which adversely affect A's own case; or adversely affect party B's case; or support B's case; or any
other documents which A is required to disclose by a relevant practice direction.[86]
For this purpose, a 'document' is 'anything in which information of any description is recorded', thus including non-paper sources, for example, electronic information.[87] It is important that the recipient of information disclosed under legal
compulsion should only use this material for the purpose of the present proceedings, and that he should not divulge it to strangers at any point.[88] Accordingly, the
so-called 'Implied Undertaking' provides:[89]

---

[82] Neil Andrews, *English Civil Procedure* (Oxford UP, 2003), ch 26.

[83] CPR Part 31.

[84] CPR 31.10(2) and 31.15, subject to certain qualifications added at CPR 31.3(2).

[85] CPR 31.6.

[86] The court can order narrower disclosure in special situations: CPR 31.5(1) & (2).

[87] CPR 31.4.

[88] As Lord Hoffmann explained in *Taylor v Serious Fraud Office* [1999] 2 AC 177,
207, HL: 'The concept of an implied undertaking originated in the law of discovery in civil
proceedings. A solicitor or litigant who receives documents by way of discovery is treated
as if he had given an undertaking not to use them for any purpose other than the conduct
of the litigation. As Hobhouse J pointed out in *Prudential Assurance Co Ltd v Fountain
Page Ltd* [1991] 1 WLR 756, 764 the undertaking is in reality an obligation imposed by
operation of law by virtue of the circumstances in which the document or information is
obtained. The reasons for imposing such an obligation were explained by Lord Keith of
Kinkel in *Home Office v Harman* [1983] 1 AC 280, 308, HL: "Discovery constitutes a
very serious invasion of the privacy and confidentiality of a litigant's affairs. It forms part
of English legal procedure because the public interest in securing that justice is done
between parties is considered to outweigh the private and public interest in the maintenance of confidentiality. But the process should not be allowed to place upon the litigant
any harsher or more oppressive burden than is strictly required for the purpose of securing
that justice is done.'

[89] CPR 31.22; even in situation (a), however, the court has power to make a special order

'a party to whom a document has been disclosed may use the document only for the purpose of the proceedings in which it is disclosed, except (a) where the document has been read to or by the court, or referred to, at a hearing which has been held in public; or (b) the court gives permission;[90] or (c) the party who disclosed the document and the person to whom the document belongs agree.'

Evidence at Pre-trial Hearings

2.38   There is hardly ever any presentation of oral evidence at such hearings, although formally the rules do permit this in exceptional circumstances (see, for example, 5.03). And so the court only receives oral testimony from witnesses at trial. At a pre-trial hearing, witness evidence is received in the form of sworn statements. There is opportunity for the judge and the parties' lawyers to discuss the content of these statements. Given that few actions reach trial, pre-trial hearings have considerable practical importance. At such a hearing, the court can grant interim injunction or make interim payment orders, or strike out claims or defences, or dispense summary justice (see chapter 5 on this pre-trial range of interim or accelerated judgments).

Trial

2.39   The general rule is that a hearing must be in public.[91] The court can order that the identity of a party or of a witness must not be disclosed where this is necessary to protect that person's interest.[92] Adjudication at trial is nearly always by a single judge, who sits without a jury.[93] The civil jury's virtual disappearance has transformed the rules of evidence. Civil evidence now displays a strong trend towards 'free evaluation', that is, assessment of relevant evidence liberated from the fetters of types of inadmissible evidence. English law reflects the transnational movement towards 'free evaluation', a concept embraced in

---

restricting or prohibiting use of a document: CPR 31.22(2): *McBride v The Body Shop International Plc* [2007] EWHC 1658 (QB), noting *Lilly Icos Ltd v Pfizer Ltd* [2002] 1 WLR 2253, CA.

[90] *SmithKline Beecham Biologicals SA v Connaught Laboratories Inc* [1999] 4 All ER 498, CA.

[91] CPR 39.2(1); CPR 39.2(3) and PD (39) 1.5 set out exceptions; the primary source is s 67, Supreme Court Act 1981; J Jaconelli, *Open Justice* (Oxford UP, 2002).

[92] CPR 39.2(4); PD (39) 1.4A emphasises the need to consider the requirement of publicity enshrined in Art 6(1) of the European Convention on Human Rights (incorporated into English law, Human Rights Act 1998, Sch 1).

[93] Jury trial is confined to serious criminal cases (for example, murder, rape, armed robbery) and civil actions for defamation or misconduct by the police (the torts of defamation, malicious prosecution, and false imprisonment).

the American Law Institute/UNIDROIT's *Principles of Transnational Civil Procedure*.[94] Factual witness testimony is the main type of evidence at trial.[95] Witnesses can be compelled to attend a trial (or other hearing) by the issue of a 'witness summons'.[96] The witness must be offered compensation for travelling to and from court and for loss of time.[97]

The trial proceeds as follows: counsel's opening speech (although this can be dispensed with);[98] examination-in-chief of claimant's witnesses (although this will not be oral where, as usual, the witness statement is received as a substitute for oral testimony);[99] cross-examination of claimant's witnesses by defendant's counsel; re-examination of witnesses; examination-in-chief of defendant's witnesses (although this will not be oral where, as usual, the witness statement is received as a substitute for oral testimony);[100] cross-examination of the same by claimant's counsel; re-examination of the same; defendant counsel's final speech; claimant counsel's final speech (the reason this is the last party intervention at trial is that the claimant bears the burden of proof, and so deserves the last say); judgment;[101] an order for costs, including in appropriate cases a summary assessment of costs[102] (as suggested at **2.23**

2.40

---

[94] Rule 25: accessible at: http://www.unidroit.org/english/principles/civilprocedure/main.htm.

Also published as *ALI/UNIDROIT: Principles of Transnational Civil Procedure* (Cambridge UP, 2006), pp 137 ff; the working group's membership was as follows: Neil Andrews, Clare College, Cambridge, UK; Professor Frédérique Ferrand, Lyon, France; Professor Pierre Lalive, University of Geneva and practice as an arbitrator, Switzerland; Professor Masanori Kawano, Nagoya University, Japan; Madame Justice Aida Kemelmajer de Carlucci, Supreme Court, Mendoza, Argentina; Professor Geoffrey Hazard, USA; Professor Ronald Nhlapo, formerly of the Law Commission, South Africa; Professor Dr iur Rolf Stürner, University of Freiburg, Germany. The two General Reporters for the UNIDROIT project were Professors Hazard and Stürner; the two reporters for the ALI project were Professors Hazard (Hastings College of the Law, San Francisco) and Taruffo (University of Pavia, Italy).

[95] Detailed account: Neil Andrews, *English Civil Procedure* (Oxford UP, 2003) 31.41 to 31.51.

[96] This phrase replaces the hallowed terms subpoena ad testificandum (order to attend to give oral evidence) and subpoena duces tecum (order to attend with relevant documents or other items): CPR 34.2.

[97] CPR 34.7; PD (34) 3, referring to provisions applicable also to compensation for loss of time in criminal proceedings.

[98] Fast-track: PD (28) 8.2; multi-track: PD (29) 10.2; detailed account: Neil Andrews, *English Civil Procedure* (Oxford UP, 2003) 31.21 to 31.24.

[99] CPR 32.5(2).

[100] ibid.

[101] Or direction to the jury; for rules concerning judgments, CPR 40 and PD (40); on the court's discretion whether to complete judgment once it has begun to deliver it (or to deliver it initially in draft form) *Prudential Assurance Co v McBains* [2000] 1 WLR 2000, CA; on the court's power to re-open a case before perfecting a judgment, *Stewart v Engel* [2000] 3 All ER 518, CA.

[102] CPR 44.3, 44.7(a).

'costs' is English procedure's most 'bewilderingly knotty topic'; for details, see chapter 9).

Appeals[103]

2.41   This topic is considered at **8.12**. The main points are. First, all appeals now require permission,[104] which can be granted by the first instance court or by the appeal court.[105] Secondly, most appeals proceed directly (without 'leap-frogging') to the next level of civil judge (district judge to circuit judge, Master to High Court judge, circuit judge to High Court judge, High Court judge to Court of Appeal).[106] Thirdly, the appeal court will rarely receive oral evidence. Nor will it consider new evidence (evidence not presented to the lower court) if a party, by exercise of 'reasonable diligence', could have found, appreciated, and furnished this in the lower court's proceedings (**8.16**). But the appeal court can 'draw any inference of fact which it considers justified on the evidence'.[107] Fourthly, the court will allow an appeal when the lower court's decision was 'wrong' or 'unjust because of a serious procedural or other irregularity in the proceedings in the lower court.'[108]

Enforcement

2.42   This topic is examined at **8.28** ff. The court's judgments or orders are open to enforcement, at the victorious party's request. For example, money judgments can be enforced, at the creditor's initiative, according to various official processes: enforcement agents 'taking control' of the debtor's goods (see **8.30** for statutory changes, introduced in 2007); attachment of earnings orders; garnishee proceedings ('third party debt orders'); or charging orders against real

---

[103] Detailed account: Neil Andrews, *English Civil Procedure* (Oxford UP, 2003) ch 38; CPR Part 52; for US comparisons, PS Atiyah and R Summers, *Form and Substance in Anglo-American Law* (Oxford UP, 1987) ch 10; Sir Henry Brooke, D di Mambro, L di Mambro (eds), *Manual of Civil Appeals* (2nd edn, 2004); for comparative perspectives on appeals, JA Jolowicz, *On Civil Procedure* (Cambridge UP, 2000), chs 14 to 16; for reflections on the private and public functions of civil appeals, especially in the highest chamber, see the reports by JA Jolowicz, P Lindblom, S Goldstein in P Yessiou-Faltsi (ed), *The Role of the Supreme Courts at the National and International Level* (Thessaloniki, Greece, 1998).

[104] CPR 52.3(1): except decisions affecting a person's liberty, namely appeals against committal orders, refusals to grant habeas corpus and secure accommodation orders made under s 25, Children Act 1989.

[105] CPR 52.4(2).

[106] PD (52).

[107] CPR 52.11(2) and (4).

[108] CPR 52.11(3).

property. There are special procedures relating to the recovery of movable and immovable property. Disobedience to injunctions and other coercive orders can be punished by contempt of court proceedings ('committal proceedings', 8.35).

Chapter 3

Commencement of Proceedings and Case Management

Contents

(1) The Pre-Action Stage

3.01   The CPR system introduced an important set of 'pre-action protocols' (see also **2.27, 3.01, 6.07, 11.09**). These establish a framework of responsibilities for prospective parties and their legal representatives. The protocols are intended to enable each side to know the strengths and weaknesses of his opponent's case.[1] It is hoped that compliance with the protocols' duties to disclose information will promote informed settlement.[2] The Civil Justice Council is considering whether a consolidated pre-action protocol might be attractive. For the moment (July 2007), specific protocols apply to the following topics: 'Construction and Engineering Disputes', 'Defamation', 'Personal Injury Claims', 'Clinical Disputes', 'Professional Negligence', 'Judicial Review', 'Disease and Illness Claims', 'Housing Disrepair Cases', and 'Possession Claims based on Rent Arrears'.[3]

3.02   The protocols also contain a 'general provision' ('Practice Direction on Protocols') which states:[4] 'In all cases not covered by any approved protocol, the court will [also] expect the parties ... to act reasonably in exchanging informa-

---

[1] On the related topic of pre-action disclosure, see **2.27** and **6.12** to **6.20**.

[2] For comments on pre-action protocols, *Carlson v Townsend* [2001] EWCA Civ 511; [2001] 3 All ER 663, CA; *Ford v GKR Construction Ltd* [2000] 1 WLR 802, 807, CA.

[3] A new version of the 'Construction and Building Disputes' protocol was issued in April 2007: see http://www.justice.gov.uk/civil/procrules_fin/menus/protocol.htm.

[4] 'Practice Direction on Protocols', 4.1.

tion and documents relevant to the claim and generally in trying to avoid the necessity for the start of proceedings.' If a dispute proceeds to formal civil proceedings, the court's discretionary powers when making costs orders enable it to express disapproval of a person's failure to comply with a protocol. Thus the court can modify the normal costs order in favour of the victorious party (see **9.06**), with the result that the victorious party will not receive his costs, or at least these will be reduced.[5] Such a costs sanction is applicable to all categories of civil litigation.[6] But no costs sanction is justified against a party who has conscientiously abandoned issues during the pre-action action phase.[7]

A pre-action admission of liability can be withdrawn when the defence is   **3.03** pleaded (on pleadings, see **3.08** below), provided this change of position will neither involve an abuse of process nor 'obstruct the just disposal of the case'.[8] The problem of such an 'obstruction' might arise, for example, if evidence has been lost or destroyed as a result of the earlier admission.

(2) Commencement of a Civil Action

In the ordinary case, an action begins when the claimant obtains from the   **3.04** court a dated claim form (see **3.05** below, for details). The case is later allocated to the appropriate 'track': small claims litigation, fast-track litigation, or multi-track.[9] In addition, multi-track litigation must be further allocated to a county court or the High Court, and within the latter court to the appropriate division (the three divisions are Queen's Bench, Chancery, and Family) and even to a specific constituent 'court', for example, the Commercial Court or Technology and Construction Court, which are parts of the Queen's Bench Division. If the case is to be defended, both the claimant and defendant must produce a sworn 'statement of case' setting out the main aspects of the claim or defence. Until the CPR, 'statements of case' were known as 'pleadings' (see further **3.08** below). There is no need to include in a 'statement of case' any detailed evidence or details of legal argument. The claimant should also specify the relief he is seeking.

---

[5] CPR 44.3(5)(a); PD (Protocols) 2.3; eg, *Straker v Tudor Rose (A Firm)* [2007] EWCA Civ 368 (where the court held that the first instance judge had over-reacted and made too severe a costs reduction).

[6] *Ford v GKR Construction Ltd* [2000] 1 WLR 1397, 1403, CA.

[7] *McGlinn v Waltham Contractors Ltd* [2005] EWHC 1419 (TCC); [2005] 3 All ER 1126, at [14].

[8] *Walley v Stoke-on-Trent CC* [2006] EWCA Civ 1137; [2007] 1 WLR 352 at [34], [35] (note Brooke LJ's plea for reform at [45]); considering *Sowerby v Charlton* [2005] EWCA Civ 1610; [2006] 1 WLR 568.

[9] Respectively, CPR Parts 27 to 29; court fees are governed by the Civil Proceedings Fees (Amendment) (No 2) Order 2007 (SI 2007/2176): schedule 1.

3.05   The main form of commencement is by claim form.[10] An alternative 'Part 8
          procedure' is used where the claimant seeks 'the court's decision on a question
          which is unlikely to involve a substantial dispute of fact'.[11] No claim can be
          commenced in the High Court unless the sum in issue is for more than £15,000
          or, in the case of damages for personal injuries, more than £ 50,000.[12] Alloca-
          tion of business to the High Court and county court is determined by reference
          to the claim's 'value', 'complexity' and public importance.[13] The claimant can
          choose whether to include in the claim form the particulars of claim or to serve
          these later.[14] Accompanying the particulars of claim, the claimant must serve
          forms enabling the defendant to defend the claim, or to admit the claim, and to
          acknowledge service.[15] The time of commencement of civil proceedings is
          when the court enters the date on the claim form.[16] The same date governs the
          lis alibi pendens rules under the Brussels jurisdictional regime.[17] The topics of
          'Group Litigation Orders' and representative proceedings are discussed in
          chapter 14.[18]

---

    [10] CPR 7.2; PD (7) 3, 4.

    [11] CPR 8.1(6).

    [12] Respectively, PD (7) 2.1, 2.2; for transfers between these courts, CPR Part 30.

    [13] PD (7) 2.4.

    [14] CPR 7.4.

    [15] CPR 7.8(1).

    [16] CPR 7.2(2); for limitation purposes, the date can be earlier: when the claim form was
received in the court office: PD (7) 5.1; thus in *Barnes v St Helens MBC* [2006] EWCA Civ
1372; [2007] 1 WLR 879 (noted J Sorabi [2007] CJQ 166) held that a claim was 'brought'
when a claimant's request for the issue of a claim form was delivered to the correct court office during its opening hours on the day before the expiry of the limitation period, even
though the claim was not issued by the court office until four days later, by which date it was
out of time.

    [17] Art 30, Jurisdiction Regulation, (EC) No 44/2001 of 22 December 2000 on 'jurisdic-
tion and the recognition and enforcement of judgments in civil and commercial matters':
[2001] OJ L 12/1; interpreted in *Benatti v WPP Holdings Italy SRL* [2007] EWCA Civ 263
at [65] ff.

    [18] See also Neil Andrews, *English Civil Procedure* (Oxford UP, 2003); R Mulheron, *The
Class Action in Common Law Legal Systems: A Comparative Perspective* (2004) (reviewed, S Gibbons (2006) 122 LQR 336); 'Some Difficulties with a Group Litigation Order
– and Why a Class Action is Superior' (2005) CJQ 40; J Seymour, 'Justice and the Representative Parties Rule: An Overriding Interest?' (2006) LS 668; C Hodges, 'The Europeanisation of Civil Justice: Trends and Issues' (2007) CJQ 96, which includes reference to the
DTI's consultation on an 'UK Representative Actions mechanism': http://www.dti.gov.uk/
consultations/page30259.html

(3) Service of Process

The court will serve the claim form (provided the defendant's address for ser-   **3.06**
vice is specified in the claim form)[19] unless the claimant tells the court that he
wishes to do so, or there is rule, practice direction, or order releasing the court
from itself serving the process.[20] Where the claim form is to be served outside
the jurisdiction, the period is six months.[21] As for service of the claim form
within England and Wales, this must normally occur within four months from
the claim form's date of issue.[22] The parties can agree an extension of this period, but this agreement and extension must be recorded in writing.[23] The
claimant can seek an extension of this period for service either before the period
for service has elapsed[24] or after.[25] There has been elaborate judicial discussion
of the court's discretionary powers to grant extension of the period for service
of the claim form.[26] Where the period has not yet elapsed, the courts have
declared that the applicant must show a 'very good reason', and not a 'weak'

---

[19] CPR 6.13; the topic of 'service' is under review: on 5 July 2007, the Ministry of Justice
published a consultation paper entitled, 'Review of Part 6 of the CPR: Service of Documents'.
[20] CPR 6.3.
[21] CPR 7.5 (3); *Habib Bank Ltd v Central Bank of Sudan* [2006] EWHC 1767 (Comm);
[2007] 1 WLR 470 (validity of service abroad); distinguished, *Olafsson v Gissurarson* [2006]
EWHC 3162 (QB); [2007] 1 All ER 88 (invalid service in Iceland could not be cured under
CPR 3.10); service at a person's last known address within the jurisdiction will be valid even
though he was at the time resident outside the jurisdiction, provided the latter fact was not
known to the claimant at the time of posted service: *City & Country Properties Ltd v Kamali* [2006] EWCA Civ 1879; [2007] 1 WLR 1219 (noted J Sorabi (2007) 26 CJQ 279);
Neuberger LJ (as he then was) explained: '[26] … it is clear that, before a claim form can be
served on a defendant's last known residence in this country, the claimant has to have made
reasonable investigations to find out where the defendant actually resides or carries on business … If, as a result of those investigations, the claimant discovers where the defendant is
living abroad, then of course the claimant cannot rely on CPR 6.5 and must serve in accordance with Section III of CPR 6 [viz serve outside the jurisdiction]. [27] If the claimant has
made reasonable investigations and cannot locate the defendant abroad, then he can issue
proceedings and proceed to judgment, serving the claim form on the defendant's previous
residence in this country with the defendant not knowing. But, if that leads to judgment being entered against him, the defendant can, provided he acts promptly on learning what has
happened, apply to set aside the judgment. If he has an arguable defence or there is some
other unfair prejudice, then judgment can normally be expected to be set aside.'
[22] CPR 7.5(2).
[23] *Thomas v The Home Office* [2006] EWCA Civ 1355; [2007] 1 WLR 230, considering
CPR 2.11; noted J Sorabi [2007] CJQ 168.
[24] CPR 7.6(2).
[25] *Thomas* case, ibid.
[26] *Collier v Williams* [2006] EWCA Civ 20; [2006] 1 WLR 1945 examining, in particular, *Hashtroodi v Hancock* [2004] EWCA Civ 652; [2004] 1 WLR 3206; and case law cited
below at n 41.

reason such as sheer forgetfulness.[27] But if the four month period has already
elapsed at the time the claimant applies for an extension, the rules explicitly
impose the following restrictive criteria: 'the court has been unable to serve the
claim form' or 'the claimant has taken all reasonable steps to serve the claim
form but has been unable to do so' and, in either case, 'the claimant has acted
promptly in making the application'.[28]

3.07   The modes of service, whether by the court or by the claimant, are: in accordance with a prior contract;[29] personal service[30] upon the defendant
(whether an individual, company or partnership);[31] first class post[32] (the place
for valid service by this method is specified in the rules;[33] when service is made
by the court, postal service is the normal method);[34] leaving the claim form at
an address (which can include the relevant office of the defendant's solicitor)
specified in advance for these purposes by the defendant;[35] leaving the claim
form at the defendant's 'usual or last known residence'[36] (in the case of an individual, business proprietor, or firm) or other place specified in the rules;[37]
through a document exchange (unless prohibited in advance by the intended
defendant);[38] by fax or other electronic means (both these modes are in fact
circumscribed);[39] the court can order service by some alternative method;[40] or
the court can even dispense with service.[41] The rules specify the 'deemed day
of service' in these various situations.[42]

---

[27] *Hashtroodi v Hancock* [2004] EWCA Civ 652; [2004] 1 WLR 3206, at [19] and
[20].
[28] CPR 7.6(3); criteria considered in *Carnegie v Drury* [2007] EWCA Civ 497.
[29] CPR 6.15.
[30] CPR 6.2(1)(a).
[31] CPR 6.4(3), (4), (5).
[32] CPR 6.2(1)(b).
[33] CPR 6.5(6).
[34] PD (6) 8.1.
[35] CPR 6.5(1)-(4).
[36] CPR 6.5(6); *Collier v Williams* [2006] EWCA Civ 20; [2006] 1 WLR 1945 at [63] ff
(and rejecting the view that C's reasonable belief that D resided in a particular place is
enough if in fact D never resided there).
[37] CPR 6.5(6).
[38] CPR 6.2(1)(d); PD (6) 2.
[39] CPR 6.2(1)(e); PD (6) 3 (restrictive both for faxes and e-mail); *Kuenyehia v International Hospitals Group Ltd* [2006] EWCA Civ 21; [2006] CP Rep 34.
[40] CPR 6.8.
[41] CPR 6.9; however, the courts will not use CPR 6.9 to relieve liberally against ineffective,
defective, or late service: see the statement of principle by Neuberger LJ, in the *Kuenyehia*
case, [2006] EWCA Civ 21; [2006] CP Rep 34 at [26], considering a farrago of cases, especially *Godwin v Swindon BC* [2001] EWCA Civ 1478; [2002] 1 WLR 997, CA, *Anderton v
Clwyd CC* [2002] EWCA Civ 933; [2002] 1 WLR 3174 and *Cranfield v Bridegrove* [2003]
EWCA Civ 656; [2003] 1 WLR 2441.
[42] CPR 6.7; *Akram v Adam* [2004] EWCA Civ 1601; [2005] 1 WLR 2762, at [42] and [43]
(service effective under this deeming regime even if notice was never received).

(4) Pleadings

The matters in dispute are to be ascertained from the 'statement of case'.[43]   **3.08**
This phrase embraces the claim form, particulars of claim (if separate from the
claim form), the defence, a possible reply to the defence, as well as 'further information'[44] (formerly 'further and better particulars') and a counterclaim or
third party proceeding.[45] The claim form must contain a concise statement of
the nature of the claim and specify the remedy sought.[46] But the court can
grant a remedy even if it is unspecified in the claim form.[47] The particulars of
claim must include 'a concise statement of the facts on which the claimant relies' and include any claim for interest.[48] The claimant is not required to adduce at this early stage details of his intended evidence. The defendant can respond by stating which allegations in the particulars of claim he (i) denies or
(ii) requires to be proved or (iii) admits.[49] The defendant will be 'taken to admit' a particular allegation if his defence contains no response to it, whether
direct or indirect.[50] A party can include in a statement of claim 'any point of
law on which his claim or defence ... is based', and 'the name of any witness he
proposes to call', and 'a copy of any document which he considers is necessary
to his claim or defence ... (including any expert's report to be filed in accordance with [CPR] Part 35).' 'Statements of case' must be verified by a statement of truth.[51] A dishonest statement can lead to contempt proceedings (see
8.35).[52] Special rules govern amendment of statements of case.[53] Documents

---

[43] For this wide definition, CPR 2.3(1).

[44] CPR 18.1; this rule has been used to require a defendant to disclose details of its liability
insurance, *Harcourt v Fef Griffin (Representative of Pegasus Gymnastics Club)* [2007]
EWHC 1500 (QB), Irwin J.

[45] For reasons of space, the complicated law concerning set-off has been omitted from this
work: see Neil Andrews, *English Civil Procedure* (Oxford UP, 2003) 11.07 ff; and for the law
concerning counterclaims, ibid, 11.65 ff; for comparative discussion, R Zimmermann, *Comparative Foundations of a European Law of Set-off and Prescription* (Cambridge UP,
2002).

[46] CPR 16.2(1); PD (16), 12 to 14 for matters which must be included in defences.

[47] CPR 16.2(5).

[48] CPR 16.4.

[49] CPR 16.5(1).

[50] CPR 16.5(5).

[51] CPR 22.1(1)(a).

[52] PD (22) 3.1.

[53] Limitation Act 1980, s 35; CPR 17.4; *Charles Church Developments v Stent Foundations Ltd* [2006] EWHC 3158 (TCC); [2007] 1 WLR 1203; *O'Byrne v Aventis Pasteur
MSD Ltd* [2006] EWHC 2562, (QB); [2007] 1 WLR 757; *BP plc v AON Ltd* [2005] EWHC
2554 (Comm); [2006] 1 Lloyd's Rep 549 at [46] to [63]; *Martin v Kaisary* [2005] EWCA Civ
594; [2005] CP Rep 35; *Goode v Martin* [2001] EWCA Civ 1899; [2002] 1 All ER 620; Neil
Andrews, *English Civil Procedure* (Oxford UP, 2003) 10.78 ff; *Zuckerman on Civil Procedure* (2006) 6.36 ff.

referred to in statements of case become subject to the disclosure regime (see **6.22**).

(5) Limitation of Actions (or 'Prescription')[54]

3.09 The general position adopted in English law is that expiry of a limitation period does not extinguish the claimant's right. And so a limitation defence must be pleaded in the defendant's statement of case.[55] If that defence is not raised, the action cannot be defeated on that basis.[56] However, the contrary principle of automatic extinction of the underlying claim (the 'cause of action') applies in a few exceptional contexts,[57] notably foreign limitation period rules.[58] It should also be noted that the general statutory regime of limitation periods does not apply to claims for injunctive relief or specific performance. Instead claims for those types of remedy are subject to the special 'equitable' bars of 'laches' and acquiescence.[59] The court must then consider in a broad fashion whether the claimant's delay and the impact that this has had on the defendant's position justify withholding these special equitable remedies.

3.10 A person under a 'disability' (lacking mental capacity or a minor) must bring proceedings within three years from the date the disability ceases; or, in the case of a former minor, three years from the time he reaches the age of 18.[60] There

---

[54] Andrews, ibid, ch 12 and *Zuckerman*, ibid, 24.4 ff; A McGee, *Limitation Periods* (2006); Law Commission's discussion, *Limitation of Actions* (Law Com No 270, HC 23, 2001 and L Com CP No 151, 1998); on which, Neil Andrews [1998] CLJ 588; R James (2003) 22 CJQ 41.

[55] PD (16) 13.1.

[56] *Ketteman v Hansel Properties* [1987] AC 189, 219, HL.

[57] L Com CP No 151, 1998, para 9.4, noting certain international conventions, eg, *Payabi v Armstel Shipping Corpn* [1992] QB 907 (the Hague Rules); claims made under the Consumer Protection Act 1987; the tort of conversion, Limitation Act 1980, s 3(2); recovery of land, 1980 Act, s 17; see also discussion in *Financial Services Compensation Scheme Ltd v Larnell (Insurances) Ltd* [2005] EWCA Civ 1408; [2006] QB 808 at [40] ff.

[58] Foreign Limitation Periods Act 1984; eg, *Gotha City v Sotheby's The Times* 8 October 1998; on the mixed systems of prescription (extinction) and limitation (non-extinctive) in Scotland, *Majrowski v Guy's and St Thomas's NHS Trust* [2006] UKHL 34; [2007] 1 AC 224 at [47], per Lord Hope.

[59] *P & O Nedlloyd BV v Arab Metals Co* [2006] EWCA Civ 1717; *Cattley v Pollard* [2006] EWHC 3130 (Ch); [2007] 3 WLR 317, at [151] citing recent authorities, notably *Re Loftus* [2006] EWCA Civ 1124; [2007] 1 WLR 591, at [42]; for literature and other authorities, see Neil Andrews, *English Civil Procedure* (Oxford UP, 2003) 12.81 ff; L Com CP No 151, 1998, paras 9.12 to 9.22; L Com No 270, HC 23, 2001, paras 2.97 to 2.99.

[60] Limitation Act 1980, s 28; L Com CP No 151, 1998, paras 8.2 to 8.10; noting *Headford v Bristol & District Health Authority* [1995] PIQR P180, CA (proceedings commenced in 1992 concerning hospital incident in 1964; claimant permanently brain-damaged at birth).

are special provisions in three situations:[61] where the action is based on the defendant's fraud; secondly, where facts relevant to the claim have been deliberately concealed by the defendant; thirdly, if the action is for relief from the consequences of mistake.[62] The main limitation periods will now be set out (see **3.11** for tort and contract claims and **3.12** for other types of claim).

Tort or Contract Claims: **3.11**

(i) *defamation and malicious falsehood* claims are subject to a one year rule;[63]

(ii) *personal injury and fatal accident* claims: the claimant has three years from the date of damage, or from the (later) date when he acquired 'knowledge' of the wrong;[64] there is a discretionary power to lift the statutory bar in the case of actions for personal injury or fatal accidents;[65]

(iii) *assault claims*, including instances of alleged sexual abuse: a *non-extendable* (compare (ii) above) six year period governs;[66]

(iv) *negligence claims in tort for 'latent damage'*: that is, forms of damage or loss which are not reasonably apparent to the victim at the time of the initial breach of duty; such instances of 'latent damage' are subject either to a six year period, reckoned from the date at which the cause of action accrued, or a three year period running from the 'starting date' (when the claimant acquired know-

---

[61] 1980 Act, s 32.

[62] As for fraud, see, eg, *Cattley v Pollard* [2006] EWHC 3130 (Ch); [2007] 3 WLR 317, at [151; as for deliberate concealment, *Cave v Robinson, Jarvis and Rolf* [2002] UKHL 18; [2003] 1 AC 368, HL (T Prime (2002) 21 CJQ 357) considered in *Williams v Fanshaw Porter & Hazelhurst* [2004] EWCA Civ 157; [2004] 1 WLR 3185; as for relief from the consequences of mistake, *Kleinwort Benson Ltd v Lincoln CC* [1999] 2 AC 349, HL; but, as noted by Lord Mance in *Sempra Metals Ltd v Inland Revenue Commissioners* [2007] UKHL 34; [2007] 3 WLR 354, at [200]: 'from 8th September 2003 … s 320 of the Finance Act 2004 in fact means that the provisions of s 32(1)(c) of the Limitation Act 1980 no longer apply to mistakes of law *relating to a taxation matter under the care and management of the [Inland] Revenue.*'

[63] 1980 Act, ss 4A, 32A.

[64] 1980 Act, ss 11, 12 to 14; L Com CP No 151 (1998) paras 3.38 ff; *Adams v Bracknell Forest Borough Council* [2004] UKHL 29; [2005] 1 AC 76; R Moules (2005) CJQ 37; *Young v South Tyneside MBC* [2006] EWCA Civ 1534; [2007] 2 WLR 1192; *McCoubrey v Ministry of Defence* [2007] EWCA Civ 17; [2007] 1 WLR 1544.

[65] 1980 Act, s 33; *Adams v Bracknell Forest Borough Council* [2004] UKHL 29; [2005] 1 AC 76; R Moules (2005) CJQ 37; *KR v Bryn Alyn Community (Holdings) Ltd* [2003] EWCA Civ 85; [2003] QB 1441; *Horton v Sadler* [2006] UKHL 27; [2006] 2 WLR 1346: reversing *Walkley v Precision Forgings Ltd* [1979] 1 WLR 606, HL.

[66] 1980 Act, s 2; *A v Hoare* [2006] EWCA Civ 395; [2006] 1 WLR 2320, applying *Stubbings v Webb* [1993] AC 498, HL; but negligence claims against the employers of sexual assaulters are subject to the (extendable) three year period (on which see the preceding two notes): *Young v South Tyneside MBC* [2006] EWCA Civ 1534; [2007] 2 WLR 1192.

ledge of the claim and of his capacity to bring it);[67] a 'long-stop' provision bars a latent damage claim once fifteen years have elapsed since the act of alleged negligence;[68] it should be noted that the latent damage rules apply only to negligence pleaded in tort (and not in contract);[69] these provisions only concern *damage to property or economic loss*; a common situation is an allegation of defective building or design, or negligent accounting or other professional service; the latent damage provisions do *not* concern claims for personal injury or fatal accidents (for which see (ii) above);

(v) *general regime for tort or contractual claims*: subject to (i) to (iv), other tort actions (for damages) or contractual claims (for damages or debt) are subject to a six year rule;[70] occasionally, the starting point for this period of limitation can differ depending on whether the claim is in tort or in contract; this is because, as Lord Nicholls succinctly observed, in contractual cases 'the cause of action for breach of contract arises *at the date of the breach of contract*' but 'in cases in *tort* the cause of action arises, not when the culpable conduct occurs, but *when the plaintiff first sustains damage*.'[71] The House of Lords, in another case concerning a claim in tort for negligent accounting, held that the failure to identify a contingent financial liability does not constitute 'damage'. Instead the relevant date is when damage actually materialises.[72] Where there are overlapping rights in contract and tort, that is, a 'concurrence' of claims, a claimant can sue both in contract and tort, or in either.[73]

(vi) *specific performance*:[74] This remedy is only available if the contract is supported by consideration (that is, the promise was not gratuitous, but some-

---

[67] 1980 Act, s 14A, added by Latent Damage Act 1986; *Haward v Fawcetts (a firm)* [2006] UKHL 9; [2006] 1 WLR 682; J O'Sullivan, 'Limitation, Latent Damage and Solicitors' Negligence' (2004) 20 Journal of Professional Negligence 218.

[68] 1980 Act, s 14B.

[69] *Iron Trade Mutual Insurance Co Ltd v J K Buckenham Ltd* [1990] 1 All ER 808; affmd *Société Générale de Réeassurance v Eras (International) Ltd* (note) [1992] 2 All ER 82, CA.

[70] 1980 Act, ss 2 and 5 respectively.

[71] *Nykredit Mortgage Bank plc v Edward Erdman Group Ltd (No 2)* [1997] 1 WLR 1627, 1630, HL.

[72] *Law Society v Sephton & Co (a firm)* [2006] UKHL 22; [2006] 2 AC 543.

[73] *Henderson v Merrett Syndicates Ltd* [1995] 2 AC 145, 184–194, HL.

[74] The leading modern study is GH Jones and W Goodhart, *Specific Performance* (2nd edn, 1996), superseding as the practitioner's text the out-dated *Fry on Specific Performance* (6th edn, 1921); AS Burrows, *Remedies for Torts and Breach of Contract* (3rd edn, Oxford UP, 2004) ch 20; Burrows in P Birks (ed), *English Private Law* (Oxford UP, 2000), 18–168 to 18–185; *Chitty on Contracts* (29th edn, 2004) ch 28; D Harris, D Campbell, R Halson, *Remedies in Contract and Tort* (2nd edn, 2002, reprinted Cambridge UP, 2005) ch 12; Canada: R Sharpe, *Injunctions and Specific Performance* (looseleaf edn, Toronto, 2002); S Waddams, *The Law of Contract* (4th edn, Ontario, 1999), ch 20; Australia: Meagher, Gummow and Lehane, *Equity: Doctrines and Remedies* (4th edn, Sydney, 2003) ch 20; S Hepburn in P Parkinson (eds), *Principles of Equity* (Sydney, 1996), ch 17; *Spry's Equitable Remedies* (6th edn, Sydney 2001) ch's 3 (specific performance), 4 (injunctions), 5 (injunctions and contracts), and 7 (damages and Lord Cairns's

thing was given or promised in return) and the remedies of damages or debt would provide inadequate relief; only in the context of agreements for the transfer of land or shares in private companies is specific performance the primary remedy;[75] the reason specific performance is regularly granted in those situations is that the relevant subject-matter is, or is regarded as, 'unique'; the Court of Appeal has held that the remedy of specific performance for breach of contract is not subject to the six year rule applicable to contractual claims for damages or debt;[76] instead, this equitable remedy is subject to the doctrines of laches and acquiescence (see **3.09** above).[77]

(vii) *actions on deeds*: In the case of claims for damages or non-payment of debt claims arising from breach of a deed, the period is twelve years[78] (a 'deed' is also known as a 'covenant'; it is a formal written contract, signed by the covenantor, who makes the promise, witnessed by a third party, and 'delivered', normally by face-to-face transfer, to the covenantee).[79]

(viii) *third party claims upon contracts*: The Contracts (Rights of Third Parties) Act 1999 applies the six year rule and twelve year rule, respectively, to third party claims upon simple contracts[80] and contracts founded upon deeds, on which see (vii).[81]

Other Limitation Periods: 3.12

(ix) *statutory contribution claims*: a two year limitation period applies;[82]

(x) *restitution claims*: (for example, in respect of mistaken payments) there is no general provision governing actions for restitution, but the statutory limitation rules have been applied in a piece-meal way to many such claims;[83]

Act); comparative account: GH Treitel, *Remedies for Breach of Contract: A Comparative Account* ch III (Oxford UP, 1988) (comparative discussion; common law, ibid, at 63 ff); Yorio, *Contract Enforcement: Specific Performance and Injunctions* (USA, 1989).

[75] eg, specific performance to compel transfer of shares in a private company: *Harvela v Royal Trust Bank of Canada* [1986] AC 207, HL.

[76] *P & O Nedlloyd BV v Arab Metals Co* [2006] EWCA Civ 1717; [2007], WLR 2483, at [52].

[77] ibid, at [55] ff.

[78] 1980 Act, s 8.

[79] For the formalities of a deed, s 1(2)(3) Law of Property (Miscellaneous Provisions) Act 1989; GH Treitel, *The Law of Contract* (12th edn, 2007) 5–008; *Bolton MBC v Torkington* [2004] Ch 66, CA.

[80] A 'simple contract' is a legally enforceable agreement other than one made by deed.

[81] Contracts (Rights of Third Parties) Act 1999, s 7(3).

[82] Limitation Act 1980, s 10 (claims under the Civil Liability (Contribution) Act 1978); *Aer Lingus v Gildacroft Ltd* [2006] EWCA Civ 4; [2006] 1 WLR 1173 (date runs from time that primary liability is quantified).

[83] L Com No 270, HC 23, 2001, paras 2.48 to 2.51.

(xi) *actions for recovery of land, or concerning mortgages*: special provisions apply;[84]

(xii) *non-fraudulent breaches of trust*: special provisions apply.[85]

(6) Case Management[86]

3.13   As examined in the next paragraph, the courts possess extensive 'case management' powers. In his reports of 1995–6[87] Lord Woolf adopted this technique as the mainstay for actions on the 'multi-track' (see **3.04** above), thus including all High Court litigation.[88] The court must ensure that matters are properly focused, procedural indiscipline checked, expense reduced, progress accelerated, and that just outcomes are facilitated or awarded. Case management has three main functions:[89] to encourage the parties to pursue mediation, where this is practicable (generally, see chapter 11); secondly, to prevent the case from progressing too slowly and inefficiently; finally, to ensure that judicial resources are allocated proportionately, as required by 'the Overriding Objective' in CPR Part One. This aspect of Part One requires the court and parties to consider the competing demands of other litigants who wish to gain access to judges, whose court-room availability represent the court's 'scarce resources'.[90]

3.14   The CPR lists various managerial responsibilities. These are not intended to be exhaustive statements of the court's new active role.[91] Judges, especially at first instance, have the following managerial responsibilities: *co-operation and settlement*: encouraging co-operation between the parties;[92] helping parties to

---

[84] 1980 Act, ss 15–17 (recovery of land); s 20 (mortgages).

[85] ibid, s 21; for a careful review of the ambit of this provision, see *Cattley v Pollard* [2006] EWHC 3130 (Ch); [2007] 3 WLR 317 (summary of conclusions at [158]).

[86] On the new system from the perspective of the traditional adversarial principle, Neil Andrews, 'A New Civil Procedural Code for England: Party-Control "Going, Going, Gone"' (2000) 19 CJQ 19–38; Neil Andrews, English Civil Procedure (Oxford UP, 2003) 13.12 to 13.41; 14.04 to 14.45; 15.65 to 15.72.

[87] Lord Woolf's two reports are: *Access to Justice: Interim Report* (1995) and *Access to Justice: Final Report* (1996): for comment, A Zuckerman and R Cranston, *The Reform of Civil Procedure: Essays on 'Access to Justice'* (Oxford UP, 1995); see also R Cranston, *How Law Works: The Machinery and Impact of Civil Justice* (Oxford UP, 2006) ch 5.

[88] eg, Neil Andrews, *English Civil Procedure* (Oxford UP, 2003) chs 13, 14, 15; *Zuckerman on Civil Procedure* (2006) at 1.74 ff, ch 10, 11.53 ff.

[89] On case management and settlement, S Roberts, 'Settlement as Civil Justice' (2000) 63 MLR 739, 745–7.

[90] eg Neil Andrews, *English Civil Procedure* (Oxford UP, 2003) chs 13, 14, 15; *Zuckerman on Civil Procedure* (2006) at 1.74 ff, ch 10, 11.53 ff.

[91] CPR 1.4(2); CPR 3.1(2); CPR Parts 26, 28, 29.

[92] CPR 1.4(2)(a).

settle all or part of the case;[93] encouraging alternative dispute resolution;[94] if necessary, staying the action to enable such extra-curial negotiations or discussions to be pursued (see **11.31**);[95] *determining relevance and priorities:* helping to identify the issues in the case;[96] deciding the order in which the issues are to be resolved;[97] deciding which issues need a full trial and which can be dealt with summarily;[98] *making summary decisions:*[99] deciding whether to initiate a summary hearing (under CPR Part 24);[100] or whether the claim or defence can be struck out as having no prospect of success (including making striking out the automatic result of failure to comply with a procedural order);[101] or whether to dispose of a case on a preliminary issue;[102] excluding issues from consideration;[103] *maintaining impetus:* fixing time-tables and controlling in other ways the progress of the case;[104] giving directions which will bring the case to trial as quickly and efficiently as possible;[105] *regulating expenditure:* deciding whether a proposed step in the action is cost-effective,[106] taking into account the size of the claim ('proportionality').[107] Lord Woolf commented on these powers:

'... judges have to be trusted to exercise the wide discretions which they have fairly and justly ... [Appeal courts] should not interfere unless judges can be shown to have exercised their powers in some way which contravenes the relevant principles.'[108]

A party must obtain permission to appeal from a case management decision, but this will be difficult to obtain (generally on permission to appeal, **8.12**).[109]

---

[93] CPR 1.4(2)(f).

[94] CPR 1.4(2)(e).

[95] CPR 3.1(2)(f).

[96] CPR 1.4(2)(a).

[97] CPR 1.4(2)(d); 3.1(2)(j).

[98] CPR 1.4(2)(c).

[99] On summary judgment, see **5.18**, on striking out, **5.23**, and on preliminary issues, **5.17**.

[100] PD (26) 5.1, 5.2.

[101] CPR 3.4(2); as for striking out for failure to comply with an 'unless' order, see **2.21** at n 62, examining *Marcan Shipping (London) Ltd v Kefelas* [2007] EWCA Civ 463; [2007] 1 WLR 1864, at [33] to [36].

[102] CPR 3.1(2)(l).

[103] CPR 3.1(2)(k).

[104] CPR 1.4(2)(g).

[105] CPR 1.4(2)(l).

[106] eg, suggestion that video-conferencing be used for short appeals: *Black v Pastouna* [2005] EWCA Civ 1389; [2006] CP Rep 11, per Brooke LJ.

[107] CPR 1.4(2)(h) and 1.1(2)(c).

[108] *Biguzzi v Rank Leisure plc* [1999] 1 WLR 1926, 1934 F, CA, per Lord Woolf MR.

[109] PD (52) 4.4, 4.5: 'Case management decisions include decisions made under rule 3.1(2) [containing a long list of procedural powers] and decisions about disclosure, filing of witness statements, or experts' reports, directions about the timetable of the claim, adding a party to a claim, and security for costs.' In this context, a decision concerning permission to appeal requires consideration whether 'the issue is of sufficient significance to justify the costs of an appeal', 'the procedural consequences of an appeal (eg loss of trial date) outweigh

Appellate courts are prepared to show considerable deference to judges' case management decisions, unless they are incorrect in principle.[110]

3.15   Sir Anthony Clarke, the Master of the Rolls, in a lecture in 2007, encapsulated the essence of the case management regime:[111]

'Taken together, the Overriding Objective [in CPR Part One] and active judicial case management [notably CPR 3.1] seek to ensure that each case is afforded no more than a proportionate amount of judicial and party resources, that the real issues in dispute are identified early and concentrated upon by the court and the parties, and that the claim is dealt with expeditiously.'

He added that the knife of judicial management, whetted by the principles of proportionality and expedition, permits:

'a simple and straightforward procedural system to be tailored effectively to the needs of the court, the parties and to litigants in general so that justice in the individual case can be achieved at a reasonable costs and within a reasonable timeframe.'

3.16   The foreign reader will be especially interested in the style of judicial case management practised in the Commercial Court in London.[112] This court is part of the Queen's Bench Division within the High Court. It has its own detailed procedural code: 'The Admiralty and Commercial Courts Guide'.[113] Its judges hear all pre-trial applications, including case management hearings.[114] This contrasts with the general pattern in the Queen's Bench Division where full High Court judges ('puisne judges') are generally involved in civil litigation only at trial and Masters hear many pre-trial matters.[115]

3.17   There are two important pre-trial hearings, the 'case management conference' ('CMC') and the 'pre-hearing review'. The following documents must be

---

the significance of the case management decision', and whether 'it would be more convenient to determine the issue at or after trial'.

[110] *Thomson v O'Connor* [2005] EWCA Civ 1533 at [17] to [19], per Brooke LJ; *Three Rivers DC v Bank of England* [2005] EWCA Civ 889; [2005] CP Rep 46, at [55] see also the authorities cited in Neil Andrews, *English Civil Procedure* (Oxford UP, 2003) 13.61 to 13.68, 38.49; *Zuckerman on Civil Procedure* (2006) 23.193 ff.

[111] Sir Anthony Clarke MR, 'The Supercase-Problems and Solutions', 2007 Annual KPMG Forensic Lecture: available at http://www.judiciary.gov.uk/docs/speeches/kpmg_speech.pdf.

[112] Supreme Court Act 1981, s 6(1)(2); A Colman, *Commercial Court* (5th edn, 2000) ch 5; S Sugar and R Wilson (eds), *Commercial and Mercantile Courts Litigation Practice* (2004).

[113] The Admiralty and Commercial Courts Guide (7th edn, 2006) available at http://www.hmcourts-service.gov.uk/publications/guidance/admiralcomm/index.htm; A Colman, *Commercial Court* (5th edn, 2000) 19–20; S Sugar and R Wilson (eds), *Commercial and Mercantile Courts Litigation Practice* (2004); R Cranston, 'Complex Litigation: the Commercial Court' (2007) 26 CJQ 190.

[114] A Colman, *Commercial Court* (5th edn, 2000) 6–7; S Sugar and R Wilson (eds), *Commercial and Mercantile Courts Litigation Practice* (2004).

[115] 'Puisne' is the adjective used to describe High Court judges who are knighted or decorated as 'Dame'; see also **2.04**.

prepared for a CMC: (i) an agreed case memorandum,[116] that is, a 'short and uncontroversial description' of 'what the case is about'; (ii) a 'list of issues' which should comprise: 'important ... issues of fact and issues of law' and 'what is common ground between the parties ...';[117] (iii) two 'case management information sheets'[118] setting out the parties' respective proposals regarding documentary disclosure, preliminary issues, factual and expert witnesses (names or at least their fields of expertise), and an estimate of readiness for, and length of, trial;[119] (iv) a draft order (agreed by the parties) for consideration by the judge and a statement signed by each advocate explaining plans for ADR or why the dispute is not suitable for that technique;[120] (v) the claimant must also prepare a case management bundle.[121] A CMC is generally oral.[122] Clients need not attend, unless the court orders. Each party should send a solicitor and at least one advocate.[123] The judge will discuss with the advocates the issues raised in the case, and fix the pre-trial timetable,[124] including a 'progress monitoring date'.[125] The judge might make an 'ADR order'[126] and 'stay' the proceedings (see **11.38**). Finally, the judge will consider 'the possibility of the trial of preliminary issues' (see **5.17**) which might shorten the action. After this conference, the parties must arrange with the clerk to the court a fixed date for trial.

The aim of the 'pre-trial review' is to ensure that trial proceeds efficiently and fairly:[127] 'The judge may set a timetable for the trial and give such other directions for the conduct of the trial as he considers appropriate.'[128] Each   **3.18**

---

[116] The Admiralty and Commercial Courts Guide (7th edn, 2006), D5; Colman, ibid, 64–5; for an example, Colman, ibid, 83; S Sugar and R Wilson (eds), *Commercial and Mercantile Courts Litigation Practice* (2004).

[117] The Guide, ibid, D6; Colman, ibid, 65–6, and for an example, 84; S Sugar and R Wilson (eds), *Commercial and Mercantile Courts Litigation Practice* (2004).

[118] The Guide, ibid, D8.5 and Appendix 6; see also PD (58) 10.7; Colman, ibid, 66; S Sugar and R Wilson (eds), *Commercial and Mercantile Courts Litigation Practice* (2004).

[119] Various questions are posed in the case management information sheet (see Appendix 6 to the Guide, at [15]).

[120] The Guide, ibid, D8.3(e).

[121] The Guide, ibid, D7; Colman, ibid, 67; S Sugar and R Wilson (eds), *Commercial and Mercantile Courts Litigation Practice* (2004).

[122] The Guide, ibid, D8.3; Colman, ibid, 69–70; S Sugar and R Wilson (eds), ibid.

[123] The Guide, ibid, D8.2; Colman, ibid; S Sugar and R Wilson (eds), ibid.

[124] The Guide, ibid, D8.10, D8.11.

[125] ibid, D12.

[126] Such an 'order' is a misnomer; it does not compel the parties to engage in ADR, but at most to take 'such serious steps as they may be advised to resolve their disputes by ADR procedures ...' (see **11.37**); and for details of the Commercial Court's special version of this 'order', see Appendix 7 of the Guide.

[127] The Guide, D18.

[128] ibid, D18.4.

party must later confirm that he has satisfied these directions and is ready for trial.[129]

(7) 'Supercases' and Scope for Refinement of Case Management

3.19   In a lecture in 2007 the Master of the Rolls, Sir Anthony Clarke, acknowledged that the CPR still provides opportunity for litigation to spin out of control.[130] His Lordship was discussing the so-called 'Supercase' problem. He cited two recent pieces of litigation, both before the Commercial Court in London (which forms part of the Queen's Bench Division of the High Court). These two cases have several things in common: they were prolonged and expensive; the claims were ultimately abortive; in each case the three-headed monster of extreme cost, great delay and complexity had warped the legal process. Trial in the Commercial Court in the first of these, *Equitable Life Assurance v Ernst & Young*, began in April 2005 and was settled in November 2005 (the whole litigation took four years).[131] Trial in the second Commercial Court case, *Three Rivers District Council and others v Governor of the Bank of England*, lasted almost two years (the litigation as a whole twelve years; see **5.28**).

3.20   Such monster cases are an embarrassment. They bring the law into disrepute. They sap confidence in the capacity of the court system to marshal disputes effectively. However, the Master of the Rolls is correct to observe that such cases are atypical, in fact freakish. The reality is that most cases litigated under the CPR system are handled with reasonable speed, the issues are efficiently identified, and the costs, although heavy, do not exceed the GNP of various smaller nations.

3.21   Among the lessons that might be drawn from such 'monster' litigation, the following issues stand out: (i) whether the judges should be still more robust, when exercising their case management powers, to ensure that complex cases are conducted efficiently; (ii) possibly greater use, where appropriate, of electronic assistance, especially with regard to exchange of documents during disclosure; (iii) whether mediation might be employed more imaginatively and perhaps earlier; for example, it has been suggested that mediation might re-

---

[129]   ibid, D14, states: 'Not later than three weeks before the date fixed for trial each party must send to the Listing Office (with a copy to all other parties) a completed check-list confirming final details for trial (a 'pre-trial checklist') in the form set out in Appendix 13 [to the Guide].'

[130]   Sir Anthony Clarke MR, 'The Supercase – Problems and Solutions', 2007 Annual KPMG Forensic Lecture: available at http://www.judiciary.gov.uk/docs/speeches/kpmg_speech.pdf.

[131]   R Reed, 'Company Directors: Collective or Functional Responsibility' (2006) 27 Co Lawyer 170.

solve 'internal' or 'mini' procedural issues, such as the scope of disclosure; (iv) whether to adopt a special code to govern especially complex commercial cases (an idea which has not been adopted); (v) recognising the isolation and pressures experienced by judges involved in complex and prolonged commercial litigation;[132] in response to this, taking steps to support judges by use of judicial associates and adjunct judges, the latter to be used as 'sounding boards' for pre-trial decisions in complex and protracted cases; (vi) introducing a deeper and more trenchant approach to striking out claims and defences, to avoid trial of weak issues.

In October 2006, a symposium was held to examine litigation within the **3.22** Commercial Court. It is in this court where recent examples of 'monster' litigation have occurred.[133] Addressing the points mentioned in the preceding paragraph, it is reported that 'the key suggestions emerging from the 2006 symposium' concerned the following matters:[134] (i) widespread allocation of cases to specific judges; (ii) listing of cases to ensure adequate reading time; (iii) more vigorous exercise of case management powers; (iv) the facility for indications from the judge as to the merits of the claim; (v) restrictions on expensive disclosure of electronic material; (vi) limitation of length and cost of witness statements; (vii) the imposition of more realistic but nonetheless strict timetables.

---

[132] R Cranston, 'Complex Litigation: The Commercial Court' (2007) 26 CJQ 190, 204–5.

[133] See preceding and next notes for details.

[134] 'Report of the Commercial Court and the Admiralty Courts' (2005–6): www.judiciary.gov.uk/docs/annual_report_comm_admiralty_ct_0506.pdf.

Chapter 4

Protective Relief

Contents

(1) Introduction

4.01   Let us begin by considering four issues: (i) the nature of 'protective relief'; (ii) the various forms of such relief; (iii) when it can be sought; and (iv) specialist literature on this topic. As for (i), its nature, a distinction can be drawn between (a) 'protective relief' and (b) interim or (c) accelerated final justice concerning the substantive merits of the case: the topics of interim, summary, peremptory ('striking out'), and default relief, orders, or judgments are examined in chapter 5). Common to all three heads, (a) to (c), is the fact that orders or judgments are issued without trial. But protective relief, category (a), differs from categories (b) and (c) because it does not concern relief with respect to the substantive merits (an interim or final award offering substantive relief). Protective relief is, therefore, merely ancillary to the substantive claim. Its function is not to anticipate the final result by giving some portion or temporary enjoyment of that final relief (compare interim payments and interim injunctions), nor does protective relief involve accelerated adjudication or disposal of the substance of the claim (compare summary judgment, striking out orders, and default judgments). As for issue (ii), in England protective relief operates to preserve assets against disposal by the defendant, or to preserve evidence, or to secure eventual payment of costs ('security for costs' orders). Turning to issue (iii), freezing injunctions and search orders are normally sought before, or at an early stage of, the substantive proceedings; or they might be sought in England (or elsewhere) in support of primary proceedings intended or pending in a foreign legal system. Finally, issue (iv), protective relief is examined in the English literature on civil procedure,[1] in dis-

---

[1] Neil Andrews, *English Civil Procedure* (Oxford UP, 2003), ch 17; *Zuckerman on Civil*

cussion of commercial arbitration,[2] comparative procedure,[3] and it is recognised within the American Law Institute/UNIDROIT's canon of 'transnational' principles of civil litigation.[4]

Protective relief to secure the *claimant's* interests takes two main[5] forms: **4.02** first, orders for the freezing of the defendant's assets (freezing injunctions, formerly *Mareva* injunctions); secondly, orders for the seizure and preservation of evidence (search orders, formerly *Anton Piller* orders). Both are commonly sought before trial and 'without notice' to the defendant: that is, (to use the former English terminology), they are awarded *ex parte*.[6] A third form of protective relief operates, unlike the first two just mentioned, in favour of a *defendant*. This is an order for security of costs against a claimant. This protects the defendant against the risk that the claimant might be unwilling or unable to

---

Procedure (2006) ch 9; IS Goldrein (ed), *Commercial Litigation: Pre-emptive Remedies* (International Edition, 2005).

[2] International commercial arbitration, A Redfern, 'Interim Measures' in LW Newman and RD Hill (eds), *The Leading Arbitrators' Guide to International Arbitration* (Bern, 2004), at 217 ff and F Knoepfler 'Les Mésures Provisoires et l'Arbitrage' in L Cadiet, E Jeuland, T Clay (eds), *Médiation et Arbitrage: Alternative Dispute Resolution-Alternative a la justice ou justice alternative? Perspectives comparatives* (Lexis Nexis: Litec, Paris, 2005); for the position in international commercial arbitration, A Redfern, 'Interim Measures' in LW Newman and RD Hill (eds), *The Leading Arbitrators' Guide to International Arbitration* (Bern, 2004), 217–43; H van Houtte, 'Ten Reasons Against a Proposal for Ex Parte Interim Measures of Protection in Arbitration' (2004) 20 Arbitration International 85; A Baykitch and J Truong, 'Innovations in Internaitonal Commercial Arbitration: Interim Measures a Way Forward or Back to the Future' (2005) 25 The Arbitrator and Mediator 95; and on the same context, M Mustill and S Boyd, *Commercial Arbitration* (2001, Companion Volume) at 314–6, 323–4, considering, respectively, ss 39, 44, Arbitration Act 1996; see also on those provisions the Departmental Advisory Committee (on the Arbitration legislation), on clauses 39, 44 (the report is reproduced in M Mustill and S Boyd, *Commercial Arbitration* (2001, Companion Volume) and in *Russell on Arbitration* (2003, Appendix 3); the arbitral tribunal has power under s 39, 1996 Act, but only if the parties consent, to make a 'provisional' decision on the substance of the case, for example for an interim payment; the High Court has power under s 44, 1996 Act, to award (ex parte) freezing relief or a search order in support of pending or contemplated arbitration proceedings, if the matter is 'urgent'; therefore, the arbitral tribunal itself lacks power to award ex parte freezing relief or search orders.

[3] Neil Andrews, 'Provisional and Protective Measures: Towards an Uniform Provisional Order' (2001) Uniform L Rev (Rev dr unif) vol VI 931; Stephen Goldstein, 'Revisiting Preliminary Relief in Light of the ALI/UNIDROIT Principles and the New Israeli Rules' in *Studia in honorem: Pelayia Yessiou-Faltsi* (Athens, 2007) 273–96.

[4] *ALI/UNIDROIT: Principles of Transnational Civil Procedure* (Cambridge UP, 2006), principle 8; on which Stephen Goldstein, 'Revisiting Preliminary Relief in Light of the ALI/UNIDROIT Principles and the New Israeli Rules' in *Studia in honorem: Pelayia Yessiou-Faltsi* (Athens, 2007) 273.

[5] A minor remedy, discussed below at **4.43**, concerns orders designed to prevent a defendant, or prospective defendant, from fleeing the jurisdiction.

[6] cf the argument against grant of ex parte relief by commercial arbitrators, H van Houtte, 'Ten Reasons Against a Proposal for Ex Parte Interim Measures of Protection in Arbitration' (2004) 20 Arbitration International 85.

pay the defendant's costs if the action ends with a costs order in favour of the defendant. These various forms of protective relief will now be examined.

(2) Preservation of Assets: Freezing Injunctions[7]

Nature

4.03   Once known as *Mareva* injunctions, later ratified by Parliament,[8] they are now called 'freezing injunctions',[9] the standard form being provided within CPR Part 25.[10] The injunction's function is to preserve assets from dissipation pending final execution against the defendant. A freezing injunction is an *in personam* order which compels a defendant to refrain from dealing with his assets. It also imposes a collateral restraint upon non-parties, such as the defendant's bank. It does not give the applicant any proprietary interest in the defendant's assets.[11]

4.04   This order commonly applies to the defendant's bank account assets. The terms of the order normally provide that a portion of those assets, above a protected sum, should remain 'unfrozen'. The defendant is permitted to satisfy his ordinary domestic or business expenses, and to pay for legal advice when resisting the order.[12]

4.05   The injunction operates at first 'without notice' (*ex parte*), usually before the main proceedings against the defendant have commenced. Its essence is a surprise procedural strike, but the merits of the order are reviewed at an *inter partes* hearing, when the court must decide whether the order should be continued or discharged. In fact applications for freezing relief can be made in anticipation of proceedings (whether the main proceedings will be heard in

---

[7] The leading work is S Gee, *Commercial Injunctions* (2004); see also N Andrews, *English Civil Procedure* (Oxford UP, 2003), ch 17; *Zuckerman on Civil Procedure* (2006) 9.139 ff; IS Goldrein (ed), *Commercial Litigation: Pre-emptive Remedies* (International Edition, 2005) ch 2; for extensive bibliographical details on this topic, see N Andrews, op cit, 17.01 at n 7 and Neil Andrews 'Provisional and Protective Measures: Towards a Uniform Provisional Order' (2001) Uniform L Rev (Rev dr unif) vol VI pp 931–49, at n 4 (this article contains analysis of a possible 'blue-print' for an international code or practice relating to freezing relief, preservation of evidence, and asset disclosure orders).

[8] s 37(3), Supreme Court Act 1981.

[9] CPR 25.1(1)(f) renames the injunction.

[10] PD (25): accessible at http://www.justice.gov.uk/civil/procrules_fin/menus/rules.htm.

[11] *Cretanor Maritime Co Ltd v Irish Marine Maritime Ltd* [1978] 3 All ER 164, CA; *Capital Cameras Ltd v Harold Lines Ltd* [1991] 1 WLR 54; *Flightline v Edwards* [2003] 1 WLR 1200, CA.

[12] PD (25); for examination of the legal expenses exception, *United Mizrahi Bank v Doherty Ltd* [1998] 1 WLR 435.

England or elsewhere, see **4.24** below); or after commencement but before judgment on the substance of the dispute; or after judgment.[13]

An unsuccessful applicant should not make repeated applications for freez-   **4.06** ing relief on the same facts, unless either he uncovers new evidence or there is a justifiable change of legal argument. Subject to this, therefore, the proper course is to appeal from refusal of such an application.[14] However, issue estoppel (on which **8.24**) does not arise from an unsuccessful application for 'without notice' relief.[15]

Most freezing injunctions are awarded by the High Court rather than the   **4.07** county courts (on these two first instance courts, see **2.03**).[16] This reflects the draconian nature of this type of order.[17] In the interests of consistency and judicious decision-making, exercise of this delicate discretion is safeguarded if the remedy is confined to experienced, high-ranking, and specialist civil judges, members of the English High Court. Only full 'puisne' judges, and not Masters, are permitted to issue injunctions, a restriction which includes freezing relief (see also **2.04**).

Assets Disclosure Orders

A freezing injunction is nearly always supplemented by an asset disclosure or-   **4.08** der. This compels the respondent to disclose details of his assets in England (or, where appropriate, elsewhere),[18] whether or not the assets are in his own name, and whether or not solely owned.[19] For example, freezing relief can be made against a respondent who holds assets as trustee or nominee for another. Cross-examination of a respondent on the accuracy of this disclosure is possible even though the respondent has already disclosed an amount of assets sufficient to cover the applicant's substantive claim.[20] A person (including non-

---

[13] eg, post-judgment, *Flightwise Travel Service Ltd v Gill The Times* 5 December 2003, Neuberger J; [2003] EWHC 3082 (Ch).

[14] *Laemthong International Lines Co Ltd v ARTIS* [2005] 1 Lloyd's Rep 100; [2004] 2 All ER (Comm) 797, Colman J at [24].

[15] ibid at [65].

[16] PD (25): Masters or District judges can make such orders only in special cases.

[17] *Fourie v Le Roux* [2007] UKHL 1; [2007] 1 WLR 320 recently emphasised this feature.

[18] *Derby & Co Ltd v Weldon (No 1)* [1990] Ch 48, CA; *Derby & Co Ltd v Weldon (Nos 3 & 4)* [1990] Ch 65, 86, 94–5, CA; *Bank of Crete SA v Koskotas* [1991] 2 Lloyd's Rep 587, CA; LA Collins (1989) 105 LQR 262, 286 ff; C McLachlan 'The Jurisdictional Limits of Disclosure Orders: Transnational Fraud Litigation' (1998) ICLQ 3.

[19] PD (25); *AJ Bekhor & Co Ltd v Bilton* [1981] 1 QB 923, CA; *A v C (Note)* [1981] 1 QB 956, Goff J; *Bankers Trust Co v Shapira* [1980] 1 WLR 1274, CA.

[20] *Motorola Credit Corpn v Uzan (No 2)* [2004] 1 WLR 113, CA [138] to [147], per Millett LJ.

parties, see next paragraph) who is subject to such an ancillary order can sometimes invoke the privilege against self-incrimination (see **6.26**) to provide information.[21]

4.09   A non-party can be compelled to provide certain information if he has assisted, albeit innocently, another's wrongdoing.[22]

Dangers of 'Without Notice' Proceedings

4.10   Freezing injunctions[23] must be handled with the utmost care because they are available upon an application 'without notice' (formerly denoted as *'ex parte'*).[24] And so the respondent has, at first, no opportunity to contradict the applicant's submissions.

Criteria for Grant of Freezing Injunctions[25]

4.11   The following conditions must be satisfied before a freezing injunction can be awarded. First, the applicant must show a good arguable case that he is entitled to damages or some other underlying relief. This is a low threshold.[26] However, the House of Lords in 2007 held that a freezing injunction had been invalidly awarded when the applicant had made no attempt at all to indicate

---

[21] *Sonangol v Lundqvist* [1991] 2 QB 310, CA; information disclosed under a disclosure order, including in response to cross-examination, ancillary to a freezing order can be used for contempt purposes, *Dadourian Group International Inc v Simms* [2006] EWCA Civ 1745; [2007] 2 All ER 329.

[22] On the 'mere witness' rule, see *Norwich Pharmacal Co v Customs and Excise* [1974] AC 133, HL and, in the present context, *Bankers Trust Co v Shapira* [1980] 1 WLR 1274, CA, *Arab Monetary Fund v Hashim (No 5)* [1992] 2 All ER 911, Hoffmann J; on the whole topic, besides **6.16** ff, see Neil Andrews, *English Civil Procedure* (Oxford UP, 2003) 26.102 to 26.128.

[23] And search orders, on which see **4.26** below.

[24] *Fourie v Le Roux* [2007] UKHL 1; [2007] 1 WLR 320 emphasises the draconian nature of this jurisdiction and the need to maintain appropriate safeguards; Lord Hope at [6] and [7] referred to Scottish authorities which consider possible conflict with European human rights law (Article 1 of the First Protocol to the European Convention on Human Rights) unless such safeguards are maintained, citing *Karl Construction Ltd v Palisade Properties plc* 2002 SC 270; *Advocate General for Scotland v Taylor* 2003 SLT 1340

[25] *Flightwise Travel Service Ltd v Gill The Times* 5 December 2003, Neuberger J; [2003] EWHC 3082 (Ch) at [18] to end, contains a good re-statement of various forms of protection aimed at ensuring that freezing relief is applied fairly.

[26] *Ninemia Maritime Corpn v Trave* [1983] 2 Lloyd's Rep 600, per Mustill J (approved [1983] 1 WLR 1412, CA, per Kerr LJ); on different perceptions of an applicant's claim by successive Commercial Court judges, see the facts of *Laemthong International Lines Co Ltd v ARTIS* [2005] 1 Lloyd's Rep 100; [2004] 2 All ER (Comm) 797, Colman J.

the nature of its substantive claim.[27] The lower courts' award of indemnity costs in this case was not disturbed (on 'indemnity costs' see **9.12**). Secondly, the court must also be satisfied that the underlying cause of action has 'accrued', that is, a breach of duty or a debt obligation has arisen. Such liabilities cannot be merely anticipated.[28]

Thirdly, there must also be a real risk that the respondent's assets will be removed or dissipated unless the injunction is granted:[29] there must be clear and strong evidence of such a risk.[30] 'Dissipation' includes any act of alienation or charging of property,[31] with the exception of innocent transactions made in the ordinary course of business.[32] However, anticipated dissipation need not be 'unconscionable' in nature: it is enough that the court is satisfied that the applicant's eventual judgment will go unsatisfied unless a freezing injunction is granted.[33] Fourthly, the court must be satisfied that the applicant will be unable to receive satisfaction of the claim unless he receives an injunction.[34] The court will take into account whether the applicant already has adequate security against such a risk.[35] Finally, the injunction must be a necessary and fair response, on the facts:

4.12

---

[27] *Fourie v Le Roux* [2007] UKHL 1; [2007] 1 WLR 320.

[28] *Veracruz Transportation Inc v VC Shipping Co Inc ('The Veracruz')* [1992] 1 Lloyd's Rep 353, CA, noted LA Collins (1992) 108 LQR 175–81 (expressing the hope that the House of Lords might reverse this decision); *Zucker v Tyndall Holdings plc* [1992] 1 WLR 1127, CA, noted R Harrison (1992) New LJ 1511–2; *Dicey, Morris and Collins on the Conflict of Laws* (14th edn, 2006) 8–009 (also 8–022 ff) also criticise the *Veracruz* case, noting Lord Nicholls's doubts in the *Mercedes Benz* case [1996] AC 284, 312, PC (in a dissenting judgment on another aspect), and preferring contrary Australian authority, *Patterson v BTR Engineering (Australia) Ltd* (1989) 18 NSWLR 319, NSWCA; W Kennett, *The Enforcement of Judgments in Europe* (Oxford UP, 2000), 161, n 97, notes that the *Veracruz* position is not adopted in Austria, Germany, and Belgium; see also the discussion in *Swift-Fortune Ltd v Magnifica Marine SA (Capaz Duckling)* [2007] EWHC 1630 (Comm).

[29] *Refco Inc v Eastern Trading Co* [1999] 1 Lloyd's Rep 159, 171, CA, per Morritt LJ (no such risk on the facts).

[30] *Laemthong International Lines Co Ltd v ARTIS* [2005] 1 Lloyd's Rep 100; [2004] 2 All ER (Comm) 797, Colman J at [60], citing *Thane Investments Ltd v Tomlinson* [2003] EWCA Civ 1271.

[31] Dispositions, pledges, charges; in *CBS UK Ltd v Lambert* [1983] Ch 37, 42, CA, per Lawton, LJ and in *Z Ltd v A-Z* [1982] 1 QB 558, 571, CA, per Lord Denning MR, both citing the words 'otherwise dealing with' in s 37(3), Supreme Court Act 1981.

[32] PD (25).

[33] *Ketchum International plc v Group Public Relations Holdings Ltd* [1997] 1 WLR 4, 13, CA; *Commissioner of Customs & Excise v Anchor Foods Ltd* [1999] 1 WLR 1139 (if D's proposed transaction is bona fide, the court's discretion to grant an injunction should be exercised very circumspectly); this factor was not satisfied in *Re Q's Estate* [1999] 1 All ER (Comm) 499, Rix J.

[34] *Etablissements Esefka International Anstalt v Central Bank of Nigeria* [1979] 1 Lloyd's Rep 445.

[35] *Refco Inc v Eastern Trading Co* [1999] 1 Lloyd's Rep 159, 171, CA, per Morritt LJ.

'... the court [must be] satisfied that any damage which the respondent may suffer through having to comply with the order is compensatable under the cross-undertaking or that the risk of uncompensatable loss is clearly outweighed by the risk of injustice to the applicant if the order is not made.'[36]

Undertakings by the Applicant[37]

4.13   The injunction's standard provisions require the applicant, *inter alia*, to: (i) indemnify the respondent if the injunction is wrongly granted; the applicant should provide a guarantee to support this undertaking;[38] (the court can order the applicant to provide a guarantee bond in case it becomes necessary to compensate the respondent by invoking this cross-undertaking);[39] (ii) to indemnify the reasonable costs of any non-party complying with the order, or compensate for any loss caused by the order (subject to the court's control), whether or not the injunction is properly granted;[40] (iii) to issue and serve his claim form straightaway, unless this is inappropriate because the main proceedings are to take place, or are pending, in another jurisdiction; and (iv) to return to court for a 'with notice' hearing (formerly described as the *'inter partes* review'), when the court decides whether to continue the injunction.

Duties of the Court and Applicant

4.14   The court must be cautious because of the self-evident danger that such an *ex parte* order (see **4.10** above) might be unjustly damaging to the respondent's interests.[41] Furthermore, both the applicant and his lawyer(s) must respect the interests of justice. An applicant must reveal to the court all material considerations and facts (including principles of law).[42] He should take reasonable steps

---

[36] *Re First Express Ltd The Times* 8 October, 1991, per Hoffmann J.

[37] PD (25).

[38] ibid.

[39] ibid.

[40] Such protection of non-parties is not standard practice for all types of injunctions: *Smithkline Beecham plc v Apotex Europe Ltd* [2006] EWCA Civ 658; [2007] Ch 71 at [23] ff.

[41] *Memory Corporation plc v Sidhu (No 2)* [2000] 1 WLR 1443, 1460, CA; on the problem of multiple applications before different judges on essentially the same facts, *Laemthong International Lines Co Ltd v ARTIS* [2004] 2 All ER (Comm) 797, Colman J, or at [2005] 1 Lloyd's Rep 100.

[42] PD (25); leading cases are: *Brink's Mat Ltd v Elcombe* [1988] 1 WLR 1350, CA; *Lloyds Bowmaker Ltd v Britannia Arrow Holdings plc* [1988] 1 WLR 1337, CA; *Behbehani v Salem* [1989] 1 WLR 723, CA; and (an important survey) *Memory Corporation plc v Sidhu (No 2)* [2000] 1 WLR 1443, 1453–6, CA, per Robert Walker LJ; *Re S (A Child)*

to investigate matters.[43] The applicant's lawyers (counsel and solicitor) must also refrain from misleading the court. They too must make full and frank disclosure.[44] An applicant's failure to make full disclosure will normally cause the injunction to be summarily set aside unless: the failure probably made no difference to the decision to grant the injunction;[45] or the value of providing freezing relief, especially to combat fraud, outweighs this aspect of procedural fairness.[46]

Variation or Termination of the Freezing Injunction

The respondent has 'a right to ask the Court to vary or discharge' the injunc-   **4.15** tion.[47] The injunction will cease to apply if the respondent pays into court a sum specified in the injunction or provides security as agreed with the applicant's lawyers.[48]

Contempt by the Respondent

A respondent will be in contempt of court (see **8.35**) if he breaches an injunc-   **4.16** tion.[49] Contempt in this context need not be deliberate: gross or prolonged negligence suffices. For example, a company might fail to ensure that its officers,

---

(Family Division: Without Notice Orders) [2001] 1 WLR 211, 219, 222–3 Munby J; *Knauf UK GmbH v British Gypsum Ltd* [2002] 1 WLR 907, CA; cf for an instance where there was a positive lie by an applicant for an interim injunction, *Browne v Associated Newspapers Ltd* [2007] EWCA Civ 295; [2007] 3 WLR 289, at [66] ff; for failure to reveal to a Singaporean court the salient principles of English case law, *Swift-Fortune Ltd v Magnifica Marine SA (Capaz Duckling)* [2007] EWHC 1630 (Comm).

[43] *Bird v Hadkinson The Times* 7 April, 1999.

[44] *Memory Corporation plc v Sidhu (No 2)* [2000] 1 WLR 1443, 1455, CA, per Robert Walker LJ.

[45] *Brink's Mat Ltd v Elcombe* [1988] 1 WLR 1350, 1358, CA; *Lloyds Bowmaker v Britannia Arrow Holdings plc* [1988] 1 WLR 1337, 1347, CA (these two statements were cited in *Memory Corporation plc v Sidhu (No 2)* [2000] 1 WLR 1443, 1454 CA); *Behbehani v Salem* [1989] 1 WLR 723, CA; *Gulf Interstate Oil Corpn LLC v Ant Trade & Transport Ltd of Malta ('The Giovanna')* [1999] 1 Lloyd's Rep 867; in *Laemthong International Lines Co Ltd v ARTIS* [2005] 1 Lloyd's Rep 100; [2004] 2 All ER (Comm) 797, Colman J at [64] held that a failure to reveal a comment made by another judge in an earlier and unsuccessful 'without notice' application did not satisfy this 'decisive influence' test.

[46] *Marc Rich & Co Holdings GmbH v Krasner* CA, unreported, 17 January, 1999.

[47] PD (25).

[48] PD (25).

[49] *Motorola Credit Corpn v Uzan (No 2)* [2003] EWCA Civ 752; [2004] 1 WLR 113, CA [45]-[58], [148]-[156]; *Federal Bank of the Middle East Ltd v Hadkinson* [2000] 2 All ER 395, 411, CA; information disclosed under a disclosure order, including in response to cross-examination, ancillary to a freezing order can be used for contempt purposes, *Dadourian Group*

employees or agents comply with the order.[50] If his breach is aggravated ('contumacious'), he can be fined, imprisoned or, in the case of a company, suffer sequestration of assets. An applicant will also be in contempt if he fails to satisfy the numerous undertakings given or implied when the order was granted (see **4.13** above).

Non-Parties

4.17   Freezing injunctions do not confer proprietary rights upon successful applicants.[51] Nor do they prevent a non-party from honouring its contractual obligations owed to other non-parties.[52] Non-parties can apply to the court to authorise the respondent to pay a pre-existing debt. Furthermore, the injunction should not apply to property manifestly belonging to a non-party. However, freezing injunctions can apply to property jointly owned by the respondent and a non-party[53] or where the latter has acquired the relevant assets from the respondent in suspicious circumstances.[54] It is common to notify the respondent's bank(s) of the injunction even before he receives notice. Once notified, a non-party is obliged not to act inconsistently with the terms of the injunction.[55] The bank must refrain from undermining the injunction's efficacy by continuing to honour its client's cheques and instructions, except where such dealings are permitted by the order.[56] Non-parties are entitled to an indemnity from the applicant for expenses incurred in respecting or carrying out the injunction, for example, the expense incurred by a bank when searching its records to find the respondent's account(s).[57]

4.18   Such a non-party bank will be in contempt (see **8.35**) if it deliberately or 'knowingly' acts, or omits to act, with the result that the injunction is under-

International Inc v Simms [2006] EWCA Civ 1745; [2007] 2 All ER 329; a sentence of 18 months imprisonment was imposed in *Lexi Holdings Plc v Shaid Luqman* [2007] EWHC 1508 (Ch), at [182]ff.

[50]   *Z Bank v D1* [1994] 1 Lloyd's Rep 656, Colman J, consistent with dictum of Steyn LJ in *Guildford BC v Valler The Times* 15 October, 1993, CA; on the duty to respond to an order for information, *Bird v Hadkinson The Times* 4 March, 1999, Neuberger J (respondent to answer accurately after exercising reasonable care).

[51]   *Cretanor Maritime Co Ltd v Irish Marine Maritime Ltd* [1978] 3 All ER 164, CA; *Capital Cameras Ltd v Harold Lines Ltd* [1991] 1 WLR 54; *Flightline v Edwards* [2003] 1 WLR 1200, CA.

[52]   *Galaxia Maritime SA v Mineralimportexport* [1982] 1 WLR 539, CA.

[53]   *SCF v Masri* [1985] 1 WLR 876, CA; injunctions can be granted against joint bank accounts, PD (25).

[54]   An instructive case is *Mercantile Group (Europe) AG v Aiyela* [1994] QB 366, CA (spousal transfer).

[55]   PD (25).

[56]   *Z Ltd v A* [1982] QB 558, CA.

[57]   PD (25); earlier, *Searose Ltd v Seatrain (UK) Ltd* [1981] 1 WLR 894, CA.

mined, or if it aids and abets the respondent's breach of the order.[58] This duty is owed to the court, and it is sanctioned by contempt of court penalties (fines, for example, payable to the court) rather than a duty to compensate a private party (see next paragraph). The bank need not inquire closely into the propriety of every transaction proposed by its client: 'No bank need enquire as to the application or proposed application of any money withdrawn by the Respondent if the withdrawal appears to be permitted by this Order.'[59]

However, the non-party is only liable to the court, in accordance with the **4.19** contempt of court principle, just mentioned. In *Customs & Excise Commissioners v Barclays Bank plc* (2006) the House of Lords[60] (reversing the Court of Appeal)[61] held that the non-party (a bank) owes no duty of care to the recipient of freezing relief. The facts were as follows. The bank had mistakenly transferred funds covered by these injunctions after receiving notification of the relevant order. As a result, the claimants could only recover a small percentage of their debts from the respondent creditors. And so the claimants alleged that the bank owed a duty of care in the tort of negligence to apply the freezing injunction properly applied to its customer's accounts (the bank's customer being the defendant, and debtor, in the main proceedings). Lord Bingham gave various reasons for denying such a duty.[62] Perhaps the most telling point was this:

'... it cannot be suggested that the customer owes a duty to the party which obtains an order, since they are opposing parties in litigation and no duty is owed by a litigating party to its opponent [citing authorities]. It would be a strange and anomalous outcome if an action in negligence lay against a notified party [viz, a non-party] who allowed the horse to escape from the stable but not against the owner who rode it out.'

---

[58] PD (25); *Z Ltd v A* [1982] QB 558, 567, CA, per Eveleigh LJ; cf, consistently, *Re Supply of Ready Mixed Concrete (No 2)* [1995] 1 AC 456, HL; and *Att-Gen v Newspaper Publishing plc* [1997] 3 All ER 159, 169, CA.

[59] PD, (25); *Ryan v Friction Dynamics Ltd The Times* 2 June, 2000, Neuberger J.

[60] [2006] UKHL 28; [2007] 1 AC 181, HL (reversing [2004] EWCA Civ 1555; [2005] 1 WLR 2082).

[61] The Court of Appeal, in the decision which was reversed by the House of Lords, had held that the contempt regime is inadequate for two reasons: first, contempt in this context requires proof of knowing non-compliance by the non-party Bank, as distinct from mere negligence; secondly, the sanction for contempt is punishment administered by the court, rather than an order to compensate the injured party.

[62] ibid at [18], [19] and [23].

Foreign Assets[63]

4.20   Freezing injunctions can apply to assets located outside England and Wales. 'Worldwide' freezing injunctions are now common.[64] The applicant can gain both an *in personam* order affecting the relevant foreign assets and a disclosure order compelling the respondent to provide information relating to such assets. The disclosure order can operate on a worldwide basis even where the restraining element of the same injunction is confined to assets situated in England.[65] A post-judgment disclosure order can operate without such a restraint upon any assets.[66]

4.21   Sir Lawrence Collins, now a Lord Justice of Appeal, and Lord Millett, have suggested that the 'worldwide' disclosure order is of greater practical and tactical importance than the main freezing injunction.[67] This is because the latter is merely a 'holding operation' to give the claimant time to apply to the relevant foreign court(s) for appropriate supplementary or substantive relief.[68]

4.22   An applicant cannot make a related application for enforcement of a worldwide English freezing order in a foreign jurisdiction without first obtaining the English court's permission.[69] The fear is that such parallel litigation might become oppressive. To guard against that danger, the Court of Appeal in *Dadourian Group International Inc v Simms* (2006) enumerated

---

[63] C McLachlan, 'Extraterritorial Court Orders Affecting Bank Deposits' in Meessen (ed), *Extraterritorial Jurisdiction in Theory and Practice: Symposium Held at Dresden on 8–10 October 1993* (Deventer, 1996).

[64] PD (25); *Babanaft Co SA v Bassatne* [1990] Ch 13, CA; *Republic of Haiti v Duvalier* [1990] QB 202, CA; *Derby & Co v Weldon* (No 1) [1990] Ch 48, CA; *Derby & Co Ltd v Weldon (Nos 3 & 4)* [1990] Ch 65, CA; LA Collins, 'The Territorial Reach of *Mareva* Injunctions' (1989) 105 LQR 262–99; LA Collins, chs VIII and IX, in *Essays in International Litigation* (Oxford UP, 1993); *Dicey, Morris and Collins on the Conflict of Laws* (14th edn, 2006) 8–011 ff; D Capper, 'Worldwide *Mareva* Injunctions' (1991) 54 MLR 329–48; A Malek and C Lewis, 'Worldwide Injunctions – The Position of International Banks' [1990] LMCLQ 88; Rogers [1991] LMCLQ 231; the English Court cannot grant worldwide relief in the context of *post-judgment relief* under Art 47(1) of the (Brussels) Jurisdiction Regulation, *Banco Nacional De Comercio Exterior SNC v Empresa De Telecomunicationes De Cuba SA* [2007] EWCA Civ 662 (reversing Steel J in [2006] EWHC 19 (Comm)).

[65] *Gidrxslme Shipping Co Ltd v Tantomar-Transportes Maritimos Lda* [1994] 4 All ER 507, 519, Colman J.

[66] ibid, 519–20, per Colman J; if the freezing relief is sought *pre*-judgment, it seems the freezing element is a sine qua non for the disclosure order: *Grupo Torras SA v Sheikh Fahad Mohammed Al-Sabah* CA, unreported, 16 February, 1994), summarized (1994) New LJ 942; for other developments, K Lloyd (1994) New LJ 1482 and 1556.

[67] *Dicey, Morris and Collins on the Conflict of Laws* (14th edn, 2006) 8–011 ff; *Credit Suisse Fides Trust SA v Cuoghi* [1998] QB 818, 827–8, CA, per Millett LJ.

[68] *Babanaft International Co SA v Bassatne* [1990] Ch 13, 41, CA, per Nicholls LJ.

[69] PD (25).

eight principles, but for reasons of space, these will not be recited here.[70] Non-parties resident in other jurisdictions are protected by the so-called, '*Babanaft* proviso':[71]

'The terms of this Order do not affect or concern anyone outside the jurisdiction of this Court until it is declared enforceable or is enforced by a Court in the relevant country and then it shall affect him only to the extent it has been declared enforceable or has been enforced *UNLESS* such person is: a person to whom this Order is addressed or an officer of or an agent appointed by a power of attorney of such a person; or a person who is subject to the jurisdiction of this Court and (a) has been given written notice of this Order at his residence or place of business within the jurisdiction of this Court and (b) is able to prevent acts or omissions outside the jurisdiction of this Court which constitute or assist in the breach of the terms of this order.'

Conflict between the English Freezing Injunction and Foreign Law

The Court of Appeal in *Bank of China v NBM LLC and Others* made the following amendment (the so-called, '*Baltic* proviso') to those freezing injunctions which have extra-jurisdictional effect:[72] **4.23**

'... nothing in this order shall, in respect of assets located outside England or Wales, prevent [the non-party bank] or any of its subsidiaries from complying with what it reasonably believes to be its obligations, contractual or otherwise, under the laws and obligations of the country or state in which those assets are situated or under the proper law of any bank account in question; and any orders of the courts of that country or state provided reasonable notice of any application for such an order by [the non-party bank] or any of its subsidiaries (to the extent such notice is permitted by the criminal law of such country or state), is given to the claimant's solicitors.'

---

[70] [2006] EWCA Civ 399; [2006] 1 WLR 2499; [2006] CP Rep 31 at [25] with commentary on each at [26] ff; noted T Rutherford (2006) NLJ 837.

[71] Incorporated in PD (25); this protection originated in *Babanaft Co SA v Bassatne* [1990] Ch 13, CA.

[72] [2002] 1 All ER 717, CA; noting the proviso's genesis in *Baltic Shipping v Translink Shipping Ltd* [1995] 1 Lloyd's Rep 673, Clarke J; the proviso is now incorporated into PD (25).

Supporting Primary Litigation Pending or Contemplated in Foreign Jurisdictions[73]

4.24   The English High Court can grant freezing injunctions and connected orders for disclosure of assets in support of pending or prospective[74] substantive civil proceedings throughout the world. This supportive English jurisdiction applies whether or not the relevant foreign jurisdiction is party to the Brussels or Lugano jurisdictional regimes.[75]

4.25   The Court of Appeal in *Motorola Credit Corpn v Uzan (No 2)* identified five factors regulating the discretion to issue this type of supportive relief:[76] (i) 'whether the making of the [English supportive] order will interfere with the management of the case in the primary [foreign] court, eg, where the order is inconsistent with an order in the primary court or overlaps with it'; (ii) 'whether it is the policy in the primary jurisdiction not itself to make worldwide freezing/disclosure orders'; (iii) 'whether there is a danger that the orders made will give rise to disharmony or confusion and/or risk of conflicting inconsistent or overlapping orders in other jurisdictions, in particular in the courts of the state where the person enjoined resides or where the assets affected are located. If so, then respect for the territorial jurisdiction of that state should discourage the English court from using its unusually wide powers against a foreign defendant'; (iv) 'whether at the time the order is sought there is likely to be a potential conflict as to jurisdiction rendering it inappropriate and inexpedient to make a worldwide order'; (v) 'whether in a case where jurisdiction is resisted and disobedience to be expected, the court will be making an order which it cannot enforce.' In the *Motorola* case, this last factor justified discharging

---

[73] *Dicey, Morris and Collins on the Conflict of Laws* (14th edn, 2006) 8–024; G Maher and BJ Rodger, 'Provisional and Protective Remedies: The British Experience of the Brussels Convention' (1999) 48 ICLQ 302 (a detailed account; also examining Scots decisions); see also Andrews and Johnson at n 76 below.

[74] '... proceedings have been or are to be commenced in a [Brussels or Lugano] Contracting State [or a regulation state]': s 25(2) 1982 Act: see next note.

[75] Civil Jurisdiction and Judgments Act 1982 s 25; Civil Jurisdiction and Judgments Act 1982 (Interim Relief) Order 1997 (SI 1997, No 302) (the 1982 Act, s 25, gives effect to the United Kingdom's obligation to effectuate Article 24 of the 1968 Brussels Convention (now Article 31 of the Brussels I Regulation); from 1 April, 1997, the English High Court's jurisdiction to grant interim relief under the 1982 Act was extended to include non-Convention and non-Member States; and to apply to civil proceedings outside the rather restricted scope of Article 1 of the Brussels Convention and its successor, the Jurisdiction Regulation: (EC) No 44/2001 of 22 December 2000 on 'jurisdiction and the recognition and enforcement of judgments in civil and commercial matters': [2001] OJ L 12/1.

[76] [2004] 1 WLR 113, CA at [115] (the earlier case law is analysed in N Andrews, *English Civil Procedure* (Oxford UP, 2003) 17.74 ff and by A Johnson in M Andenas, N Andrews, R Nazzini (eds), *The Future of Transnational Civil Litigation* (reprinted British Institute of International and Comparative Law, 2006), ch 11.

freezing relief aimed at two co-defendants resident in Turkey, and who did not have assets in England.[77] However, the remaining co-defendants did have residential and proprietary connexions with England, and so the court maintained freezing relief against these.[78]

(3) Preservation of Evidence: Civil Search Orders[79]

Nature

Now known as 'civil search orders' (formerly '*Anton Piller* orders'),[80] these have been ratified by primary legislation,[81] and codified in CPR Part 25.[82] The civil search order enables the applicant to swoop like a hawk upon the defendant and seize vital evidence before it can be conveniently lost or destroyed. This relief has been especially useful in tackling breaches of intellectual property rights and confidentiality. They are not nearly as common as freezing injunctions (discussed at **4.03** ff above). Deliberate destruction by a prospective defendant of documents or deletion of e-mails can involve criminal liability, as held in *Douglas v Hello! Ltd* (2003),[83] approving Australian guidance.[84]   **4.26**

Search orders are ancillary injunctions requiring the respondent to permit the applicant to inspect premises and to remove or secure evidence of any alleged wrongdoing. The order, made *ex parte* (see **4.10** above), authorises a limited number of persons, normally the applicant or his lawyer and an independent solicitor, to enter the respondent's premises (**4.32**). It is oppressive to execute a search order at the weekend, or before 9.30 am or later than 5.30 pm   **4.27**

---

[77] ibid at [125] and [126].

[78] ibid at [127] and [128].

[79] Re-named as such, CPR 25.1(1)(h); the standard order is prescribed by PD (25); the leading discussion is S Gee, *Commercial Injunctions* (2004); see also N Andrews, *English Civil Procedure* (Oxford UP, 2003) ch 17; *Zuckerman on Civil Procedure* (2006) 14.175 ff; IS Goldrein (ed), *Commercial Litigation: Pre-emptive Remedies* (International Edition, 2005) ch 3; the CPR, their accompanying PDs, and various 'Guides' to parts of the High Court's practice, are accessible at http://www.justice.gov.uk/civil/procrules_fin/menus/court_guides.htm

[80] *Anton Piller v Manufacturing Processes* [1976] Ch 55, CA is the eponymous decision.

[81] s 7, Civil Procedure Act 1997, following recommendation of a Committee of Judges appointed by the Judges' Council, 'Anton Piller Orders: A Consultation Paper' ('the Staughton Committee'), Lord Chancellor's Department, November 1992; for comment, M Dockray and K Reece Thomas, (1998) 17 CJQ 272); see also s 72, Supreme Court Act 1981 (privilege against self-incrimination; s 7(7), Civil Procedure Act 1997 Act, also acknowledges this privilege).

[82] PD (25).

[83] [2003] 1 All ER 1087 (brief note); [2003] EWHC 55 (Ch), at [86].

[84] ibid at [173].

during a weekday.[85] The 'premises' searched can be commercial, business or domestic premises, or a 'vehicle'.[86] The premises or vehicle must be situated in England and Wales.

4.28   A search order can be granted before or after the main proceedings have commenced, or even after judgment.[87] When granted in anticipation of the main proceedings, the applicant must undertake to commence and serve notice of the main action without delay.[88] Only the High Court can issue such an order.[89]

4.29   The search, supervised by an independent solicitor (**4.32**), will be confined to evidence, property or other material encompassed by the order. After the respondent is served with the order, he has a short period within which to consult a lawyer. This period for consultation cannot exceed two hours. But, even if the respondent exercises this right to receive legal advice, he must immediately allow the applicant and independent solicitor, to enter the premises. Therefore, the period for legal consultation is merely a pause before commencement of the detailed search. The respondent commits contempt of court (see **8.35**) if he fails to admit the applicant.[90] Once the detailed search begins, the applicant is entitled to remove the material so that it can be safeguarded, or take copies, samples, or make records.[91]

Criteria for Award

4.30   The five criteria are: (i) such an order must not be used as a means of fishing for a cause of action;[92] (ii) the applicant must have a very strong prima facie case on the substance of the main complaint;[93] (iii) there must be a very serious risk of damage to the applicant's interests unless this special order is granted;[94] (iv) the court must be satisfied both that the respondent possesses relevant material and that he will destroy this material unless subjected to a surprise search;[95] (v) 'the harm likely to be caused by the execution of the ... order to the respon-

---

[85] ibid.

[86] s 7(8), Civil Procedure Act 1997.

[87] On this last situation, *Distributori Automatici Italia SpA v Holford General Trading Co Ltd* [1985] 1 WLR 1066.

[88] PD (25).

[89] s 7(8), Civil Procedure Act 1997.

[90] PD (25).

[91] s 7(4)(b), Civil Procedure Act 1997.

[92] *Hy-trac v Conveyors International* [1983] 1 WLR 44, CA.

[93] *Anton Piller KG v Manufacturing Processes Ltd* [1976] Ch 55, 62, CA, per Ormrod LJ.

[94] ibid.

[95] ibid, at 59–60, per Lord Denning: 'grave danger that vital evidence will be destroyed'.

dent and his business affairs must not be excessive or out of proportion to the legitimate object of the order.'[96]

Supporting Disclosure Order

Search orders often require the respondent to reveal the identity of co-wrong-   **4.31**
doers.[97] The applicant can use information concerning non-parties to launch separate or related proceedings against those co-wrongdoers.[98] But he must not disclose these details to other non-parties, such as the Police, Customs and Excise and the Inland Revenue.[99]

Protecting the Respondent

Search orders and freezing injunctions share many procedural features (see   **4.32**
discussion at **4.13** above of the applicant's undertaking to indemnify the re-spondent if the order is later held to have been wrongly granted and at **4.14** of his duty to make full disclosure of material facts before receiving the order). The standard civil search order also contains numerous provisions aimed at controlling the process of executing these orders, especially the seizure of ma-terial.[100] There should be an independent and supervisory solicitor present to ensure fair-play and prevent oppression.[101] He must not be an employee or member of the applicant's firm of solicitors and should be suitably experi-enced.[102] A criminal search warrant and a civil search order should not be si-multaneously executed at the same premises, because that would be oppres-sive.[103]

---

[96] Criterion proposed by the report into 'Anton Piller Orders', (Consultation Paper, Lord Chancellor's Department, 1992), para 2.8, following *Columbia Picture Industries v Robin-son* [1987] 1 Ch 38, 76, and *Lock International plc v Beswick* [1989] 1 WLR 1268, 1281.

[97] PD (25); earlier, *EMI Ltd v Sarwar & Haider* [1977] FSR 146; and see s 7(5), Civil Pro-cedure Act 1997.

[98] *Sony Corpn v Anand* [1981] FSR 398.

[99] *Customs & Excise Commrs v AE Hamlin & Co* [1984] 1 WLR 509 (but Falconer J gave permission for the information to be used by a non-party); *EMI Records Ltd v Spillane* [1986] 1 WLR 967 and *General Nutrition Ltd v Pattni* [1984] FSR 403 (in both cases permis-sion for such use was refused).

[100] ibid; for earlier comment, *Columbia Picture Industries Inc v Robinson* [1987] Ch 38.

[101] PD (25); eg, *IBM v Prima Data International Ltd* [1994] 1 WLR 719, 724–5.

[102] PD (25); for a rogue execution of a civil search order, where the supervisory solicitor lacked sufficient experience, *Gadget Shop Ltd v Bug.Com Ltd* [2001] CP 13, Rimer J, noted L Mulcahy, *Human Rights and Civil Practice* (2001) para 10.62.

[103] PD (25).

4.33   The respondent need not disclose material protected by legal professional privilege (on which **6.28**) or the privilege against self-incrimination (see **6.26**).[104] Statutory provisions partially override the latter privilege in the context of offences under the theft legislation or in respect of protection of rights in intellectual property.[105] Subject to these qualifications, privileged material will be excluded from the search. This material will be checked and held safely by the supervisory solicitor.[106]

4.34   The respondent can apply to the court for the order to be discharged or varied at the 'with notice' review, that is, on the 'return day'[107] specified in the main order. The defendant need not wait until then and can apply 'at any time' to have the order varied or discharged.[108]

---

[104] On the **nature** of the privilege: defined by Civil Evidence Act 1968, s 14, as follows: 'The right of a person in any legal proceedings other than criminal proceedings to refuse to answer any question or produce any document or thing if to do so would tend to expose that person [or his or her spouse] to proceedings for an offence or for the recovery of a penalty [under UK law].' A majority in *C plc v P* [2007] EWCA Civ 493; [2007] 3 WLR 437 ([26] to [38], per Longmore LJ, and Sir Martin Nourse at [74]) held that there is no privilege in things or documents existing prior to the order compelling their production (applying the European Court of Human Rights' decision in *Saunders v UK* (1996) 23 EHRR 313), at [69]); but Lawrence Collins LJ, agreeing that the majority's approach was attractive in principle at [46], nevertheless observed at [63] to [73] that the majority's decision in this case, supported by a line of Strasbourg jurisprudence, could not be reconciled with settled House of Lords' authority (at first instance, Evans-Lombe J in *C plc v P* [2006] EWHC 1226 (Ch); [2006] Ch 549, noted Neil Andrews [2007] CLJ 47, had used the Human Rights Act 1998 to declare that the privilege must yield to the need to protect the human rights of children against pornographic exploitation); for **statutory overriding of the privilege**: notably, s 72, Supreme Court Act 1981; and s 13, Fraud Act 2006, considered in *Kensington International Ltd v Republic of the Congo* [2007] EWCA Civ 1128; on the background, see N Andrews, *English Civil Procedure* (Oxford UP, 2003) 29.24 to 29.28 and (on possible reform) 29.56 ff; B Thanki (ed), *The Law of Privilege* (Oxford UP, 2006) ch 8; *Cross and Tapper on Evidence* (11th edn, 2007) 449 ff; IH Dennis, *The Law of Evidence*, (2nd edn, 2002) ch 5; C Hollander, *Documentary Evidence* (9th edn, 2006) ch 17 (reproducing, also by C Hollander, *Phipson on Evidence* (16th edn, 2005) 24–40 ff); *Zuckerman on Civil Procedure* (2nd edn, 2006) ch 17; see also 'The Privilege against Self-incrimination in Civil Proceedings' (Consultation Paper, Lord Chancellor's Dept, 1992); I Dennis, 'Instrumental Protection, Human Right or Fundamental Necessity? Re-assessing the Privilege against Self-incrimination' [1995] 54 CLJ 342.

[105] Notably, s 72, Supreme Court Act 1981, and s 13, Fraud Act 2006 (considered in *Kensington International Ltd v Republic of the Congo* [2007] EWCA Civ 1128.

[106] PD (25).

[107] ibid.

[108] ibid.

(4) Protection of the Defendant: Security for Costs[109]

Nature

A defendant can seek an order for security for costs against a claimant. The **4.35**
security might take the form of a payment into court, or a banker's guarantee,
or some other undertaking. A claimant who fails to comply with such an order
will find either that the action is stayed until security is given or even that the
action is dismissed (a 'stay' is a judicial order holding proceedings in suspense,
but not an outright dismissal).

The purpose of such a security for costs order is to protect the defendant **4.36**
against the risk that the claimant might not pay the defendant's costs if the
claimant eventually becomes liable, or agrees as a term of settlement, to pay
the defendant's costs. Such an order can in fact be directed one of these three
problems: the claimant lacks sufficient funds; or he is a shifty litigant manifestly disposed to avoid liability for costs; or the procedural chase against the
claimant would be uncertain or difficult because the foreign jurisdiction where
he resides does not provide a dependable or straightforward system for enforcing an English costs order.

Main Gateways

There is no general right to security for costs. Instead such orders are discre- **4.37**
tionary.[110] The rules specify various 'gateways', any one of which the defendant must ordinarily[111] establish. The latter must then further satisfy the court
that security should be awarded in exercise of its discretion (on the latter, see
4.38 below).[112] The three main gateways are: (i) 'the claimant is resident out of
the English and Welsh jurisdiction but not resident in a Member State of the
European Union or a Lugano Convention Contracting State'; or (ii) 'the claim-

---

[109] Neil Andrews, *English Civil Procedure* (Oxford UP, 2003), ch 37; MJ Cook, *Cook on Costs* (2007); P Hurst, *Civil Costs* (4th edn, 2007); *Zuckerman on Civil Procedure* (2006) 9.182 ff; IS Goldrein (ed), *Commercial Litigation: Pre-emptive Remedies* (Interna-tional Edition, 2005) ch 4; *Dicey, Morris and Collins on the Conflict of Laws* (14th edn, 2006) 8–092 ff.

[110] CPR 25.13(1) states: 'The court may make an order for security for costs … if (a) it is satisfied, having regard to all the circumstances of the case, that it is just to make such an order.'

[111] In *Olatawura v Abiloye* [2002] EWCA Civ 998; [2003] 1 WLR 275, the court recog-nised a power to make an order for a security payment by an individual claimant resident out-side the jurisdiction, and having modest financial means; this power subsists independently of the general regime concerning security for costs contained in CPR Part 25, Section II.

[112] CPR 25.13(2) (s 726, Companies Act 1985 will be repealed by October 2008; it dupli-cates CPR 25.13(2)(c)).

ant is a company or other body (whether incorporated inside or outside Great Britain) and there is reason to believe that it will be unable to pay the defendant's costs if ordered to do so'; or (iii) 'the claimant has taken steps in relation to his assets that would make it difficult to enforce an order for costs against him.'[113]

Factors Regulating the Discretion to Order Security

4.38   The case law has identified the following (non-exhaustive) factors which the court should consider when exercising its discretion whether to award security for costs:[114] (i) the action is a sham or is made in good faith; (ii) the claimant has a reasonably good prospect of success in the case; (iii) there is an admission by the defendant in the statement of case or elsewhere that the money is due or the claim is otherwise sound; (iv) there is a substantial payment into court or offer to settle; (v) the application is being used by the defendant to stifle an honest and sound claim; (vi) the claimant's lack of funds has been caused by, or aggravated by, the defendant's failure to pay; (vii) the application for security for costs has been made late.

Individual Not Subject to Security Merely on Ground of Poverty

4.39   The court cannot make a security for costs order against a claimant who is an *individual* and resident in England (or another part of the United Kingdom) or in a 'Brussels or Lugano State' simply because of his financial inability to pay costs. To impose security against such a claimant would bar his access to justice. By contrast, an impecunious *corporate* claimant enjoys no such favourable treatment.

Claimant Resident outside England and outside the Territories of the Brussels and Lugano Conventions

4.40   Most non-UK residents are likely to be non-UK citizens. And so the foreign residence ground, cited above, has the potential to infringe Article 14 of the European Convention on Human Rights (now Schedule 1, Human Rights Act

---

[113] *Harris v Wallis* (Ch D, 15 March 2006, All England Reporter) on the phrase 'taken steps in relation to his assets that would make it difficult to enforce an order for costs against him'; no need to show improper motivation by claimant.

[114] *Sir Lindsay Parkinson v Triplan Ltd* [1973] QB 609 at 626–7, CA, per Lord Denning MR.

1998, UK). That provision prohibits direct or indirect discrimination by reference to: 'any ground such as sex, race, colour, language, religion, political or other opinion, national or social origin, association with a national minority, property, birth or other status.'[115]

The Court of Appeal in the *Nasser* case (2002) achieved the following reconciliation between the non-residence ground for awarding security for costs regime and the human rights provision concerning direct or indirect 'anti-discrimination', just cited.[116] To avoid conflict with that provision, the court rejected 'any inflexible presumption that any person not resident in a Brussels or Lugano state should provide security for costs'. Instead, the court declared that an order for security must be based on 'objectively justified grounds relating to obstacles to or the burden of enforcement in the context of the particular foreign claimant or country concerned', such as 'substantial obstacles to or a substantial extra burden, for example, costs or delay, in enforcing an English judgment ...' In the case itself, the claimant was resident in the USA. The English court was satisfied that enforcement of an English costs order in the relevant US state would be rather difficult and expensive. This finding established an 'objective' justification for security against the American claimant. **4.41**

Security for the Costs of a Pending Civil Appeal

The *Tolstoy* case (1995), long-running litigation resembling 'War and Peace', culminated in proceedings before the European Court of Human Rights, began as an English defamation trial. That hearing lasted forty days. Judgment was given against the defendant author, Tolstoy (a descendant of the Russian novelist). He appealed to the Court of Appeal. That court required Tolstoy to provide £ 126,000 as security for the respondent's prospective costs in this appeal. Tolstoy unsuccessfully challenged this English security for costs award before the European Court of Human Rights.[117] The latter held that the English award met the following human rights criterion: that any 'restrictions [on appeal] must pursue a legitimate aim and there must be a reasonable relationship of proportionality between the means employed and the aim sought to be achieved'. **4.42**

---

[115] *Nasser v United Bank of Kuwait* [2002] 1 All ER 401, CA (main judgment by Mance LJ); for a review of this context, *Al-Koronky v Time-Life Entertainment Group Ltd* [2006] EWCA Civ 1123; [2006] CP Rep 47, at [24].

[116] ibid.

[117] *Tolstoy Miloslavsky v UK* (1995) 20 EHRR 442, ECtHR.

(5) Civil Orders for Custody of Passports

4.43   The English courts can restrain a defendant, or prospective defendant, from leaving the jurisdiction and compel him to surrender his passport (*'Bayer v Winter* orders').[118]

---

[118] Neil Andrews, *Principles of Procedure* (1994), 8–50 to 8–053; *Dicey, Morris and Collins on the Conflict of Laws* (14th edn, 2006), 8–010, 19–022; leading modern cases are *Bayer v Winter (No 1)* [1986] 1 WLR 497, CA; *Re Oriental Credit* [1988] Ch 204; *Lipkin Gorman v Cass The Times* 29 May, 1985; *Al Nakhel for Contracting and Trading Ltd v Lowe* [1986] QB 235, Tudor-Evans J (decided 2 days before the *Bayer* case); *Allied Arab Bank v Hajjar* [1988] QB 787, Leggatt J; the court has a statutory power in the case of a bankrupt, s 333, Insolvency Act 1986, on which see *Morris v Murjani* [1996] 1 WLR 848, CA; for academic discussion, see L Anderson, 'Antiquity in Action ...' (1987) 103 LQR 246; and case notes by C Harpum [1986] CLJ 189 and Neil Andrews [1988] CLJ 364; for Israeli abandonment of this protective remedy, Stephen Goldstein, 'Revisiting Preliminary Relief in Light of the ALI/UNIDROIT Principles and the New Israeli Rules' in *Studia in honorem: Pelayia Yessiou-Faltsi* (Athens, 2007) 273–96; in South Africa, civil orders restraining prospective defendants from fleeing the jurisdiction ('arrest tamquam suspectus de fuga') have a long tradition: Wouter de Vos (Rhodes University) report to the Brazil (2007) World Congress (South African national report on the 'pre-action phase', for details, see Andrews, op cit, at **2.26** n 73).

Chapter 5

Interim Relief and Final Judgements
Without Trial[1]

Contents

(1) Introduction

This chapter is concerned with various interim or final forms of judgment or   **5.01**
relief which are available without trial. The topics to be covered are as follows:
(i) interim or provisional forms of relief; (ii) 'preliminary issues', that is, the
hearing of discrete issues before the main trial, or selection of issues before the
remainder of the trial; (iii) 'summary judgment' and 'striking out', that is, accelerated judicial powers to dismiss the claim or defence by reference to the
factual or legal merits, but without the apparatus of oral examination at trial;
and (iv) judgments in default of a defence. Their function is either to supply
short-term relief, pending the case's final resolution at trial, or to dispose in a
speedy way of the whole case, or part of it. These procedures have two things
in common: they precede trial; and they are concerned with the substance of
the dispute (the latter feature provides the distinction between the material in
this chapter and 'protective relief', as explained at **4.01**).[2]

---

[1] Generally on the material examined in this chapter, see Neil Andrews, *English Civil
Procedure* (Oxford UP, 2003) chs 18 to 21, and 37, section A; *Zuckerman on Civil Pro-
cedure* (2006) chs 8, 9; IS Goldrein (ed), *Commercial Litigation: Pre-emptive Remedies*
(International Edition, 2005), chs 1–6.

[2] Protective relief, on which see ch 4 of this book, does not concern any element of the
substantive relief, but merely provides ancillary protection or security (freezing relief, search
orders to preserve evidence, and security for costs).

5.02   The subject-matter of the present chapter must be further introduced. As
for (i), interim or provisional forms of relief, it has been found to be imperative
that the courts should have power to issue interim relief pending final disposal
of the action. This is because the road to trial can be long, slow and procedurally circuitous. An interim payment gives the claimant a portion of the final
monetary relief sought at trial. An interim injunction normally[3] operates to
restrain the defendant temporarily. It concerns conduct which the claimant
seeks to restrain permanently at trial. The claimant obtains temporary satisfaction of his interest in obtaining perpetual restraint. Remarkably, the English courts lacked power to order interim payments until 1969, whereas the
equitable jurisdiction to issue interim injunctions is much older (on the latter,
see **5.08** below). As for (ii), preliminary issues, the applicant might wish to obtain the court's accelerated judgment on a particular issue on which the rest of
the dispute might hang. Although referred to as 'preliminary', such decisions
are in fact final judgments on aspects of the case. The issue selected has the
potential to bring the whole proceedings to an efficient conclusion, for example, when a point of limitation (or 'prescription') (see **3.09**) is considered
and the court decides that the action is statute-barred.

5.03   The remaining categories are (iii) summary judgment, (iv) striking out, and
(v) default judgment. These are accelerated and stream-lined procedures without oral examination of factual evidence (on the absence of oral examination
of witnesses at pre-trial hearings, see **2.38**). Each of these forms of pre-trial
procedure can dispose of the whole case (although species (iii) and (iv) might
be confined to only part of the action). Summary judgment and 'striking out',
respectively (iii) and (iv), require examination of the substantive merits of the
claim in a pre-trial hearing. By contrast, default judgment is obtained without
a hearing. However, if the defendant challenges this judgment, there can be a
hearing of the merits to determine whether the default judgment should be
maintained (see **5.32**).

(2) Interim Payments[4]

Outline

5.04   Because litigation can take considerable time, it is expedient for the courts to
have power to issue provisional or interim relief pending final disposal of the
action. In fact the courts lacked power to order interim payments until 1969,

---

    [3] See, below, **5.12** at (iii) for the less common situation where the interim injunction aims
to compel the defendant to perform a positive act: a 'mandatory' injunction.
    [4] CPR 25.6 to 25.9; and PD (25) 'Interim Payments'; on which Neil Andrews, *English
Civil Procedure* (Oxford UP, 2003) 18–04 ff; *Zuckerman on Civil Procedure* (2006)

whereas the equitable jurisdiction to issue interim injunctions is much older. Interim payments were at first confined to protect plaintiffs in personal injury or fatal accident claims.[5] In 1978 the system of interim payments was expanded to cover all damages or debt claims.[6] An interim payment order enables the claimant to obtain advance payment, often well before trial.[7] The payment will be reckoned as at least a 'reasonable proportion' of the claim. The court can order an interim payment if the defendant has admitted liability or the court 'is satisfied' that, if the case went to trial, the claimant would obtain judgment for a 'substantial' monetary award against the defendant, other than costs. After receiving such an award, the claimant cannot discontinue the proceedings unless the defendant consents in writing or the court gives permission.[8] The interim payment will not be disclosed to the court at trial until all questions concerning liability have been considered.[9]

General Conditions

Such an order enables the claimant to recover at least a reasonable proportion   **5.05** of a money claim months or even a year or more before trial. This is fair, provided the claim has been admitted by the defendant or the court can provisionally decide that the claim has real strength on the merits. The rules permit such an order to be made in any of these three situations:[10] (1) the defendant admits liability but there are outstanding issues on the damages or other relief sought, and so the action must proceed further, normally to a hearing on the unresolved matter; or (2) the claimant has obtained judgment against the defendant with the amount to be assessed (the difference between (1) and (2), therefore, is that in (2) the question of liability required judgment rather than party settlement); or (3) the court 'is satisfied' that, if the case went to trial, the claimant would obtain judgment for a 'substantial' monetary award against the defendant, other than costs. The word 'satisfied' (see above) has been held to require 'something more than a prima facie case ... but not proof beyond reasonable doubt'; 'the burden is high'; 'but it is a civil burden on the balance of probabil-

---

9–205 ff; IS Goldrein (ed), *Commercial Litigation: Pre-emptive Remedies* (International Edition, 2005) 590 ff.

    [5] s 20, Administration of Justice Act 1969.
    [6] Responding to the criticism made in *Associated Bulk Carriers Ltd v Koch Shipping Inc* [1978] 2 All ER 254, CA, of the narrowness of this regime.
    [7] CPR 25.1(1)(k) defines an interim payment as: 'an order (referred to as an order for interim payment) under rule 25.6 for payment of any damages, debt or other sum (except costs) which the court may hold the defendant liable to pay.'
    [8] CPR 38.2(2)(b).
    [9] CPR 25.9.
    [10] CPR 25.7.

ities, not a criminal burden.'[11] In another case, the court said that 'the burden is a high one: it is not enough that the court thinks it likely that the [claimant] will succeed at trial.'[12] It might be suggested that the courts approach this in terms of a 75 per cent threshold of conviction that the claimant is likely to succeed: somewhere between certainty and a bare 'more likely than not' sense of success.

Amount Awarded

5.06   The sum awarded as interim payment must not exceed a reasonable proportion of the likely amount of the final judgment.[13] Furthermore, the court must take into account (a) contributory negligence and (b) any relevant set-off or counterclaim.[14] For example, the court might conclude that the claimant is unlikely to obtain any net award at trial because the defendant's counterclaim, which is for a greater amount, is likely to be upheld at trial.[15] Or, where the claim is for, say, £ 500,000, but the court is confident that a contributory negligence defence of, say, 50 per cent, is likely to succeed at trial, the court would arrive at a provisional award of £ 250,000. When deciding, next, how much to award as an interim payment, the court must exercise its discretion and fix a 'reasonable proportion' of that 'likely amount'. For this purpose the court can take account of the following factors: (1) the strength of the claimant's claim; (2) whether the claim has been admitted; (3) whether the defendant has made a Part 36 payment into court, and the amount of that payment (generally on settlement offers, see **10.25** ff);[16] (4) the interval which is likely to elapse between the date of the award and the trial or final disposal of the case; (5)

---

[11] *Shearson Lehman Inc v MacLaine, Watson & Co Ltd* [1987] 1 WLR 480, 489, CA, per Lloyd LJ; *Gibbons v Wall The Times* 24 February, 1988, CA, cited *British & Commonwealth Holdings plc v Quadrex Holdings plc* [1989] 1 QB 842, 865, CA.

[12] *British & Commonwealth* case, ibid, at 866, CA, per Browne-Wilkinson V-C, which was cited by Balcombe LJ in *Andrews v Schooling* [1991] 1 WLR 783, 787, CA; *Crimpfil Ltd v Barclay's Bank plc The Times* 24 February, 1995, CA (held that a court can form impressionistic view of merits of an application even where liability and quantum are highly contentious and the issues are complicated).

[13] CPR 25.7(2).

[14] CPR 25.7(3); for reasons of space, the complicated law concerning set-off has been omitted from this work: see Neil Andrews, *English Civil Procedure* (Oxford UP, 2003) 11.07 ff; and for the law concerning counterclaims, ibid, 11.65 ff; for comparative discussion, R Zimmermann, *Comparative Foundations of a European Law of Set-off and Prescription* (Cambridge UP, 2002).

[15] eg *Shanning International Ltd v George Wimpey International Ltd* [1988] 3 All ER 475, CA.

[16] *Fryer v London Transport Executive The Times* 4 December, 1982, CA, supports this aspect of the discretion.

whether the defendant can afford to pay;[17] (6) whether the claimant has a pressing need for the money; (7) the likelihood of the defendant's defences of contributory negligence and set-off[18] succeeding in fact at trial; (8) the likely amount of final judgment; (9) the reasons why the claimant believes that the general conditions for awarding an interim payment are satisfied in the present case;[19] (10) details of special damages and past and future loss, in actions for personal injury; (11) in a fatal accident claim, details of the person(s) on whose behalf the claim is made and the nature of the claim.

Protection of the Defendant

There are three elements of protection. First, to avoid the danger of pre-judg- **5.07** ment at trial, the existence of an interim payment will not be disclosed to the court at trial until all questions concerning liability have been considered, unless 'the court directs', or the defendant agrees otherwise.[20] Secondly, a claimant who has received an interim payment cannot discontinue the proceedings unless the defendant consents in writing or the court gives permission.[21] This rule protects the defendant against the risk that if the case had proceeded to trial it might have been shown that the sum was not in fact owed, or at least not in full. Thirdly, a claimant might need to repay an interim payment, in whole or in part, in any of these situations: (1) because he has discontinued or settled the claim in circumstances where the interim payment becomes repayable; or (2) he has lost at trial; or (3) he has received final judgment for less than the interim payment; or (4) the court has otherwise varied or discharged an interim payment order.

---

[17] eg *Newton Chemical Ltd v Arsenis* [1989] 1 WLR 1297; *British & Commonwealth Holdings plc v Quadrex Holdings plc* [1989] 1 QB 842, CA.

[18] For reasons of space, the complicated law concerning set-off has been omitted from this work: see Neil Andrews, *English Civil Procedure* (Oxford UP, 2003) 11.07 ff; for comparative discussion, R Zimmermann, *Comparative Foundations of a European Law of Set-off and Prescription* (Cambridge UP, 2002).

[19] See CPR 25.7.

[20] CPR 25.9.

[21] CPR 38.2(2)(b).

(3) Interim Injunctions[22]

5.08   There are many divisions between types injunction: (1) (a) interim or (b)final; (2) (a) mandatory ('positive') or (b) prohibitory ('negative'); (3) (a) 'without notice' or (b) 'with notice' to the defendant (formerly, *ex parte* or *inter partes*, respectively);[23] (4) (a) *quia timet* (that is, anticipatory of a legal wrong) or (b) injunctions which apply *ex post facto*; (5) (a) injunctions obtained before or (b) after commencement of the main proceedings; (6) or (a) before or (b) after judgment.[24] The court's statutory power to grant injunctions includes the power to issue interim injunctions where the relief sought at trial is a final injunction.[25] This sub-section concerns interim injunctions, whether mandatory or prohibitory, awarded *inter partes* ('with notice'). 'Freezing injunctions' and 'search orders', discussed in chapter 4, do not concern the substantive dispute but instead operate in a 'protective' fashion to maintain the monetary or evidential viability of pursuing or enforcing the main claim.

5.09   Recipients of interim injunctions are normally bound by an implicit 'cross-undertaking' (an implied promise to the court for the benefit of the other litigant) to indemnify the respondent if the interim order is subsequently held, for whatever reasons, to have been improperly granted. This duty to indemnify will apply if court discharges the interim order or the claimant later concedes during a settlement arrangement that the interim injunction should not have been granted.[26]

General 'Embargo' on Examination of The Substantive Merits

5.10   In general, the House of Lords' decision in *American Cyanamid Ltd v Ethicon Ltd* (1974) governs this practice.[27] This leading case establishes the general rule that, on an application for an interim injunction, the court must not attempt to consider the 'merits' (that is, the strength of the substantive claim and defence).

---

[22] Neil Andrews, *English Civil Procedure* (Oxford UP, 2003) 18–41 ff; S Gee, *Commercial Injunctions* (2004) ch 2; IS Goldrein (ed), *Commercial Litigation: Pre-emptive Remedies* (International Edition, 2005), pp 1 ff; *Zuckerman on Civil Procedure* (2006) 9.5 ff.

[23] CPR 25.3.

[24] CPR 25.2(1), for these last two dichotomies.

[25] s 37, Supreme Court Act 1981.

[26] *F Hoffmann – La Roche & Co AG v Secretary of State for Trade & Industry* [1975] AC 295, 360–1, HL, *American Cyanamid Co v Ethicon Ltd* [1975] AC 396, 407–9, HL; on enforcement of the cross-undertaking, *Cheltenham & Gloucester Building Society v Ricketts* [1993] 1 WLR 1545, CA, *Goldman Sachs International v Philip Lyons The Times* 28 February, 1995, CA, *Barratt Manchester Ltd v Bolton MBC* [1998] 1 WLR 1003, CA, *Customs & Excise Commissioners v Anchor Foods Ltd* [1999] 1 WLR 1139.

[27] [1975] AC 396, HL.

Instead the court will assess the litigants' competing interests in, respectively, gaining interim restraint of the defendant's alleged misconduct, and preserving freedom from that restraint. The court must strive to balance the hardship to the applicant caused by refusal of relief against the hardship to the other party if he is temporarily bound by an injunction. According to the *American Cyanamid* doctrine, consideration of the case's factual merits would be just and proper only if the court discovered no real difference in weight between the parties' respective potential hardships. Thus the five elements of this doctrine are as follows. (1) Has the claimant proved that there is a serious question to be tried? If so, one must proceed to the next question. (2) Would damages adequately protect the claimant's interests? (3) If the answer to (2) is 'no', the next question is whether the defendant would be adequately protected by the indemnification available under the claimant's cross-undertaking if the defendant won the case at trial (see **5.09** above)? (4) If the answer to question (3) is 'no', the court must next consider whether the 'balance of convenience' justifies the award or refusal of the interim injunction, taking into account all the circumstances, but especially these: [A] the need to preserve the status quo; [B] the extent of non-compensatable disadvantage to each party if he should succeed at trial having lost at the interim stage; [C] the relevant strength of each party's case on the basis of the documentary material and lawyers' submissions made at the interim hearing. (5) Consideration of the case's factual merits would be just and proper only if, at stage (4) [B] of this inquiry, the court discovers no real difference in weight between the parties' respective potential hardships.

As for stage (4) [C] of the inquiry, Laddie J in the *Series 5 Software* case **5.11** (1996)[28] attractively suggested that the courts will often be well positioned to make reliable assessment of the 'case's strength' on the factual merits and that the embargo should be reserved for really difficult issues of fact requiring prolonged investigation at trial, including oral examination of witnesses.[29] This had in fact been precisely the situation facing the House of Lords in the *American Cyanamid* case. That had been an application for an interim injunction to prevent an alleged infringement of a patent. The facts had concerned highly complex questions of fact, involving hydro-carbons. Proceedings in the lower courts had already occupied many days of judicial time. Against that back-

---

[28] *Series 5 Software Limited v Clarke* [1996] 1 All ER 853; see also Laddie J in *Antec International v Southwestern Chicks (Warren) Ltd* [1997] FSR 278 and in *Direct Line Group Ltd v Direct Line Estate Agency and Others Ltd* [1997] FSR 374, 376; for comment on the *Series 5 Software* case, *Barnsley Brewery Co Ltd v RBNB* [1997] FSR 462, Robert Walker J and *SIG Architectural Products Ltd v Castle House Windows Ltd* (unreported 20 June 1996), Robert Walker J; and see Jacob J in *Cable and Wireless plc v British Telecommunications plc* (unreported, 8 December, 1997).

[29] *Series 5 Software* case [1996] 1 All ER 853.

ground, Laddie J's explanation in the *Series 5 Software* case (1996) of the 1974 *American Cyanamid* decision makes complete sense. He said:

'... what is intended is that the court should not attempt to *resolve difficult issues of fact or law*[30] on an application for interlocutory relief. If, on the other hand, the court is able to come to a view as to the strength of the parties' cases on the credible evidence, then it can do so. In fact, ... it is frequently the case that it is easy to determine who is (more) likely to win the trial on the basis of the [documentary material].'[31]

It should also be noted that, in the context of summary judgment, the courts refuse to permit 'mini-trials' of complicated factual issues (see **5.20** below).

5.12   Decisions continue to cite the *American Cyanamid* decision. It remains the starting-point for analysis.[32] However, decisions since 1974 have deftly established various situations where efficiency and fairness demand pre-trial examination of the 'merits' (as explained above). The most important contexts are as follows:[33]

(i) *urgent cases*: the matter is highly urgent and there is not enough time to wait until trial, for example, when the delay necessitated by waiting for trial would render the central dispute a 'non-issue' (for example, if a restrictive covenant clause has only three months to run);[34] in such a case, it would be unjust to ignore that the grant of interim relief will effectively dispose of the whole litigation; therefore, the merits can be legitimately appraised at the interim stage;

(ii) *transparent cases*: these are instances where the factual merits of the application are 'plain and uncontroversial', or perhaps the case is plainly hopeless; in such cases, the courts should not hesitate to consider the substantive merits of the case;[35]

(iii) *applications for mandatory injunctions*: such an order compels the defendant actively to do something, such as 'thou shall build the wall, as agreed'; this type of injunction is more intrusive than a negative or prohibitory order (for example, 'do not build the proposed wall'); furthermore, it would be incon-

---

[30] It is submitted that it will be rare for a point of law to be so complicated that the matter cannot be conveniently adjudicated at the interim stage; admittedly, some legal points, requiring very prolonged discussion, might not be conveniently considered at this stage of proceedings; furthermore, some points of law might require complicated issues of fact to have been resolved.

[31] *Series 5 Software* case [1996] 1 All ER 853, 865.

[32] eg, *Intelsec Systems Ltd v Grech-Cini* [1999] 4 All ER 11, 25 and *R v Secretary of State for Health, ex p Imperial Tobacco Ltd* [2000] 1 All ER 572, 598, CA, per Laws LJ ('*American Cyanamid* is the ordinary rule by which applications for interlocutory injunctions in private law proceedings are decided every day ...'); *R v Secretary of State for Health ex p Imperial Tobacco Ltd* [2001] 1 WLR 127, 131, 135, HL; and *Att-Gen v Punch* [2002] UKHL 50; [2003] 1 AC 1046, at [74], [99], [100].

[33] Neil Andrews, *English Civil Procedure* (Oxford UP, 2003) 18.53 to 18.65.

[34] *Cayne v Global Natural Resources Ltd* [1984] 1 All ER 225, CA.

[35] *Office Overload Ltd v Gunn* [1977] FSR 39, 44, CA, per Bridge LJ.

venient, wasteful and unjust to make an interim order to build and then for the court at trial to change its appreciation of the case and instead to require the defendant to demolish. And so, to avoid such procedural tergiversation, the interim decision to make such a positive order requires a 'high degree of assurance that the claimant will win at trial;[36]

(iv) *freedom of expression*: where the case concerns the respondent's freedom of expression, section 12 (3) of the Human Rights Act 1998 states that interim injunctions must be clearly justified on the merits: 'No such relief is to be granted so as to restrain publication before trial unless the court is satisfied that the applicant is likely to establish that publication should not be allowed'; there has been extensive recent judicial examination of this context;[37]

(v) *matters of real public importance*: occasionally such cases have been held to justify examining the case's substantive merits at the interim stage.[38]

Conclusion on the American Cyanamid Approach

The highly complex nature of the factual issues in the *American Cyanamid* (1974) plainly justified the House of Lords' decision not to permit further investigation of the case's substantive merits. The House of Lords' introduction of a new test was a rational allocation of the court's scarce appellate resources on those peculiarly complex facts.[39] It is, however, questionable whether the decision's general proscription upon judicial consideration of 'factual merits' was   **5.13**

---

[36] *Shephard Homes Ltd v Sandham* [1971] Ch 340, Megarry J; see also *Locabail v Agro-export ('The Sea Hawk')* [1986] 1 WLR 657, CA affirming this exception to *American Cyanamid*; cf *Akai Holdings Limited (in compulsory liquidation) v RSM Robson Rhodes LLP and Another* [2007] EWHC 1641, Briggs J (*RSM RR contractually bound to provide Akai with expert advice in pending civil litigation between Akai and GT; interim injunction to restrain RSM RR, accountancy firm, from merging with GT; prospect of conflict of interest; injunction granted against RSM RR*).

[37] s 12(3), Human Rights Act 1998: *Cream Holdings Inc v Banerjee* [2004] UKHL 44; [2005] 1 AC 253; *Browne v Associated Newspapers Ltd* [2007] EWCA Civ 295; [2007] 3 WLR 289 at [23] and [40] ff: 'the approach required by section 12 arises in this way. The court should first consider whether this is a case in which article 8 is engaged. It should then consider whether article 10 is engaged and, critically, whether the applicant for relief has shown that he is likely to establish at a trial that publication should not be allowed within the meaning of section 12(3) of the HRA.' For consideration of the *Cream Holdings* case and 'freedom of expression' in the context of interim relief to restrain a trade mark infringement, *Boehringer Ingelheim Ltd v Vetplus Ltd* [2007] EWCA Civ 583. In *HRH The Prince of Wales v Associated Newspapers Limited* [2006] EWCA Civ 1776; [2007] 3 WLR 222 the claimant succeeded in obtaining a permanent injunction to restrain breaches of confidentiality and of copyright, employing the process of summary judgment (on which generally, **5.18**).

[38] *Smith v Inner London Education Authority* [1978] 1 All ER 411, CA; *Express Newspapers Ltd v Keys* [1980] IRLR 247; *Thanet DC v Ninedrive Ltd* [1978] 1 All ER 703.

[39] Anticipating the last limb of 'the Overriding Objective', in CPR Part 1: see **2.14**.

justified. As Laddie J said in the *Series 5 Software* case (1996) (see **5.11** above), High Court judges hearing applications for interim injunctions acquire much experience in discerning who is more likely to win, even on the basis of merely documentary evidence presented at this interim stage (on this evidential restriction, see **2.38, 5.03**). It would be useful for the House of Lords at some point to re-visit this important topic. What are the arguments for and against retaining the *American Cyanamid* doctrine as the starting-point in this area (for situations where that decision has been effectively by-passed, see the list at **5.12** above)?

5.14   Two arguments can be made to support general refusal to consider the merits on an interim application for an injunction. First, the courts will spare themselves a heavy interlocutory workload and so have more time to devote to hearing trials.[40] Secondly, sometimes a court cannot safely assess the factual merits until the case has been fully prepared and witnesses have been cross-examined.[41] Furthermore, most applications for interim injunctions precede disclosure of the parties' relevant documents under CPR Part 31 (on which **6.21**). It might sometimes be dangerous and unfair to consider the merits of the case before that stage because one party might be disadvantaged.[42]

5.15   However, there are three arguments against the *American Cyanamid* doctrine. First, the old requirement of a prima facie case was satisfactorily applied in many cases.[43] Parties often agreed that they would abide by the result of the interlocutory decision on the merits. Secondly, Part 1 of the CPR ('the Overriding Objective', for the text see **2.14**) emphasises the importance of providing an efficient, cheap, expeditious and proportionate means of resolving civil disputes.[44] Grant of interim injunctions not only accelerates justice, but also promotes swift and informed settlement. These benefits can be secured only if the court makes a provisional assessment of the merits of each side's case, often months before the trial date.[45] Finally, procedural conditions have changed since the *American Cyanamid* case was decided. Since 1998 English courts no longer face the crisis of long queues for trial (on this decline in litigation, **2.22, 5.15, 10.08, 13.12**). Whereas in 1974 this problem existed, and the position worsened in the 1980s.

5.16   It is submitted that the court should avoid considering a case's substantive merits when deciding whether to grant an interim injunction only if such provisional adjudication of the facts would be perilous in that particular case. This danger arises only if reliable assessment of the facts will require scrutiny of oral

---

[40] eg, comments in *Derby & Co Ltd v Weldon (No 6)* [1990] 1 WLR 1139, 1153, CA.

[41] *American Cyanamid Ltd v Ethicon Ltd* [1975] AC 396, 406, HL.

[42] *Cayne v Global Natural Resources Ltd* [1984] 1 All ER 225, 229, CA.

[43] See comments by an experienced intellectual property and Chancery practitioner: Peter Prescott, (1975) 91 LQR 168–71 (case note); see also the approach of Laddie J in the *Series 5 Software Ltd v Clarke* [1996] 1 All ER 853.

[44] CPR 1.1(2) (the Overriding Objective).

[45] As emphasised by P Prescott (1975) 91 LQR 168–71 (case note).

witness evidence, a process confined to trial (factual evidence during pre-trial hearings is presented instead in written form and there is no opportunity for cross-examination). Otherwise, the courts should cut the Gordian knot and make an interim assessment on the basis of both documentary material (provided it is not too voluminous) and counsel's submissions.

(4) Preliminary Issues[46]

The court can be asked to pronounce in final form on a preliminary issue: either a point of pure law or 'construction' (that is, interpretation) of a document. The preliminary matter can be heard before the factual issues have been investigated. Such a 'preliminary' decision is not provisional, but final. Often the point singled out for this accelerated treatment is a 'crux' on which the entire fate of the litigation might depend. Even if the preliminary decision does not determine the rest of the dispute, it might provide the basis for settlement of the remaining issues, or at least reduce the scope or length of the ensuing process. Thus considerations of speediness, proportionality, and efficiency justify measured use of this technique. Typical 'preliminary issues' are: points concerning limitation of actions ('prescription'; generally see **3.09**);[47] consensual time bars upon valid proceedings[48]; exclusion clauses;[49] disputes on a preliminary point of substantive law, for example whether the defendant owes a duty of care on the present facts.[50]

5.17

(5) Summary Judgment[51]

This procedure allows claimants *or defendants* (a change introduced in the CPR in 1998) to gain final judgment if they can show that their opponent's claim or defence lacks a 'real prospect' of success. It is a stream-lined procedure. It enables the applicant to avoid the delay, expense and inconvenience

5.18

---

[46] Neil Andrews, *English Civil Procedure* (Oxford UP, 2003) 9.33, 9.34, 34.17.

[47] ibid, 9.33 n 39; eg, *Haward v Fawcetts* [2006] UKHL 9; [2006] 1 WLR 682, on s 14A, Limitation of Actions Act 1980.

[48] *Senate Electrical Wholesalers Ltd v Alacatel Submarine Networks Ltd* [1999] 2 Lloyd's Rep 243, CA, 355–7; *Laminates Acquisition Co v BTR Australia* [2003] EWHC 2540 (Comm), Cooke J.

[49] *Cremdean Properties v Nash* (1977) 244 EG 547, CA.

[50] eg *Customs & Excise v Barclays Bank plc* [2006] UKHL 28; [2007] 1 AC 181, on which **4.19**; *Deep Vein Thrombosis and Air Travel Group Litigation* [2005] UKHL 72; [2005] UKHL 72; [2006] 1 AC 495.

[51] Neil Andrews, *English Civil Procedure* (Oxford UP, 2003) ch 20; IS Goldrein (ed), *Commercial Litigation: Pre-emptive Remedies* (International Edition, 2005) ch 6; *Zuckerman on Civil Procedure* (2006) 8.39 ff.

of taking the case to trial. Factual issues are considered on the basis of written evidence. Such evidence takes the form of witness statements and statements of truth.[52]

Test

5.19   Normally a party applies for summary judgment, but the court can itself initiate a summary judgment hearing. Summary judgment is available both to test the legal (including points of construction of documents) and factual merits of a claim or defence, or any part thereof. [53] The governing rule states:[54]

> 'The court may give summary judgment against a claimant or defendant on the whole of a claim or on a particular issue if (a) it considers that (i) that claimant has no real prospect of succeeding on the claim or issue; or (ii) that defendant has no real prospect of successfully defending the claim or issue and (b) there is no other reason why the case or issue should be disposed of at a trial.'

5.20   This CPR reformulation of the old law (formerly known as 'RSC Order 14') increases the court's power to sift bad or hopeless claims or defences. The pre-CPR test gave the respondent the benefit of the doubt in more situations. In essence, the old pre-CPR test was whether the defence was arguable: 'is there a fair or reasonable probability of the defendant having a real or bona fide defence?'[55] That generous approach to defences gave the defendant the benefit of the doubt. But, since 1998, the CPR test is whether the defence or claim has a 'real' chance of succeeding as opposed to a merely fanciful chance of success. As Lord Woolf said in *Swain v Hillman* (2001), the new words ('no *real* prospect' of success) 'speak for themselves' and he refused to gloss this language (other than accepting that 'realistic' means the same as 'real').[56] He added that the function of CPR Part 24 would be distorted if summary judgment hearings were allowed to become 'mini-trials' (see the analogy with the practice concerning interim injunctions, at **5.11** above). Instead, issues involving detailed

---

[52] CPR 24.5.

[53] PD (24) 1.2, 1.3; points of construction are amenable to summary judgment, as explained in *ICI Chemicals & Polymers Ltd v TTE Training Ltd* [2007] EWCA Civ 725 at [12], per Moore-Bick LJ: 'if the court is satisfied that it has before it all the evidence necessary for the proper determination of the question and that the parties have had an adequate opportunity to address it in argument, it should grasp the nettle and decide it.'

[54] CPR 24.2.

[55] *National Westminster Bank plc v Daniel* [1993] 1 WLR 1453, 1457, CA.

[56] *Swain v Hillman* [2001] 1 All ER 91, 92, CA; for other judicial observations on this test, see the references collected by Blackburne J in *HRH The Prince of Wales v Associated Newspapers Limited* [2006] EWHC 522 (Ch); [2007] 3 WLR 222, 227, at [11]; for comment on the CPR test, Derek O'Brien, 'The New Summary Judgment: Raising the Threshold of Admission' (1999) 18 CJQ 132, esp 137, 145–8.

factual investigation require the case to progress through disclosure under CPR 31 and preparation of witness statements, perhaps culminating in cross-examination at trial.[57] It has been persuasively contended that, sensibly applied, summary judgment does not infringe Article 6(1) of the European Convention on Human Rights, which accords a right to a 'fair hearing'.[58]

The primary 'real prospect of success' test, just explained, is subject to a **5.21** secondary or safety-valve provision, introduced to safeguard the wider interests of justice. The courts are here administering 'procedural equity', an ancient virtue not yet outlawed in the modern (sometimes rather obsessive) quest for procedural efficiency (on 'procedural equity' see also comments at **2.21**). The same test is also a manifestation of the court's 'Overriding Objective' to ensure that the case is decided justly.[59] This secondary tests applies as follows: even though the court would ordinarily award summary judgment against the 'summary hearing respondent' (whether he be the defendant or claimant), because he has not shown a cogent factual or legal case, the court must further consider whether 'there is no other compelling reason why the case or issue should be disposed of at a trial.'[60] This gives the 'summary respondent' a further opportunity to avoid defeat. Litigants in person, in particular, might benefit from this 'safety-valve' if they have not presented their claim or defence so as to disclose a 'real' chance of success. At the same time, however, the courts should not be too quick to give hopeless claims or defences the benefit of the doubt. This 'safety-vale' test requires excellent judgement.

The Court's Options at a Summary Judgment Hearing

The court has three options. First, the court can give judgment (summary judg- **5.22** ment) for the applicant, whether this is the claimant or the defendant, and whether this is on the whole of the claim or merely on a particular issue[61] (summary judgment can be expressed as a decision to strike out or dismiss the

---

[57] Even so, a party should not be allowed to drag out a case to trial if there is no real prospect of new evidence becoming available and the summary judgment hearing is instead already soundly supported: *ICI Chemicals & Polymers Ltd v TTE Training Ltd* [2007] EWCA Civ 725 at [12]; and summary judgment against the defendant, following a three day hearing (without, of course, oral examination of witnesses) before a Master, was upheld on appeal by Peter Smith J, even though the claims involved allegations of dishonesty: *Hanco ATM Systems Ltd v Cashbox ATM Systems Ltd* [2007] EWHC 1599 (Ch), at [18] to [30] (containing valuable analysis of the practice).

[58] L Mulcahy, *Human Rights and Civil Practice* (2001) 10.52.

[59] CPR 1.1. and 1.2.

[60] CPR 24.2(b); and PD (24) 2(3)(b).

[61] CPR 24.1 and 24.2; PD (24) 5.1(1)(2); for the situation where there is a counterclaim and the main claim is brought by the liquidators of an insolvent claimant, *Swissport (UK) Ltd v Aer Lingus Ltd* [2007] EWHC 1089 (Ch).

claim or a particular issue, on which see **5.23** below).[62] This first option involves victory for the summary judgment applicant, whether in respect of the whole or any part of the case. The second option is that the court can dismiss outright the application for summary judgment.[63] This option involves defeat for the summary judgment applicant, but not overall defeat in the main action, which survives intact and might proceed ultimately to trial. The third option is that the court can grant a conditional order (discussed below) where 'it appears to the court that a claim or defence may succeed but improbable that it will do so'.[64] In this last situation, the conditional decision will permit the claim or defence to proceed to trial only if the relevant party satisfies a stipulated condition.[65] A pre-CPR decision reinvigorated this jurisdiction to make such conditional decisions at summary judgment hearings[66] (endorsed in decisions under the CPR).[67] Possible conditions are: a payment into court or some other 'specified step'.[68] A payment into court will protect the intended beneficiary against the payor's insolvency.[69]

(6) Striking Out Claims or Defences[70]

Introduction

5.23   Sometimes the court can strike out a claim or defence, usually at a very early stage of the proceedings. The power to strike out a pleading (now known as a 'statement of case', whether it is a claim, defence, reply, or counterclaim, or any part of one) is exercisable in any of these situations:[71] *the statement of case discloses no reasonable grounds for bringing or defending the claim; or the statement of case is an abuse of the court's process[72] or is otherwise likely to*

---

[62] PD (24) 5.1(2), which should be construed in the light of CPR 24.1 and 24.2 where 'claim' is clearly used compendiously to embrace both an active claim and a possible defence to that active claim.

[63] PD (24) 5.1(3).

[64] PD (24) 4; *Yorke Motors Ltd v Edwards* [1982] 1 WLR 444, HL.

[65] PD (24) 4 (see also PD (24) 5).

[66] *Yorke Motors Ltd v Edwards* [1982] 1 WLR 444, HL.

[67] eg, *Foot & Bowden v Anglo Europe Corporation Ltd* (CA, unreported 17 February, 2000); *Chapple v Williams* (CA, unreported 8 December, 1999)

[68] Note to CPR 24.6, cross-referring to CPR 3.1(3); PD (24) 5.2.

[69] *Re Ford* [1900] 2 QB 211.

[70] Neil Andrews, *English Civil Procedure* (Oxford UP, 2003) ch 21; *Zuckerman on Civil Procedure* (2006) 8–30 ff.

[71] CPR 3.4(2).

[72] Generally on abuse of process, Neil Andrews, *English Civil Procedure* (Oxford UP, 2003) ch 16.

obstruct the just disposal of the proceedings; or failure to comply with a rule, practice direction or court order.[73]

Striking out can be exercised whether or not a party makes an application to the court; and striking out can be specified as a 'sanction', that is, prescribed as the automatic consequence of failure to comply with an 'unless' order (see further on this last possibility, **2.19**).[74] One of the grounds for striking out (because *'the statement of case discloses no reasonable grounds for bringing or defending the claim'*) can overlap with the court's jurisdiction to award summary judgment under CPR Part 24 (on which see **5.19** and **5.20** above). Both pre-trial procedures serve the function of enabling the court to weed out bad or tenuous claims or defences. Both are subject to the evidential constraint that the court can only receive oral evidence at trial (on the absence of oral examination of witnesses at pre-trial hearings, see **2.38** and **5.16**). As we shall see, the summary judgment sieve has slightly finer mesh than the striking out jurisdiction. **5.24**

The Court of Appeal in *S v Gloucestershire CC* (2000)[75] confirmed that summary judgment and striking out procedures can be applied concurrently. At first instance in this case the defendant municipal authorities had unsuccessfully attempted to strike out negligence suits under CPR Part 3, but there had been no consideration of a summary judgment under CPR Part 24.[76] This case was unusual. All the evidence was available in documentary form (clinical notes composed by social workers). By contrast, most negligence claims will ordinarily require postponement of final decision until trial. Only then can the court receive oral evidence from witnesses, especially by cross-examination.

On appeal, it was held that the validity of these claims could be considered as a concurrent striking out (under CPR Part 3) and summary judgment application (under CPR Part 24, on the basis that the claims should be dismissed as lacking any real prospect of success).[77] Applying pre-CPR authorities,[78] the court said that striking out on the factual or legal merits (see rule 3.4(2)(a) cited at **5.23** above) is justified only in 'the clearest case'.[79] The test for sum- **5.26**

---

[73] CPR 3.4(2)(a) to (c).

[74] The court can take the initiative and order a summary judgment hearing: CPR 24.5(3); on 'unless' orders in this context, see 2.21 n 62, explaining *Marcan Shipping (London) Ltd v Kefelas* [2007] EWCA Civ 463; [2007] 1 WLR 1864, at [33] to [36]; considering CPR 3.8(1) (sanctions take effect automatically); and CPR 3.9 (relief from sanctions); and CPR 3.5 (innocent party's right to file for judgment with costs if opponent's whole defence or claim is struck out automatically for non-compliance with an 'unless' order).

[75] [2000] 3 All ER 346, 370–3, CA.

[76] CPR 3.4(2).

[77] *S v Gloucestershire CC* [2000] 3 All ER 346, 372; for another example, see *Murray v Express Newspapers plc* [2007] EWHC 1908 (Ch) (noted at **6.27** n 108) (the JK Rowling application).

[78] See the authorities collected at Neil Andrews, *Principles of Civil Procedure* (1994) 10–23.

[79] *S v Gloucestershire CC* [2000] 3 All ER 346, 373.

mary judgment under CPR Part 24 offers slightly greater scope for disposing of the relevant claim or defence (see **5.19** and **5.20** above).

5.27   And so the two tests have the same function (to eliminate unsound claims or defences without trial); and they apply to the same raw material, because at a pre-trial hearing, (whether for summary judgment or striking out), the court can only receive written evidence;[80] but the tests are slightly differently calibrated, summary judgment allowing slightly more searching review of the relevant issue. As the Court of Appeal said:

> 'For a summary judgment application to succeed in a case such as this where a strike out application would not succeed [because the latter requires proof of the "clearest case" that the striking out application is justified], the court will first need to be satisfied that all substantial facts relevant to the allegations of negligence, which are reasonably capable of being presented to the court, are indeed before the court; that these facts are undisputed or that there is no real prospect of successfully disputing them; and that there is no real prospect of oral evidence affecting the court's assessment of the facts.'[81]

Provided there are no gaps in the evidence which might still be filled, 'there will ... have been proper judicial scrutiny of the detailed facts of the particular case such as to constitute a fair hearing in accordance with Article 6 of the [European Convention on Human Rights].'[82]

5.28   The House of Lords, in the notorious application known as *Three Rivers DC v Bank of England (No 3)* (2001), also noted the concurrent application of striking out and summary judgment procedures.[83] Three members of the House of Lords fatefully allowed this case to proceed to trial. The trial lasted two years. The claimant eventually discontinued it before judgment, on 'day 256' of the trial.[84] The author (at **3.19** and elsewhere)[85] has lamented this ill-calculated refusal to dismiss a claim. According to Lord Millett, one of the dissentients, even taking into account the voluminous pre-trial papers, the claim was objectively 'most implausible', 'scarcely credible' and 'extravagant'.[86]

---

[80] ibid, at 372–3.

[81] ibid, at 373.

[82] ibid; May LJ added, at 371 that 'in an appropriate case, a defendant is entitled to a fair summary hearing of a case which, when it is properly investigated, has no real prospect of success.'

[83] [2001] 2 All ER 513, HL, notably at [90] ff, and [134] ff.

[84] *Three Rivers DC v Bank of England* [2006] EWHC 816 (Comm) (12 April 2006), Tomlinson J at [1].

[85] Neil Andrews, *English Civil Procedure* (Oxford UP, 2003) 20–15 to 20–19; see also A Zuckerman, 'A Colossal Wreck – the BCCI/Three Rivers Litigation' (2006) CJQ 287; and see Sir Anthony Clarke MR, 'The Supercase-Problems and Solutions', 2007 Annual KPMG Forensic Lecture: available at http://www.judiciary.gov.uk/docs/speeches/kpmg_speech.pdf.

[86] *Three Rivers* case [2001] 2 All ER 513, HL, [90] ff, and [134] ff, esp at [180], [181].

This 'supercase' or 'monster litigation' (generally, see **3.19**) demonstrates   **5.29**
that appeal courts should be slow to upset a striking out decision, even if the
case is 'complicated' and involves 'extensive documentation'. English law
should also consider a focused pre-trial *oral* hearing to probe weak claims
which might otherwise proceed to lengthy trial. This requires abandonment of
the practice that oral evidence must always be postponed until trial.

Compatibility of Striking Out Procedure and Article 6 of the European Convention on Human Rights

The European Court of Human Rights ('ECtHR') in *Osman v UK* (1998) cas-   **5.30**
tigated the English courts for employing striking out to dismiss *legally* un-
founded claims. It held that there had been a violation of Article 6 on the facts
of that litigation. But the European Court in *Z v UK* (2001) acknowledged that
such a pre-trial *legal* filter is compatible with the human right to a 'fair hearing',
provided the English court only decides to strike out a claim (or possibly a defence) after considering possible pertinent differences between factual situations.[87] For convenience, the four essential passages of the judgment in *Z v UK*
(2001) are cited here:[88]

'The [ECtHR] observes, firstly, that the applicants were not prevented in any practical manner from bringing their claims before the domestic courts. Indeed, the case
was litigated with vigour up to the House of Lords ...'[89]

'There is no reason to consider the striking-out procedure which rules on the existence of sustainable causes of action as per se offending the principle of access to a
court. In such a procedure, the plaintiff is generally able to submit to the court the
arguments supporting his or her claims on the law and the court will rule on those issues at the conclusion of an adversarial procedure ...'[90]

'The [ECtHR] considers that its reasoning in *Osman v United Kingdom* (1999) was
based on an understanding of the law of negligence which has to be reviewed in the
light of the clarifications subsequently made by the domestic courts and notably by
the House of Lords ...'[91]

'In [*Z v United Kingdom*] the [ECtHR] is led to the conclusion that the inability of the
applicants to sue the local authority flowed not from an immunity but from the appli-

---

[87] *Z v United Kingdom* – 29392/95 [2001] ECHR 333 (10 May 2001); (2001) 10 BHRC
384, (2002) 34 EHRR 333; [2001] 2 FCR 246, [2001] 2 FLR 612; ECtHR, not following
Osman v UK (1998) BHRC 293; (1999) 29 EHRR 245; for comment Neil Andrews, *English
Civil Procedure* (Oxford UP, 2003) 7–64 ff; ACL Davies (2001) 117 LQR 521 and other literature cited Andrews, op cit, p 167 nn 114 ff.

[88] *Z v United Kingdom*, ibid.

[89] ibid at [95].

[90] ibid at [97].

[91] ibid at [100].

cable principles governing the substantive right of action in domestic law. There was no restriction on access to a court ... .'[92]

(7) Default Judgments[93]

Nature

5.31   Judgment by default is an important means of accelerating the legal process. It involves judgment without trial where a defendant (a) has failed to file an acknowledgment of service; or (b) has failed to raise a defence.[94] A claimant can obtain default judgment if the claim is for: 'a specified amount of money';[95] or 'an amount of money to be decided by the court';[96] or delivery of goods where the claim form gives the defendant the alternative of paying their value.[97] In these situations, the claimant can normally apply for judgment by administrative process without troubling a judge.[98] If the claimant seeks some other remedy, default judgment must be sought by specific application to the court.[99] Certain classes of claim are not amenable to default judgment.[100]

Setting Aside Default Judgments if Substantive Merits Justify

5.32   A judgment by default is regarded as not as strong as a judgment obtained after a full contest between the parties. In the classic statement, Lord Atkin said: 'The principle obviously is that unless and until the court has pronounced a judgment upon the merits or by consent, it is to have the power to revoke the expression of its coercive power where that has been obtained by a failure to follow any of the rules of procedure.'[101] If a default judgment is challenged by the defendant in good time, the court can set aside or vary a regular judgment if 'the defendant has a real prospect of successfully defending the claim' or 'there is some other good reason' why judgment should be set aside or

---

[92] ibid.

[93] Neil Andrews, *English Civil Procedure* (Oxford UP, 2003) ch 19; IS Goldrein (ed), *Commercial Litigation: Pre-emptive Remedies* (International Edition, 2005) ch 5; *Zuckerman on Civil Procedure* (2006) 8–3 ff.

[94] CPR 12.1 and 12.3; see also CPR 10.2 and CPR 15.3.

[95] Formerly known as 'liquidated claims'.

[96] Formerly known as 'unliquidated claims'.

[97] CPR 12.4(1)(a)-(c).

[98] For exceptions, CPR 12.9, 12.10, 12.11.

[99] CPR 12.4(2), 12.10, 12.11.

[100] CPR 12.2; PD (12) 1.2.

[101] *Evans v Bartlam* [1937] AC 473, 480, HL, per Lord Atkin.

varied.[102] The court will consider whether the defence has objective merits and why the defendant failed to acknowledge service or file a defence.[103]

When asked to set aside a default judgment, the court should not dismiss   **5.33** too peremptorily a (newly presented) defence, even it is has been merely sketched by the defendant. The court should not lean too far in its scepticism:[104]

'... the [defendant's suggested] arguable case must carry some degree of conviction but judges should be very wary of trying issues of fact on evidence where the facts are apparently credible and [those facts] are to be set aside against the facts being advanced [by the claimant]. Choosing between them is the function of the trial judge ...'[105]

When the default judgment was obtained on the question of liability, the power to set aside exists whether or not there was a further failure to contest the quantification of liability.[106]

A default judgment which survives a review on the merits, as just explained,   **5.34** in fact becomes a stronger form of judgment: the claimant now holds a judgment on the merits, capable of being reconsidered only on appeal.[107] Finally, the court can impose a condition upon the setting aside of a regular judgment. The condition can either require the defendant to provide security for the claimant's costs,[108] or to make a payment into court.[109]

Setting Aside Procedurally Defective Default Judgments

The court must uphold the defendant's application to set aside a procedurally   **5.35** defective default judgment in any the following situations: (i) because judgment was procedurally premature (it preceded expiry of the time for acknowledging service or filing a defence);[110] or (ii) an application for summary judgment was still pending[111] or (iii) the defendant had fully discharged the claim

---

[102] CPR 13.3.

[103] The leading pre-CPR (but still illuminating) decision is *Alpine Bulk Transport Co Inc v Saudi Eagle Shipping Co Inc (The Saudi Eagle)* [1986] 2 Lloyd's Rep 221, CA; considered in *Allen v Taylor* [1992] 1 Personal Injury and Quantum Reports P 255, CA and *Shocked v Goldschmidt* [1998] 1 All ER 372, 376, CA (the last case in fact concerned with non-appearance at trial).

[104] *Day v RAC Motoring Services Ltd* [1999] 1 WLR 2150, CA.

[105] ibid, 2157.

[106] *Strachan v The Gleaner Co Ltd* [2005] 1 WLR 3204, PC.

[107] *Clapp v Enron* [2005] EWCA Civ 1511 at [36] ff, citing *Odyssey (London) Ltd v OIC Run-off* [2001] Lloyd's Rep (Insurance) 1.

[108] *Burchmore v Hills* (1935) 79 Law Journal Newspaper 30.

[109] *City Construction Contracts (London) Ltd v Adam*, *The Times* 4 January, 1988, CA.

[110] CPR 13.2, 12.3(1), (2).

[111] CPR 13.2, 12.3(3).

(including any costs claim);[112] or (iv) the defendant had admitted liability in full and requested more time to pay.[113]

5.36   If the defendant satisfies the court that he was unaware of the relevant claim form, the court will 'normally' set aside the default judgment 'unless it is pointless to do so.'[114] There is a cognate power to set aside judgment where the relevant party fails to attend trial and his claim or defence is struck out.[115]

---

[112] CPR 13.2(c), 12.3(3)(b).

[113] CPR 13.2, 12.3(3)(c), 14.4, 14.7.

[114] *Godwin v Swindon BC* [2001] 4 All ER 641, CA, at [49], per May LJ, considering CPR 13.3(1)(b); *Akram v Adam* [2004] EWCA Civ 1601; [2005] 1 WLR 2762, at [42] and [43]: service is technically effective under the deemed service regime even if notice was never received; but not where there is no reasonable basis for the proposed defence and the defendant has delayed in applying to have the default judgment set aside, eg, *City & Country Properties Ltd v Kamali* [2006] EWCA Civ 1879; [2007] 1 WLR 1219, at [17], noted J Sorabi (2007) 26 CJQ 279.

[115] CPR 39.3(5); which requires, among other things, proof of a 'good reason' for non-attendance at trial; see *Estate Acquisition and Development Ltd v Wiltshire* [2006] EWCA Civ 533; this topic has led to confusion: eg, *Nelson v Clearsprings (Management) Ltd* [2006] EWCA Civ 1854; [2007] 2 All ER 407; for the general common law principles governing this context, *Gaydamak v UBS Bahamas Ltd & Anor (Bahamas)* [2006] UKPC 8; [2006] 1 WLR 1097; cf **8.03** n 16 for the situation where the court proceeds with a trial of the merits despite the defendant's non-appearance.

Chapter 6

Disclosure and Privileges

Contents

(1) Introduction

This chapter concerns two inter-related topics: first, the system of documentary disclosure, especially between parties after English civil proceedings have commenced (on this, the main context, see **6.21** ff)[1]; secondly, the main 'privileged' exceptions to the party's obligation to disclose relevant documents, namely legal advice and litigation privileges (**6.28** and **6.36**).[2]   **6.01**

We can begin by considering why the common law system has permitted, indeed long since required, scrupulous disclosure by each party to the other of relevant documentation.[3] Such 'disclosure' (formerly known as 'discovery') between adversaries (prospective or present parties) serves four main functions   **6.02**

---

[1] Neil Andrews, *English Civil Procedure* (Oxford UP, 2003) ch 26; P Matthews and H Malek, *Disclosure* (3rd edn, 2007); C Hollander, *Documentary Evidence* (9th edn, 2006) chs 7 to 10; *Zuckerman on Civil Procedure* (2nd edn, 2006) ch 14.

[2] These and other heads of privilege are examined in Neil Andrews, *English Civil Procedure* (Oxford UP, 2003) chs 25, 27 to 30; other sources are *Cross and Tapper on Evidence* (11th edn, 2007) chs IX and X; C Hollander, *Documentary Evidence* (9th edn, 2006) chs 11 to 20; *Phipson on Evidence* (16th edn, 2005) chs 23 to 26; C Passmore, *Privilege* (2nd edn, 2006); B Thanki (ed), *The Law of Privilege* (Oxford UP, 2006); *Zuckerman on Civil Procedure* (2nd edn, 2006) chs 15–18; see also, J Auburn, *Legal Professional Privilege: Law and Theory* (Hart, Oxford, 2000).

[3] For succinct remarks on the discovery system's historical roots in the practice of the

(and a similar list of benefits was compiled before the CPR)[4]: it can achieve equality of access to information; secondly, it can facilitate settlement of disputes; thirdly, it avoids so-called 'trial by ambush', that is, the situation when a party is unable to respond properly to a surprise revelation at the final hearing; and, finally, it assists the court in reaching accurate determinations of fact when entering judgment on the merits.[5]

6.03   As we shall see (**6.22**), the changes introduced in Part 31 of the CPR, when compare with the pre-CPR aarrangements, involve a more restrictive approach to the exchange of documents between the parties in preparation for trial.[6] Before the CPR, the so-called '*Peruvian Guano*' (1882) test of relevant documents was much too broad.[7] It included peripheral documents. The idea was that if an opponent were permitted to inspect these 'outer' documents, this might enable him, by a side-ways investigation (a 'train of inquiry'), to uncover centrally important matters. In the 1880s this broad test did little harm. There was little commercial printing. This was the era of the 'quill-pen', laborious clerking, and 'copper-plate' handwriting (still visible on conveyancing documents preserved from that era). But in the last part of the twentieth century, the legal process was battered by the documentary tidal-waves of photo-copying and word-processing. During the dicovery process, it would be necessary for lawyers to sift through two masses of papers, those held by their clients and those released by opponents for inspection in accordance with the disclosure obligation. In determining which documents should be released for the opponent to inspect, each side had to apply the broad *Peruvian Guano* case's test to identify 'relevant' documents. The recipient party then had to absorb the material disclosed according to that broad test. This process of release and inspection could result in large legal fees. The discovery process also caused delay. Finally, the same process could be used to intimidate, because one side could

---

Court of Chancery, abolished as a separate court in the Judicature Act reforms during the 1870s, Sir Jack Jacob, *The Fabric of English Civil Justice* (1987) 93.

    [4] Jacob, ibid, (1987) 94: 'The process of discovery operates as a powerful procural instrument to produce fairness, openness and equality in the machinery of English civil justice. It enables each party to be informed or to be capable of being informed of all the relevant material evidence, whether in the possession of the opposite party or not; it ensures that as far as possible there should be no surprises before or at the trial; it reveals to the parties the strengths and weakness of their respective cases, and so produces procedural euqlaity between them; and it encourages fair and favourable settlements, shortens the lengths of trials and saves costs.'

    [5] *Tweed v Parades Commission for Northern Ireland* [2006] UKHL 53; [2007] 2 All ER 273 at [2], per Lord Bingham.

    [6] For the inspiration, Lord Woolf, *Access to Justice: Interim Report* (1995) ch 21, paras 1–9.

    [7] The '*Peruvian Guano*' test: *Compagnie Financière v Peruvian Guano Co* (1882) 11 QBD 55, 63, CA.

cynically bury the other in an avalanche of paper.[8] Lord Woolf's new 'standard disclosure' test (effective since 1999) is an attempt to avoid these hazards and to render the process proportionate to the nature of the claim.[9] Each party must now disclose and allow inspection of:[10] documents on which he wishes to rely; or which adversely affect his case or his opponent's case, or which support the latter's case.[11] An order for 'standard disclosure' is the usual provision, except for 'small claims' litigation.[12]

However, technological change continues to challenge the discovery system. **6.04** Under the CPR, the word 'document' refers to 'anything in which information of any description is recorded':[13] whether paper or electronic; literary, pictorial, visual or 'audio'. It thus encompasses 'e-mail', 'e-commerce', information held on answer-phones, and details recorded in mobile phones. Most people's trails of 'e-foot-prints' are now extensive. These burgeoning sources of private and commercial information have intensified the need for a focused and disciplined approach to disclosure. Since 1998 the rules have been amended to deal with the question of disclosure of electronic data.[14]

In October 2006, a symposium was held to examine aspects of litigation **6.05** within the Commercial Court.[15] It is clear that this was a response to the problems encountered in two recent 'super' or 'monster' cases which proceeded to trial that court (see also **3.19**).[16] Sir Anthony Clarke, the Master of the Rolls, addressed those problems in his 2007 'KPMG' lecture.[17] For present purposes, two topics examined at the symposium stand out: possibly greater use, where appropriate, of electronic assistance, especially with regard to exchange of documents during disclosure; and the question whether mediation might be

---

[8] Sir Johan Steyn (later Lord Steyn), preface to Hodge and Malek, *Discovery* (1992); R Cranston, 'Complex Litigation: the Commercial Court' (2007) 26 CJQ 190, 203.

[9] Especially, CPR 31.3(2), 31.7(2), 31.9(1).

[10] CPR 31.6.

[11] The court can vary the width of disclosure in special situations: CPR 31.5(1)(2).

[12] CPR 31.5; CPR 28.3; PD (28) 3.9; PD (29) 4.10(2).

[13] CPR 31.4.

[14] See PD (31) at (new) paragraph 2A on the duty to disclose electronic data, including ostensibly 'deleted' documents: see the Appendix to this chapter at **6.41**.

[15] R Cranston, 'Complex Litigation: The Commercial Court' (2007) 26 CJQ 190, 204–5.

[16] *Equitable Life Assurance v Ernst & Young*, trial began in April 2005 and was settled in November 2005 (the whole litigation took four years); trial in the second Commercial Court case, *Three Rivers District Council and others v Governor of the Bank of England*, lasted almost two years (the litigation as a whole twelve years); on the latter case, Neil Andrews, *English Civil Procedure* (Oxford UP, 2003) 20.15 to 20.19, and A Zuckerman, 'A Colossal Wreck – the BCCI/Three Rivers Litigation' (2006) CJQ 287; see also the next note.

[17] Sir Anthony Clarke MR, 'The Supercase-Problems and Solutions', 2007 Annual KPMG Forensic Lecture: available at http://www.judiciary.gov.uk/docs/speeches/kpmg_speech.pdf

employed more imaginatively and perhaps earlier; for example, to resolve procedural issues, such as the scope of disclosure (generally on mediation see chapter 11 of this book).[18] Certainly the 'Report of the Commercial Court and the Admiralty Courts' (2005–6) states that the symposium recognised 'the need for restrictions on expensive disclosure of electronic material'.[19]

6.06   Apart from the CPR's redefinition of 'relevance' (see **6.03** above and **6.22** below), and the challenge presented by burgeoning electronic documentation (see **6.04** and **6.05**), the main issues in this field are, first, fixing the legitimate scope of obligations to disclose information *before commencement of proceedings* (normally associated with the so-called 'no fishing rule'); the second issue (overlapping with the question of pre-action disclosure) is the appropriate extent of the jurisdiction to *require non-parties, in anticipation of trial, to provide information* for use in pending or contemplated litigation, a topic normally referred to as 'exceptions to the "mere witness rule"' (for general discussion of the law's development in these two contexts, see **6.19** and **6.20**). We turn immediately to the pre-action context, beginning with the English 'pre-action protocol' system.

(2) Pre-Action 'Protocols'

6.07   Following Lord Woolf's reports (1995–6) on the reform of English civil justice,[20] the CPR (1998) system introduced a set of 'pre-action protocols'.[21] Such protocols prescribe 'obligations' which the prospective parties and their legal representatives must satisfy before commencing formal proceedings. Andrews commented in 2003: 'English law is right to have made this bold entrance into a zone which, traditionally, has been largely left to private negotiation or adversarial posturing.'[22] And Brooke LJ, a leading authority on the CPR system, praised Lord Woolf for this imaginative innovation:[23]

'... [the] introduction of pre-action protocols ... represents a major step forward in the administration of justice ... Under the [pre-CPR system], in many disputed cases of any substance nothing very effective seemed to happen until a [case began] ... [These protocols] are guides to good litigation and pre-litigation practice, drafted and agreed by those who know all about the difference between good and bad practice.'

---

[18] Neil Andrews, *English Civil Procedure* (Oxford UP, 2003) 20–15 to 20–19; see also A Zuckerman, 'A Colossal Wreck – the BCCI/Three Rivers Litigation' (2006) CJQ 287.

[19] For the year ending July 2006: www.judiciary.gov.uk/docs/annual_report_comm_admiralty_ct_0506.pdf

[20] *Access to Justice* (interim report, 1995, final report, 1996); both reports are available on line: *http://www.dca.gov.uk/civil/reportfr.htm*

[21] http://www.justice.gov.uk/civil/procrules_fin/menus/protocol.htm

[22] Neil Andrews, *English Civil Procedure* (Oxford UP, 2003) 7–8.

[23] *Carlson v Townsend* [2001] 3 All ER 663, CA, at [24], [28], [31], per Brooke LJ.

Pre-action protocols are intended to promote efficient exchange of informa-   **6.08**
tion between the parties. For example, a person who alleges that he was the
victim of medical negligence, without the expenses or dealy of seeking a court
order, can gain access to hospital or medical records under this system of pre-
action protocols. That is why protocols receive emphasis here in a chapter concerned with 'disclosure'. In the context of the pre-action exchange of information, their obvious aim is to promote and enhance settlement, thus avoiding
formal proceedings, or at least to prepare the way for better focused and more
efficient litigation, if it cannot be avoided. As Lord Woolf had explained:[24]

'What is needed is a system which enables the parties to a dispute to embark on mean-
ingful negotiation as soon as the possibility of litigation is identified, and ensures that
as early as possible they have the relevant information to define their claims and make
realistic offers to settle.'

Judge LJ said in *Ford v GKR Construction Ltd* (2000):[25]

'Civil litigation is now developing a system designed to enable the parties involved to
know where they stand in reality at the earliest possible stage, and at the lowest practicable cost, so that they may make informed decisions about their prospects and the
sensible conduct of their cases.'

In (the first half of) 2007 English protocols applied to nine subject areas.[26]   **6.09**
This topic-by-topic approach has the advantage that the protocol is tailored to
suit the particular features of each type of dispute. But it has the demerit of being somewhat fragmented and producing an overall appearance of complexity.
The (English) Civil Justice Council is considering whether a consolidated pre-
action protocol might be attractive (consultation on this question ended in
April 2007). Even without a general pre-action protocol, the current rules have
some general application. Both prospective claimants[27] and defendants[28] must
comply with their obligations to reveal information specified in each particular protocol.[29] Thus the 'Practice Direction on Protocols' states:[30]

---

[24] *Access to Justice: Final Report* (1996), ch 10.
[25] [2000] 1 WLR 802, 807, CA.
[26] (1) 'Construction and Engineering Disputes'; (2) 'Defamation'; (3) 'Personal Injury
Claims'; (4) 'Clinical Disputes'; (5) 'Professional Negligence'; (6) 'Judicial Review'; (7)
'Disease and Illness Claims'; (8) 'Housing Disrepair Cases'; and (9) 'Possession Claims based
on Rent Arrears'; a new version of the 'Construction and Building Disputes' protocol was
issued in April 2007: see http://www.justice.gov.uk/civil/procrules_fin/contents/protocols/
prot_ced.htm
[27] 'Practice Direction-Protocols', at 2.1.
[28] ibid at 3.2.
[29] On the question whether there are restrains on the manner in which such information
might be used by the recipient, S Gibbons, 'Protecting Documents Disclosed under Pre-Action Protocols against Subsequent Use' (2002) CJQ 254.
[30] 'Practice Direction-Protocols', at 4.1.

'In all cases not covered by any approved protocol, the court will expect the parties ... to act reasonably in exchanging information and documents relevant to the claim and generally in trying to avoid the necessity for the start of proceedings.'

6.10 If the dispute does proceed to a formal action, the court has power to sanction a person's failure to comply with a protocol. The sanction is the making of an adverse costs order.[31] The high cost of litigation in England ensures that this is a most potent threat and, accordingly, that compliance with protocols remains high.

6.11 An early study of the protocol system suggested that there has been some improvement in the quality of pre-action communication between opponents' lawyers.[32] But this report discovered that protocols had not speeded up the disposal of medium-sized personal injury disputes. It also revealed that 'front-loading' of procedure has increased overall litigation costs above the rate of general economic inflation (see also **6.19** below). The German experience concerning pre-action ADR appears also to endorse the anxiety that elaborate pre-action mechanisms might engender unacceptable expense.[33]

(3) Pre-Action Judicial Orders for Disclosure

6.12 The previous section concerned the self-executing obligations to make pre-action disclosure in accordance with protocols. In this section we are concerned with judicial civil orders or criminal sanctions concerning preservation, inspection or disclosure of evidence or information. Four regimes deserve mention. First, specific judicial orders can be made to preserve property, for example, factory equipment awaiting inspection.[34] Secondly, a judicial 'civil search order'[35] can be made to prevent a prospective defendant from destroy-

---

[31] ibid, at 2.3; eg, *Straker v Tudor Rose (A Firm)* [2007] EWCA Civ 368 (where the court held that the first instance judge had over-reacted and made too severe a costs reduction).

[32] T Goriely, R Moorhead, P Abrams, *More Civil Justice? The Impact of the Woolf Reforms on Pre-Action Behaviour* (Law Society and Civil Justice Council, London, 2001) (based on 54 interviews with lawyers and insurers and a study of 300 case files).

[33] Michael Breyer, Düsseldorf, German National Report for the World Congress 2007, Bahia, Brazil: 'New Trends in Pre-Action', in P Gilles and T Pfeiffer (eds), *Neue Trends im Prozessrecht – Deutsche Landesberichte zum 13. Weltkongress für Prozessrecht 2007* (Nomos-Verlag, forthcoming 2007): 'For the pre-action phase, legislative efforts have been aimed at directly prescribing mediation and settlement: § 15a EGZPO of 1999 and § 278(2) ZPO of 2001.' But 'experience has already showed, these means have not improved proceedings but have rather caused more cost and delay'.

[34] Supreme Court Act 1981, s 33, providing for a court order regarding 'the inspection, photographing, preservation, custody and detention of property which appears to the court to be property which may become the subject-matter of subsequent proceedings ... or as to which any question may arise in such proceedings.'

[35] Re-named as such, CPR 25.1(1)(h); the standard order is prescribed by PD (25); the lead-

ing vital evidence (formerly known as '*Anton Piller*' orders)[36] (see **4.26** for discussion of such orders). Thirdly, it is an offence for a prospective defendant to destroy documents, or other potential evidence, in order to spoil his opponent's chances of winning the relevant case.[37] Fourthly, and most importantly, there is a general rule empowering the court to make a pre-action *documentary* disclosure order against any type of prospective defendant.[38] When first introduced in 1999, it seemed that the pre-action disclosure system might expand very significantly. However, in *Black v Sumitomo Corporation* (2002) the Court of Appeal refused to countenance 'deep-sea fishing' expeditions, at least in commercial contexts,[39] that is, speculative applications when the applicant has no hard evidence at all to support his allegations of civil wrongdoing (for further comment on this, see **6.19** below).

In preparation for the 2007 World Congress in Brazil the author was fortunate to receive comparative materials and remarks from many national reporters concerning pre-action disclosure conducted under court order in their various systems. The following two paragraphs are derived from his General Report (see **2.26** at n 73). Development of English judicial pre-action disclosure orders is considered above at **6.12**.   **6.13**

There is a link between access to information and access to justice (or access to court, as it is known in European human rights law; on this connection, see   **6.14**

---

ing discussion is S Gee, *Commercial Injunctions* (2004); see also Neil Andrews, *English Civil Procedure* (Oxford UP, 2003), ch 17; *Zuckerman on Civil Procedure* (2006) 14.175 ff; IS Goldrein (ed), *Commercial Litigation: Pre-emptive Remedies* (International Edition, 2005) ch 3; the CPR, their accompanying PD's, and various 'Guides' to parts of the High Court's practice, are accessible at http://www.justice.gov.uk/civil/procrules_fin/menus/court_guid es.htm

[36] [1976] Ch 55, CA; now endorsed by legislation: s 7, Civil Procedure Act 1997, following recommendation of a Committee of Judges appointed by the Judges' Council, 'Anton Piller Orders: A Consultation Paper' ('the Staughton Committee'), Lord Chancellor's Department, November 1992; for comment, M Dockray and K Reece Thomas, (1998) 17 CJQ 272.

[37] *Douglas v Hello! Ltd* [2003] EWHC 55 (Ch); [2003] 1 All ER 1087 (brief note), Morritt V-C.

[38] CPR 31.16 (3) states: 'The court may make an order under this rule only where –
(a) the respondent is likely to be a party to subsequent proceedings;
(b) the applicant is also likely to be a party to those proceedings;
(c) if proceedings had started, the respondent's duty by way of standard disclosure, set out in rule 31.6, would extend to the documents or classes of documents of which the applicant seeks disclosure; and
(d) disclosure before proceedings have started is desirable in order to –
   (i) dispose fairly of the anticipated proceedings;
   (ii) assist the dispute to be resolved without proceedings; or
   (iii) save costs.

[39] [2002] 1 WLR 1562, CA; Neil Andrews, *English Civil Procedure* (Oxford UP, 2003) 26.70; for a successful application in a commercial context, *Landis and Gyr Ltd v Scaleo Chip ET* [2007] EWHC B3 (QB).

further **6.19**).[40] This link received special comment in the USA report for the Brazil meeting.[41] Often a complainant knows less about the alleged wrong than the respondent. Even the most relaxed requirements of pleading presuppose that the plaintiff can delineate in bare outline the gist of his complaint. The German report explained that where pleading rules require a higher threshold of detail than modern common law pleading, pre-action access to information becomes especially crucial.[42] In Israel the problem has been 're-solved' by tolerating a 'scatter-gun' style of unverified pleading by plaintiffs.[43] Sometimes the complainant might not even know the other's identity.[44] It can

---

[40] This is an implied right within, or an offshoot from, Article 6(1) of the European Convention on Human Rights (1950), as developed by the European Court of Human Rights at Strasbourg in a long line of cases: eg *Golder v UK* (1975) 1 EHRR 524, ECHR; *Airey v Ireland* (1979) Series A, No 32; 2 EHRR 305, at [24], ECHR; *Ashingdane v UK* (1985) 7 EHRR 528, ECHR; for discussion, A Le Sueur, 'Access to Justice in the United Kingdom' [2000] EHRLRev 457, 461 ff; Neil Andrews, *English Civil Procedure* (Oxford UP, 2003) ch 7.

[41] Richard Marcus, Hastings College of the Law, San Francisco, USA National Report for the World Congress 2007, Bahia, Brazil: 'The American reality for many plaintiffs (and defendants) is that formal discovery is an essential source of information regarding matters in litigation. If not unique, American litigation is almost unique in its reliance on broad discovery. Without discovery, many American litigants might be reluctant to address settlement seriously'.

[42] Michael Breyer, Düsseldorf, German National Report for the World Congress 2007, Bahia, Brazil: 'New Trends in Pre-Action', in P Gilles and T Pfeiffer (eds), *Neue Trends im Prozessrecht – Deutsche Landesberichte zum 13. Weltkongress für Prozessrecht 2007* (Nomos-Verlag, 2007): 'A system like the German one, which knows fact pleading and a loser-pays rule, creates a special interest in pre-action access to information as distinct from the interest in having access after formal commencement of proceedings. Under German pleading rules, parties have to furnish the detailed factual basis of the legal contentions which justify their claims or affirmative defenses. In addition, parties must identify specific means of proof supporting their specific factual allegations to the extent not admitted by the other party. The plaintiff further has to specify the remedy sought. For money claims this means as a general principle that the amount sought has to be specified. The courts, however, accept that money claims need not be specified in cases in which the amount due may only be determined by judicial estimation. Typically, this is the case for damages for pain and suffering. If the burden of allegation (Darlegungslast) or the burden of seeking a specific remedy is not met, the claim or defense is dismissed without the taking of any evidence.'

[43] Stephen Goldstein, Hebrew University, Jerusalem, Israeli National Report for the World Congress 2007, Bahia, Brazil: 'Israel requires detailed fact pleadings but does not provide for pre-action access to information. The problem has been "solved" traditionally by a plaintiff who does not know the facts pleading every possible fact situation. This could be done since there was no [general] obligation to verify the facts by affidavit and no penalty for pleading unnecessary facts ... If affidavits were to be generally required in Israeli proceedings, we would have to adopt some form of pre-action disclosure.'

[44] In England (see further **6.17** below) there is a general equitable power to order pre-action disclosure, in respect of information or documents, and against non-parties, see Neil Andrews, *English Civil Procedure* (Oxford UP, 2003) 26–102 ff on these various categories; leading decisions are *Norwich Pharmacal Co v Customs & Excise* [1974] AC 133, HL and *Ashworth Hospital Authority v MGN Ltd* [2002] 1 WLR 2033, HL.

even happen that a pre-action demand for information is necessary to discover whether a wrong has been suffered behind a person's back. This is exemplified by an English case, where a person suspected that the reason he had been dismissed from employment was that someone had made untrue and defamatory comments about him to his employer.[45]

Krans has noted the generous system of 'provisional examination' of witnesses available under Dutch civil procedure[46] and pre-action mechanisms to elicit or preserve information.[47] The Dutch 'provisional examination' system provides pre-action mechanisms for the production of 'evidence'[48] (as distinct from merely unattested 'information' and as distinct from a system of pre-action discovery of documents).[49] Dutch law also provides pre-action expert investigations[50] (pre-action reference to expert opinion is also a feature of Eng-   **6.15**

---

[45] *P v T Ltd* [1997] 1 WLR 1309, Scott V-C: see further **6.17** below.

[46] Bart Krans, University of Groningen, Dutch National Report for the World Congress 2007, Bahia, Brazil: '… In some cases the parties use the provisional examination of witnesses as a fishing expedition … [Quite often] parties call up large numbers of witnesses … The Council for the Judiciary has suggested three ways of restricting the provisional examination of witnesses: limitation of the provisional examination of witnesses to emergency cases, limitation of the provisional examination of witnesses to cases with a prominent financial interest, and raising the court registry fee for petitions for the provisional examination of witnesses. The Council also suggests that the courts should be given more authority to deny calling up some witnesses. Parties could be obliged to motivate their choice for the witnesses they want to hear.'

[47] Bart Krans, ibid, commenting: 'Provisional production of evidence … Prior to the formal commencement of a claim, the court, in response to the petition of a party, can appoint a provisional examination of witnesses by a judge (voorlopig getuigenverhoor). The court can also order a provisional expert's report (voorlopig deskundigenbericht) or a provisional court inspection of the premises (plaatsopneming en bezichtiging). These three forms of provisional production of evidence are based on the Dutch CCP: Art 186–193 CCP (voorlopig getuigenverhoor) and Art 202–207 CCP (voorlopig deskundigenbericht and voorlopige plaatsopneming and bezichtiging).'

[48] Bart Krans, ibid, commenting: 'The word 'provisional' might, in this context, be misleading. When witnesses are examined by a judge in a provisional hearing, … their testimonies have the same evidential value as testimonies made during formal proceedings.'

[49] Bart Krans, ibid, commenting: 'It is argued that in Dutch law an enforceable pre-trial disclosure of documents should be introduced, supervised by the court. The authors of the fundamental review prefer the suggestions of the working group chaired by Professor Storme in 1994. That working group proposed as substantial a disclosure or communication of documents as reasonably possible: Marcel Storme (ed), *Rapprochement du Droit Judiciaire de l'Union européenne/Approximation of Judiciary Law in the European Union*, (Dordrecht: Martinus Nijhoff, 1994) 97; cf their proposal for a European Directive on discovery, (Art 4.1.1. and Art 4.1.2. – 4.5.2).'

[50] Bart Krans, ibid, commenting: 'Provisional expert examination (voorlopig deskundigenonderzoek) and provisional court inspection of a site (voorlopige descente) … In the pre-action phase, evidence can also be produced by a provisional expert examination (voorlopig deskundigenonderzoek) or a provisional court inspection of a site (voorlopige descente) … The decisions of the courts on this issue do not set high standards for these petitions …'

lish pre-action protocols, and of the Japanese system[51]). Settlement can be
stimulated and indeed enhanced by such judicially controlled pre-action 'evidence'-gathering,[52] including pre-action conferences with Dutch judges regarding such 'evidence',[53] and by provisional decisions on the substance of the
case.[54]

(4) Disclosure Against Non-Parties
(Pre- and Post-Commencement)

6.16 Traditionally, the starting point under English Law[55] has been that non-parties are compellable to supply evidence only as 'witnesses', that is, by court order in connection with trial. Thus the 'good citizen' principle that non-parties
should assist in providing documents or information relevant to others' litigation has been confined, in general, to evidence at trial and not earlier. This restriction on litigants' (and prospective litigants') access to information held by
non-parties is known as the 'mere witness rule'. This rule is old, but was re-
stated by the House of Lords in 1974 as follows: 'It is settled, rightly or wrongly,
that you cannot get discovery against someone who has no connection with
the litigious matter other than that he might be called as a witness either to
testify or to produce documents at trial.'[56] More recently, Lord Woolf CJ said
in *Ashworth Hospital Authority v MGN Ltd* (2002) that the 'mere witness'
rule remains the starting point when considering the position of non-parties

---

[51] Masanori Kawano, Nagoya University, Japanese National Report for the World Congress 2007, Bahia, Brazil.

[52] Bart Krans, University of Groningen, Dutch National Report for the World Congress
2007, Bahia, Brazil: 'Many formal proceedings have probably been prevented because a pre-
action settlement could be reached based on the outcomes of provisional evidence.'

[53] Bart Krans, ibid, commenting: 'Pre-action conference (preprocessuele comparitie) ...
a pre-action hearing is possible in connection with a provisional examination of witnesses.
By virtue of art 191 CCP, at the request of the parties or ex officio the judge may order the
parties to appear at a court hearing after a provisional examination of witnesses. This hearing may serve to attempt to reach a settlement, to provide information or to make procedural arrangements ... However, it has been observed in various quarters that at this point
the court would have insufficient information to be of service to the parties.'

[54] Bart Krans, ibid, commenting: 'Provisional relief proceedings (kort geding) ... provisional relief proceedings make it possible to provide temporary relief in the short term in
urgent cases ... After the claimant's summons a hearing takes place in which claimant and
defendant put forward their positions orally ... The legal rules of evidence do not apply ... In
a large number of cases eventually no full-length proceedings are initiated.'

[55] More precisely, under the procedure administered by the Common Law courts, as distinct from the pre-1875 Court of Chancery, which provided a parallel but distinct system of
procedure: see the 'historical note' at the end of this paragraph.

[56] *Norwich Pharmacal Co v Commissioners for Customs and Excise* [1974] AC 133, 203,
HL, per Lord Kilbrandon.

within the system of pre-trial disclosure.[57] (Historical note: By 1875 the Supreme Court of Judicature Acts had abolished the old court system and the jurisdictional distinction between the Common Law and Chancery courts. Henceforth the High Court and the county courts could administer both Common Law and Equity in the same case. But in modern law the interaction of 'common law' and 'equitable' doctrines[58] and remedies[59] persists: indeed the distinction remains fundamental.)

However, in the nineteenth century Equity had recognised an exception to **6.17** the 'mere witness' rule. That exception is now known as a '*Norwich Pharmacal order*'. This is a *non-statutory* jurisdiction to compel a person (not necessarily a prospective defendant) to disclose documents or non-documentary information if that person was 'involved', whether culpably or innocently, in an alleged civil wrong.[60] This judge-made jurisdiction can be exercised, therefore, against non-parties (for a related, but more narrow, statutory power, see the next paragraph). A *Norwich Pharmacal* order is normally made before the main proceedings have begun. The order can be used to provide information concerning any of the following matters:[61] the main wrongdoer's identity;[62] or, secondly, the location,

---

[57] [2002] 1 WLR 2033, HL.

[58] eg, the equitable doctrines of undue influence, unconscionability, and relief against forfeiture of possessory or proprietary interests, equitable bars upon rescission; the common law doctrines of 'mistake' or duress; some recent decisions have tended to diminish the common law/equitable distinction; see, for denial of a separate doctrine of shared 'equitable' mistake, '*The Great Peace*' [2003] QB 679, CA; and for absence of separate equitable principles of construction of contracts, *BCCI v Ali* [2001] UKHL 8; [2002] 1 AC 251, HL, at [17] per Lord Bingham; and the discussion of rescission in *Halpern v Halpern (No 2)* [2007] EWCA Civ 291; [2007] 3 All ER 478 at [54] to [76]; although this is not a consistent policy; for discussion of the continuing distinction between common law and equitable analysis, A Burrows, 'We do this at Common Law but that in Equity' (2002) 22 Ox JLS 1).

[59] Claims for payment of debt, or for damages, are common law remedies (unless damages are awarded under a stuatory power as a substitute for an injunction or specific performance); claims for injunction, specific performance, or and an account of profits, at 11–33, are equitable remedies: for details, see Neil Andrews, *English Civil Justice and Remedies: Progress and Challenges: Nagoya Lectures* (Shinzan Sha Publishers, Tokyo, 2007) ch 11.

[60] In *Ashworth Hospital Authority v MGN Ltd* [2002] UKHL 29; [2002] 1 WLR 2033, HL, Lord Woolf CJ re-stated the principles governing this jurisdiction, which was resuscitated in *Norwich Pharmacal v Customs & Excise Commrs* [1974] AC 133, HL; and see next note; the power is exercisable in support of foreign proceedings, *Equatorial Guinea v Bank of Scotland International (Guernsey)* [2006] UKPC 7 at [5]; but the jurisdiction is one of last resort, *Mitsui & Co Ltd v Nexen Petroleum UK Ltd* [2005] EWHC 625 (Ch); [2005] 3 All ER 511, [18] ff, esp [24], [28], [37], [39]; for the sequel to the *Ashworth* case, *Mersey Care NHS Trust v Ackroyd* [2006] EWHC 107 (QB); *The Times* 9 February, 2006.

[61] Neil Andrews, *English Civil Procedure* (Oxford UP, 2003) 26.102 ff on these various categories; note also *Carlton Film Distributors Ltd v VCI plc* [2003] EWHC 616; [2003] FSR 47, Jacob J (non-party holding records of amount of film copies made in suspected violation of prospective defendant's contract with applicant; information necessary to enable applicant to plead breach of contract and sign a statement of truth).

[62] *Norwich Pharmacal Co v Commissioners for Customs and Excise* [1974] AC 133, HL

nature and value of the prospective defendant's assets;[63] or, thirdly, whether the applicant has fallen victim of a civil wrong, such as defamation, committed behind his back;[64] or, finally, to identify and discipline a dishonest or defaulting employee within the applicant's organisation.[65]

6.18   Furthermore, *after commencement* of proceedings, the court has a *statutory* power to order disclosure of *documents* against a non-party in any type of case (the words underlined bring out the points of contrast between this and the broader judge-made jurisdiction, 'Norwich Pharmacal orders', discussed in the preceding paragraph).[66] This statutory power, in rule CPR 31.17, requires the applicant to satisfy the court that the required document (or class of documents) is 'likely' to be supportive in those proceedings. The word 'likely' has been held to require only something weightier than a mere 'fanciful chance' that the document might assist the applicant.[67] The future development of non-party disclosure orders is considered below (see **6.20**).

(5) Assessment of Pre-Action and Non-Party Disclosure

6.19   Pre-action disclosure can be effective in two main ways: it can encourage and enhance settlement by assisting disputants to make a more solid assessment of the dispute's merits; secondly, it can reduce litigation expenses; this is achieved by advancing the stage at which disputants focus upon the essential matters in dispute; in short, pre-action disclosure can reduce the need for post-action orders for disclosure. Perhaps with these potential benefits in mind, as well as the question of promoting 'access to justice' (for this connection, see **6.14**), the American Law Institute's/UNIDROIT's 'Principles of Transnational Civil Procedure'[68] state that potential parties, litigants, and the court should each enjoy

---

(government department having details of imports of pharmaceutical drugs into the UK; suppliers' names and addresses needed by applicant to ascertain identity of alleged infringer of applicant's patent rights).

[63] *Mercantile Group (Europe) AG v Aiyele* [1994] QB 366, CA (if the information is sought to assist enforcement after judgment, Hoffmann LJ observed that the 'mere witness' rule is in any case inapplicable).

[64] *P v T Ltd* [1997] 1 WLR 1309, Scott V-C.

[65] *Ashworth Hospital Authority v MGN Ltd* [2002] UKHL 29; [2002] 1 WLR 2033, HL.

[66] CPR 31.17; this rule concerns only documents: see CPR 31.17(3)(4); cf CPR 18.1 ('further information'): this rule has been held to require a defendant to disclose details of its liability insurance, *Harcourt v Fef Griffin (Representative of Pegasus Gymnastics Club) [2007] EWHC 1500 (QB), Irwin J.*

[67] *Three Rivers DC v Bank of England (No 4)* [2002] EWCA Civ 1182; [2003] 1 WLR 210 CA at [32], [33].

[68] *American Law Institute/UNIDROIT Principles of Transnational Civil Procedure* (Cambridge UP, 2006), Principle 16.1

appropriate 'access to information'.[69] However, there are three counter-constraints: the problem of 'fishing', that is, an applicant's 'roving' request for evidence to make out a contemplated claim which is wholly speculative; secondly, the question of non-parties' reasonable expectations in maintaining confidentiality and privacy (whether in respect of their own private information, or to satisfy duties of confidentiality owed to fourth parties); and, thirdly, the danger that judicially adminsitered orders for pre-action disclosure can increase the expense of resolving disputes. These three constraints will now be explained further.

'Fishing': First, the traditional principle in England has been that a prospective claimant cannot 'fish' for information. The Court of Appeal in *Black v Sumitomo* (2002) re-affirmed this in the context of 'commercial wrongs'.[70] That context should be contrasted with the liberal approach displayed towards applications for pre-action disclosure by persons claiming to have been the victims of personal injury wrongfully inflicted, or alleging wrongful damage to their employment prospects.[71] This willingness to assist such prospective claimants involves a judicial value-judgement (consistent with the legislative history of this disclosure jurisdiction, which first allowed pre-action disclosure in the context of personal injury or fatal accident claims, but later broadened the power). In short, English pre-action disclosure rules give priority to claims concerning bodily or personal harm rather than commercial or corporate loss. It is submitted that the Court of Appeal in the *Sumitomo* case was right to resist a wholesale relaxation of the 'no fishing' principle. It is one thing to have the power to issue 'fishing permits', but another matter to decide who should receive them. It is clear that prospective claimants for personal injury damages will continue to be given priority. The *Sumitomo* decision shows that, outside that favoured context, the courts will continue to adopt a cautious approach, mindful of the danger of encouraging 'fishing expeditions' to support truly speculative claims.

Confidentiality and Non-Parties: The second constraint upon pre-action disclosure concerns protection of non-parties' confidentiality and privacy. An applicant must provide a strong reason in support of a pre-action disclosure order to elicit confidential information from banks, doctors, government departments, and other 'non-parties'. In England non-parties cannot be ordered to supply such information unless the court is convinced that the demand is

---

[69] Hence the title to Part VII ('Access to Information: Disclosure and Evidence') of Neil Andrews, *English Civil Procedure* (Oxford UP, 2003).

[70] *Black v Sumitomo Corporation* [2002] 1 WLR 1562, CA; considering CPR 31.16 (3); for comment, Neil Andrews, *English Civil Procedure* (Oxford, UP, 2003) 26.70; for rjection of a 'fishing' objection to an application for a 'letter of request' for evidence from a foreign jurisdiction, *Honda Giken Kogyou Kabushiki Kaisha v KJM Superbikes* [2007] EWCA Civ 313; on that context see Andrews (2003) ch 33.

[71] As indicated in the *Black* case, ibid.

justified in the interests of justice and that no other source of information exists (see also **6.20** below).[72]

Expensive Court-Based Disclosure: The third constraint concerns expense and efficiency. Expansion of pre-action duties to disclose information will increase the expense of complying with 'the pre-action phase'. This is an example of 'front-loading' (see also **6.11** above). The advantage of pre-action protocols is that they render the process of disclosure largely automatic and so dispense with the need for expensive and time-consuming applications to the court for disclosure orders.

6.20   What of disclosure orders against non-parties? The tendency of both the CPR (see **6.18** above) and the *Norwich Pharmacal* jurisdiction (see **6.17** above) is towards greater use of disclosure orders against non-parties prior to trial. Indeed it might be suggested that the distinction between 'disclosure' and 'evidence' will lose its historical significance within the Common Law systems once it is acknowledged that both are instruments whose common purpose is to provide potential parties, litigants and the court with 'access to information.'[73] Already the 'mere witness' rule (see **6.17**) has been eroded. What of the future? It is submitted that the courts, whether deciding to order disclosure by non-parties prior to trial, or even before commencement of formal proceedings, should balance the importance of the material sought and the strength of the applicant's prospective case against the non-parties' interests in protection against oppression and against unjustified interference with his rights or duties of confidentiality, and his right of privacy.[74] Non-parties should not be ordered to supply such information unless the demand is strongly justified ('in the interests of justice') and no other source of information exists.[75]

---

[72] *Mitsui & Co Ltd v Nexen Petroleum UK Ltd* [2005] EWHC 625 (Ch); [2005] 3 All ER 511, [18] ff, esp [24], [28], [37], [39]; Lightman J, emphasising that disclosure against non-parties, especially pre-action, is a process of last resort, and that other channels of information must have been exhausted.

[73] See **6.19** above at n 68 for American Law Institute/UNIDROIT's approach to this concept.

[74] These factors have been articulated in the context of CPR 31.17; recent leading judicial discussion of 'confidentiality' and 'privacy' is collected at n 108 below.

[75] *Mitsui & Co Ltd v Nexen Petroleum UK Ltd* [2005] EWHC 625 (Ch); [2005] 3 All ER 511, [18] ff, esp [24], [28], [37], [39]; Lightman J, emphasising that disclosure against non-parties, especially pre-action, is a process of last resort, and that other channels of information must have been exhausted.

(6) Disclosure of Documents During the Main Proceedings

Automatic or case management directions require each party to prepare a list **6.21** of documents on which he will rely, or which might assist the other party.[76] A party is obliged both to provide a list of documents ('disclosure') and to allow inspection of these by the other side.[77] Such information only becomes evidence if it is 'adduced' by one party for the purpose of a trial or other 'hearing'. The CPR defines a 'document' as 'anything in which information of any description is recorded', including electronic sources (see also **6.41**).[78] That definition does not catch information held in a human memory. Nor does it cover non-documentary 'things', such as the claimant's body, physical chattels, or immovable property.[79] The CPR rules now contain special provision for disclosure of electronic information (and see **6.41** below for the text of the rule).[80]

'Standard disclosure' concerns documents which satisfy one of the follow- **6.22** ing criteria:[81] documents on which a party will rely; or which adversely affect his case; or adversely affect the opponent's case; or support the opponent's case; or any other documents of which disclosure is required under a practice direction.[82] The obligation to make disclosure applies to 'documents' (defined at **6.21** above), whether or not they are currently available, and whether they were created before or during the relevant litigation.[83] These documents must either fall within the scope of standard disclosure (as discussed above), or they must have been referred to in that party's statement of case (see also **3.08**), a witness statement or summary, affidavit, or (subject in the last case to special judicial control) in that party's expert report(s).[84] A party's duty to make 'disclosure' embraces documents which 'are or have been in [the relevant party's] control'; and 'control' refers to material which 'is or was in his physical possession', or other material to which he has or has had a 'right to possession' or 'a right to inspect or take copies'.[85] However, there is no obligation to produce

---

[76] CPR Part 31.

[77] CPR 31.10(2) and 31.15, subject to certain qualifications added at CPR 31.3(2); Form N 265, available on-line, is instructive.

[78] CPR 31.4.

[79] eg, Civil Evidence Act 1968, s 14.

[80] PD (31) 2A.1

[81] CPR 31.6.

[82] The court can order narrower disclosure in special situations: CPR 31.5(1),(2).

[83] On the continuing duty to make disclosure until the end of the relevant proceedings, CPR 31.11.

[84] CPR 31.14.

[85] CPR 31.8; *Three Rivers DC v Bank of England (No 4)* [2002] EWCA Civ 1182; [2003] 1 WLR 210, CA, at [46] to [51] (application to obtain disclosure held by non-party, HM Treasury, at the National Archive, Kew, London; held that the defendant, the Bank of England, had no possession of these documents; nor any right to possess them; nor any right to inspect them).

for inspection (as distinct from listing during the first stage of discovery) material which is subject to any of the various privileges (for the list of privileges, see **6.26** below).[86] In applications for judicial review, disclosure of documents is not automatic, nor is it as broad as the scope of disclosure applicable to ordinary civil proceedings. However, the House of Lords has recognised the need for a slightly more liberal approach to disclosure in such proceedings.[87]

6.23   The duty to make disclosure extends to non-privileged confidential material.[88] However, when deciding whether to order disclosure and inspection of confidential material, the courts will consider three questions:[89] is the information available to the other side from some other convenient source;[90] secondly, might sensitive material be blanked out;[91] thirdly, might the class of recipients be restricted?[92]

6.24   The 'implied undertaking' ensures that the recipient can use the information only in the present proceedings.[93] The same undertaking also obliges him not to reveal the information to any non-party.[94] The recipient's lawyer is similarly constrained.[95] The CPR provides: 'a party to whom a document has been disclosed may use the document only for the purpose of the proceedings

---

[86] CPR 31.3(1)(b).

[87] *Tweed v Parades Commission for Northern Ireland* [2006] UKHL 53; [2007] 2 All ER 273.

[88] *Wallace Smith Trust Co v Deloitte Haskins & Sells* [1997] 1 WLR 257, CA.

[89] eg, when deciding whether to order specific disclosure under CPR 31.12.

[90] See the *Wallace Smith* case [1997] 1 WLR 257, CA.

[91] *GE Capital etc v Bankers Trust Co* [1995] 1 WLR 172, CA.

[92] Neil Andrews, *Principles of Civil Procedure* (1994) 11–056.

[93] As Lord Hoffmann explained in *Taylor v Serious Fraud Office* [1999] 2 AC 177, 207, HL: 'The concept of an implied undertaking originated in the law of discovery in civil proceedings. A solicitor or litigant who receives documents by way of discovery is treated as if he had given an undertaking not to use them for any purpose other than the conduct of the litigation. As Hobhouse J pointed out in *Prudential Assurance Co Ltd v Fountain Page Ltd* [1991] 1 WLR 756, 764 the undertaking is in reality an obligation imposed by operation of law by virtue of the circumstances in which the document or information is obtained. The reasons for imposing such an obligation were explained by Lord Keith of Kinkel in *Home Office v Harman* [1983] 1 AC 280, 308, HL: "Discovery constitutes a very serious invasion of the privacy and confidentiality of a litigant's affairs. It forms part of English legal procedure because the public interest in securing that justice is done between parties is considered to outweigh the private and public interest in the maintenance of confidentiality. But the process should not be allowed to place upon the litigant any harsher or more oppressive burden than is strictly required for the purpose of securing that justice is done."'

[94] eg, *Omar v Omar* [1995] 1 WLR 1428; *Watkins v AJ Wright (Electrical) Ltd* [1996] 3 All ER 31; *Miller v Scorey* [1996] 1 WLR 1122; SMC Gibbons, 'Subsequent use of documents obtained through disclosure in civil proceedings . . .' (2001) 20 CJQ 303.

[95] *Bowman v Fels* [2005] EWCA Civ 226; [2005] 1 WLR 3083, at [88], per Brooke LJ: 'In so far as a lawyer gains information from documents disclosed by another party to adversarial litigation and not read in open court, he will be committing a contempt of court if he discloses them to a third party without the express or implied permission of the court or express, clear, Parliamentary sanction.'

in which it is disclosed,[96] except (a) where the document has been read to or by the court, or referred to, at a hearing which has been held in public; or (b) the court gives permission;[97] or (c) the party who disclosed the document and the person to whom the document belongs agree.'[98]

A person will be in contempt of court if he presents a deliberately false state- **6.25** ment contained in a statement of case, witness statement, disclosure declaration (under CPR Part 31), or in an expert's report (see **8.35** on contempt). The court can also dismiss a claim or defence if there has been deliberate destruction or falsification of evidence. For example, in *Arrow Nominees Inc v Blackledge* (2001), a litigant had falsified documents. The Court of Appeal concluded that the litigant's behaviour had destroyed all credibility in his evidence.[99] The court can also draw adverse inferences against a party who has failed to comply with the disclosure rules in CPR Part 31[100] (such a 'soft sanction' is more generally recognised in other legal systems as a response to procedural disobedience).[101] It is also an offence for a prospective defendant to destroy documents, or other potential evidence, in order to spoil his opponent's chances of winning the relevant case.[102]

---

[96] cf, under the pre-CPR practice, 'collateral' use had included certain uses in same action: *Milano Assicurazioni SpA v Walbrook Insurance Co Ltd* [1994] 1 WLR 977; and *Omar v Omar* [1995] 1 WLR 1428; respectively, proposed amendments to writ or statement of claim.

[97] *SmithKline Beecham Biologicals SA v Connaught Laboratories Inc* [1999] 4 All ER 498, CA.

[98] CPR 31.22; even in situation (a) however, the court can make a special order restricting or prohibiting use of a document: CPR 31.22(2); on the latter point, *McBride v The Body Shop International Plc* [2007] EWHC 1658 (QB), noting *Lilly Icos Ltd v Pfizer Ltd* [2002] 1 WLR 2253, CA.

[99] [2000] 2 BCLC 167; [2001] BCC 591, CA; Chadwick LJ said: 'it is no part of the court's function to proceed to trial if to do so would give rise to a substantial risk of injustice', and Ward LJ said: 'Striking out is not a disproportionate remedy for such an abuse … Deception of this scale and magnitude will result in a party's forfeiting his right to continue to be heard.' On 'unless' orders in this context, see **2.21 n 62**, explaining *Marcan Shipping (London) Ltd v Kefalas* [2007] EWCA Civ 463; [2007] 1 WLR 1864, at [33] to [36]; considering CPR 3.8(1) (sanctions take effect automatically); and CPR 3.9 (relief from sanctions); and CPR 3.5 (innocent party's right to file for judgment with costs if opponent's whole defence or claim is struck out automatically for non-compliance with an 'unless' order); the *Marcan* case contains a review of many decisions, including the *Arrow Nominees* case.

[100] eg the first instance decision in *Infabrics v Jaytext* [1985] FSR 75 (affmd [1987] FSR 529, CA) decided under the old rules, but still relevant.

[101] *ALI/UNIDROIT: Principles of Transnational Civil Procedure* (Cambridge UP, 2006), Principles 17.3, 21.3, acknowledge this 'soft sanction'.

[102] *Douglas v Hello! Ltd* [2003] EWHC 55 (Ch); [2003] 1 All ER 1087, Morritt V-C.

(7) Privileges in General

6.26   'Evidential privileges' in English law confer upon the privilege holder (which can be a person, company or organisation) immunity against legal compulsion to supply information, whether at trial or at some other stage of the legal process. The potential compulsion can arise in two main[103] contexts: as an order for a witness to give evidence at a civil or criminal trial; or, secondly, during the pre-trial process of information gathering (known in English civil proceedings as 'disclosure', on which see **6.16** ff above).[104] In England, the following heads of privilege apply:[105] confidential discussion between lawyer and client ('legal advice privilege'); documents created for the dominant purpose of use in pending or contemplated criminal or civil proceedings (including arbitration proceedings) ('litigation privilege'); settlement negotiations explicitly or implicitly conducted on a secret basis ('without prejudice communications privilege'; on which **10.01**, but especially **11.49**); mediation or conciliation negotiations conducted on a confidential basis ('mediation privilege'; on which **11.49** ff); the privilege against self-incrimination (statutory provisions partially override this pivilege in the context of offences under the theft legislation or in respect of protection of rights in intellectual property);[106] and 'public interest

---

[103] Sometimes the privilege is asserted outside the context of the formal legal process: eg *R (on the Application of Morgan Grenfell & Co Ltd) v Special Commissioners of Income Tax* [2002] UKHL 21; [2003] 1 AC 563 (legal advice privilege available against a tax inspector's demand for documents); B Thanki (ed), *The Law of Privilege* (Oxford UP, 2006) 1–05.

[104] Predominantly covered by CPR Part 31; Neil Andrews, *English Civil Procedure* (Oxford UP, 2003) ch 26; C Hollander, *Documentary Evidence* (9th edn, 2006) chs 7 to 10; *Zuckerman on Civil Procedure* (2nd edn, 2006) ch 14.

[105] Neil Andrews, *English Civil Procedure* (Oxford UP, 2003) chs 25, 27 to 30; *Cross and Tapper on Evidence* (11th edn, 2007) chs IX and X; C Hollander, *Documentary Evidence* (9th edn, 2006) chs 11 to 20; P Matthews and H Malek, *Disclosure* (3rd edn, 2007); *Phipson on Evidence* (16th edn, 2005) chs 23 to 26; C Passmore, *Privilege* (2nd edn, 2006); B Thanki (ed), *The Law of Privilege* (Oxford UP, 2006); *Zuckerman on Civil Procedure* (2nd edn, 2006) chs 15 to 18; see also, J Auburn, *Legal Professional Privilege: Law and Theory* (Hart, Oxford, 2000).

[106] **Nature:** Defined by Civil Evidence Act 1968, s 14, as follows: 'The right of a person in any legal proceedings other than criminal proceedings to refuse to answer any question or produce any document or thing if to do so would tend to expose that person [or his or her spouse] to proceedings for an offence or for the recovery of a penalty [under UK law].' A majority in *C plc v P* [2007] EWCA Civ 493; [2007] 3 WLR 437 ([26] to [38], per Longmore LJ, and Sir Martin Nourse at [74]) held that there is no privilege in things or documents existing prior to the order compelling their production (applying the European Court of Human Rights' decision in *Saunders v UK* (1996) 23 EHRR 313), at [69]); but Lawrence Collins LJ, agreeing at [46] that the majority's approach was attractive in principle, nevertheless observed at [63] to [73] that the majority's decision in this case, supported by a line of Strasbourg jurisprudence, could not be reconciled with settled House of Lords' authority; see R Moules [2007] CLJ 528 (at first instance, in *C plc v P* [2006] EWHC 1226 (Ch); [2006] Ch 549, noted Neil Andrews [2007] CLJ 47, Evans-Lombe J had used the Human

immunity',[107] that is protection against use in civil proceedings of information protected in the public interest, for example, high-level state secrets or information supplied to identify criminal wrongdoers.

(8) Privilege and 'Confidentiality'[108]

Non-confidential information cannot be privileged. If information ceases to   **6.27**
be confidential, privilege will also lapse. As a matter of 'substantive law', con-

---

Rights Act 1998 to declare that the privilege must yield to the need to protect the human rights of children against pornographic exploitation); on the background, see Neil Andrews, *English Civil Procedure* (Oxford UP, 2003) 29.24 to 29.28 and (on possible reform) 29.56 ff; B Thanki (ed), *The Law of Privilege* (Oxford UP, 2006) ch 8; *Cross & Tapper on Evidence* (11th edn, 2007) 449 ff; IH Dennis, *The Law of Evidence*, (2nd edn, 2002) ch 5; C Hollander, *Documentary Evidence* (9th edn, 2006) ch 17 (reproducing, also by C Hollander, *Phipson on Evidence* (16th edn, 2005) 24–40 ff); *Zuckerman on Civil Procedure* (2nd edn, 2006) ch 17; see also 'The Privilege against Self-incrimination in Civil Proceedings' (Consultation Paper, Lord Chancellor's Dept, 1992); I Dennis, 'Instrumental Protection, Human Right or Fundamental Necessity? Re-assessing the Privilege against Self-incrimination' [1995] 54 CLJ 342; see also **4.08**; **4.33**; as for **statutory overriding of the privilege**, see, notably, s 72, Supreme Court Act 1981; and s 13, Fraud Act 2006, considered in *Kensington International Ltd v Republic of the Congo* [2007] EWCA Civ 1128.

[107] Neil Andrews, *English Civil Procedure* (Oxford UP, 2003) ch 30.

[108] Recent leading judicial discussion of 'confidentiality' and 'privacy' includes: (i) *Douglas v Hello! Ltd* [2007] UKHL 21; [2007] 2 WLR 920; ibid, at [272], Lord Walker conveniently summarised modern House of Lords' decisions on the topic: '… the law of confidentiality has been, and is being developed in such a way as to protect private information:' (referring to *Wainwright v Home Office* [2003] UKHL 53; [2004] 2 AC 406, HL [28] to [30], *Campbell v MGN Ltd* [2004] UKHL 22; [2004] 2 AC 457, HL, [11] to [22], [43] to [52], [85], [86], [105] to [113], [132], [141], [166], [167]); (ii) *Browne v Associated Newspapers Ltd* [2007] EWCA Civ 295; [2007] 3 WLR 289; (iii) *McKennit v Ash* [2006] EWCA Civ 1714; [2007] 3 WLR 194; (iv) *HRH The Prince of Wales v Associated Newspapers Limited* [2006] EWCA Civ 1776; [2007] 3 WLR 222; (v) *Murray v Express Newspapers plc* [2007] EWHC 1908 (Ch) (photograph taken in public of child of JK Rowling (author of the 'Harry Potter' series); child not yet two years old; summary judgment hearing to strike out claims for injunction and compensation; claims struck out; Patten J at [66] stating: 'the law does not in my judgment (as it stands) allow the [claimants, suing on behalf of their child] to carve out a press-free zone for their children in respect of absolutely everything they choose to do. Even after [Von Hannover v Germany [2004] EMLR 21 (the Princess Caroline of Monaco case)] there remains, I believe, an area of routine activity which when conducted in a public place carries no guarantee of privacy. [T]his is just such a case. [T]here is no allegation of any direct harm or distress being caused to the [child] or to his parents at the time and I am not persuaded that his mother's understandable sensitivity to and upset caused by her children being photographed on any occasion can of itself be allowed to dictate what the legal boundaries of protection should be.' Earlier seminal cases on confidentiality are: *Prince Albert v Strange* (1849) 2 De G & Sm 652; *Duchess of Argyle v Duke of Argyle* [1967] Ch 302; *Coco v Clark (Engineers) Ltd* [1969] RPC 41 and *Fraser v Evans* [1969] 1 QB 349. On the grant of interim injunctions in this context, see the *Browne* case, and see **5.12 at (iv)**. On English law's absorption of European Human Rights law, and the balancing of Art 8 (pro-

fidential information can be protected by the equitable remedy of injunction,[109] and by pecuniary remedies.[110] But not all confidential information is privileged. For example, confidential discussion between a person and a priest or religious advisor, or between a patient and doctor, and in many other professional relationships,[111] is undoubtedly subject to legal protection through injunctions and pecuniary relief. But the holder of those types of confidentiality cannot invoke privilege if ordered by the court to give evidence or produce documents relating to this information. In short, privilege is confidentiality admitted to a higher level of legal protection; but not all confidential relations are raised to that level.

(9) Legal Advice Privilege[112]

6.28 This is undoubtedly the most important head of evidential privilege. In the United States it is known as 'attorney-client' privilege (see, for example, discussion of *Upjohn Co v United States* (1981) at **6.35** below). Protection of confidential legal consultation is also recognised as a human right under the Euro-

---

tection of privacy) and Art 10 (freedom of expression), see Buxton LJ in the *McKennit* case, at [8] and [11]; on the Strasbourg 'privacy case law, see especially *Murray v Express Newspapers plc* [2007] EWHC 1908 (Ch) at [36] ff; where there is no previous relationship between the parties, and the complaint concerns the defendant's unlawful acquisition or proposed use of confidential information, Lord Nicholls in *Campbell v MGN* [2004] UKHL 22; [2004] 2 AC 457 at [14] suggested that 'the essence of the tort is better encapsulated now as misuse of private information.'

[109] Whether by interim injunction (*Browne v Associated Newspapers Ltd* [2007] EWCA Civ 295; [2007] 3 WLR 289, and see **5.12 at (iv)**) or final injunction (*HRH The Prince of Wales v Associated Newspapers Limited* [2006] EWCA Civ 1776; [2007] 3 WLR 222); see also the abundant case law concerning protection of 'client information' by injunctions: *Marks and Spencer Group plc v Freshfields Bruckhaus Deringer* [2004] EWCA Civ 741; *Koch Shipping Inc v Richards Butler* [2002] EWCA Civ 1280; *GUS Consulting GmbH v Leboeuf Lamb, Greene & McCrae* [2006] EWCA Civ 683; [2006] CP Rep 40; *Bolkiah v KPMG* [1999] 2 AC 222, HL; the topic is considered in C Hollander and S Salzedo, *Conflicts of Interest and Chinese Walls* (2nd edn, 2005); for US and comparative discussion: G Hazard and A Dondi, *Legal Ethics* (Stanford UP, 2004) ch 5, 'Loyalty', and ch 6, 'Confidentiality'.

[110] On the remedies of damages and 'account' in this context, *Douglas v Hello! Ltd (No 3)* [2005] EWCA Civ 595; [2006] QB 12 at [237] to [250] (there have been further developments in this litigation, but not on this precise point: *Douglas v Hello! Ltd* [2007] UKHL 21; [2007] 2 WLR 920 at [108] to [136], per Lord Hoffmann, [242] to [262], per Lord Nicholls, [265] to [300] per Lord Walker, [323] to [330] per Lord Brown; however, see the summary of remedies, ibid, at [376] per Lord Walker).

[111] R Pattenden, *The Law of Professional – Client Confidentiality: Regulating the Disclosure of Confidential Personal Information* (Oxford UP, 2003).

[112] Neil Andrews, *English Civil Procedure* (Oxford UP, 2003), chs 27, 28; other sources are *Cross and Tapper on Evidence* (11th edn, 2007), 466 ff; C Hollander, *Documentary Evidence* (9th edn, 2006), chs 11–15, esp 13, 14; P Matthews and H Malek, *Disclosure* (3rd

pean Convention on Human Rights,[113] and as part of European Community law.[114] In English law, legal advice operates as an absolute privilege in two senses. First, this head of privilege cannot be disapplied by exercise of judicial discretion.[115] Secondly, unless privilege is waived by a privilege holder (or his authorised agent),[116] protection endures beyond the immediate occasion or context of the privileged communications.[117] Summing up legal advice privilege's adamantine qualities, Lord Millett said in 2002:

'Some principles are well established[118] ... First, the privilege remains after the occasion for it has passed: unless waived "once privileged, always privileged". Secondly, the privilege is the same whether the documents are sought for the purpose of civil or criminal proceedings and whether by the prosecution or the defence. Thirdly, the refusal of the claimant to waive his privilege for any reason or none cannot be questioned or investigated by the Court. Fourthly, save in cases where the privileged communication is itself the means of carrying out a fraud [see 6.33], the privilege is absolute. Once the privilege is established, the lawyer's mouth is "shut for ever".'[119]

---

edn, 2007); *Phipson on Evidence* (16th edn, 2005), ch 20 esp 20–04 to 20–24; C Passmore, *Privilege* (2nd edn, 2006) ch 2; B Thanki (ed), *The Law of Privilege* (Oxford UP, 2006); *Zuckerman on Civil Procedure* (2nd edn, 2006) ch 15; J Auburn, *Legal Professional Privilege: Law & Theory* (Hart, Oxford, 2000); HL Ho, 'History and Judicial Theories of Legal Professional Privilege' (1995) Sing J L Studies 558.

[113] For references, Neil Andrews, *English Civil Procedure* (Oxford UP, 2003) 27.16 and B Thanki (ed), *The Law of Privilege* (Oxford UP, 2006) 1.60 to 1.64; see the judicial surveys (1) by Brooke LJ in *Bowman v Fels* [2005] EWCA Civ 226; [2005] 1 WLR 3083 at [74] ff and (2) by Lord Hoffmann in *R (on the Application of Morgan Grenfell & Co Ltd) v Special Commissioners of Income Tax* [2002] UKHL 21; [2003] 1 AC 563 at [7]; ibid, per Lord Hoffmann, commenting, '[legal advice privilege] is a fundamental human right long established in the common law ... It has been held by the European Court of Human Rights to be part of the right of privacy guaranteed by Article 8 of the Convention (*Campbell v United Kingdom* (1992) 15 EHRR 137 [46], [48]; *Foxley v United Kingdom* (2000) 31 EHRR 637, at [29], referring to Art 8; at [50] remarking on Art 6) and held by the European Court of Justice to be a part of Community law: *A M & S Europe Ltd v Commission of the European Communities (Case 155/79)* [1983] QB 878' at [18] [25]; in the criminal context Art 6(3)(c) is also germane: *Brennan v UK* – 39846/98 [2001] ECHR 596 at [58]; in the *Morgan Grenfell* case [2002] UKHL 21; [2003] 1 AC 563 at [39], Lord Hoffmann added: 'the European Court of Human Rights has said that [the privilege] is a fundamental human right which can be invaded only in exceptional circumstances: see *Foxley v United Kingdom* (2001) 31 EHRR 637, para 44.'

[114] *A M & S Europe Ltd v Commission of the European Communities* (Case 155/79) [1983] QB 878, ECJ, at [18] and [25]; B Thanki (ed), ibid, 1.59.

[115] *R v Derby Magistrates' Court, Ex p B* [1996] AC 487, HL; *B v Auckland District Law Society* [2003] UKPC 38; [2003] 2 AC 736, PC, at [50] to [56], per Lord Millett; B Thanki (ed), ibid, 1.26 to 1.30.

[116] Neil Andrews, *English Civil Procedure* (Oxford UP, 2003) ch 28.

[117] *B v Auckland District Law Society* [2003] UKPC 38; [2003] 2 AC 736, PC at [44]; B Thanki (ed), ibid, 1.52 to 1.58.

[118] Noting Lord Taylor's analysis in *R v Derby Magistrates' Court, Ex p B* [1996] AC 487, 503G-H, HL.

[119] Lord Millett, *Auckland* case, ibid, at [44], citing for this last proposition, *Wilson v Rastall* (1792) 4 Durn & E 753, 759, per Buller J.

6.29   The leading English decision on legal advice privilege is *Three Rivers DC v Governor and Company of the Bank of England (No 6) (2004)*.[120] In that case the House of Lords held that legal advice privilege is not confined to confidential consultation between a lawyer and his client concerning the latter's legal rights and obligations. For example, it can include so-called 'presentational' advice to a client on how to formulate submissions to an inquiry into alleged wrongdoing or commercial default.

6.30   In the House of Lords in the *Three Rivers (No 6)* case, Baroness Hale said that 'legal advice is not confined to telling the client the law; it must include advice as to what should prudently and sensibly be done in the relevant context.'[121] She added:[122]

'We want people to obey the law, enter into valid and effective transactions, settle their affairs responsibly when they separate or divorce, make wills which will withstand the challenge of the disappointed, and present their best case before all kinds of court, tribunal and inquiry in an honest and responsible manner.'

The House of Lords approved the opinion of Advocate-General Slynn, given before the European Court of Justice in the *A M & S Europe Ltd* case (1983):[123]

'[Legal advice privilege] springs essentially from the basic need of a man in a civilised society to be able to turn to his lawyer for advice and help, and if proceedings begin, for representation; it springs no less from the advantages to a society which evolves complex law reaching into all the business affairs of persons, real and legal, that they

---

[120] [2004] UKHL 48; [2005] 1 AC 610; noted Neil Andrews (2005) CJQ 185; S Partington and J Ward [2005] JBL 231; J Seymour [2005] CLJ 54; C Tapper (2005) 121 LQR 181; the leading historical survey conducted by an English court is Lord Taylor of Gosforth CJ's remarkable speech in *R v Derby Magistrates Court, Ex p B* [1996] AC 487, HL; and see HL Ho, 'History & Judicial Theories of Legal Professional Privilege' (1995) Sing J L Studies 558.

[121] [2004] UKHL 48; [2005] 1 AC 610, at [62], referring to Taylor LJ's statement in *Balabel v Air India* [1988] Ch 317, 330, CA.

[122] [2004] UKHL 48; [2005] 1 AC 610, at [62].

[123] ibid, at [95], citing *A M & S Europe Ltd v European Commission* (Case 155/79) [1983] QB 878, 913 (ECJ, Opinion of Advocate-General Slynn); similarly, Lord Scott at [34] in the *Three Rivers* case approved AAS Zuckerman's suggestion that legal advice privilege is linked to the 'rule of law' (Adrian Zuckerman, *Civil Procedure* (2003), 15.8 to 15.10; see now *Zuckerman on Civil Procedure* (2nd edn, 2006) 15.09 ff); see, earlier, Neil Andrews, *Principles of Civil Procedure* (1994) at 12–009, quoted at next footnote; in Lord Scott's words, at [34] in the *Three Rivers* case, this means that: 'it is necessary in our society, a society in which the restraining and controlling framework is built upon a belief in the rule of law, that communications ... whereby clients are hoping for the assistance of the lawyers' legal skills in the management of their ... affairs, should be secure against the possibility of any scrutiny from others, whether the police, the executive, business competitors, inquisitive busybodies or anyone else ... . B Thanki (ed), *The Law of Privilege* (Oxford UP, 2006), 1–15 attractively presents a composite rationale, based on the right of access to legal advice, and on the need for candour so as to facilitate free and informed legal consultation.

should be able to know what they can do under the law, what is forbidden, where they must tread circumspectly, where they run risks.'

In other words, 'modern society accepts that there is an important constitutional value in obtaining "free, confident, and candid" legal consultation'.[124]

According to the House of Lords in the *Three Rivers* case (2004), legal advice privilege must arise from a 'relevant legal context', including 'presentational' advice for participation in an inquiry.[125] As Lord Brown of Eaton-under-Heywood said:[126] '... the process by which a client seeks and obtains his lawyer's assistance in the presentation of his case for the purposes of any formal inquiry – whether concerned with public law or private law, whether adversarial or inquisitorial in form, whether held in public or private, whether or not directly affecting his rights or liabilities – attracts legal advice privilege.' He added: 'Such assistance to my mind clearly has the character of legal business. It is precisely the sort of professional service for which lawyers are ordinarily employed by virtue of their expertise and experience.' **6.31**

However, legal advice privilege does not extend to a lawyer's advice or assistance in a general commercial capacity if the same can be provided equally well by a non-lawyer. This last point is known as the 'mere man of business' limitation.[127] And so there must be a distinctive 'legal input'. This element will place the confidential advice in a different category from, say, general commercial advice given by a banker, surveyor, property developer, or insurer. Lord Scott in the *Three Rivers (No 6)* case re-emphasised the 'mere man of business' limitation:[128] 'If a solicitor becomes the client's "man of business", and some solicitors do, responsible for advising the client on all matters of business, including investment policy, financial policy and other business matters, the advice may lack a relevant legal context. There is, in my opinion, no way of avoiding difficulty in deciding in marginal cases whether the seeking of advice from or the giving of advice by lawyers does or does not take place in a relevant legal context ... '. It is submitted that the courts should not too readily dismiss a claim to privilege under this 'mere man of business' rule. The boundaries of legal activity are fluid. There is a danger that clients might be trapped into supposing that information disclosed to lawyers will be privileged. If lawyers fail to point out that discussions at some point 'are conducted on thin ice', the upshot might be that suits for professional negligence are made by clients against their lawyers. Fear of such liability might lead to over-cautious dealings between lawyers and clients. This is exactly the converse of that 'free, confident, **6.32**

---

[124] Neil Andrews, *Principles of Civil Procedure* (1994) at 12–009.

[125] *Three Rivers (No 6)* [2004] UKHL 48; [2005] 1 AC 610, at [120].

[126] ibid, at [120].

[127] ibid, at [38]; on this problematic topic, B Thanki (ed), *The Law of Privilege* (Oxford UP, 2006) 2–115 ff.

[128] [2005] 1 AC 610; [2004] UKHL 48, at [38]; B Thanki (ed), ibid, 2–115 ff.

and candid' communication which the privilege is intended to engender (see the formulation cited at **6.30** above).[129]

6.33   Three other limitations on legal advice privilege must be briefly noted. First, the House of Lords in the *Three Rivers* case (2004) accepted without proper analysis the assumption that this type of privilege will apply only if the dominant purpose of that communication was the eliciting or giving of legal advice.[130] Secondly, a trickle, fortunately not a torrent, of statutes has overridden this head of privilege in specific contexts.[131] But only clear legislation can suppress privilege.[132] Thirdly, the rule in *R v Cox & Railton* (1884)[133] prevents privilege from attaching to legal advice or assistance concerning the client's intended commission of a crime or 'fraud'. Nor does privilege apply where the client is being manipulated for fraudulent purposes by a third party.[134] 'Fraud' in this context includes, it seems, all species of dishonest conduct. But it does not extend to ordinary breaches of contract, nor to the torts of conversion of

---

[129] Neil Andrews, *Principles of Civil Procedure* (1994) at 12–009.

[130] [2005] 1 AC 610; [2004] UKHL 48 at [35], per Lord Scott, [57], per Lord Rodger, [70] and [73], per Lord Carswell, also citing the Court of Appeal in *Three Rivers (No 5)* [2003] QB 1556, CA, at [35], per Longmore LJ; there is acute discusssion of this question in the Australian decision, *Esso Australia Resources Ltd v Commr of Taxation of the Commonwealth of Australia* [1999] HCA 67; (1999) 210 CLR 49 (High Ct of Aust), cited but not examined in the speeches by the House of Lords; B Thanki (ed), *The Law of Privilege* (Oxford UP, 2006) 2.169 to 2.176; earlier, Neil Andrews, *English Civil Procedure* (Oxford UP, 2003) 27.07, 27.08; C Passmore, *Privilege* (2nd edn, 2006) 2.079 ff contends that the dominant purpose test has neither been authoritatively adopted by the House of Lords, nor should it be adopted; his argument is that the 'relevant legal context' test serves satisfactorily as a criterion, ibid at 2.080; but Passmore's first point seems dooubtful; as for the Court of Appeal's authority, it is arguable that the dominant purpose test was adopted by the Court of Appeal (*Three Rivers (No 5)* [2003] QB 1556, CA, at [35]; again Passmore is unpersuaded: ibid, at 2.083, describing the Court of Appeal's rather short reference to this test as 'strictly obiter').

[131] B Thanki (ed), *The Law of Privilege* (Oxford UP, 2006) 4.73 to 4.77; Neil Andrews, *English Civil Procedure* (Oxford UP, 2003) 26.17 to 27.18; note also the distinction between innocent consultation with a lawyer to parry a charge or meet an accusation, and nefarious attempts to conceal and stifle legal investigation or destroy evidence or concoct false or misleading evidence; on that distinction see *Derby & Co Ltd v Weldon (No 7)* [1990] 1 WLR 1156, 1174 E-G, per Vinelott J; *O'Rourke v Darbishire* [1920] AC 681, 613, HL, per Lord Sumner.

[132] *R (on the Application of Morgan Grenfell & Co Ltd) v Special Commissioners of Income Tax* [2002] UKHL 21; [2003] 1 AC 563 (legal advice privilege available against a tax inspector's demand for documents); statutory suppression of this privilege requires explicit language or 'necessary implication': *Morgan Grenfell* case, ibid, at [45], [46], and remarks by Lord Millett in *B v Auckland District Law Society* [2003] UKPC 38; [2003] 2 AC 736, PC at [57] ff, and by Brooke LJ in *Bowman v Fels* [2005] EWCA Civ 226; [2005] 1 WLR 3083 at [85] ff.

[133] (1884) 14 QBD 153, Stephen J; C Passmore, *Privilege* (2nd edn, 2006) ch 8; see also 7.30 for discussion of the fraud/iniquity exception in the context of litigation privilege.

[134] *R v Central Criminal Court, ex p Francis & Francis* [1989] AC 346, HL.

goods or trespass. This is because each of these legal wrongs ordinarily lacks the taint of dishonesty or sufficiently reprehensible 'iniquity'.[135]

A 'lawyer'[136]-'client' relationship is normally easy to identify when the client **6.34** is an individual. Even so there are limits. It has been suggested that a lawyer's 'advice about your love life' might not be privileged.[137] To ask a lawyer for the time might not be privileged (although he might charge you for his time, rounding up his 'unit'). The real question, however, is not the subject-matter of the discussion but the circumstances in which the lawyer was consulted. The test must be whether a lawyer's professional knowledge or wisdom has been at least implicitly sought or offered.[138] However, delineating the scope of a lawyer-client relationship has become problematic if communications occur beween a lawyer (including an in-house lawyer) and a company or organisation. This topic is presently governed by the Court of Appeal's decision in *Three Rivers (No 5)*.[139] Unfortunately, the House of Lords in the *Three Rivers (No 6)* case chose not to examine this authority. And so this question remains governed by *Three Rivers (No 5)*.[140] Based on that perhaps debatable Court of Appeal

---

[135] B Thanki (ed), *The Law of Privilege* (Oxford UP, 2006) 4.33 to 4.63; Neil Andrews, *English Civil Procedure* (Oxford UP, 2003) 26.19 to 27.20.

[136] 'Lawyer', in England and Wales, includes an 'in house lawyer' (C Passmore, *Privilege* (2nd edn, 2006) 4.041 to 4.046): but not under the law of the EU, *A M & S Europe Ltd v Commission of the EC* [1987] QB, ECJ, B Thanki (ed), *The Law of Privilege* (Oxford UP, 2006), 1.41 to 1.44, and C Passmore, ibid, 4.047 ff; in England, legal advice privilege has been extended to trade mark and patent agents, and certain other 'quasi-legal' advisors, mostly by statute, for references see Neil Andrews, *English Civil Procedure* (Oxford UP, 2003) 27.03 at nn 10 – 15 and B Thanki (ed), ibid, 1.40 to 1.51, Passmore, ibid 1.144; attention is also drawn to proposed changes to legal practices – see the Legal Services Bill, clause 182, referring to legal professional privilege; the text of the Bill, which is being debated in Parliament in early 2007. The Bill is available at: *http://www.publications.parliament.uk/pa/pabills/200607/legal_services.htm*. For general comment on that Bill, K Underwood, 'The Legal Services Bill-Death by Regulation?' (2007) 26 CJQ 124. In *Bolkiah v KPMG* [1999] 2 AC 222, HL, privilege arose in the dealings between 'forensic accountants' and potential witnesses; but this seems to have been rooted in litigation privilege, C Passmore, *Privilege* (2nd edn, 2006) 1.145.

[137] B Thanki (ed), *The Law of Privilege* (Oxford UP, 2006) 1.46; generally, ibid, 1.45 ff; thus the advice must be given in a professional capacity, as distinct from a merely social one (although, notoriously, lawyers at social parties are frequently 'button holed' for informal advice; moral, attend only parties with other lawyers; or, if laity is present, pass oneself off as a 'sociologist').

[138] See the author's earlier discussion in Neil Andrews, *Principles of Civil Procedure* (1994) 339 n 95, citing *O'Rourke v Darbishire* [1929] AC 581, 602, HL; *Minter v Priest* [1930] AC 558, 568, HL, per Lord Buckmaster.

[139] *Three Rivers DC v Governor and Company of the Bank of England (No 5)* [2003] EWCA Civ 474; [2003] QB 1556.

[140] *Three Rivers DC etc (No 5)* [2003] EWCA Civ 474; [2003] QB 1556; *Zuckerman on Civil Procedure* (2nd edn, 2006) 15.37 ff; *Three Rivers (No 5)* was applied in *National Westminster Bank v Rabobank Nederland* [2006] EWHC 218 (Comm); for comment, J Loughrey, 'Legal Advice Privilge and the Corporate Client' (2005) 9 E & P 183; M Stock-

authority (see further the next paragraph and discussion elsewhere),[141] the present law can be formulated as follows: when an event involving or affecting a company (or other organisation) is being investigated or considered, English law does not extend legal advice privilege to confidential communications between the lawyer and all the various members and echelons within that client company or other organisation. This is so, even though this legal discussion is designed to gather the facts surrounding the relevant event. The Court of Appeal in *Three Rivers (No 5)* held that the 'client' should be defined narrowly to comprise only a small segment of the company or organisation. Legal consultation beyond that 'core' 'client' group of officials or employees will not attract legal advice privilege. Admittedly, legal consultation beyond this 'core' 'client' group might be privileged on the basis of 'litigation' privilege (on which see **6.36** below). However, litigation privilege is confined to confidential communications in relation to 'adversarial' proceedings, as distinct from an inquiry (on the latter point, see point (iv) at **6.37** below).[142]

6.35   By contrast, the US Supreme Court in *Upjohn Co v United States* (1981) adopted a broader approach than the English Court of Appeal's (on which see the preceding paragraph) to the question of a 'corporate client'.[143] The American case involved a confidential 'internal trawl' conducted by in-house counsel for information from a company's employees. The US Supreme Court held that attorney-client privilege attaches to documents and communications which enable lawyers (in-house counsel in the *Upjohn* case) to give confidential legal advice to the company's leading officials. The internal inquiry in this case involved allegations of wrongdoing. The case is conveniently analysed by Thanki.[144] The House of Lords in *Three Rivers (No 6)* chose not to decide whether they regarded the *Upjohn* decision as offering an attractive approach. English commentators are divided on this point. Charles Hollander QC (writing both in his own book and in *Phipson on Evidence*),[145] Thanki's *Law of*

---

dale and R Mitchell, 'Who is the Client? An Exploration of Legal Professional Privilege in the Corporate Context' (2006) 27 Company Lawyer 110.

[141] Neil Andrews, English Civil Justice and Remedies: Progress and Challenges: Nagoya Lectures (Shinzan Sha Publishers, Tokyo, 2007) 7.20 ff.

[142] *Re L* [1997] AC 16, HL.

[143] 449 US 383 (1981); cf the US material collected at *Zuckerman on Civil Procedure* (2nd edn, 2006) 15.43 ff, at nn 70 to 82, also noting J Sexton, 'A Post-*Upjohn* Consideration of Corporate-Client Privilege' (1982) 57 NYULR 442; on the danger of corporate 'cloaking', B Thanki (ed), *The Law of Privilege* (Oxford UP, 2006) 2.28 n 73, noting Australian discussion, most recently in *Esso v Federal Commissioner of Taxation* (1999) 201 CLR 49 (considering *Grant v Downs* (1976) 135 CLR 674); Thanki, ibid, at 2–39, notes the non-binding view of Lord Scott in argument in *Three Rivers (No 6)* that the (entire) company is normally the client.

[144] B Thanki (ed), *The Law of Privilege* (Oxford UP, 2006) 2.41 ff; Thanki at 2.45 notes Burger CJ's test at 449 US 383, 402–3 (1981).

[145] C Hollander, *Documentary Evidence* (9th edn, 2006) 13.12; *Phipson on Evidence*

Privilege,[146] and Passmore,[147] support a wide approach to corporate legal advice privilege; but Zuckerman[148] is firmly against such a wide approach; and Tapper[149] is (arguably) equivocal. Perhaps the arguments just tip in favour of maintaining the current and restrictive English law, even though this presents difficulty for companies engaged in internal fact-finding. The problem has been analysed elsewhere by the author.[150]

(10) Litigation Privilege[151]

This privilege shields a party's (or lawyer's) attempt to prepare a case for litigation conducted *inter partes*. Each party's (or prospective party's, see next paragraph) private investigation into the case's facts and background can be conducted in the knowledge that an opponent cannot discover either the target or fruit (or empty handedness) of the other party's forensic investigation. There is no general duty, therefore, to reveal 'bad points' discovered during this process (for an exceptional positive duty to disclose 'bad points' in the context of 'without notice' applications, see **4.14**). However, a litigant or lawyer must not positively mislead the court. **6.36**

The elements of 'litigation privilege' are: (i) it covers confidential[152] communication (including the creation of documentary material) between third parties and either the client or lawyer; (ii) the communication must have occurred, or this material must have been created, for the dominant purpose[153] of use in **6.37**

(16th edn, 2005) 23.58 to 23.61 (highly critical of *Three Rivers DC (No 5)* [2003] QB 1556, CA; [2003] EWCA Civ 474).

[146] B Thanki (ed), *The Law of Privilege* (Oxford UP, 2006) 2.168 (Thanki QC had been counsel for the Bank of England).

[147] C Passmore, *Privilege* (2nd edn, 2006) 2.029 ff, 4.008 ff (also noting inconsistency between the common law approach and the statutory approach to the scope of privilege afforded to dealings with patent agents and trade mark agents, ibid at 2.038).

[148] *Zuckerman on Civil Procedure* (2nd edn, 2006) 15.37 to 15.51.

[149] C Tapper's case note (2005) 121 LQR 181, 182 is equivocal on this point, but the tenor of his note is hostile to expansion of legal advice privilege.

[150] Neil Andrews, *English Civil Justice and Remedies: Progress and Challenges: Nagoya Lectures* (Shinzan Sha Publishers, Tokyo, 2007) at 7.20 ff, considering the arguments for and against adoption of the *Upjohn* approach.

[151] For details, Neil Andrews, *English Civil Procedure* (Oxford UP, 2003) 27–21 ff; C Hollander, *Documentary Evidence* (9th edn, 2006) ch 14; B Thanki (ed), *The Law of Privilege* (Oxford UP, 2006) ch 3; *Zuckerman on Civil Procedure* (2nd edn, 2006) ch 15.

[152] An unsolicited communication with a potential witness would be privileged even if the witness has not indicated that he intends to respect confidence: *ISTIL Group Inc v Zahoor* [2003] 2 All ER 252; [2003] EWHC 165 (Ch) at [63] per Lawrence Collins J; B Thanki (ed), *The Law of Privilege* (Oxford UP, 2006) 3.35.

[153] On the 'dominant purpose' test, B Thanki (ed), *The Law of Privilege* (Oxford UP, 2006) 3–73 ff.

pending or anticipated proceedings; if not already commenced, the relevant proceedings must be in reasonable prospect;[154] (iii) the proceedings for which the
communication was intended can be criminal or civil, foreign[155] or domestic,
and involve courts, tribunals or arbitration (but see the next restriction); (iv)
however, the proceedings must be adversarial in nature, as distinct from an inquisitorial procedure.[156] Element (iv) appears to prevent this head of privilege
attaching to communications with third parties relating to any type of 'inquiry'.
Such communications can only be protected under the aegis of 'legal advice
privilege' (on which see **6.28** ff above). However, legal advice privilege only applies to direct communications between client and lawyer. But this 'inquisitorial' proceeding bar upon litigation privilege needs to be re-examined as a matter of principle, and certainly it can be contended that the point is less secure
than often supposed.[157] Other commentators are similarly unconvinced.[158]

6.38   What is the relationship between legal advice and litigation privileges? Legal advice privilege applies to lawyer-client consultation, whether or not the
relevant advice concerns litigation: whereas litigation privilege is concerned
with communications between the privilege holder (the 'party') and a third
party or the privilege holder's lawyer and a third party. Litigation privilege,
therefore, unlike legal advice privilege, concerns confidential discussion or investigation outside the lawyer/client relationship.[159] It is submitted that the

---

[154] A 'real prospect' rather than a 'mere possibility': *USA v Philip Morris Inc (No 1)*
[2004] EWCA Civ 330; [2004] 1 CLC 811; Brooke LJ at [66] to [69] explained that Moore-
Bick J's 'real likelihood' test at first instance, [2003] EWHC 3028 (Comm) at [46], was perhaps not an improvement on the traditional formulation of a 'real prospect'; that the level of
likelihood did not have to be 50 per cent or higher; and that a 'mere possibility' of proceedings was insufficient; B Thanki (ed), *The Law of Privilege* (Oxford UP, 2006) 3.47 ff.

[155] *Re Duncan* [1968] P 306; *Minnesota Mining and Manufacturing Co v Rennicks
(UK) Ltd* [1991] FSR 97, 99; *Société Francaise Hoechst v Allied Colloids Ltd* [1992] FSR
66; *International Computers (Ltd) v Phoenix International Computers Ltd* [1995] 1 All
ER 413, 427 ff.

[156] *Re L* [1997] AC 16, HL.

[157] In the *Three Rivers* litigation, counsel for the Bank had conceded that the Bingham
Inquiry was not an 'adversarial' procedure and that 'litigation privilege' could not, therefore, apply (on the basis of *Re L* [1997] AC 16, HL); with respect, it might be contended that
the special context of that case – child protection proceedings – should be taken to restrict
the ambit of that decision; however, that concession appears to have been later supported by
Lord Scott in the *Three Rivers* appeal [2004] UKHL 48; [2005] 1 AC 610, at [10]; cf, Lord
Rodger, ibid, at [53], who suggested that the 'adversarial' and 'inquisitorial' distinction
might require further examination (also noting that Lord Nicholls, a dissentient in *Re L*,
ibid at 31 G to 32 L, had cautioned against a rigid distinction); see also the critical comments
in *Zuckerman on Civil Procedure* (2nd edn, 2006) 15.110 ff.

[158] B Thanki (ed), *The Law of Privilege* (Oxford UP, 2006) 3.57 to 3.65; C Passmore,
Privilege (2nd edn, 2006) 3.058 ff.

[159] Several Law Lords in *Three Rivers (No 6)* [2004] UKHL 48; [2005] 1 AC 610 acknowledged this distinction between legal advice and litigation privilege: see Lord Scott at
[10], Lord Rodger at [50] and [51], and Lord Carswell at [65] and [72]; Lord Rodger at [51]

better view is that there is no overlap between these privileges.[160] A communication or document should be analysed as privileged under one head rather the other, and not as privileged under both.[161]

Finally, it should be noted that litigation privilege has become controversial. The two main arguments in its favour, reiterated rather bluntly in most of the cases,[162] are: (i) each litigant (or prospective litigant), in preparation for the case (or prospective action), should be free to communicate confidentially with third parties (notably potential witnesses, experts – on which see also **7.30, 7.31** –, or non-legal advisors), without fear that the opponent will invade, feed off, or take advantage of, such exploratory communication; (ii) potential witnesses and experts, no less than clients, should feel secure that they can state their recollection of the relevant events, or venture their opinion, 'fully and candidly'.[163] There are also subsidiary arguments supporting litigation privilege.[164] But in modern

6.39

---

noted that Lord Edmund-Davies in *Waugh v BR Board* [1980] AC 521, 541–2, HL, had said that this distinction had not always been borne in mind, and that lawyers had sometimes loosely spoken of a global 'legal professional privilege' doctrine; in *Waugh's* case it was also made clear that litigation privilege is subject to a 'dominant purpose' test; the House of Lords in the *Three Rivers* case assumed that a 'dominant purpose' test also applies to legal advice privilege; on this last issue, B Thanki (ed), *The Law of Privilege* (Oxford UP, 2006) 2–169 ff.

[160] B Thanki (ed), ibid, 1–08, 3–08 to 3–09; C Passmore, *Privilege* (2nd edn, 2006) 3.002 ff

[161] cf the contention that there is overlap: *Zuckerman on Civil Procedure* (2nd edn, 2006) 15.17.

[162] eg '... as you have no right to see your adversary's brief, you have no right to see that which comes into existence merely as materials for the brief': *Anderson v Bank of British Columbia* (1876) 2 Ch D 644 at 656, per James LJ; cited with approval by Lord Simon of Glaisdale in *Waugh v British Railways Board* [1980] AC 521, 537, HL.

[163] As for argument (i), besides the judicial statements listed at Neil Andrews, *English Civil Procedure* (Oxford UP, 2003), 27.25 to 27.27 (notably, Simon Brown LJ in *Robert Hitchins Ltd v International Computers Ltd* [1996] EWCA Civ 1163, also cited in C Passmore, *Privilege* (2nd edn, 2006) 3.205 ff) see the more recent remarks of Lord Rodger in the *Three Rivers (No 6)* case [2005] 1 AC 610; [2004] UKHL 48 at [52], who offered strong support for this head of privilege: 'Litigation privilege ... is based on the idea that legal proceedings take the form of a contest in which each of the opposing parties assembles his own body of evidence and uses it to try to defeat the other ... In such a system each party should be free to prepare his case as fully as possible without the risk that his opponent will be able to recover the material generated by his preparations.' He also approved a leading American discussion of this privilege: 'In the words of Justice Jackson in *Hickman v Taylor* [US Supreme Court, 329 US 495, 516 (1947)], "Discovery was hardly intended to enable a learned profession to perform its functions either without wits or on wits borrowed from the adversary."' Charles J has also supported this privilege, doubting the cogency of the judicial dicta attacking litigation privilege: *S County Council v B* [2000] Fam 76, as noted by C Passmore, *Privilege* (2nd edn, 2006) 3.019. Argument (ii) (see text above) is noted by C Passmore, ibid, 3.018, citing Lord Wilberforce in *Waugh v BR Board* [1980] AC 521, 531, HL, and ibid, at 3.117, citing in the context of experts, Lord Denning MR in *Re Saxton* [1962] 1 WLR 968, 972, CA and Canadian decisions

[164] Additional, although perhaps subsidiary, arguments are: the prospect of nit picking cross-examination concerning the drafting of witness statements, Thanki (ed), op cit,

times it has become almost fashionable for judges to express scepticism or outright hostility towards litigation privilege. There are two lines of attack. First,
some emphasise the value of intensifying the programme of '(all) cards [face-up]
on the table' (a point made by Sir Lawrence Collins in the *Istil* case (2003),[165]
and by others).[166] The second attack rests on the radical suggestion that litigation privilege is a chimera, a doctrinal impostor having no convincing claim to
independent existence. According to this view, legal advice privilege (confidential lawyer-client consultation) is the only true basis for protection in this context (see dicta of Lord Scott in the *Three Rivers DC* case (2004),[167] and earlier
as Scott V-C in *Secretary of State for Trade and Industry v Baker* (1998);[168] and
the statement by Sir Lawrence Collins, already cited).[169]

3–128, and the financial free-rider problem, Neil Andrews, *English Civil Procedure* (Oxford UP, 2003) 27–34 ff.

[165] *ISTIL Group Inc v Zahoor* [2003] 2 All ER 252; [2003] EWHC 165 (Ch), at [56] and
[57] per Lawrence Collins J: '[56] The rationale for litigation privilege was said to be that
"... the solicitor is preparing for the defence or for bringing the action, and all communications he makes for that purpose, and the communications made to him for the purpose of
giving him the information, are, in fact, the brief in the action, and ought to be protected"
(*Wheeler v Le Marchant* (1881) 17 Ch D 675, 684–5, per Cotton LJ) or "... as you have no
right to see your adversary's brief, you have no right to see that which comes into existence
merely as materials for the brief" (*Anderson v Bank of British Columbia* (1876) 2 Ch D 644
at 656, per James LJ, cited with approval by Lord Simon of Glaisdale in *Waugh v British
Railways Board* [1980] AC 521, 537). [57] That rationale is not very attractive, and is perhaps ripe for reconsideration in the light of reforms which are designed to make litigation
more open and less like a game of poker. More attractive as a rationale is the consideration
that preparation of a case is inextricably linked with the advice to the client on whether to
fight or to settle, and if so, on what terms.'

[166] For these and other judicial statements on this issue, B Thanki (ed), *The Law of Privilege* (Oxford UP, 2006) 3.110 to 3.129 and in Neil Andrews, *English Civil Procedure* (Oxford UP, 2003) 27.29 to 27.32; as *Zuckerman on Civil Procedure* (2nd edn, 2006) 15.30 and
Thanki (ed), op cit, at 3.88 to 3–90 observe, preparations for trial *by a litigant in person*
should be privileged.

[167] [2005] 1 AC 610; [2004] UKHL 48 at [29], 'I do not ... agree that [litigation privilege is
easily justified] in relation to those documents which although having the requisite degree of
connection with litigation neither constitute nor disclose the seeking or giving of legal advice.'

[168] *(No 2)* [1998] Ch 356, 362–71 (on which see Neil Andrews, *English Civil Procedure*
(Oxford UP, 2003) 27.29 to 27.41). Sir Richard Scott V-C said: '... documents brought into
being by solicitors for the purposes of litigation were afforded privilege because of the light
they might cast on the client's instructions to the solicitor or the solicitor's advice to the client regarding the conduct of the case or of the client's prospects. There was no general privilege that attached to documents brought into existence for the purposes of litigation independent of the need to keep inviolate communications between client and legal adviser. If
documents for which privilege was sought did not relate in some fashion to communications
between client and legal adviser, there was no element of public interest that could override
the ordinary rights of discovery and no privilege. So, for example, an unsolicited communication from a third party, a potential witness, about the facts of the case would not, on this
view, have been privileged. And why should it be? What public interest is served by according privilege to such a communication?'

[169] *ISTIL Group Inc v Zahoor* [2003] 2 All ER 252; [2003] EWHC 165 (Ch), at [57] per

Arguably there is a *via media* between outright abolition of litigation privi- **6.40**
lege and maintaining the present law without modification. The author has
considered that question in detail elsewhere.[170] Zuckerman also supports such
an approach. He has attractively suggested that evidence given at civil trial
should be open to 'probing' beyond the limits currently set.[171] My own conclusion on this point is as follows:[172]

'Root-and-branch abolition of litigation privilege is unjustified. Instead measures [for
details of which, see the next two footnotes] should be taken to promote greater openness or "transparency" in the exchange and presentation of factual[173] or expert[174]
evidence by litigants. These proposed measures would tend to protect the integrity of
witness statements and expert reports by countering the vices of "witness coaching",
"expert shopping", and "interference with experts". These proposed changes would
tighten the rules governing parties' disclosure of expert reports and so restrict opportunity for misleading presentation.'

Lawrence Collins J: 'More attractive as a rationale is the consideration that preparation of a
case is inextricably linked with the advice to the client on whether to fight or to settle, and if
so, on what terms.'

[170] Neil Andrews, *English Civil Justice and Remedies: Progress and Challenges: Nagoya
Lectures* (Shinzan Sha Publishers, Tokyo, 2007) 7.28 to 7.40.

[171] *Zuckerman on Civil Procedure* (2nd edn, 2006) 15.73.

[172] Andrews, *Nagoya Lectures*, ibid, at 7–41.

[173] Andrews, *Nagoya Lectures*, ibid, at 7–39: 'The author suggests that the law should
be changed to require that a "witness statement" must contain the following declaration:
that the witness has not received any assistance in writing the statement; where he has received assistance, he should further state whether this concerned the "contents" or "matters
of spelling, grammar and punctuation"'. For judicial support for a more scrupulous approach to witness statement preparation, see *Aquarius Financial Enterprises Inc v Certain
Underwriters at Lloyd's ('The Delphine')* [2001] 2 Lloyd's Rep 542, at [49], per Toulson J,
cited in S Sugar and R Wilson (eds), *Commercial and Mercantile Courts Litigation Practice*
(2004) 9.27; the Solicitors' Code of Conduct (2007), issued by the Solicitors Regulation Authority: Rule 11.01, Guidance, at point (12)(e), prohibits a solicitor from 'attempting to influence a witness, when taking a statement from that witness, with regard to the contents of
their statement …'

[174] Andrews, *Nagoya Lectures*, ibid, at 7–40: '(1) The instructing party should reveal to
the expert ("the chosen expert"): any previous report or comments received by the instructing party from another expert in connection with the present litigation; the reason why the
instructing party chose not to use any other expert previously instructed to produce a report
with a view to it being used in evidence. (2) The matters mentioned at (1) will become part of
the "range of opinion" which the chosen expert must consider in his report. (3) The chosen
expert must state in his report whether he has received information from the instructing
party for the purpose of (1) above; if so, details should be given; if not, a "nil return" explicitly made. (4) The expert should also state in his report whether he has amended his report,
to satisfy the instructing party's suggestion; if he has, he should indicate whether the change
concerned the content of his report or merely its language and presentation; if the content,
he should give details by reference to specific paragraphs of his report and append the relevant portion of the earlier draft.'

(11) Appendix: Disclosure of Electronic Data[175]

6.41 The English rule currently states:[176]

2A.1 CPR 31.4 contains a broad definition of a document. This extends to electronic documents, including e-mail and other electronic communications, word processed documents and databases. In addition to documents that are readily accessible from computer systems and other electronic devices and media, the definition covers those documents that are stored on servers and back-up systems and electronic documents that have been 'deleted'. It also extends to additional information stored and associated with electronic documents known as metadata.

2A.2 The parties should, prior to the first Case Management Conference, discuss any issues that may arise regarding searches for and the preservation of electronic documents. This may involve the parties providing information about the categories of electronic documents within their control, the computer systems, electronic devices and media on which any relevant documents may be held, the storage systems maintained by the parties and their document retention policies. In the case of difficulty or disagreement, the matter should be referred to a judge for directions at the earliest practical date, if possible at the first Case Management Conference.

2A.3 The parties should co-operate at an early stage as to the format in which electronic copy documents are to be provided on inspection. In the case of difficulty or disagreement, the matter should be referred to a Judge for directions at the earliest practical date, if possible at the first Case Management Conference.

2A.4 The existence of electronic documents impacts upon the extent of the reasonable search required by CPR 31.7 for the purposes of standard disclosure. The factors that may be relevant in deciding the reasonableness of a search for electronic documents include (but are not limited to) the following:
  (a) The number of documents involved.
  (b) The nature and complexity of the proceedings.
  (c) The ease and expense of retrieval of any particular document. This includes:
      (i) The accessibility of electronic documents or data including e-mail communications on computer systems, servers, back-up systems and other electronic devices or media that may contain such documents taking into account alterations or developments in hardware or software systems used by the disclosing party and/or available to enable access to such documents.
      (ii) The location of relevant electronic documents, data, computer systems, servers, back-up systems and other electronic devices or media that may contain such documents.
      (iii) The likelihood of locating relevant data.

---

[175] On this topic, see also **3.22** and **6.04, 6.05**.
[176] PD (31), para 2A.

(iv) The cost of recovering any electronic documents.

(v) The cost of disclosing and providing inspection of any relevant electronic documents.

(vi) The likelihood that electronic documents will be materially altered in the course of recovery, disclosure or inspection.

(d) The significance of any document which is likely to be located during the search.

2A.5 It may be reasonable to search some or all of the parties' electronic storage systems. In some circumstances, it may be reasonable to search for electronic documents by means of keyword searches (agreed as far as possible between the parties) even where a full review of each and every document would be unreasonable. There may be other forms of electronic search that may be appropriate in particular circumstances.

Chapter 7

Expert Evidence

Contents

(1) Introduction[1]

7.01 Experts are needed in the civil process because (as a non-judge has had the temerity to suggest) 'no judge is omniscient' and 'we cannot demand of the judges that they have knowledge of every branch of science, of every art and of the

---

[1] Neil Andrews, *English Civil Procedure* (Oxford UP, 2003) ch 32; L Blom-Cooper (ed), *Experts in Civil Courts* (Oxford UP, 2006); S Burn, *Successful Use of Expert Witnesses in Civil Disputes* (2005); *Cross and Tapper on Evidence* (11th edn, 2007) 578 ff; IR Freckleton, *The Trial of the Expert* (Oxford UP, 1987); T Hodgkinson and M James, *Expert Evidence: Law and Practice* (2nd edn, 2006) (the leading English discussion); C Hollander, *Documentary Evidence* (9th edn, 2006) ch 24; M Iller, *Civil Evidence: the Essential Guide* (2006) ch 12; *Phipson on Evidence* (16th edn, 2005) ch 33; *Zuckerman on Civil Procedure* (2nd edn, 2006) ch 20; other discussion includes, A Edis, 'Privilege and Immunity: Problems of Expert Evidence' (2007) 26 CJQ 40, and DM Dwyer, 'The Duties of Expert Witnesses of Fact and Opinion' (2003) 7 E & P 264; Dwyer, 'Changing Approaches to Expert Evidence in England and Italy' (2003) International Commentary on Evidence (http://www.bepress.com/ice/vol1/iss2/art4/); Dwyer, 'The Effective Management of Bias in Civil Expert Evidence' (2007) 26 CJQ 57; on the history of expert witnesses, L Blom-Cooper (ed), *Experts in Civil Courts* (Oxford UP, 2006) ch 1; DM Dwyer, 'Expert Evidence in the English Civil Courts 1550–1800' Jo of Legal History (forthcoming); T Hodgkinson and M James, *Expert Evidence: Law and Practice* (2nd edn, 2006) 1–009–1–011; see also: Law Reform Committee's 17th Report 'Evidence of Opinion and Expert Evidence' (Cmnd 4489, 1970); Lord Woolf, *Access to Justice, Interim Report* (1995) ch 23, and *Access to Justice, Final Report* (1996) ch 13: both available on-line at: *http://www.dca.gov.uk/civil/reportfr.htm.*

mysteries of every profession.'[2] This chapter concerns expert *witnesses* in English court proceedings[3] (and apart from court assessors)[4] rather than background expert advisors to litigants. Advisory consultation with experts is not covered by the CPR regime, that is, where a litigant obtains an opinion from an expert, but that opinion is not for use as evidence in the case (see further **7.22** below).[5]

The system of expert witnesses has become complex. For convenience, these   **7.02**
are the main points to be discussed in this chapter.

(i) Under the CPR (1998), English law allows matters of expert evidence to be admitted by use of a 'single, joint expert', by party-appointed experts, or by court assessors (see **7.04**).

(ii) All types of expert owe their primary duty to the court (see **7.05**).

(iii) Compared with the system of party-appointed experts, a 'single, joint expert' is more likely to enjoy neutrality and objectivity, and one expert is normally cheaper than two (or more) (see **7.10**).

(iv) However, the major problem with the 'single, joint expert' system (see **7.12** ff) is the danger of inaccuracy. Under this system, a court is invited to rely upon only a single opinion. But experts can be fallible. Therefore, the court must form an independent view, or permit a party to contradict an unsatisfactory single, joint expert's opinion and place before the court an opinion given by a party-appointed expert.

(v) It is submitted that English law is correct to retain the system of party-appointed experts for appropriately difficult types of case, notably large or complex litigation (see **7.18** to **7.20**) or as a 'safety-net' for unsatisfactory 'single, joint expert' evidence in particular cases (see **7.13, 7.14**).

(vi) The court must give permission to present expert evidence, including evidence from party-appointed experts. Normally such permission will be ex-

---

[2] JA Jolowicz, *On Civil Procedure* (Cambridge UP, 2000) 225.

[3] Experts are also important in arbitration; they can be party-appointed, or appointed by the arbitral tribunal; see M Mustill and S Boyd, *Commercial Arbitration* (Companion volume, 2001) 311–2, or J Tackaberry and A Marriott, *Bernstein's Handbook of Arbitration and Dispute Resolution Practice* (4th edn, 2003) 2–845 ff (a perceptive overview): both works also comment on s 37, Arbitration Act 1996 (England, Wales and Northern Ireland), which empowers the tribunal (unless the parties otherwise agree) to appoint 'experts, legal advisers or assessors', but it requires the tribunal to afford the parties opportunity to comment on their reports or opinion; such a tribunal-appointed expert etc can be used to supplement party-appointed expert opinion, *Bernstein's Handbook* 2–858; in arbitration proceedings, instructions to experts are not covered by the CPR regime.

[4] For court assessors, see **7.04**.

[5] eg 'Protocol for the Instruction of Experts to Give Evidence in Civil Claims' (Civil Justice Council, 2005), which supplements CPR Part 35 and PD 35, covers 'steps taken for the purpose of civil proceedings by experts or those who instruct them on or after 5th September 2005', provided the relevant experts are 'governed by Part 35' (see, Protocol, at 5.1); however, it does not cover experts who are not instructed to give evidence 'for the purpose of civil proceedings in a Court in England and Wales'.

pressed by reference to the 'field' of expertise rather than an individual expert (see **7.21**).

(vii) The parties are required to exchange their experts' reports (see **7.24**).

(viii) English courts often require party-appointed experts to conduct 'discussions' and to produce 'joint statements' identifying common ground and points of unbridgeable disagreement (see **7.32** to **7.34**). Such contact between experts can enable the parties to reach a settlement and so avoid trial, or at least permit them to narrow the issues in dispute and so reduce costs.

(ix) Witnesses, including experts, enjoy immunity from civil liability in tort or contract for negligence, fraud, or defamation (see **7.35**, **7.36**); but not immunity from professional disciplinary proceedings (see **7.37**). Expert witnesses, however, can be rendered liable for 'wasted costs' caused by their 'gross dereliction of duty' (see **7.38**).

(2) The CPR System's Aims Concerning Experts

7.03 The CPR aims to curb the perceived excesses of the party-appointed 'battle of experts'. The three problems experienced before the CPR system were: first, the tendency for expert witnesses hired by a litigant to lose objectivity and tailor their report to suit that party's case; secondly, the need to control the number of experts involved in a particular case, especially with a view to achieving proportionality between their use and the case's value or importance;[6] thirdly, the need to promote 'equality of arms' between rich and poor parties. Under the CPR system the main rule is that no expert evidence can be presented in a case unless the court has granted permission (see **7.21** below).[7] This control is a facet of the court's case management powers.[8]

7.04 Under the CPR, there are three ways in which the ordinary civil courts can receive expert opinion: by a 'single, joint expert', party-appointed experts, and court assessors.[9] These will be introduced in turn in the ensuing discussion.

---

[6] CPR 35.1 states: 'Expert evidence shall be restricted to that which is reasonably required to resolve the proceedings.'

[7] CPR 35.4(1) to (3).

[8] Generally on case management, see **3.13**.

[9] The decision-making members of the relevant tribunal might themselves be 'expert': cf the constitution of Coroners Courts, medical appeal tribunals, etc. This specialisation is not available amongst the ordinary judiciary.

(3) Roles of the Court and the Expert(s)

All expert witnesses in civil proceedings owe a duty to the court 'to help the court on the matters within his expertise'.[10] This duty 'to help the court' overrides any obligation owed by the expert to the instructing party.[11] In short, experts must exercise independent judgement. They must not become the pawns of litigants. Nor should they become attached to their own dogmas. **7.05**

An expert can file a written request to the court for 'directions to assist him in carrying out his function as an expert'.[12] Because they enjoy direct access to the court in this manner, this rule elevates expert witnesses into a higher category of witness. So far, however, experts have seldom sought such direct contact.[13] The expert's report must 'contain a statement that the expert understands his duty to the court, and has complied with that duty'.[14] The expert has been styled a 'quasi-officer of the court', who can be ordered to pay the other side's wasted costs if his opinion is wrong or exaggerated as a result of reckless or gross dereliction of his duty (see **7.38** below).[15] In his report, the expert must sign a special 'statement of truth' (see also **7.26** below): 'I confirm that insofar as the facts stated in my report are within my own knowledge I have made clear which they are and that I believe them to be true, and that the opinions I have expressed represent my true and complete professional opinion.'[16] **7.06**

The leading textbook distinguishes four categories of expert evidence, although the expert might give evidence under more than one of these heads: 'opinion on facts adduced before the court'; '[evidence] to explain technical **7.07**

---

[10] CPR 35.3(1); in *Anglo Group plc, Winther Brown & Co Ltd v Winter Brown & Co Ltd, BML (Office Computers) Ltd, Anglo Group plc, BML (Office Computers) Ltd* [2000] EWHC Technology 127 (8th March, 2000) at [108] to [110], Judge Toulmin QC, summarised '*The Ikarian Reefer*' guidelines ('*The Ikarian Reefer*' [1993] 2 Lloyds Rep 68, at 81–2, per Cresswell J); Judge Toulmin added: 'It is clear from the Judgment of Lord Woolf MR in *Stevens v Gullis* [2000] 1 All ER 527, CA that the new Civil Procedure Rules underline the existing duty which an expert owes to the Court as well as to the party which he represents'; T Hodgkinson and M James, *Expert Evidence: Law and Practice* (2nd edn, 2006) 7–005 helpfully present a 14 point enumeration of the elements of this duty; and on the expert's duty to the court, L Blom-Cooper (ed), *Experts in Civil Courts* (Oxford UP, 2006) ch 11.

[11] Or duty owed to 'the instructing parties', in the case of a 'single, joint witness' under CPR 35.7(2); or 'any obligation' owed by the expert to the person 'by whom [the expert] is paid'); see CPR 35.3.

[12] CPR 35.14(1).

[13] Master John Leslie, Queen's Bench Division, states (2007) that he has only encountered two instances since April 1999; in one case the problem arose between a litigant in person and his appointed expert.

[14] CPR 35.10(2).

[15] *Phillips v Symes (No 2)* [2005] 1 WLR 2043, Peter Smith J.

[16] PD (35), para 2.4; para 2.5 refers to the consequences of making a false statement – contempt of court, on which see **8.35**.

subjects or technical words'; 'evidence of fact only observable, comprehensible, or open to description by experts'; 'admissible hearsay of a specialist nature'.[17] The Civil Justice Council's Protocol (on Experts) states that experts should be capable of 'addressing questions of fact and opinion', even 'material facts in dispute', but it exhorts experts to keep issues of fact and opinion 'separate and discrete'.[18] The following indicates the range of possible topics: 'is the claimant suffering from illness X?'; 'is it likely that the relevant collision would have caused injury to Y?'; 'what are the chances of P recovering fully from this injury, and when?'; 'is this manner of accounting recognised as good practice amongst the British accounting profession?'; 'what is the range of rents for this type of property in this district of London, if the property is subject to these planning restrictions?' Expertise can be focused, therefore, upon past, present or future physical events or states or matters of social perception ('what is professionally acceptable in this context?').[19]

7.08   It is established that the court has the ultimate say on matters of expertise. Brooke LJ recently approved the remark that 'We do not have trial by expert in this country; we have trial by judge.'[20] This comment encapsulates two interrelated points: (i) experts are not infallible; (ii) the judge is the final arbiter; he must not delegate to others his fact-finding and evaluative power; if ultimate decision-making were ceded to the expert, this would involve a 'usurpation [by the expert] of the constitutional function of the judge'.[21]

7.09   The court should give a reason for preferring one expert's evidence to another's,[22] or for not acting on a single, joint expert's opinion (see further,

---

[17] T Hodgkinson and M James, *Expert Evidence: Law and Practice* (2nd edn, 2006) 1–012, 2–006; adding that sometimes an expert can refer to facts as a necessary preliminary to his expert evidence.

[18] 'Protocol for the Instruction of Experts to Give Evidence in Civil Claims' (Civil Justice Council, 2005) 13.9 to 13.11.

[19] For discussion of this range, see Law Reform Committee's 17th Report, 'Evidence of Opinion and Expert Evidence' (Cmnd 4489, 1970) pp 1 ff; JA Jolowicz, *On Civil Procedure* (Cambridge UP, 2000), 224–5; PL Murray and R Stürner, *German Civil Justice* (Durham, USA, 2004) 280–2; in *Morgan Chase Bank v Springwell Navigation Corporation* [2006] EWHC 2755 (Comm), Aikens J noted, at [30] to [32], that expert evidence will not be admissible from a lawyer on construction of commercial contracts which are subject to English law; this is a question of (English) law for the court; unless the parties have used technical expressions outside the expertise of the judge; eg, *Kingscroft Insurance Co Ltd v Nissan Fire & Marine Insurance Co Ltd (No 2)* [1999] Lloyd's Insurance and Reinsurance Reports, 603 at 622, per Moore-Bick J.

[20] *Armstrong v First York Ltd* [2005] 1 WLR 2751, CA; [2005] EWCA Civ 277 at [28], approving *Liddell v Middleton* [1996] PIQR P36 at p 43.

[21] Law Reform Committee's 17th Report, 'Evidence of Opinion and Expert Evidence' (Cmnd 4489, 1970) p 5.

[22] Generally on judicial reasons and compliance with Art 6(1) of the European Convention on Human Rights and for a survey of the English case law, Neil Andrews, *English Civil Procedure* (Oxford UP, 2003) 5.39 ff.

on the latter possibility, **7.15** below). But although the judge cannot remain mute, nor even monosyllabic, he need not become loquacious. His explanation need not be technical.[23] Some tolerance is discernible.[24] It is enough to say, for example, that expert Y seemed to be more 'cogent' or 'persuasive' than expert X, other than simply the burden of proof.[25] This approach seems to be justified for two reasons. First, it is unrealistic to expect judges to provide elaborate ratiocination on arcane and technical matters. Secondly, often a judge's preference for one side's expert is a matter of well-educated 'impression'.

(4) The 'Single, Joint Expert' System

In relatively straightforward claims, or peripheral matters in large litigation,[26] the expert will be a 'single, joint expert', appointed to act for both parties.[27] The parties can agree on the relevant individual, failing which the court can select him from lists supplied or agreed by the parties.[28] The parties share the   **7.10**

---

[23] Arden LJ in *Armstrong v First York Ltd* [2005] 1 WLR 2751, CA at [33], noting the leading decision *English v Emery Reimbold and Strick* [2002] 1 WLR 2409, CA at [20] (in the *English* case the CA stated at [20] that the judge should 'simply provide an explanation as to why he has accepted the evidence of one expert and rejected that of another. It may be that the evidence of one or the other accorded more satisfactorily with facts found by the Judge. It may be that the explanation of one was more inherently credible than that of the other. It may simply be that one was better qualified, or manifestly more objective, than the other. Whatever the explanation may be, it should be apparent from the judgment.' And at [21] it said: 'The essential requirement is that the terms of the judgment should enable the parties and any appellate tribunal readily to analyse the reasoning that was essential to the Judge's decision.'

[24] *DN v London Borough of Greenwich* [2004] EWCA Civ 1659, at [28] to [30], where the Court of Appeal was unimpressed by the judge's statement of reasons on a point of rival expert opinion, but declined to order a new trial.

[25] For a judge's unjustified resort to the burden of proof to resolve a conflict of expert evidence: *Stephens v Cannon* [2005] EWCA Civ 222; CP Rep 31.

[26] Sometimes proportionality will justify use of a 'single, joint expert' on a relatively short issue which forms only a part of a more substantial litigation; for example, the quantification of liability in an action for professional negligence against a defendant accountant might be the subject of a single, joint expert's report, but the (prior) question of liability might be the subject of party-appointed experts; I am grateful to Master John Leslie, Queen's Bench Division, for this observation.

[27] L Blom-Cooper (ed), *Experts in Civil Courts* (Oxford UP, 2006) ch 5; T Hodgkinson and M James, *Expert Evidence: Law and Practice* (2nd edn, 2006) ch 5; as CPR 35.7 mentions, this presupposes that more than one party wishes to adduce expert evidence on a particular issue.

[28] I am grateful to Master John Leslie, Queen's Bench Division, for the following insight into this practice: 'If the parties cannot agree on a 'single, joint expert', I direct that they are to exchange the CVs of three (or some other number) experts, each party listing them in their order of preference; that they are then to send in written reasons as to why they do not

cost of the expert.[29] Each party has an opportunity to instruct the expert and to ask written questions. Such an expert should not communicate, meet, or discuss the case or his evidence with one party, independently of the opponent.[30]

7.11   The single, joint expert's report must summarise any 'range of opinion' on the relevant issue and give reasons for preferring the view adopted.[31] Although, in the interest of economy,[32] the courts at first expressed a strong disinclination to hear oral evidence from such an expert, the Court of Appeal has since confirmed that a court can give permission for a 'single, joint expert' to be cross-examined.[33]

7.12   The 'single, joint expert' system carries the risk of inaccuracy.[34] This is because the court receives no adversarial debate. It might find itself beguiled by the single, joint expert's opinion. It might be sceptical but have no means of ventilating its doubts. The fact that this is the only expert opinion at first available, and the danger that it might be inaccurate and so mislead the decision-maker, explain the English courts' willingness, in appropriate circumstances, to allow such evidence to be challenged by resort to party-appointed experts (see the limiting factors mentioned in at **7.13, 7.14,** as well as the court's ultimate power not to act on a single, expert's opinion, **7.15**).

7.13   The test for supplementing evidence submitted by a 'single joint expert' is as follows. The court will give permission for a party to adduce supplementary party-appointed expert evidence if (i) that party can show reasons which are 'not fanciful' for supplementing the 'single, joint expert' report; (ii) use of a par-

---

accept the opponent's proposed experts and why they say that their own are to be preferred and justifying their order of preference.'

[29] A cheaper 'single, joint expert' might be appointed, if the more expensive expert's fees are disproportionate to the case's value: *Kranidotes v Paschali* [2001] EWCA Civ 357; [2001] CP Rep 81; T Hodgkinson and M James, *Expert Evidence: Law and Practice* (2nd edn, 2006) 4–018.

[30] *Peet v Mid-Kent Care Healthcare Trust* [2002] 1 WLR 210 at [24]: see also 'Protocol for the Instruction of Experts to Give Evidence in Civil Claims' (Civil Justice Council, 2005), at 17.12.

[31] PD (35), para 2.2(6).

[32] *Daniels v Walker* [2000] 1 WLR 1382, 1388 A, CA, where Lord Woolf admitted that cross-examination of a single, joint evidence is a possibility; similarly, *Peet v Mid-Kent Care Healthcare Trust* [2002] 1 WLR 210, at [28], per Lord Woolf CJ.

[33] *R v R* [2002] EWCA Civ 409 at [14] to [18], per Ward LJ; L Blom-Cooper (ed), *Experts in Civil Courts* (Oxford UP, 2006) 5.37 to 5.39 noting also remarks in *Popel v National Westminster Bank plc* [2002] EWCA Civ 42, [2002] CPLR 370, at [28] and [29], per Dyson LJ, and *Austen v Oxfordshire CC* [2002] All D 97 (CA); 17 April 2002 (noting that it is settled law that where a single expert has been appointed, there is no general need for that expert's evidence to be amplified by oral evidence or tested in cross-examination; but the Court of Appeal said that the court might permit cross-examination where the need arose; in the unusual circumstances of this case, cross-examination was allowed).

[34] DM Dwyer, 'The Effective Management of Bias in Civil Expert Evidence' (2007) 26 CJQ 57, 78.

ty-appointed experts will not result in disproportionate costs; (iii) the party who seeks the court's permission to adduce additional expert evidence will be expected already to have asked written questions of the expert and to have received manifestly unsatisfactory answers.[35]

The approach just explained was established in *Daniels v Walker* (2000).[36] It **7.14** was soon refined in *Peet v Mid-Kent Healthcare Trust* (2002).[37] Lord Woolf CJ there noted that Part One of the CPR ('the Overriding Objective') is relevant. CPR Part One's broad procedural 'directives' ensure that the courts must be constantly mindful of the need for 'proportionality' and expedition, at the same time taking into account still broader questions of fairness (which must include the search for accurate decisions).[38]

---

[35] Practice reported to author by Master John Leslie, Queen's Bench Division.

[36] [2000] 1 WLR 1382 CA; Neil Andrews, *English Civil Procedure* (Oxford UP, 2003) 32.68 to 32.74; see also *Cosgrove v Pattison* [2001] CP Rep 68; *The Times* 13 February 2001, Neuberger J, on which S Burn and B Thompson in L Blom-Cooper (ed), *Experts in Civil Courts* (Oxford UP, 2006) 5.21; Neuberger J suggested eight factors, and then allowed a second expert's report to be adduced; the latter had already become involved in the case; there would be no delay; his eight factors are: (i) nature of the dispute; (ii) number of issues requiring expertise; (iii) reasons for requiring second expert; (iv) amount and number of issues at stake; (v) possible impact of second expert on conduct of trial; (vi) possible delay caused; (vii) special features; (viii) overall justice to the parties; on this last aspect, resting on the 'Overriding Objective' in CPR Part 1, see the discussion in *Stallwood v David* [2006] EWHC 2600 (QB); [2007] 1 All ER 206, Teare J (on which see **7.34** below, concerning permission to call a new expert after a meeting of experts) (case noted A Zuckerman (2007) 26 CJQ 159); Teare J said: [32] 'In *Cosgrove v Pattison* ... Neuberger J ... considered the approach to be followed when a party who was dissatisfied with the report of a single joint expert might be granted permission to adduce evidence from another expert ... .He listed a number of factors to be taken into account, the last two of which were any special features of the case and the overall justice of the case. In considering the overall justice of the case he asked himself two questions which he thought were of help. The first was, if the applicant was not entitled to call the additional evidence sought and lost the case would he have an understandable sense of grievance judged objectively and the second was, if the applicant was entitled to call the additional evidence and won the case would the respondent have an understandable sense of grievance judged objectively. It was submitted that I should follow that approach in this case. [33] Although Neuberger J was dealing with a case in which a single joint expert had been instructed and I am not, the Court must always have regard to the overriding objective to deal with the case justly and in that regard the approach of Neuberger J is apposite.'

[37] [2002] 1 WLR 210, CA, at [28]; his Lordship emphasised that these matters of discretion are governed by the 'Overriding Objective' in CPR Part 1; this discretion applies to the following issues: whether to use such an expert; whether to allow further clarification of his report by written answers beyond the 'once only' scope of CPR 35.6(2); whether to supplement his report by appointing party-nominated experts; and whether to allow a 'single, joint expert' to appear and be cross-examined at trial; this discretion is emphasised at [14] of the *Peet* case.

[38] [2002] 1 WLR 210, CA, at [28]; his Lordship emphasised that these matters of discretion are governed by the 'Overriding Objective' in CPR Part 1; this discretion applies to the following issues: whether to use such an expert; whether to allow further clarification of his report by written answers beyond the 'once only' scope of CPR 35.6(2); whether to supple-

7.15   In most cases the court will adopt the 'single joint expert', but a judge can reject it if it appears to be unsound. As the Civil Justice Council's Protocol states: 'It is for the court to determine the facts.'[39] The Court of Appeal affirmed this point in *Armstrong v First York Ltd* (2005), where Brooke LJ said: 'we do not have trial by expert in this country; we have trial by judge' (see also below).[40] The Court of Appeal held that the court is likely to adopt the 'single, joint expert' report when it is the only evidence on a matter of a technical nature, such as the valuation of a property.[41] However, it noted that the trial judge is not bound by an expert's opinion, even that of a single, joint expert, when it contradicts the factual evidence given by one party. The judge can here decide to prefer the party's factual evidence, even if the same judge lacks the technical capacity to repudiate the expert's evidence.[42]

(5) Court Assessors[43]

7.16   Assessors are mainly used in cases concerning maritime collisions, some patent litigation, and occasional appeals concerning technical questions of costs. Thus English courts have not adopted this model of court-annexed 'expertise' for all types of technical issues. By contrast, in civilian systems, court-appointed experts are used extensively. Indeed several such regimes might operate within each jurisdiction.[44] In England the assessor's task is to advise the judge on the evaluation of disputed matters of fact. For example, it has been said: 'The nautical assessor's function is to enlarge the field of matters of which the judge

---

ment his report by appointing party-nominated experts; and whether to allow a 'single, joint expert' to appear and be cross-examined at trial; this discretion is emphasised at [14] of the *Peet* case.

   [39] 'Protocol for the Instruction of Experts to Give Evidence in Civil Claims' (Civil Justice Council, 2005), at 17.14; this document, which does not have the force of law, ibid, at 2.1, supplements CPR Part 35 and PD 35.

   [40] Brooke LJ in *Armstrong v First York Ltd* [2005] 1 WLR 2751, CA; [2005] EWCA Civ 277 at [28], approving a comment in *Liddell v Middleton* [1996] PIQR P36 at 43.

   [41] [2005] 1 WLR 2751, CA; [2005] EWCA Civ 277.

   [42] For other cases on this topic: *Jakto Transport v Derek Hall* [2005] EWCA Civ 1327; *Montracon v Whalley* [2005] EWCA Civ 1383; *Montoya v Hackney LBC* (unreported).

   [43] CPR 35.15; PD (35) 7.1 to 7.4; see the observations of Lord Bingham in T Bingham, *The Business of Judging* (Oxford UP, 2000) 19–24; Neil Andrews, *English Civil Procedure* (Oxford UP, 2003) 32–76 to 32–77; L Blom-Cooper (ed), *Experts in Civil Courts* (Oxford UP, 2006) ch 8; DM Dwyer, 'The Future of Assessors under the CPR' (2006) 25 CJQ 219; T Hodgkinson and M James, *Expert Evidence: Law and Practice* (2nd edn, 2006) ch 5.

   [44] JA Jolowicz, *On Civil Procedure* (Cambridge UP, 2000) ch 12; L Cadiet et E Jeuland, *Droit Judiciare Privé* (4th edn, Litec, Paris, 2004) 454 ff; PL Murray and R Stürner, *German Civil Justice* (Durham, USA, 2004) 280 ff.

may take judicial notice so as to include matters of navigation and general seamanship.[45]

Assessors' advice must be disclosed to the parties. After the parties have had their say, it would be wrong for assessors to retire with the judge to present further comment. To do so would infringe the right of the parties to contradict all relevant issues or matters of opinion.[46]

7.17

(6) Party-Appointed Experts: A Common Law Tradition

In complex or relatively large claims, each party will seek permission to appoint his own expert or experts (see further **7.21** below). If permission is granted, the court will also order the parties to exchange their reports (see further **7.24** below). Although party-appointed experts are required to be impartial and must acknowledge that their overriding duty is to the court (**7.05**), it has often been observed or suspected that their evidence might be tailored to suit the appointing party. As Lord Bingham (as he now is) commented in a 1996 decision: 'For whatever reason, and whether consciously or unconsciously, the fact is that expert witnesses instructed on behalf of parties to litigation often tend, if called as witnesses at all, to espouse the cause of those instructing them to a greater or lesser extent, on occasion becoming more partisan than the parties.'[47]

7.18

But the problem of lack of neutrality is easily exaggerated. It should be recalled that the court has the final say (**7.15**). The party-appointed expert system injects often salutary scepticism, debate, even 'intellectual honesty', into the process of taking a 'view' on debatable matters of opinion. This is acknowledged in Professor Hazard Jr's comment in the American Law Institute/UNIDROIT's *Principles of Transnational Civil Procedure*:[48]

7.19

'... Court appointment of a neutral expert is the practice in most civil-law systems and in some common-law systems. However, party-appointed experts can provide valuable assistance in the analysis of difficult factual issues. Fear that party appointment

---

[45] Law Reform Committee's 17th Report, 'Evidence of Opinion and Expert Evidence' (Cmnd 4489, 1970) p 6.

[46] *Owners of the Ship Bow Spring* [2005] 1 WLR 144, CA.

[47] Sir Thomas Bingham MR in *Abbey National Mortgages plc v Key Surveyors Ltd* [1996] 1 WLR 1534, 1542, CA (a pre-CPR case concerning appointment of a court expert under the old RSC Ord 40); on the question of party expert partiality and the question of transparency, besides discussion elsewhere in this book of litigation privilege and party-appointed experts, see A Edis, 'Privilege and Immunity: Problems of Expert Evidence' (2007) 26 CJQ 40, and DM Dwyer, 'The Effective Management of Bias in Civil Expert Evidence' (2007) 26 CJQ 57.

[48] Principle 22.4; accessible at: http://www.unidroit.org/english/principles/civilprocedure/main.htm. Also published as *ALI/UNIDROIT: Principles of Transnational Civil Procedure* (Cambridge UP, 2006).

of experts will devolve into a "battle of experts" and thereby obscure the issues is generally misplaced. In any event, this risk is offset by the value of such evidence ...'

7.20 Certainly, many English litigation lawyers wish to retain the party-appointed expert system in order to exert some influence over issues of expertise. As Lord Bingham has commented:

'The [English] neglect of court experts is ... explicable. The chances and changes of litigation are formidable enough as it is, but parties do at least feel able (sometimes ... mistakenly) to rely with confidence on their expert saying what he has committed himself to say. They are naturally reluctant to forgo this assurance for an independent expert whom they do not engage, do not directly pay, cannot decline to call if his opinion is entirely hostile and cannot, perhaps, cross-examine so effectively.'[49]

Furthermore, Lord Woolf in his 1996 report on the civil justice system said that

'in large and strongly contested cases the full adversarial system, including oral cross-examination of opposing experts, is the best way of producing a result. That will apply particularly to issues on which there are several tenable schools of thought, or where the boundaries of knowledge are being extended.'[50]

We now consider the party-appointed expert system in greater detail.

(7) Selection and Approval of Party-Appointed Expert Witnesses

7.21 In large claims (or complicated 'middling actions'), it will be inappropriate to use a 'single, joint expert'. Instead each party will seek permission from the court to use his own expert or experts as a witness in the case. The court's permission will be expressed either in relation to 'the expert named' or 'the field identified'.[51] If permission exists to call a 'named' expert, that party must obtain the court's further permission to substitute another expert.[52] But such further permission will be conditional on that party's disclosing the first expert's

[49] T Bingham, *The Business of Judging* (Oxford UP, 2000) 23 (Lord Bingham).

[50] Lord Woolf, *Access to Justice: Final Report* (1996) ch 13, at [19].

[51] CPR 35.4(2); generally on 'court management' of experts, L Blom-Cooper (ed), *Experts in Civil Courts* (2006) ch 4; in *Morgan Chase Bank v Springwell Navigation Corporation* [2006] EWHC 2755 (Comm) Aikens J noted, at [30] to [32], that expert evidence will not be admissible from a lawyer on construction of commercial contracts (subject to English law); this is a question of law for the court; unless the parties have used technical expressions outside the expertise of the judge; eg, *Kingscroft Insurance Co Ltd v Nissan Fire & Marine Insurance Co Ltd (No 2)* [1999] Lloyd's Insurance and Reinsurance Reports page 603 at 622, per Moore-Bick J.

[52] *Vasiliou v Hajigeorgiou* [2005] EWCA Civ 236; [2005] 1 WLR 2195, CA: applying *Beck v Ministry of Defence* [2003] EWCA Civ 1043; [2005] 1 WLR 2206 (note), even though in the *Beck* case the relevant order had not mentioned an expert by name.

report.[53] 'Transparency' can then be achieved. However, this condition cannot be imposed if permission has been expressed in terms of a 'field' of expertise.[54] In that situation, there is no check upon so-called 'expert shopping'.

The CPR covers only experts who give evidence, or prepare to do so.[55] A **7.22** litigant can *consult* (as distinct from adducing civil evidence from) any number of experts without seeking the court's permission.[56] But the experts' fees for such consultation will not be recoverable as costs in the action. However, such consultation with experts will be covered by litigation privilege, provided the 'dominant' purpose of such consultation was to assist in preparing the pending or contemplated civil case (**7.30**). But one cannot pre-emptively buy up experts. There is 'no property in a witness', whether the witness is a potential expert or a layperson (a 'witness of fact').[57] Furthermore, the CPR provides: 'where a party has disclosed an expert's report, any party may use that expert's report as evidence at the trial.'[58]

The expert selected should be: competent,[59] available,[60] and free from any **7.23** potential conflict of interest.[61] It is improper to pay an expert witness on a con-

---

[53] *Vasiliou* case (applying *Beck* case) ibid.

[54] *Vasiliou* case, ibid considering CPR 35.4(2)(a); eg, in a recent High Court case involving very severe brain injury, assessment of the claimant's mental capacity to conduct the litigation without Court of Protection direction was assessed by six experts: two neurologists, two neuro-psychologists, two neuro-psychiatrists; I am grateful to Master John Leslie, Queen's Bench Division, for this illustration.

[55] Thus CPR 35.2 provides: 'a reference to an "expert" in this Part is a reference to an expert who has been instructed to give or prepare evidence for the purpose of court proceedings.' Nor does the 'Protocol for the Instruction of Experts to Give Evidence in Civil Claims' (Civil Justice Council, 2005) cover advisory consultation with experts, for example, where a litigant obtains confidential comments from an expert on a single, joint expert's report: ibid, at 5.2; T Hodgkinson and M James, *Expert Evidence: Law and Practice* (2nd edn, 2006) 4–011.

[56] *Vasiliou v Hajigeorgiou* [2005] 1 WLR 2195, CA, at [20].

[57] *Harmony Shipping Co SA v Davis* [1979] 1 WLR 1380, 1384–5, CA, per Lord Denning MR: 'The reason is because the court has a right to every man's evidence. Its primary duty is to ascertain the truth. Neither one side nor the other can debar the court from ascertaining the truth either by seeing a witness beforehand or by purchasing his evidence or by making communication with him.'

[58] CPR 35.11.

[59] On the question of 'accreditation' and 'training', L Blom-Cooper (ed), *Experts in Civil Courts* (Oxford UP, 2006) chs 2, 12.

[60] A party should not instruct an expert who would be unavailable at the trial, because this will cause unacceptable disruption and delay, N Madge in L Blom-Cooper (ed), *Experts in Civil Courts* (Oxford UP, 2006) 4.33, noting *Rollison v Kimberly Clark* [2001] EWCA Civ 1456; [2002] CP Rep 10.

[61] 'Protocol for the Instruction of Experts to Give Evidence in Civil Claims' (Civil Justice Council, 2005) 7.1; cf *Akai Holdings Limited (in compulsory liquidation) v RSM Robson Rhodes LLP and Another [2007] EWHC 1641, Briggs J (RSM RR contractually bound to provide expert advice to applicant in pending civil litigation; in present case, interim injunction sought to restrain RSM RR, accountancy firm, from merging with applicant's*

ditional or contingency fee basis.[62] He should not have any close connection
with the appointing party or persons involved in the case. Admittedly, perhaps
in the interest of economy, some decisions have permitted expert evidence to
be received from a party's employee. But the employee's manifest lack of independence will reduce the weight of his evidence.[63]

(8) Disclosure of Expert Reports

7.24   Expert evidence must be given in a written report, unless the court directs
otherwise.[64] Pre-trial disclosure of a party's expert report is also a condition
for use of that expert: a party 'may not use the report at the trial or call the
expert to give evidence orally unless the court gives permission' (see further
7.28 below).[65]

7.25   The rules prescribe the form of the expert's report.[66] He must give details of
his qualifications in his report.[67] He should not exceed his field of expertise.[68]
If he does, he should make this clear.[69] The expert must provide: 'details of any
literature or other material which the expert has relied on in making the
report';[70] additionally, he must 'summarise the range of opinion and give rea-

---

*defendant (GT) in those pending proceedings; prospect of conflict of interest; injunction
granted).*

[62] *R (Factortame Ltd) v Secretary of State for the Environment, Transport and the Regions (No 8)* [2003] QB 381, CA; [2002] EWCA Civ 932 at [54], [57], [87], [90], [91], per
Lord Phillips MR; but an expert not acting as witness can validly agree a percentage return
for litigation support: *Mansell v Robinson* (QBD 31 January 2007, All England Reporter).

[63] *Field v Leeds CC* [2000] 1 EGLR 54 CA; *R (Factortame Ltd) v Secretary of State for
the Environment, Transport and the Regions (No 8)* [2003] QB 381, CA; [2002] EWCA Civ
932, at [70]; on which, Neil Andrews, *English Civil Procedure* (Oxford UP, 2003) 32.43 to
32.45; T Hodgkinson and M James, *Expert Evidence: Law and Practice* (2nd edn, 2006)
1–030 and DM Dwyer, 'The Effective Management of Bias in Civil Expert Evidence' (2007)
26 CJQ 57.

[64] CPR 35.5; generally on expert reports, L Blom-Cooper (ed), *Experts in Civil Courts*
(Oxford UP, 2006) ch 6.

[65] CPR 35.13.

[66] CPR 35.10 and PD (35) 2.2; see also 'Protocol for the Instruction of Experts to Give
Evidence in Civil Claims' (Civil Justice Council, 2005) at 13.

[67] PD (35), 2.2(1) for the latter requirement.

[68] The need for such delineation of his legitimate field of comment is made clear in: (1)
section 3(1), Civil Evidence Act 1972 ('... where a person is called as a witness in any civil
proceedings, his opinion on any relevant matter on which he is qualified to give expert evidence shall be admissible in evidence'); and (2) CPR 35.3.1, referring to an expert's evidence
on: '... matters within his expertise'.

[69] PD (35) 1.5(a); for such a failure in the criminal context, see *Meadow v General Medical Council* [2006] EWCA Civ 1390; [2007] 2 WLR 286, discussed below at **7.37**.

[70] PD (35) 2.2(2).

sons for his own opinion';[71] finally, 'if the expert is not able to give his opinion without qualification, [he must] state the qualification'.[72]

The expert's report must 'contain a statement that the expert understands **7.26** his duty to the court, and has complied with that duty'.[73] Because his report can cover both matters of fact and, of course, opinion, the rules prescribe a special 'statement of truth':

'I confirm that insofar as the facts stated in my report are within my own knowledge I have made clear which they are and that I believe them to be true, and that the opinions I have expressed represent my true and complete professional opinion.'[74]

As for amendment at the instructing party's request, the Civil Justice Council's **7.27** Protocol states:

'experts should not be asked to, and should not, amend, expand, or alter any parts of reports in a manner which distorts their true opinion, but may be invited to amend or expand reports to ensure accuracy, internal consistency, completeness and relevance to the issues and clarity.'[75]

The court's order can be for simultaneous or sequential disclosure of reports **7.28** by the opposing parties.[76] Disclosure is confined to 'the expert's intended evidence'. It does not extend to 'earlier and privileged drafts of what might or might not become the expert's evidence', unless the final report is 'on its face' a 'partial or incomplete document'.[77] Parties can pose written questions for the attention of the other side's expert witness or the single, joint witness.[78] Answers become part of the main report.[79]

'The expert's report must state the *substance of all material instructions*, **7.29** whether written or oral, on the basis of which the report was written.'[80] 'Instructions' include 'material supplied by the instructing party to the expert as

---

[71] ibid, 2.2(6).

[72] ibid, 2.2(8).

[73] CPR 35.10(2).

[74] PD (35) 2.4; PD (35) 2.5 notes that making a false statement involves contempt of court: see **8.35**.

[75] 'Protocol for the Instruction of Experts to Give Evidence in Civil Claims' (Civil Justice Council, 2005) 15.2.

[76] Normally the exchange is simultaneous; but fairness and clarity might sometimes justify sequential disclosure: T Hodgkinson and M James, *Expert Evidence: Law and Practice* (2nd edn, 2006) 4–020.

[77] *Jackson v Marley Davenport Ltd* [2004] 1 WLR 2926, CA, at [14] and [18]; Longmore LJ commented at [18]: '... it would in my view be a retrogression and not an advance in our law if earlier reports of experts, upon which they did not intend to rely, had to be routinely disclosed before they could give evidence.'

[78] See PD (35) 5.1 to 5.3.

[79] CPR 35.6(3).

[80] CPR 35.10(3).

the basis on which the expert is being asked to advise'.[81] But a summary of these 'instructions' will do: 'The only obligation on the expert is to set out "material instructions".'[82] These do not include material lying behind a written summary presented to the expert and containing 'assumed facts'.[83]

7.30   A litigant, or prospective litigant, enjoys 'litigation privilege' in communications between him (or his lawyer) and a prospective expert if the communication is confidential and made for the dominant purpose of use in, or preparation for, criminal or civil litigation[84] which is in reasonable prospect (on that head of privilege, see also **6.36** ff).[85] There is an exception to litigation privilege if the communication was intended to further or facilitate a crime or fraud, even if the lawyer acts in good faith.[86] It is possible that communications between an instructing party and an expert might fall within this exception to litigation privilege.[87] However, the cases so far reported have concerned per-

---

[81] *Lucas v Barking, Havering and Redbridge Hospitals NHS Trust* [2003] EWCA Civ 1102; [2004] 1 WLR 220, at [34].

[82] ibid, at [36], per Waller LJ.

[83] *Morris v Bank of India* (unreported, 15 Nov 2001, Chancery), Hart J; on which Neil Andrews, *English Civil Procedure* (Oxford UP, 2003) 32.51 to 31.56; and comments in *Lucas v Barking, Havering and Redbridge Hospitals NHS Trust* [2003] EWCA Civ 1102; [2004] 1 WLR 220, at [8].

[84] See, for example, *Carlson v Townsend* [2001] 1 WLR 2415, CA; *Jackson v Marley Davenport Ltd* [2004] 1 WLR 2926, CA, at [13], [14], [22], cited in *Vasiliou v Hajigeorgiou* [2005] 1 WLR 2195, CA, at [28].

[85] On this last element, *USA v Philip Morris* [2004] EWCA Civ 330.

[86] *Kuwait Airways Corpn v Iraqi Airways Corp* [2005] EWCA Civ 286; [2005] 1 WLR 2734, at [42], where Longmore LJ concluded: '(1) the fraud exception can apply where there is a claim to litigation privilege as much as where there is a claim to legal advice privilege; (2) nevertheless it can only be used in cases in which the issue of fraud is one of the issues in the action where there is a strong (I would myself use the words "very strong") prima facie case of fraud as there was in *Dubai Aluminium v Al-Alawi* [1999] 1 WLR 1964, 1969–1970, Rix J [claimant's agents criminally impersonating defendants in order to gain access to banking details], and there was not in *Chandler v Church* (1987) 137 NLJ 451, Hoffmann J; (3) where the issue of fraud is not one of the issues in the action, a prima facie case of fraud may be enough as in *R (Hallinan Blackburn Gittings and Nott) v Crown Court at Middlesex Guildhall* [2004] EWHC 2726 (Admin); [2005] 1 WLR 766, DC.' In the *Kuwait* case, the defendant had committed perjury 'on a remarkable and unprecedented scale' (see [40]) and there was clear evidence of this; this destroyed litigation privilege in communications between the claimant and its solicitors. Author's note: it is submitted (see **6.38**) that such communications are truly classified as legal advice privilege; client/lawyer communications are covered by legal advice privilege even where no litigation is in prospect; they do not cease to be covered by that species of the privilege when litigation is contemplated or has begun; litigation privilege is better confined to communications between the lawyer or client and third parties, such as factual or expert witnesses: see B Thanki (ed), *The Law of Privilege* (Oxford UP, 2006) 3.08, citing House of Lords' authority to support the present point of classification; generally, see C Passmore, *Privilege* (2nd edn, 2006) ch 8.

[87] *The David Agmashenebeli* (2001) CLC 942, Colman J: strong prima facie evidence that claimants had procured a surveyor's report in order to present false evidence: B Thanki (ed), *The Law of Privilege* (Oxford UP, 2006) 4.45.

jury and conspiracies to pervert the course of justice by producing false *factual* evidence, from non-expert witnesses. Another pertinent rule is that the court will not grant an injunction to retrieve inadvertently disclosed privileged material (containing witness preparation, etc) if there is evidence that the privilege-holder attempted to deceive the court.[88]

The CPR has removed litigation privilege in the 'instructions', written or oral, provided by the litigant to an expert.[89] Such loss of privilege occurs only when 'the party decides that the particular report on which he wishes to rely should be disclosed.'[90]   **7.31**

(9) Discussions between Party-Appointed Experts

The court can direct that there should be a 'discussion' between party-appointed experts, followed by a 'joint statement':[91]   **7.32**

'the court may direct that following a discussion between the experts they must prepare a statement for the court showing: (a) those issues on which they agree; and (b) those issues on which they disagree and a summary of their reasons for disagreeing.'[92]

Such discussions can engender settlement, reduce the adversarial sting of the contest, narrow the scope of the dispute, and produce ideas for further streamlining the dispute. The Civil Justice Council's Protocol states:[93]

'The parties' lawyers may only be present at discussions between experts if all the parties agree or the court so directs; and if they do attend, they should not normally intervene except to answer questions put to them by the experts or to advise about the law.'

---

[88] *ISTIL Group Inc v Zahoor* [2003] EWHC 165 (Ch), [2003] 2 All ER 252, at [112], per Lawrence Collins J: 'In my judgment the combination of forgery and misleading evidence make this a case where the equitable jurisdiction to restrain breach of confidence gives way to the public interest in the proper administration of justice.'

[89] CPR 35.10(4).

[90] *Jackson v Marley Davenport Ltd* [2004] 1 WLR 2926, CA, at [22], per Peter Gibson LJ; see also A Edis, 'Privilege and Immunity: Problems of Expert Evidence' (2007) 26 CJQ 40.

[91] CPR 35.12; L Blom-Cooper (ed), *Experts in Civil Courts* (Oxford UP, 2006) ch 7.

[92] CPR 35.12(3).

[93] 'Protocol for the Instruction of Experts to Give Evidence in Civil Claims' (Civil Justice Council, 2005) 18.8; R Clements in L Blom-Cooper (ed), *Experts in Civil Courts* (2006) 7.12 ff; T Hodgkinson and M James, *Expert Evidence: Law and Practice* (2nd edn, 2006) 4–024; a lawyer's presence might be useful to avoid the embarrassment and injustice of the expert misapplying the law (eg the civil standard of proof: *Temple v S Manchester HA* [2002] EWCA Civ 1406; see **2.32** of this book for the civil standard of proof); besides next note, see A Whitfield QC's review of arguments for and against legal presence at these discussion in 'Clinical Risk' 2000 vol 6, 149; accessible at www.clinical-disputes-forum.org.uk/files/projectfiles/project3–app1.doc

Such a meeting is not contrary to the guarantee in Article 6(1) of the European Convention on Human Rights of a fair trial and process.[94] Baroness Hale (as she now is) has suggested that it would be good practice to agree that a legally qualified chairman, independent of the parties, might preside during expert discussions involving matters of sensitivity.[95]

7.33   Experts' discussions are privileged.[96] But the joint statement agreed by rival parties' experts at the end of such a session is not privileged and in fact becomes available to the court in the proceedings (CPR 35.12(3) '[the court can order that the parties' experts] must prepare a statement *for the court* ...').[97] The joint statement is not formally binding on the parties, but in practice it will be difficult to sidestep.

7.34   The Court of Appeal in *Stanton v Callaghan* (2000) held that an expert is immune from liability in negligence when agreeing a joint statement (see further on witness immunity, **7.35**, and for another aspect of the present decision, **7.36**, below). Therefore, the instructing party cannot sue him, alleging negligence or fraud.[98] What if one party wishes to substitute a new expert, following this process? In *Stallwood v David* (2006) Teare J held that permission for a substitute should be refused, except in three situations: (i) the expert plainly acted beyond his expertise; or (ii) he was incompetent for this task; or (iii), as on the facts of the present case, the application for permission to substitute a party-appointed expert was unjustly conducted (for example, by unsympathetic comments based on the judge's own personal experience; in the present case, the first instance judge's autobiographical remarks on his stoical resistance to prolonged backpain).[99] The *Stanton* and *Stallwood* cases establish important constraints. Without them, the salutary system of experts' discussions would soon unravel.

(10) Witness Immunity

7.35   This doctrine applies to both expert and factual witnesses. Lord Hoffmann in *Arthur JS Hall v Simons* (2002) said:[100]

---

[94]   *Hubbard v Lambeth, Southwark and Lewisham AHA* [2001] EWCA Civ 1455; *The Times*, 8 October 2001, at [17], per Tuckey LJ.

[95]   *Hubbard* case, ibid, at [29], per Hale LJ.

[96]   CPR 35.12(4).

[97]   *Aird v Prime Meridian Ltd* [2006] EWCA Civ 1866, at [3].

[98]   [2000] 1 QB 75, CA; the expert discussion in that case preceded the CPR and was not at the court's direction; nevertheless, the court's reasoning would seem to apply to CPR 35.12 discussions.

[99]   [2006] EWHC 2600 (QB); [2007] 1 All ER 206; noted A Zuckerman (2007) 26 CJQ 159.

[100]   [2000] UKHL 38; [2002] 1 AC 615, 697; A Edis, 'Privilege and Immunity: Problems of Expert Evidence' (2007) 26 CJQ 40; on the scope of the immunity in the context of an affidavit, *Martin Walsh v Paul Staines* [2007] EWHC 1814 (Ch).

'... a witness is absolutely immune from liability for anything which he says in court ... .[He] cannot be sued for libel, malicious falsehood, or conspiring to give false evidence ... The policy of this rule is to encourage persons who take part in court proceedings to express themselves freely.'

In *Darker v Chief Constable of the West Midlands Police* (2001) the House of Lords distinguished (i) the false presentation of evidence in court, whether deliberately or not (if deliberate the crime of perjury arises), and (ii) out-of-court steps taken to produce false evidence, such as fabrication of evidence and conduct aimed at 'setting up' an accused; or destroying evidence.[101] Matters falling within (ii) do not attract witness immunity. Therefore, a lie told in the witness box, although attracting criminal liability for perjury, will not also expose the witness to civil liability, for example in tort.

In *Stanton v Callaghan* (2000) Chadwick LJ said:[102]   7.36

'[witness] immunity does not extend to protect an expert who has been retained to advise as to the merits of a party's claim in litigation from a suit by the party by whom he has been retained in respect of that advice, notwithstanding that it was in contemplation at the time when the advice was given that the expert would be a witness at the trial if that litigation were to proceed.'[103]

But this restriction on the scope of witness immunity has been doubted.[104] A more attractive approach, it is submitted, is whether the expert advice was given with a view to possible use in pending or reasonably contemplated litigation. This should be an objective inquiry.[105]

The Court of Appeal in *Meadow v General Medical Council* (2006) held   7.37
that an expert (whether he has given evidence in a criminal or civil case) can be later subjected to disciplinary proceedings before his professional body if he is alleged by that body, or some complainant, to have given expert evidence in a thoroughly unsatisfactory way.[106] Witness immunity does not protect an expert from such disciplinary proceedings. Sir Anthony Clarke MR said:[107]

---

[101] [2001] 1 AC 435, HL; similarly, *L (A Child) v Reading BC* [2001] EWCA Civ 346; [2001] 1 WLR 1575, 1593, CA.

[102] [2000] 1 QB 75, CA.

[103] Considering *Palmer v Durnford Ford* [1992] QB 483 and *Landall v Dennis Faulkner & Alsop* [1994] 5 Med LR 268.

[104] *Karling v Purdue* [2004] ScotCS 221 (29 September 2004) (Outer House, Court of Session) at [38].

[105] On witness immunity with respect to experts' pre-hearing involvement, *Karling* case, ibid, at [65].

[106] [2006] EWCA Civ 1390; [2007] 2 WLR 286, reversing on the immunity point Collins J in [2006] EWHC 146 (Admin); on the general question of remedies against the defaulting expert, L Blom-Cooper (ed), Experts in Civil Courts (Oxford UP, 2006) ch 9 and DM Dwyer, 'The Effective Management of Bias in Civil Expert Evidence' (2007) 26 CJQ 57.

[107] [2006] EWCA Civ 1390; [2007] 2 WLR 286, at [46]; the other members agreed, at [106] and [249].

'the threat of [professional disciplinary] proceedings ... helps to deter those who might be tempted to give partisan evidence and not to discharge their obligation to assist the court by giving conscientious and objective evidence' and it 'helps to preserve the integrity of the trial process and public confidence both in the trial process and in the standards of the professions from which expert witnesses come.'

7.38   In *Phillips v Symes (Costs No 2)* (2005) Peter Smith J held that a party-appointed expert can be ordered to pay costs wasted by his reckless or grossly negligent advice (generally on 'wasted costs', see **9.18**).[108] The judge rejected the suggestion that the spectre of wasted costs liability might deter experts from giving evidence. He held that witness immunity should not preclude a wasted costs order against an expert.[109] This seems persuasive, for several reasons: experts are nearly always remunerated; the present jurisdiction requires proof of 'gross dereliction of duty or recklessness'; and the aggrieved party's primary recourse for financial compensation is against the litigant who hired the expert ('the hiring party') who is alleged to have been guilty of gross dereliction of his duty.[110] As for this last point, on the facts of the *Phillips* case, such recourse was not possible because the offending expert's instructing party was already bankrupt.

---

[108] [2004] EWHC 2330 (Ch); [2005] 1 WLR 2043; noted Neil Andrews [2005] CLJ 566.

[109] On witness immunity, *Arthur JS Hall v Simons* [2000] UKHL 38; [2002] 1 AC 615; *Taylor v Director of the Serious Fraud Office* [1999] 2 AC 177, HL; *Stanton v Callaghan* [2000] 1 QB 75, CA; *Darker v Chief Constable of the West Midlands Police* [2000] UKHL 44; [2001] 1 AC 435; *L v Reading BC* [2001] EWCA Civ 346; [2001] 1 WLR 1575; *Raiss v Palmano* [2001] PNLR 540, Eady J; *X v Bedfordshire CC* [1995] 2 AC 633, 754–5, HL; Neil Andrews, *English Civil Procedure* (Oxford UP, 2003) 31.50, 31.51,32.83 to 32.94; and see the discussion at **7.37** above of the *Meadow* case.

[110] eg *Re Colt Telecom Group plc* [2002] EWHC 2815 (Ch), at [80] and [110], where Jacob J ordered indemnity costs (on which, **9.12**) against a party who selected an expert whose report was seriously defective.

Chapter 8

'End-Game': Trial, Appeal, and Enforcement

Contents

(1) Introduction

This chapter is concerned with the 'end-game' of litigation before the courts. **8.01**
The historical centre-piece of the Common Law civil process has been 'trial'.
In the nineteenth century Common Law courts in England, trial was an oral
hearing before a judge and jury. In the United States of America civil trial before juries remains a constitutional right. England has been more pragmatic.
Nowadays English civil trials are hardly ever before a jury (except in unusual
cases concerning defamation claims, or actions for compensation involving
'malicious prosecution' or 'false imprisonment', normally brought against the
police).[1] Many actions end without trial. But, in a small percentage of cases,
trial is the culmination of the process. Thereafter, provided the claim is successful, enforcement proceedings might be brought, for example, to obtain
satisfaction of a judgment debt. Enforcement is also possible if judgment in
favour of the claimant has been obtained by some other means, for example,
by summary process (**5.18**), by 'default judgment' (**5.31**), or judgment has been
obtained because a defence has been dismissed following the defendant's failure to satisfy an 'unless order' (**2.19**), or a 'consent judgment' has been entered
(**10.15**). A final judgment on the merits of the case has a binding effect, as be-

---

[1] Neil Andrews, *English Civil Procedure* (Oxford UP, 2003) 34–06 ff; see also, **8.02** and
8.08 below.

tween the parties. The topic of 'finality', especially *res judicata*, is part of this 'end-game', therefore. Apart from appeals (see **8.12** ff), for which permission is required, English law is opposed to unnecessary re-litigation of the same issues and claim.

(2) Trial

8.02   In modern times, civil trials in England are almost invariably heard by a judge sitting alone without a jury.[2] The judge will have read a 'trial bundle' in preparation for the hearing. This will comprise:[3] the claim form (**3.05**) and statements of case (**3.08**); a case summary; witness statements 'to be relied on as evidence' (**8.04**) and witness summaries; hearsay evidence notices; plans, photographs etc;[4] medical reports and responses to them, and other expert reports and responses; any order giving directions as to the conduct of the trial. In large actions, a core bundle must also be prepared.[5]

8.03   Normally trial (and appeal)[6] must be in public[7] (see also **2.11**). To protect a person's safety,[8] the court can order that the identity of a party or of a witness must not be disclosed.[9] The courts are prepared to allow a party to give evidence by video-link, normally from abroad.[10] The trial proceeds as follows: (i)

---

[2] Jury trial in England is now confined to serious criminal cases (for example, murder, rape, armed robbery) and civil actions for defamation or misconduct by the police (the torts of defamation, malicious prosecution, and false imprisonment): Neil Andrews, *English Civil Procedure* (Oxford UP, 2003) 34–06 ff; as long ago as 1966, it became clear that the courts will unwilling to back-track on the modern trend to confine jury trial to these special categories of claim, *Ward v James* [1966] 1 QB 273, CA (applied *H v Ministry of Defence* [1991] 2 QB 103, CA; *Heil v Rankin* [2001] QB 272 at [25], CA).

[3] PD (39) 3.2.

[4] The notice requirement is strict: CPR 33.6(3).

[5] PD (39) 3.6.

[6] *Three Rivers DC v Bank of England* [2005] EWCA Civ 933; [2005] CP Rep 47.

[7] For exceptions, CPR 39.2(1), CPR 39.2(3),and PD (39) 1.5; the primary source is Supreme Court Act 1981, s 67; J Jaconelli, *Open Justice* (Oxford UP, 2002); J Jacob, *Civil Justice in the Age of Human Rights* (Aldershot, 2007), ch 2; on the question of exceptional restrictions on publicity in respect of pre-trial hearings and judgments concerning interim decisions, *Browne v Associated Newspapers Ltd* [2007] EWCA Civ 295; [2007] 3 WLR 289 at [2] to [5].

[8] But the physical frailty of a witness was not a sufficient reason in *Three Rivers DC v Bank of England* [2005] EWCA Civ 933; [2005] CP Rep 47.

[9] CPR 39.2(4); PD (39) 1.4A emphasises the need to consider the requirement of publicity enshrined in Art 6(1) of the European Convention on Human Rights (incorporated into English law, Human Rights Act 1998, Sch 1).

[10] *Polanski v Condé Nast Publications Ltd* [2005] UKHL 10; [2005] 1 WLR 637; *McGlinn v Waltham Contractors Ltd* [2006] EWHC 2322 (TCC); in neither case was the relevant absentee's reason for not coming to England held to bar use of video-linking (respectively, avoidance of extradition to the USA, and avoidance of tax liability within the UK).

counsel's opening speech (although this can be dispensed with);[11] (ii) examination-in-chief of the claimant's witnesses (although this will not be oral where, as usual, the witness statement is received as a substitute for oral testimony);[12] (iii) cross-examination of the claimant's witnesses by the defendant's counsel; (iv) re-examination of witnesses (at this stage exceptionally the court will dismiss the claim on the basis that the defendant has 'no case to answer');[13] (v) examination-in-chief of defendant's witnesses (although this will not be oral where, as usual, the witness statement is received as a substitute for oral testimony, see n 12 above); (vi) cross-examination of the same by claimant's counsel; (vii) re-examination of same; (viii) defendant counsel's final speech; (ix) claimant counsel's final speech (the reason this is the last party intervention at trial is that the claimant bears the burden of proof, and so deserves to have the last say); (x) judgment;[14] (xi) an order for costs, including in appropriate cases a summary assessment of costs (on which **9.11**).[15] In the event that the defendant does not appear at trial, judgment might be entered for the claimant (**5.36**), or the court might proceed to consider evidence, despite the defendant's absence.[16] The latter course will be necessary if the amount of damages or other pecuniary relief has still to be determined. The claimant's lawyers will be required to present arguments favourable to the other side, in a manner analogous to the applicant's role during a 'without notice' application (**4.14**).

---

[11] Fast-track: PD (28) 8.2; multi-track: PD (29) 10.2; detailed account: Neil Andrews, *English Civil Procedure* (Oxford UP, 2003) 31.21 to 31.24.

[12] CPR 32.5(2).

[13] In *Graham v Chorley Borough Council* [2006] EWCA Civ 92; [2006] CP Rep 24, at [29] ff, Brooke LJ explained (noting *Benham Ltd v Kythira Investments Ltd* [2003] EWCA Civ 1794 at [32], [36]) that a 'no case to answer' judgment for the defendant without hearing the defendant's evidence is highly perilous (eg, in the *Graham* case, the judge's decision in favour of the claimant was set aside and a re-trial ordered); cross-examination of the defendant's witnesses might have strengthened the claimant's exiguous case; before reaching 'the no case to answer' decision, the judge must give appropriate weight to the fact that the defendant elected not to call his own witnesses (drawing 'adverse inferences').

[14] Or a direction to the jury; on judgments, CPR 40 and PD (40); on the court's discretion whether to complete the giving of judgment once it has begun to deliver it (or after it has delivered it in draft form) *Prudential Assurance Co v McBains* [2000] 1 WLR 2000, CA; on the court's power to re-open a case before perfecting a judgment, *Stewart v Engel* [2000] 1 WLR 2268, CA.

[15] CPR 44.3, 44.7(a).

[16] *Braspetro Oil Services Co v FPSO Construction Inc* [2007] EWHC 1359 (Comm), Cresswell J observing at [32] and [33]: ' In view of [the defendant's] non-attendance at the trial, the Court has adopted an approach which reflects the approach followed, for example, in *Habib Bank Ltd v Central Bank of Sudan* [2006] EWHC 1767 (Comm); [2006] 2 Lloyd's Rep 412. I have required [the claimant] to draw to the Court's attention points, factual or legal, that might be to the benefit of [the defendant]. I am satisfied that [the claimant's lawyers] have complied with this direction throughout the hearing.'

(3) Evidence at Trial

8.04   Factual witness testimony is the main source of evidence at trial.[17] Witnesses can be compelled to attend a trial (or other hearing) by the issue of a 'witness summons'.[18] The witness must be offered compensation for his travel to and from court, and for loss of time.[19] The procedure for receipt of witness evidence is as follows. A proposed witness's testimony (his so-called 'evidence-in-chief') must be prepared in written form, signed, and served on the other parties.[20] In support of this 'witness statement', the witness or his legal representative must supply a 'statement of truth'. This is a solemn indication that the contents of the witness statement have been presented honestly. A modified 'statement of truth' applies to an expert's report, **7.06** and **7.26**.[21] In all these situations an untruthful 'statement of truth' carries serious consequences. It is an act of contempt of court (see **8.35**) to make, or to cause to be made, a dishonest statement of truth.[22] Normally, in the interest of economy, a witness statement will be received as evidence. This will dispense with the need for the witness to give oral evidence on behalf of the party who has called him (so-called 'examination-in-chief'), although the court can allow the witness orally to amplify his statement and to introduce matters which have subsequently arisen.[23]

8.05   At the trial, the witness will give evidence on oath (or a secular equivelent, an 'affirmation').[24] The crime of perjury is committed if false evidence is deliberately given by a witness at trial. Conviction can result in imprisonment or fines. The witness will answer questions posed by that opponent's lawyer (whether a barrister or other type of advocate, see **2.07**). This process of intense questioning is known as 'cross-examination'. During this oral process, the court does not itself conduct the examination of witnesses (see also **2.33** concerning the parties' selection of witnesses during preparation of the case for trial). Instead the judge is expected to listen to the parties' presentation of evidence. However, the judge might intervene to seek clarification, especially to assist a litigant in person (a party who is unassisted by a lawyer). It is a breach of procedure for the judge persistently to interrupt. The Court of Ap-

---

[17] Neil Andrews, *English Civil Procedure* (Oxford UP, 2003) 31.41 to 31.51.

[18] This phrase replaces the terms 'subpoena ad testificandum' (order to attend to give oral evidence) and 'subpoena duces tecum' (order to attend with relevant documents or other items): CPR 34.2.

[19] CPR 34.7; PD (34) 3, referring to provisions applicable also to compensation for loss of time in criminal proceedings.

[20] CPR 32.10.

[21] CPR 22.1(1)(c) 22.3.

[22] CPR 32.14.

[23] CPR 32.5(2)(3)(4).

[24] On affirmations, PD (32) 16.

peal in 2006 affirmed the practice of passive reception of evidence by a judge. The court declared that if the judge were to intervene excessively, he would then 'arrogate to himself a quasi-inquisitorial role', something which is 'entirely at odds with the adversarial system.'[25]

The next most important source of evidence is 'documentary evidence', which covers paper-based or electronically recorded information. 'Real evidence' refers to 'things', such as the physical objects or site relevant to the case, or body samples. As for 'expert evidence', this has been examined in chapter 7.   8.06

The court at trial has powers of 'evidential veto' in the following respects: 'the issues on which it requires evidence', 'the nature of the evidence which it requires', 'the way in which evidence is to be placed before the court';[26] excluding admissible evidence; limiting cross-examination;[27] restricting the number of witnesses (both lay and expert) used by each party;[28] restricting the time devoted to examining witnesses. These powers must be exercised with caution.[29] Preliminary questions of law or fact can be separated from other matters, in the interest of economy (**5.17**).[30] Appeals are unlikely to succeed against such trial management orders aimed at marshalling the issues.[31]   8.07

There has been much 'modernising' of civil evidence during the last few decades. The impetus for these reforms has been the civil jury's virtual disappearance in modern English practice.[32] And so various 'exclusionary rules', designed to protect the civil jury against 'potentially unreliable' material, have been removed or profoundly modified. These developments are consistent with a perceived global trend towards 'free evaluation' of evidence. American Law   8.08

---

[25] *Southwark LBC v Maamefowaa Kofiadu* [2006] EWCA Civ 281, at [148].

[26] CPR 32.1(1); *GKR Karate (UK) Ltd v Yorkshire Post Newspapers Ltd* [2000] 2 All ER 931, CA.

[27] CPR 32.1(2)(3); *Grobbelaar v Sun Newspapers Ltd The Times* 12 August, 1999, CA (prolix defence in libel action); *Three Rivers DC v Bank of England* [2005] EWCA Civ 889; [2005] CP Rep 46 (upholding the Commercial Court judge's humane restriction in a long-running trial).

[28] Fast-track: CPR 28.3(1) and PD (28) 8.4; CPR 32.1 (all tracks).

[29] A Colman (with V Lyon and P Hopkins) *The Practice and Procedure of the Commercial Court* (5th edn, 2000) 218–9, especially curtailment of the power to cross-examine the other party's witnesses; S Sugar and R Wilson (eds), *Commercial and Mercantile Courts Litigation Practice* (2004).

[30] CPR 3.1(2)(j)(l); for the pre-CPR emergence of this aspect of trial management, *Ashmore v Corporation of Lloyd's* [1992] 1 WLR 446, HL; *Thermawear Ltd v Linton The Times* 20 October, 1995, CA.

[31] *Ward v Guinness Mahon plc* [1996] 1 WLR 894, CA, *Grupo Torras Sa v Al Sabah (No 2) The Times* 17 April, 1997, CA.

[32] See the authorities cited above at n 2; on the historical influence of trial by judge and jury, Neil Andrews, *English Civil Procedure* (Oxford UP, 2003) 34–06 ff; the jury no longer sits in English civil trials except in actions for defamation, or in claims of false imprisonment or malicious prosecution; see ibid for details.

Institute/UNIDROIT's *Principles of Transnational Civil Procedure* has recognised this concept.[33] These English evidential changes will now be listed.

8.09   The English 'hearsay rule' used to provide a barrier to admitting relevant
evidence. This rule concerned second-hand or remoter reports of oral statements (for example, if the claimant wished to adduce evidence, through one of
his witnesses, who proposed to state that 'the defendant told me that his wife
had said, "let's concoct a claim against these people"'). The hearsay rule also
concerned documents composed out-of-court. But there has now been a fundamental change. Since 1995, statute has allowed a party to use out-of-court
oral statements, and documents, as evidence: 'In civil proceedings evidence
shall not be excluded on the ground that it is hearsay', that is, 'a statement
made otherwise than by a person giving oral evidence.'[34] Instead, the court
must to assess the 'weight' to be attached to the hearsay evidence. The judge is
here guided by various considerations. These include: 'whether it would have
been reasonable and practicable for the party by whom the [hearsay] evidence
was adduced to have produced the maker of the original statement as a witness' and 'whether any person involved had any motive to conceal or misrepre-
sent matters'; and 'whether the original statement was an edited account, or
was made in collaboration with another.'[35]

8.10   Two other evidential rules have been radically transformed. First, the so-
called 'best evidence rule' has been abandoned. A person is no longer obliged
to produce the original version of a document. He can instead tender a copy.
However, he must provide a satisfactory explanation for his inability to produce the original.[36] Another change is that 'similar fact' evidence is now admissible in civil cases. And so the court can legitimately take into account the
fact that very similar events have occurred. Such coincidence can be relevant
by tending to weaken a party's case.[37]

---

[33] Rule 25 in *ALI/UNIDROIT: Principles of Transnational Civil Procedure* (Cambridge UP, 2006) 137 ff.

[34] Civil Evidence Act 1995, s 1.

[35] ibid, 1995 Act, s 4; in *Polanski v Condé Nast Publications Ltd* [2005] UKHL 10;
[2005] 1 WLR 637, at [36], Lord Nicholls said: 'The principle underlying the Civil Evidence
Act 1995 is that in general the preferable course is to admit hearsay evidence, and let the
court attach to the evidence whatever weight may be appropriate, rather than exclude it altogether. This applies to jury trial [in civil cases] as well as trials by judge alone … .'; see also
S Salako, 'The Hearsay Rule and the Civil Evidence Act 1995: Where are we now?' (2000)
19 CJQ 371.

[36] In *Springsteen v Masquerade Music Ltd* [2001] EWCA Civ 513; [2001] Entertainment and Media LR 654, CA, Jonathan Parker LJ explained: 'the time has now come when
it can be said with confidence that the best evidence rule, long on its deathbed, has finally
expired. In every case where a party seeks to adduce secondary evidence of the contents of a
document, it is a matter for the court to decide, in the light of all the circumstances of the
case, what (if any) weight to attach to that evidence.'

[37] *O'Brien v Chief Constable of South Wales Police* [2005] UKHL 26; [2005] 2 AC
534.

What if evidence has been improperly obtained? If evidence (which is not   **8.11**
privileged material) has been obtained unlawfully, unfairly, or in violation of a
party's rights, the court will 'balance' the heinousness of the way it was collected against its relevance and weight if admitted into evidence. There are no
hard-and-fast rules here, as *Jones v University of Warwick* (2003) illustrates.[38]
In this case, the claimant alleged that she had suffered a serious disabling injury to her hand. The defendant did not accept this. Its investigator gained access to the claimant's home, posing as a market researcher, and took secret
video evidence of the claimant's use of her injured hand in her home.[39] Lord
Woolf CJ in the Court of Appeal held that, on balance, the evidence should be
admitted. In the court's view, the manner of its collection had not been especially 'outrageous'.

(4) Appeals[40]

Nearly all appeals require the court to give its permission (formerly known as   **8.12**
'leave'),[41] in response to the appellant's speedy request to the first instance court
(normally within fourteen days;[42] a period which cannot be extended by party
agreement).[43] If the lower court refuses permission, a fresh application for permission can be made to the appeal court. In general,[44] an appeal proceeds to the
next level of civil judge (district judge to circuit judge, Master to High Court
judge, circuit judge to High Court judge, High Court judge to Court of Appeal).[45]

---

[38] [2003] EWCA Civ 151; [2003] 1 WLR 954, CA.

[39] This involved a tort (trespass) and an invasion of privacy (as recognised by Article 8 of
the European Convention on Human Rights).

[40] Sir Henry Brooke, D di Mambro, L di Mambro (eds), *Manual of Civil Appeals* (2nd
edn, 2004); see also Neil Andrews, *English Civil Procedure* (Oxford UP, 2003) ch 38; CPR
Part 52 was examined in *Tanfern Ltd v Cameron-MacDonald* [2000] 1 WLR 1311, 1314–21,
CA; on the system requiring 'permission' in nearly all cases, IR Scott (1999) 18 CJQ 91; for
background, *Review of the Court of Appeal (Civil Division)* (report to Lord Chancellor, September 1997; the 'Bowman Report'); for US comparison, PS Atiyah and R Summers, *Form
and Substance in Anglo-American Law* (Oxford UP, 1987) ch 10; for reflections on the private and public functions of civil appeals, especially in the highest chamber, reports by JA
Jolowicz, P-H Lindblom, S Goldstein in P Yessiou-Faltsi (ed), *The Role of the Supreme Courts
at the National and International Level* (Thessaloniki, Greece, 1998); for comparative perspectives on appeals, JA Jolowicz, *On Civil Procedure* (Cambridge UP, 2000) chs 14 to 16.

[41] CPR 52.3(1): except decisions affecting a person's liberty.

[42] CPR 52.4(2); appeals out of time will only exceptionally be permitted: *Smith v Brough*
[2005] EWCA 261; [2006] CP Rep 17.

[43] CPR 52.6(1) (2).

[44] There are special rules allowing some appeals to 'hop' a level of appeal and be fast-
routed to the Court of Appeal, or even to the House of Lords.

[45] PD (52).

It has been suggested that video-conferencing should be used for short appeals.[46]

8.13   There is scope for a second appeal, but only if the appeal 'would raise an important point of principle or practice' or there is 'some other compelling reason' for the Court of Appeal to hear it.[47] A second or even third level of appeal lies from the Court of Appeal to the House of Lords. The House, however, directly controls the flow of cases to the highest chamber. It will grant for permission for final appeal only if its appeal panel is persuaded that the case raises an issue of public or other special importance. In *Callery v Gray (Nos 1 and 2)* (2002) it declared it would prefer not to become embroiled in matters of 'practice', notably in the field of conditional fee agreements, but in *Campbell v MGN (No 2)* (2005) it heard such an appeal (on which, **9.26**). [48]

8.14   A court will allow an appeal when it concludes that the lower court's decision was 'wrong' or 'unjust because of a serious procedural or other irregularity in the proceedings in the lower court'[49] (for an illustration of the latter, see **7.34**). On matters of law, appellate courts are fully prepared, indeed obliged, to make corrections. However, in general, the courts are most reluctant to hear appeals on 'academic' or 'hypothetical' points, namely matters which are of no immediate and direct concern to the parties. But an exception to this can arise if the point of law is of general public importance.[50]

---

[46] *Black v Pastouna* [2005] EWCA Civ 1389; [2006] CP Rep 11, per Brooke LJ.

[47] CPR 52.13; Sir Henry Brooke, D di Mambro, L di Mambro (eds), *Manual of Civil Appeals* (2nd edn, 2004) 4.88 ff.

[48] *Callery v Gray (Nos 1 and 2)* [2002] UKHL 28; [2002] 1 WLR 2000, at [8], per Lord Bingham, referring to the conditional fee context: '... responsibility for monitoring and controlling the developing practice in a field such as this lies with the Court of Appeal and not the House, which should ordinarily be slow to intervene. The House cannot respond to changes in practice with the speed and sensitivity of the Court of Appeal, before which a number of cases are likely over time to come ...'; and, ibid, at [17], per Lord Hoffmann: 'The Court of Appeal is traditionally and rightly responsible for supervising the administration of civil procedure. This is an area in which your Lordships have in the past seldom intervened and, it must be said, the few exceptions to this policy of self-restraint have usually tended to confirm the wisdom of the general practice.' *Campbell v MGN (No 2)* [2005] UKHL 61; [2005] 1 WLR 3394; more generally, see the observations of Lord Woolf in *Boake Allen Ltd v Revenue and Customs* [2007] UKHL 25 at [28] concerning the House of Lords' 'deference' to the Court of Appeal on questions of 'practice and procedure' ('... because the members of the [Court of Appeal] have had more recent experience of those issues than members of this House'); for discussion of the 'leap-frog' mechanism, enabling appeals to proceed straight to the House of Lords without a hearing before the Court of Appeal (under ss 12, 13, Administration of Justice Act 1969), *R (on the pplication of Jones) v Ceredigion County Council* [2007] UKHL 24; [2007] 3 All ER 781.

[49] CPR 52.11(3).

[50] *Bowman v Fels* [2005] EWCA Civ 226; [2005] 1 WLR 3083, at [7], where Brooke LJ said of the present appeal: 'The issue at the heart of the appeal is, however, an issue of public law of very great importance which is causing very great difficulties in solicitors' offices and barristers' chambers and in the orderly conduct of contested litigation through the country.'

As for the appeal courts' treatment of factual issues, there are three main **8.15** aspects: (1) the appellate court's receipt of 'fresh evidence'; (2) the appellate court's consideration of factual determinations made at first instance; (3) the appeal court's unwillingness to receive oral evidence. On this third point, it should be noted that, in general,[51] only a first instance court will hear live testimony (see further **8.18** below); for this reason, if it turns out that a just response to questions (1) or (2) requires consideration of oral evidence, the appeal court will normally remit the matter to a first instance court. Questions (1) and (2) will now be elaborated.

As for 'fresh evidence', the court will not normally consider new evidence **8.16** which was in fact clearly or reasonably available for presentation at trial. The guiding principles are:[52] (i) 'the evidence could not have been obtained with reasonable diligence for use at the trial'; (ii) the new evidence would 'probably have an important influence on the result of the case, though it need not be decisive'; (iii) the new evidence must also be 'credible, though it need not be incontrovertible.'[53]

As for the question of possible re-assessment of findings of fact, the appeal **8.17** court can 'draw any inference of fact which it considers justified on the evidence'.[54] But that court will be slow to reconsider the lower court's so-called 'conclusions of primary fact'. The appellate court's deference to the trial court's 'findings of primary fact', a somewhat complex topic, will now be explained (see **8.18** to **8.20**).

It has been attractively explained that the appellate court's capacity to re- **8.18** open findings of fact depends on the manner in which the first instance court has reached the relevant finding:[55] 'In appeals against conclusions of primary fact the approach of an appellate court will depend upon the weight to be at-

---

And Brooke LJ, ibid, noted the following leading decisions: *Sun Life Assurance Co of Canada v Jervis* [1944] AC 111, 113–4, HL per Viscount Simon LC and *Ainsbury v Millington (Note)* [1987] 1 WLR 379, 381, HL, per Lord Bridge of Harwich; *R v Secretary of State for the Home Department ex p Salem* [1999] 1 AC 450, 456 G-H, HL, per Lord Slynn of Hadley.

[51] CPR 52.11(2).

[52] Passages just cited are re-stated in *Riyad Bank v Ahli United Bank (UK) plc* [2005] EWCA Civ 1419 at [26] ff (noting that these '*Ladd v Marshall*' (1954) pre-CPR principles were re-adopted in *Hamilton v Al Fayed The Times* 13 October, 2000, CA); see also CPR 52.11(2).

[53] In the *Riyad* case, ibid, at [28] it was added that 'the Court of Appeal should be particularly cautious where what is intended is to put in, in effect, further cross-examination of a witness, including an expert, where that expert or witness has been cross-examined at a trial.'

[54] CPR 52.11(4).

[55] *Datec Electronics Holdings Ltd v United Parcels Services Ltd* [2007] UKHL 23; [2007] 1 WLR 1325, at [46], Lord Mance, quoting Clarke LJ in *Assicurazioni Generali SpA v Arab Insurance Group* [2002] EWCA Civ 1642, [2003] 1 All ER (Comm) 140; [2003] 1 WLR 577, CA.

tached to the findings of the judge and that weight will depend upon the extent to which, as the trial judge, the judge has an advantage over the appellate court; the greater that advantage the more reluctant the appellate court should be to interfere.'[56] The 'advantage' is the lower court's monopoly (under modern practice) upon hearing live testimony (see also **8.15** at point (3) above).

8.19   In the leading analysis of this context, Clarke LJ distinguished various categories of 'conclusions of primary fact':[57]

(1) those 'based almost entirely upon ... the oral evidence of the witnesses'; or

(2) based 'partly [on] oral evidence and partly [on] analysis of the documents'; or

(3) 'based entirely or almost entirely on the documents'; or

(4) findings reached as the result of 'inference from direct evidence of such facts'; or

(5) 'some conclusions of fact are, however, not conclusions of primary fact' but 'involve an assessment of a number of different factors which have to be weighed against each other'; this is 'an evaluation of the facts' and 'a matter of degree upon which different judges can legitimately differ'; such first instance determinations 'may be closely analogous to the exercise of a discretion and, in my opinion, appellate courts should approach them in a similar way.'[58]

8.20   As for categories (1) to (4) (see preceding paragraph), the correct approach is as follows:[59] 'Once the appellant has shown a real prospect (justifying permission to appeal) that a finding or inference is wrong, the role of an appellate court is to determine whether or not this is so, giving full weight of course to the advantages enjoyed by any judge of first instance who has heard oral evidence.' But in the case of category (5), the appellate court 'is essentially concerned with the correctness of an exercise of evaluation or judgment', and so the appellate court 'ought not to interfere unless it is satisfied that the judge's conclusion lay outside the bounds within which reasonable disagreement is possible.'

8.21   The Court of Appeal in *Taylor v Lawrence* (2002) held that, in very exceptional situations, it can review, and if necessary rescind or modify, one of its

---

[56] *Assicurazioni Generali*, ibid, at [15], per Clarke LJ.

[57] ibid, at [14], per Clarke LJ.

[58] ibid, at [16], per Clarke LJ; for further observations on exercises of discretion at first instance and decisions requiring the 'balancing' of nebulous factors, *Browne v Associated Newspapers Ltd* [2007] EWCA Civ 295; [2007] 3 WLR 289 at [45], citing five recent authorities.

[59] ibid, at [17], per Clarke LJ, citing Mance LJ in *Todd v Adam (trading as Trelawney Fishing Co)* [2002] EWCA Civ 509; [2002] 2 Lloyd's Rep 293, [2002] 2 All ER (Comm) 97, at [129].

own ostensibly final decisions.[60] The CPR has now codified this practice for appeals decided by the High Court or Court of Appeal.[61]

(5) *Res Judicata*: 'Cause of Action Estoppel' and 'Issue Estoppel'

The doctrine of *res judicata* bars successive litigation of the same claim or is-   **8.22** sues between the same parties.[62] It concerns 'claim or issue preclusion'.[63] The underpinning maxims are: *nemo debet bis vexari pro una et eadem causa* and *interest res publicae ut finis litium sit* ('no one should be disturbed twice in the same matter' and 'it is in the public interest that law suits should have an end'). Estoppel by *res judicata* has three elements: (i) decisions or aspects of decisions in civil matters (whether this be a final decision,[64] or a relevant type of consent order);[65] (ii) such decisions must have been made by a competent civil court or tribunal[66] (including courts recognised under English rules of private international law[67] and arbitration proceedings);[68] (iii) these decisions will be binding

---

[60] [2002] EWCA Civ 90; [2003] QB 528, CA; on which see IR Scott (2000) 21 CJQ 194 and Sir Henry Brooke, D di Mambro, L di Mambro (eds), *Manual of Civil Appeals* (2nd edn, 2004) 4.118 ff; this decision has been examined in various cases, notably, *In re Uddin* [2005] EWCA Civ 52; [2005] 1 WLR 2398, CA; *Jaffray v The Society of Lloyds* [2007] EWCA Civ 586; *First Discount Ltd v Guinness* [2007] EWCA Civ 378; see also *R v Bow Street Metropolitan Stipendiary Magistrate, Ex p Pinochet Ugarte (No 2)* [2000] 1 AC 119, HL.

[61] CPR 52.17.

[62] The leading work is Spencer Bower, Turner and Handley, *The Doctrine of Res Judicata* (3rd edn, 1996).

[63] This terminology, current in the USA and in Canada, has been adopted in *ALI/UNIDROIT's Principles of Transnational Civil Procedure* (Cambridge UP, 2006) Principles 28.2, 28.3.

[64] Including a final decision of an interim application: *R v Governor of Brixton Prison, ex parte Osman* [1991] 1 WLR 281; *Possfund v Diamond* [1996] 2 All ER 774, 779, citing *Chanel Ltd v F W Woolworth & Co Ltd* [1981] 1 WLR 485, 492–3, CA; for an example of a non-final decision, *Buehler AG v Chronos Richardson Ltd* [1998] 2 All ER 960, CA.

[65] eg *Palmer v Durnford Ford* [1992] 1 QB 483; *Green v Vickers Defence Systems Ltd* [2002] EWCA Civ 904; *The Times* 1 July 2002, CA; *Gairy v Att-Gen of Grenada* [2001] UKPC 30; [2002] 1 AC 167, PC, at [27], per Lord Bingham: 'a consent order may found a plea of res judicata even though the court has not been asked to investigate and pronounce on the point at issue.'

[66] *Green v Hampshire CC* [1979] ICR 861; *Crown Estate Commrs v Dorset CC* [1990] Ch 297.

[67] PR Barnett, *Res Judicata, Estoppel and Foreign Judgments: The Preclusive Effects of Foreign Judgments in Private International Law* (Oxford UP, 2001); P Rogerson, 'Issue Estoppel and Abuse of Process in Foreign Judgments' (1998) CJQ 91.

[68] *Ron Jones (Burton-on-Trent) Ltd v JS Hall* (unreported, 3 August 1999).

upon the parties (and their privies[69] or successors).[70] Next one must consider the distinction between 'cause of action' and 'issue estoppel', the two species of estoppel by *res judicata*.

8.23   'Cause of action estoppel' arises where the cause of action[71] in the later proceedings is the same as that adjudicated in the earlier action and the two pieces of litigation were identical both with regard to the parties (or their privies and successors in title) and subject matter.[72] This form of estoppel is an absolute bar to re-litigation of points decided in the earlier proceedings, unless fraud or collusion can be established to impugn that decision.[73]

8.24   'Issue estoppel' concerns adjudication of issues forming a necessary element in a cause of action (including foreign adjudication).[74] This estoppel applies if one of the parties to that decision seeks to re-open that issue in later proceedings between the same parties involving a different cause of action to which the same issue is relevant.[75] Unlike cause of action estoppel, issue estoppel can be relaxed in either of these situations: (i) there has been a retrospective change in the law which renders the point covered by issue estoppel 'plainly' wrong;[76] or (ii) new evidence has emerged which 'entirely changes the aspect of the case', provided that, even if he had displayed 'reasonable diligence', the relevant

---

[69] *McIlkenny v Chief Constable of the West Midlands* [1980] 1 QB 283, CA; *House of Spring Gardens Ltd v Waite* [1991] 1 QB 241, CA; *Black v Yates* [1992] 1 QB 526, 545–9; Spencer Bower, Turner and Handley, *The Doctrine of Res Judicata* (3rd edn, 1996) [231] and [232].

[70] eg, *Green v Vickers Defence Systems Ltd* [2002] EWCA Civ 904; *The Times* 1 July 2002 (consent order between victim of asbestosis and employer; held that terms of settlement included admission of liability for causation; victim's estate and dependants able to take advantage of this admission in the consent order).

[71] 'Cause of action' denotes the set of material facts supporting a recognised legal ground of claim *Cooke v Gill* (1873) LR 8 CP 107; *Brunsden v Humphrey* (1884) 14 QBD 141, CA; *Letang v Cooper* [1965] 1 QB 232, 243, CA; *Republic of India v India Steamship Co Ltd* [1993] AC 410, 419, HL; *Walkin v South Manchester Health Authority* [1995] 1 WLR 1543, 1547, CA; *Brown v KMR Services Ltd* [1995] 4 All ER 598, 640, CA; *Paragon Finance v DB Thakerar & Co* [1999] 1 All ER 400, 405–6, CA.

[72] *Arnold v National Westminster Bank plc* [1991] 2 AC 93, HL; noted Neil Andrews [1991] CLJ 419; for an example of different causes of action, *Buehler AG v Chronos Richardson Ltd* [1998] 2 All ER 960, CA.

[73] *Arnold* case [1991] 2 AC 93, 104, HL.

[74] *Carl Zeiss Stiftung v Rayner & Keeler Ltd (No 2)* [1967] 1 AC 853, HL; *Carl Zeiss Stiftung v Rayner & Keeler Ltd (No 3)* [1970] Ch 506; *The Sennar (No 2)* [1985] 1 WLR 490, 499, HL; see Dicey, Morris, and Collins, *The Conflict of Laws* (14th edn, 2006) 14–110 ff; P Rogerson, 'Issue Estoppel and Abuse of Process in Foreign Judgments' (1998) CJQ 91.

[75] *Arnold v National Westminster Bank plc* [1991] 2 AC 93, 105, HL; *Thoday v Thoday* [1964] P 181, 198, CA; *The Sennar (No 2)* [1985] 1 WLR 490, 499, HL; *Republic of India v India Steamship Co Ltd ('The Indian Grace')* [1993] AC 410, 419, HL.

[76] *Arnold* case, [1991] 2 AC 93, 112, HL (and see *Arnold* case [1990] Ch 573, 598, 600, CA; not disturbed on final appeal); *S v S (Ancillary Relief: Consent Order)* [2002] EWHC 223 Fam; [2003] Fam 1, at [30] ff.

party could not have discovered this evidence at the time of the earlier litigation.[77]

(6) Preclusion of Points that Should Have Been Raised: Finality and the Rule in *Henderson v Henderson* (1843)[78]

English law does not restrict itself to barring re-litigation of decided points. It **8.25** goes further and precludes litigation of points which might conveniently have been included by a party as part of his claim or defence in earlier civil litigation between the same parties. This will now be explained.

In 2002 the long-standing rule in *Henderson v Henderson* (1843)[79] was re- **8.26** stated as follows: '... parties who are involved in litigation are expected to put before the court all the issues relevant to that litigation. If they do not, they will not normally be permitted to have a second bite at the cherry.'[80] The rule applies not only when the first action was concluded by judgment but also when it was compromised out-of-court.[81] Unlike *res judicata* (**8.22** to **8.24**), the *Henderson* principle, therefore, does not concern adjudicated matters, but non-adjudicated matters. Those matters have only escaped decision because they were not raised, when they might have been, in earlier civil proceedings. In short, the *Henderson* principle can be regarded as an adjunct to *res judicata*; but this principle should not be confused as an aspect of *res judicata*. The House of Lords in *Johnson v Gore Wood & Co* (2002) said that the *Hender-*

---

[77] *Phosphate Sewage Co v Molleson* (1879) 4 App Cas 801, 814, HL; the *Phosphate* case test applies to the abuse of process doctrine: *Hunter v Chief Constable of West Midlands* [1982] AC 529, 545, HL and *Smith v Linskills* [1996] 1 WLR 763, 771, CA.

[78] *Henderson v Henderson* (1843) 3 Hare 100, 115, Wigram V-C; the leading modern examination is *Johnson v Gore Wood & Co* [2000] UKHL 65; [2002] 2 AC 1, HL; considered *De Crittenden v Estate of Bayliss (Deceased)* [2005] EWCA Civ 547 at [22] to [26] (earlier contract action; second action to plead a tracing action sufficiently closely tied to facts of first action; abuse of process); applied *Mohammed Nazmul Hossain v Sonali Bank and Sonali Bank UK Ltd* [2007] EWHC 1431, Eady J; and see the recent discussion cited in *Ruttle Plant Hire Ltd v The Secretary of State for the Environment, Food and Rural Affairs* [2007] EWHC 1773 (TCC); for radical comment, G Watt, 'The Danger and Deceit of the Rule in Henderson v Henderson: A New Approach to Successive Civil Actions Arising from the Same Factual Matter' (2000) 19 CJQ 287 and KR Handley, 'A Closer Look at Henderson v Henderson' (2002) 118 LQR 397.

[79] (1843) 3 Hare 100, 115, Wigram V-C.

[80] *Taylor v Lawrence* [2002] EWCA Civ 90; [2003] QB 528, at [6], per Lord Woolf; it has been (attractively) held that this rule is aimed only at countering re-litigation of points which might have been raised in earlier proceedings, and that the rule should not be stretched to control amendment of pleadings in the original action (on the basis that the point should have been raised sooner): *Ruttle Plant Hire Ltd v The Secretary of State for the Environment, Food and Rural Affairs* [2007] EWHC 1773 (TCC), at [30], per Jackson J.

[81] *Johnson* case [2000] UKHL 65; [2002] 2 AC 1, 32–3, 59, HL.

son doctrine should not be applied too zealously or mechanically.[82] Lord Millett suggested that this doctrine creates no presumption: 'the burden should always rest with the defendant [in the second action] to establish that it is oppressive or an abuse of process for him to be subjected to the second action.'[83] Sometimes litigation might be an abuse of process even when the parties in the second action are not the same as those in the first action.[84]

(7) Other Aspects of Finality

8.27   Four other rules or doctrines deserve mention. First, a claimant cannot obtain damages in successive actions in respect of the same cause of action: damages resulting from one and the same cause of action must be assessed and recovered once and for all.[85] Secondly, a court can strike out as an abuse of process an unjustified collateral attack by civil action upon a criminal conviction[86] or civil judgment[87] if 'such re-litigation would ... bring the administration of

---

[82] [2002] 2 AC 1, 22, 59, HL; *Gairy v Att-Gen of Grenada* [2001] UKPC 30; [2002] 1 AC 167, PC, at [26], [27].

[83] *Johnson* case, [2002] 2 AC 1, 59–60, HL.

[84] As suggested in the *Johnson* case, ibid, at 60; and see *Bradford & Bingley Building Society v Seddon* [1999] 1 WLR 1482, 1491–2, CA.

[85] *Brunsden v Humphrey* (1884) 14 QBD 141, 147, CA; LA Collins (1992) 108 LQR 393, 394 (case note); *Republic of India v India Steamship Co Ltd* ('*The Indian Grace*') [1993] AC 410, 420–1, HL; *Rowner v Allen & Sons* (1936) 41 Com Cas 90; *Jaggard v Sawyer* [1995] 1 WLR 269, 284, CA; *Deeny v Gooda Walker Ltd* [1995] 1 WLR 1206, 1214 (offering postponement of assessment of damages); Spencer Bower, Turner and Handley, *The Doctrine of Res Judicata* (3rd edn, 1996) ch 21; but on the need for caution in applying this rule, *Barrow v Bankside Agency Ltd* [1996] 1 WLR 257, 269, CA; *Cachia v Faluyi* [2001] 1 WLR 1966, CA, at [18] to [20].

[86] The leading case is *Hunter v Chief Constable of West Midlands Police* [1982] AC 529, HL (affirming CA sub nom *McIlkenny v Chief Constable of West Midlands Police Force* [1980] QB 283); for a luminous re-statement, *Smith v Linskills* [1996] 1 WLR 763, CA (Sir Thomas Bingham MR); the *Hunter* case was applied in *Somasunaram v M Julius Melchior & Co* [1988] 1 WLR 1394, CA, noted JA Jolowicz [1989] CLJ 196; the *Hunter* decision was distinguished in *Acton v Graham Pearce & Co* [1997] 3 All ER 904, 925 (earlier criminal conviction later set aside by CA, Criminal Division); the *Hunter* case was also distinguished in *Walpole v Partridge & Wilson* [1994] QB 106, CA (collateral attack doctrine inapplicable where possible appeal from criminal conviction not pursued, as a result of a lawyer's negligence); nor does the *Hunter* rule against collateral challenge apply when a civil *defendant* seeks to contradict his criminal conviction, *J v Oyston* [1999] 1 WLR 694 (considering Civil Evidence Act 1968, s 11(2)(a)); nor does it apply where proceedings for disqualification of a company director follow a regulatory investigation: *Re Barings (No 2)* [1999] 1 All ER 311, 335–6, 340, CA; see also Spencer Bower, Turner and Handley, *The Doctrine of Res Judicata* (3rd edn, 1996), at [447]; generally on abuse of process, Neil Andrews, *English Civil Procedure* (Oxford UP, 2003) ch 16.

[87] *Conlon v Simms* [2006] EWCA Civ 1749; [2007] 3 All ER 802 (containing a long review of authorities).

justice into disrepute.'[88] Thirdly, affiliation proceedings[89] and civil litigation concerning the welfare of children, such as care and custody proceedings,[90] do not give rise to *res judicata*: finality yields to the higher public interest in reaching accurate determinations of paternity and in promoting children's welfare. Finally, statute now bars attempts to re-litigate in England certain foreign judgments.[91] But this bar can be displaced by agreement, estoppel by convention, or acquiescence.[92]

(8) Enforcement of Money Judgments[93]

The Tribunals, Courts and Enforcement Act 2007, (Parts 3 to 5), which received royal assent on 19 July 2007, modifies the law of enforcement as follows. First, it introduces a new regime for 'taking control of goods', replacing the system of 'seizure of goods'.[94] Secondly, it creates new methods of obtaining information concerning debtor's assets and indebtedness.[95] Thirdly, it 'introduces a package of measures to help those who are willing and able to pay off their debts over time and a new personal insolvency procedure for some people who have fallen into debt but have no foreseeable way out of it' (see the various categories of protection in Part 5 of the Act).[96]   **8.28**

It remains an axiom of this procedural area that judgment creditors are free to choose from the portfolio of available enforcement methods.[97] Money judgments can be enforced by: (i) a writ of *fieri facias* or warrant of execution;[98] these are re-named 'writs of control' and 'warrants of control' by the Tribu-   **8.29**

---

[88] *Arthur JS Hall & Co v Simons* [2000] UKHL 38; [2002] 1 AC 615, 685, HL.

[89] *Hager v Osborne* [1992] Fam 94, following nineteenth century authority.

[90] *Re B (A Minor) The Times* 18 January 2000, CA, noting *Re B (Minors: Care Proceedings: Issue Estoppel)* [1997] Fam 117.

[91] Civil Jurisdiction and Judgments Act 1982, s 34; *Black v Yates* [1992] 1 QB 526; on the necessity for this provision, *Republic of India v India Steamship Co Ltd ('The Indian Endurance No 1')* [1993] AC 410, 417, HL; for the sequel, *Republic of India v India Steamship Co Ltd ('The Indian Endurance No 2')* [1998] AC 878, HL.

[92] *The Indian Endurance No 2* [1998] AC 878, HL.

[93] C Sandbrook, *Enforcement of a Judgment* (2006).

[94] Tribunals, Courts and Enforcement Act 2007, sections 62 to 70, Schs 12 and 13.

[95] Ibid, sections 95 to 105.

[96] The following background materials are available at *http://www.dca.gov.uk/legist/tribenforce.htm#b* 'Effective Enforcement: improved methods of recovery for civil court debt and commercial rent and a single regulatory regime for warrant enforcement agents', White Paper, LC Dept (Cm 5744, 2003); 'A Choice of Paths: better options to manage over-indebtedness and multiple debt' (Consultation Paper, DCA: CP23/04, 2004); 'Relief for the Indebted: an Alternative to Bankruptcy' (Consultation Paper:, Insolvency Service, 2005).

[97] CPR 70.2(2).

[98] RSC Ord 46 and 47 and CCR Ord 26, in Schs 1 and 2, CPR.

nals, Courts and Enforcement Act 2007 ('TCE Act');, see further **8.30** below;[99] (ii) a third party debt order (see **8.31**);[100] (iii) a charging order (against land; see **8.32**), stop order (against securities or funds in court), or a stop notice (against securities);[101] or (iv) by appointment of a receiver.[102] Some types of pecuniary enforcement are available only in county courts: (v) attachment of earnings orders[103] and (vi) 'administration orders'[104] (Part 5 of the TCE Act introduces various categories of protection for debtors). Enforcement of non-money judgments is unaffected by the new legislation. Such judgments can be enforced as follows: *goods*, by warrants of specific delivery or delivery (in county courts)[105] and writs of specific delivery or of delivery (in the High Court);[106] *land*, by warrants of possession (in county courts);[107] and writs of possession (in the High Court);[108] *injunctions and other orders*, by committal proceedings (see **8.35** below).[109] Judgment creditors can apply for an order compelling a judgment debtor (or in the case of a company, one of its officers) to attend the court and to supply information concerning the debtor's means and financial commitments[110] (the TCE Act creates new methods of obtaining information concerning debtor's assets and indebtedness: sections 95 to 105). The main methods of enforcement will now be explained.

8.30   Seizure of goods (re-named 'taking control of goods' by the TCE Act) is the most common form of enforcement. The traditional operation of this method of enforcement has been (i) to seize or physically secure the debtor's goods and (ii) to sell them at public auction, or threaten to sell them, (iii) in order to satisfy the judgment debt. Elements (ii) and (iii) will not be affected by the TCE Act. But this Act introduces a new approach to element (i), which will now be summarised.[111] High Court sheriffs and county court bailiffs are re-named 'enforcement agents'. The High Court writ of *fieri facias* is renamed a 'writ of control' and county court warrants of execution become 'warrants of control'.

---

[99] Tribunals, Courts and Enforcement Act 2007, sections 62 to 70, Schs 12 and 13.

[100] CPR Part 72.

[101] CPR Part 73.

[102] See RSC Orders 30 and 51, in Sch 1, CPR, which apply both in the High Court and county courts.

[103] CCR Ord 27, in Sch 2, CPR.

[104] County Courts Act 1984, s 112; such an order prevents named creditors from petitioning for bankruptcy against the judgment debtor, and makes provision for payment of creditors by instalments; the order can last for three years.

[105] CCR Ord 26, r 16 in Sch 2, CPR.

[106] RSC Ord 45, r 4 in Sch 1, CPR.

[107] CCR Ord 26, r 17 in Sch 2, CPR; or by summary proceedings for the recovery of land against trespassers, CCR Ord 24 (see Sch 2, CPR) and CPR Part 55.

[108] RSC Ord 45, r 3 in Sch 1, CPR.

[109] RSC Ord 45 and 52; CCR Ord 25, 29 in Schs 1 and 2, CPR.

[110] CPR Part 71; PD (71).

[111] Tribunals, Courts and Enforcement Act 2007, sections 62 to 70, Schs 12 and 13.

Property in all the debtor's goods (defined to cover all 'property of any description, other than land') will become 'bound' by the writ or warrant once that document is received by the enforcement agent. However, innocent third party purchasers can obtain good title to such goods if they acquired the debtor's goods 'in good faith', 'for valuable consideration', and 'without notice'. Enforcement officers can gain physical 'control' of goods. 'Control' involves physically 'securing' them (including removing them) or entering into a 'controlled goods agreement' with the debtor. Before gaining 'control', the enforcement agent must give the debtor 'notice'. Enforcement agents can use reasonable force to enter premises, including domestic premises. Force, however, is not to be exercised against a person. 'Exempt goods' will be defined by regulations.

'Third party debt orders',[112] previously known as 'garnishee orders', enable   **8.31**
a judgment creditor to divert or intercept money payable to the judgment debtor, for example money held to his order in a bank or building society.[113] In one case this process was used to obtain an order for a non-party bank to pay costs incurred in proceedings against an unincorporated association.[114] The procedure concerns 'any amount of any debt due, or accruing due, to the judgment debtor from the third party.'[115] The court must make both an interim[116] and a final order.[117] The process is not exercisable against debts 'situated' outside England and Wales,[118] even if the foreign jurisdiction is within the Brussels or Lugano jurisdictional system.[119] The relevant non-party must also be 'within the [English] jurisdiction'.[120]

---

[112] CPR Part 72; PD (72).

[113] CPR 72.1(2): provided the bank or building society 'lawfully accepts deposits in the United Kingdom'; banks and building societies can become subject to obligations to reveal details of all accounts which the judgment debtor holds with them: CPR 72.6; for money in court standing to the credit of the judgment debtor, CPR 72.10; on the threshold level of proof that a bank etc account exists, *Alawiye v Mahmood* [2006] EWHC 277 (Ch); [2007] 1 WLR 79.

[114] *Huntingdon Life Sciences Group plc v Stop Huntingdon Animal Cruelty* [2005] EWHC 2233 (QB).

[115] CPR 72.2(1)(a).

[116] *Alawiye v Mahmood* [2006] EWHC 277 (Ch); [2007] 1 WLR 79.

[117] CPR 72.2(2).

[118] *Kuwait Oil Tanker Company SAK 7 Ors v UBS AG* [2003] UKHL 31; [2004] 1 AC 300 (third party debt-a bank account in defendant's name – 'situated' in Switzerland; English judgment debt; third party bank having branch in London); *Société Eram Shipping Company Ltd v Hong Kong and Shanghai Banking Corporation Ltd* [2003] UKHL 30; [2004] 1 AC 260 (third party debt – also a bank account – 'situated' in Hong Kong; French judgment debt, recognized in England; third party bank having branch in London); reasoning criticised by P Rogerson [2003] CLJ 576.

[119] As in the *Kuwait* case [2003] UKHL; [2004] 1 AC 300.

[120] CPR 72.1(1).

8.32   Charging orders[121] can be made in respect of a money judgment, including one expressed in terms of a foreign currency.[122] CPR Part 73 governs charging orders against the judgment debtor's land or interest in land; or 'stop orders' preventing various dealings in respect of securities or funds in court; or 'stop notices' preventing various dealings in respect of securities.[123] A judgment debtor's interest in jointly held real property can be the subject of a charge.[124] A charging order can also be applied against the proceeds of sale of land held under a trust for sale.[125] In all these situations, the procedure involves an interim and a final order. The criteria for making a final charging order include:[126] '(a) the personal circumstances of the debtor and (b) whether any other creditor would be likely to be unduly prejudiced by the making of the Order.' No final order will be made if the judgment debtor becomes insolvent after the interim order. This is because such an order in that situation would disturb the insolvency legislation's scheme of distribution.[127] Final orders against interests in land should be registered.[128]

(9) Enforcement of Injunctions

8.33   Injunctions must be backed by credible threats (so too the positive order for specific performance of a contract).[129] The injunction was devised by the Court of Chancery. Before the 1870s that court had administered a separate procedure and set of rules and remedies, so-called 'Equity'. The 'Common Law' courts had a separate jurisdiction. But the Supreme Court of Judicature Acts of 1873 and 1875 amalgamated these procedural systems. The Lord Chancellors, and other Court of Chancery judges administering this 'Equitable' jurisdiction, had not been reluctant to enforce an injunction (effectively, an 'equitable order') by applying quasi-criminal sanctions against those who failed to

---

[121] CPR Part 73; PD (73); Charging Orders Act 1979.

[122] *Carnegie v Giessen* [2005] EWCA Civ 191; [2005] 1 WLR 2510, CA (English judgment payable in US dollars; valid charging order).

[123] Charging Orders Act 1979, s 2(2)(a) to (c) respectively; CPR 73, Sections I to III; notable decisions on trusts, subrogation and restitution law in this context are *Boscawen v Bajwa* [1996] 1 WLR 328, CA; *Banque Financière de la Cité v Parc (Battersea) Ltd* [1999] 1 AC 221, HL; for the types of disposition prevented by stop orders, CPR 73.13 (funds in court) and 73.14 (securities); for the types of dealing prevented by stop notices, see CPR 73.18 (securities).

[124] Charging Orders Act 1979, s 2(1)(b)(iii).

[125] *National Westminster Bank Ltd v Stockman* [1981] 1 WLR 67.

[126] Charging Orders Act 1979, s 1(5).

[127] *Roberts Petroleum Ltd v Bernard Kenny* [1983] AC 192, HL.

[128] On the effect of registration, *Clark v Chief Land Registrar* [1994] Ch 370, CA.

[129] RSC Ord 45 & 52; CCR Ord 25, 29: appended to CPR; *Arlidge, Eady and Smith on Contempt* (3rd edn, 2005).

comply with such an order (see also **8.35** below). This tough approach towards breach of injunctions has survived the procedural changes of the 1870s, just mentioned. And so a person will be guilty of contempt of court if he breaches an injunction addressed to him. It is also an act of contempt to fail to comply with an order for disclosure of assets within a freezing injunction,[130] or to fail to honour an undertaking made by a litigant (whether expressly or impliedly, under well-established rules) to the court.[131] The representative mechanism can be used for effective injunctive relief against a disruptive unincorporated association (a 'protest group').[132] In these various situations, non-compliance need not be deliberate or calculated.[133] It is normally enough that the act or omission is not accidental.[134] A party who disobeys an injunction will be guilty of contempt even if he later persuades the court to set aside the relevant order or injunction.[135] Nor is this coercive regime confined to litigants. A non-party who receives notice of an injunction is guilty of contempt if he aids or abets breach of that injunction, or acts independently to undermine it.[136]

---

[130] *Raja v Van Hoogstraten* [2004] EWCA Civ 968; [2004] 4 All ER 793; information disclosed (including in response to cross-examination) under a disclosure order ancillary to a freezing order can be used for contempt purposes, *Dadourian Group International Inc v Simms* [2006] EWCA Civ 1745; [2007] 2 All ER 329.

[131] eg, the implied undertaking applicable to information disclosed under compulsory disclosure powers, CPR 31.22 (see **6.24**); instances of contempt in that context are *Miller v Scorey* [1996] 3 All ER 18 and *Watkins v AJ Wright (Electrical) Ltd* [1996] 3 All ER 31; or the various undertakings imposed pursuant to freezing injunctions or search orders; for emphatic affirmation that breach of an undertaking is as serious as breach of an injunction, *Cobra Golf Inc v Rata* [1998] Ch 109, 128, 163, per Rimer J, citing authority; on the court's discretion to release a party from an undertaking, *Di Placito v Slater* [2003] EWCA Civ 1863; [2004] 1 WLR 1605, [27] ff.

[132] *Oxford University v Webb* [2006] EWHC 2490 (QB) Irwin J applying CPR 19.6 (see **14.03**), and considering, at [56] ff, *M Michaels (Furriers) Limited v Askew* (CA, unreported, 23 June 1983) and other authorities.

[133] *Miller v Scorey* [1996] 3 All ER 18; *Watkins v AJ Wright (Electrical) Ltd* [1996] 3 All ER 31 (both concerning breaches of the implied undertaking protecting information disclosed during discovery under CPR 31.22, see **6.24**).

[134] *Heatons Transport (St Helens) Ltd v Transport and General Workers Union* [1973] AC 15, 109, HL; applied in *Z Bank v D1* [1974] 1 Lloyd's Rep 656, Colman J; *Director General of Fair Trading v Pioneer Concrete Ltd* [1995] 1 AC 456, 478, HL; in *Bird v Hadkinson The Times* 4 March, 1999, Neuberger J refused to follow the test of deliberate breach adopted in *Irtelli v Squatriti* [1993] QB 83, CA.

[135] *Motorola Credit Corporation v Uzan (No 2)* [2003] EWCA Civ 752; [2004] 1 WLR 113, at [148] to [156] (considered in *Raja v Van Hoogstraten* [2004] EWCA Civ 968; [2004] 4 All ER 793); *Isaacs v Robertson* [1985] AC 97, PC; *Bhimji v Chatwani* [1991] 1 WLR 989; *Wardle Fabrics Ltd v Myristis (G) Ltd* [1984] FSR 263.

[136] *Seaward v Paterson* [1897] 1 Ch 545; *Elliott v Klinger* [1967] 1 WLR 1165; *Z Ltd v A-Z and AA-LL* [1982] QB 558, CA (containing a good survey of the principles); *Attorney-General v Times Newspapers Ltd* [1992] AC 191, HL; *Att-Gen v Punch Ltd* [2002] UKHL 50; [2003] 1 AC 1046.

8.34   A company is in contempt of court if it breaches an order because of the conduct of its employee. This is so even if the company expressly prohibited such conduct. It is enough that the employee's conduct took place within the course of his employment.[137]

8.35   A contemnor can be committed for contempt of court.[138] Civil contempt is classified as a quasi-criminal wrong. The standard of proof is 'beyond reasonable doubt' rather than the lower civil standard of proof 'on the balance of probabilities' (on the general standard of proof in civil cases, see **2.32**).[139] Hearsay evidence is admissible[140] (on such evidence in general, see **8.09** above), as well as statements made in earlier proceedings under compulsion.[141] A person found guilty of contempt can be imprisoned for up to two years[142] or fined. In the case of both individuals[143] and companies, the court can order 'sequestration' of their assets.[144] This involves 'sequestrators' (officers of the court, often appointed specially for the present case) seizing the contemnor's pro-

---

[137] *Re Supply of Ready Mixed Concrete (No 2)* [1995] 1 AC 456, HL; the question of corporate criminal liability was considered in *Attorney-General's Reference (No 2) of 1999* [2000] QB 796, CA, also noting: *Meridian Global Funds Management Asia Ltd v Securities Commission* [1995] 2 AC 500; *R v British Steel plc* [1995] 1 WLR 1356; *In Re Supply of Ready-Mixed Concrete (No 2)* [1995] 1 AC 456, HL; *R v Associated Octel Ltd* [1996] 1 WLR 1543; *R v Gateway Foodmarkets Ltd* [1997] ICR 382.

[138] *Arlidge, Eady and Smith on Contempt* (3rd edn, 2005); RSC Ord 52, Sch 1, CPR; CCR Ord 29, Sch 2, CPR; on the need for due process to protect contemnors, *Raja v Van Hoogstraten* [2004] EWCA Civ 968; [2004] 4 All ER 793, conclusion at [106]; *Newman v Modern Bookbinders Ltd* [2000] 1 WLR 2559, CA; for discussion of the court's willingness to commit a contemnor, despite technical procedural defects, see *Bell v Tuohy* [2002] EWCA Civ 423; [2002] 3 All ER 975, CA, at [31] to [59], examining *Nicholls v Nicholls* [1997] 1 WLR 314, 326, CA; and for problems of overlapping criminal and civil proceedings, *Lomas v Parle* [2003] EWCA Civ 1804; [2004] 1 WLR 1642.

[139] *Z Bank v D1* [1974] 1 Lloyd's Rep 656, 660, Colman J.

[140] *Daltel Europe Ltd v Makki* [2006] EWCA Civ 94; [2006] 1 WLR 2704.

[141] *Dadourian Group International Inc v Simms* [2006] EWCA Civ 1745; [2007] 2 All ER 329; *Lexi Holdings plc v Shaid Luqman* [2007] EWHC 1508 (Ch).

[142] *Harris v Harris* [2001] EWCA Civ 1645; [2002] Fam 253, CA, at [12] to [14], noting Contempt of Court Act 1981, s 14(1), restricting the period to a maximum of two years' imprisonment; also noting the statutory duty to release a contemnor who has served half of a term of less than 12 months: Criminal Justice Act 1991, s 45(3); in *Lexi Holdings plc v Shaid Luqman* [2007] EWHC 1508 (Ch), at [182] ff, a party was imprisoned for 18 months for failure to deliver up his passport and other documents, preserve evidence, disclose property assets and provide information regarding the location of funds and assets and, further, dealing with certain property and assets which fell within the ambit of the freezing order; for another instance of imprisonment, *UK (Aid) Ltd v Martin Mitchell* [2007] EWHC 1940.

[143] *Raja v Van Hoogstraten* [2004] EWCA Civ 968; [2004] 4 All ER 793 at [71] ff; although the court has such jurisdiction against individuals who are contemnors, the order was procedurally defective on the facts, see [105].

[144] Sch 1, CPR, at RSC Ord 45, rr 3 (1)(c), 4(2)(c), 5(1)(b)(i)(ii); RSC Ord 46, r 5; on the court's inherent power, *Webster v Southwark LBC* [1983] QB 698.

perty, including land,[145] and eventually selling it.[146] When deciding on the appropriateness of punishing the contemnor, the court will consider the following points: (i) whether the contemnor has 'contumaciously' flouted the law;[147] (ii) whether it has become evident that he will not accept the court's authority; (iii) the contemnor has already received adequate punishment;[148] (iv) or he has 'purged' his contempt;[149] (v) whether his conduct or omission was deliberate or negligent.[150] As for this last consideration, inadvertent breach of an injunction will not normally justify punishment.[151] The court might instead make a disciplinary costs order;[152] or strike out the contemnor's claim or defence; or bar him from bringing an appeal,[153] although in these last two respects caution is now required.[154]

---

[145] *Mir v Mir* [1992] Fam 79.

[146] On sequestrators' potential liability for negligence, *IRC v Hoogstraten* [1985] QB 1077, CA; and see *Raja v Van Hoogstraten* [2007] EWHC 1743 (Ch).

[147] *Bhimji v Chatwani* [1991] 1 WLR 989; good illustrations are *X v Y* [1988] 2 All ER 648, 666 and *Watkins v AJ Wright (Electrical) Ltd* [1996] 3 All ER 31; on the question when a litigant's defiance in open court of a judicial or court order will justify imprisonment for contempt, *Bell v Tuohy* [2002] EWCA Civ 423; [2002] 3 All ER 975, CA, [60] to [66].

[148] *Re Barrell Enterprises* [1973] 1 WLR 19, CA; RSC Ord 52, r 8, Sch 1, CPR.

[149] The court's flexibility is not without limit: *Harris v Harris* [2001] EWCA Civ 1645; [2002] Fam 253, CA (court lacks power to permit release of contemnor from prison on condition that he does not commit fresh contempt).

[150] *Guildford BC v Valler The Times* 15 October 1993, CA.

[151] eg, *Adam Phones Ltd v Gideon Goldschmidt* (unreported, 9 July 1999) (innocent failure to comply with a court order for delivery up of materials).

[152] *Miller v Scorey* [1996] 3 All ER 18; *Watkins v AJ Wright (Electrical) Ltd* [1996] 3 All ER 31.

[153] *Raja v Van Hoogstraten* [2004] EWCA Civ 968; [2004] 4 All ER 793 at [81] to [83], [112]; and see the authorities (not all of which were cited in the *Raja* case), noted at Neil Andrews, *English Civil Procedure* (Oxford UP, 2003) 39.63.

[154] *Motorola Credit Corporation v Uzan (No 2)* [2003] EWCA Civ 752; [2004] 1 WLR 113, at [81] to [83]; *Days Healthcare UK Ltd v Pihsiang MM Co Ltd* [2006] EWHC 1444 (Comm); [2007] CP Rep 1.

Chapter 9

Costs and Conditional Fee Agreements[1]

Contents

(1) Introduction

9.01 This chapter is concerned with (i) the general system of costs and (ii) 'conditional fee agreements' ('CFAs'). As for (i), the topic of 'costs' is a large, pervasive, technical, fundamental and indeed fascinating subject. In some respects it has become the most prominent and even the most vexed aspect of modern civil procedure in England. Other parts of this book contain discussion of aspects of 'costs'.[2] As for conditional fee agreements ('CFAs'), these have become the 'work-horse' of 'economic access to justice' in England[3] (on the distinction between 'formal' and 'economic' forms of access to justice, see the next para-

---

[1] Specialist works: MJ Cook, *Cook on Costs* (2007); P Hurst, *Civil Costs* (4th edn, 2007); costs generally, Neil Andrews, *English Civil Procedure* (Oxford UP, 2003) chs 35 to 37; A Zuckerman *Civil Procedure* (2nd edn, 2006) ch 26; for a recent survey, P Hurst, '... Costs including conditional fees in England and Wales' (2005) 10 ZZP 39 ff; for an Italian scholar's study of the English system, A De Luca, *L'Accesso alla Giustizia in Inghilterra: fra Stato e Mercato* (Torino, 2007); for a wide-ranging set of recommendations on access to justice and funding, Civil Justice Council's 'Improved Access to Justice – Funding Options and Proportionate costs' (August 2005) 148: www.civiljusticecouncil.gov.uk/files/Improved_Access_to_Justice.pdf

[2] **4.35** on security for costs; **10.25** on settlement offers; **11.40** ff on disciplinary costs decisions against those who unreasonably reject invitations to mediate; and **14.08, 14.10, 14.14** on aspects of costs in the context of multi-party litigation.

[3] The distinction between formal and economic or 'effective' access to justice was ac-

graph). The CFA system has enabled Government to reduce reliance upon legal aid (see also, for assessment, **9.30**). The decision to develop the conditional fee system was manifestly a response to the rise in the amount of expenditure upon civil legal aid. During the 1980s and early 1990s, this had increased at a rate exceeding general inflation.[4] The Treasury (a Government Department) noted the fiscal anomaly that expenditure on the legal aid system was not capped. This led to the political decision to replace civil legal aid with the Community Legal Service Fund. This provides public financial support for civil litigation, but only in specially deserving cases. Many categories of civil actions are excluded (for example, ordinary personal injury claims).[5]

'Formal access to justice' concerns the question whether a party *who has the financial means to do so* can have his claim or defence litigated before the courts. The Court of Appeal has encapsulated this 'fundamental principle' as follows: 'an individual (who is not under a disability, a bankrupt or a vexatious litigant) is entitled to untrammelled access to a court of first instance in respect of a bona fide claim based on a properly pleaded cause of action ... '. The same court admitted that this principle is subject to the following qualifications: '... [an individual litigant] is in peril of an adverse costs order if he is unsuccessful'; and the principle of formal access is 'subject to the further proviso that, if the court is satisfied the action is not properly constituted or pleaded, or is not brought bona fide in the sense of being vexatious oppressive or otherwise an abuse of process, then the court may dismiss the action or impose a stay ... '.[6] 'Economic access'[7] concerns the challenge of rendering the civil justice system

9.02

---

knowledged in *Hamilton v Fayed (No 2)* [2002] EWCA Civ 665; [2003] QB 1175, at [65] per Chadwick LJ, and [81] per Hale LJ; on this case see **9.14**.

[4] 'Access to Justice with Conditional Fees' (Consultation Paper, Lord Chancellor's Department, 1998), para 3.3; for further comment, *Modernising Justice* (Lord Chancellor's Department: Cm 4255, 1998) ch 2, esp at paras 2.42 ff, and ch 3; in *Callery v Gray* [2001] EWCA Civ 1117; [2001] 1 WLR 2112, at [7], Lord Woolf CJ noted the interrelated motivation behind the expansion of conditional fee arrangements: to increase effective access to justice and to reduce public expenditure on civil legal aid; there are similar comments in *Callery v Gray (Nos 1 and 2)* [2002] UKHL 28; [2002] 1 WLR 2000, at [2] per Lord Bingham, [47] and [48] per Lord Hope.

[5] Neil Andrews, *English Civil Procedure* (Oxford UP, 2003) 35.65 ff; *Cook on Costs* (2006) ch 41; for an Italian scholar's study of the English system, A De Luca, *L'Accesso alla Giustizia in Inghilterra: fra Stato e Mercato* (Torino, 2007).

[6] *Abraham v Thompson* [1997] 4 All ER 362, 374, CA, per Potter LJ, cited in *Stocznia Gdanska SA v Latvian Shipping Co (No 2)* [1999] 3 All ER 822, 829.

[7] H Genn 'Understanding Civil Justice' (1997) CLP 156–87; Lord Chancellor's Department 'Modernising Justice' (Cm 4155, 1998) chs 1–4; Lord Woolf *Access to Justice: Interim Report* (1995) and *Access to Justice: Final Report* (1996); M Zander, *The State of Justice* (2000), ch 1; for access to justice and Art 6(1) of the European Convention on Human Rights: J McBride, 'Access to Justice and Human Rights' (1998) CJQ 235; A Le Sueur, 'Access to Justice in the United Kingdom' [2000] EHRLRev 457; more generally R Abel, *English Lawyers between Market and State* (Oxford UP, 2003).

available financially to all sections of the community, its citizens, companies and other organisations. The author has discussed elsewhere the English system's adoption of 'privatised' CFA-funding, and the shift away from public legal aid.[8] The concept of 'access to court' (both in its formal and economic sense) is also prominent in the jurisprudence concerning Article 6(1) of the European Convention on Human Rights (now incorporated into English law by the Human Rights Act 1998).[9] As the European Court of Human Rights said in the *Airey* case (1979): '[Article 6(1) of the] Convention is intended to guarantee not rights that are theoretical or illusory but rights that are practical and effective. This is particularly so of the right of access to the courts in view of the prominent place held in a democratic society by the right to a fair trial.'[10]

9.03   There is widespread dissatisfaction with the expense of civil proceedings in England and Wales. Normally, the largest element in a party's expenditure upon costs is the expense of hiring a lawyer or a legal team (see also the quotation from Buxton LJ at **9.04**).[11] Solicitors are normally paid 'by the hour', although nowadays they are required to give an estimate of their likely fee to the client at the beginning of the litigation.[12] Barristers receive an agreed fee for preparing a case for a hearing and appearing at court. That fee can be supplemented if the case lasts for longer than expected. The sum to be paid as costs can be very large, both absolutely and in relation to the value of the substantive claim.[13] A shocking example is the huge costs bill, far exceeding a million pounds, incurred in an action by a 'super-model' against a newspaper. The result, only confirmed after two appeals, was that she won only four thousand pounds of damages (see the *Campbell* case, below, at **9.26**).

9.04   The reality, unpalatable to many, is that the high costs of court litigation, and the risk of incurring liability for the other side's costs, combine to deter many

---

[8] On the rise of conditional fees and the decline of legal aid, Neil Andrews, *English Civil Procedure* (Oxford UP, 2003), ch 35; see also F Regan, A Paterson, T Goriely, D Fleming (eds), *The Transformation of Legal Aid: Comparative and Historical Studies* (Clarendon Press, Oxford, 1999); T Goriely, 'The Government's Legal Aid Reforms', in AAS Zuckerman and R Cranston (eds), *Reform of Civil Procedure: Essays on 'Access to Justice'* (Oxford UP, 1995) ch 18.

[9] eg *Golder v UK* (1975) 1 EHRR 524, ECHR; *Ashingdane v UK* (1985) 7 EHRR 528, ECHR.

[10] *Airey v Ireland* (1979) Series A, No 32; 2 EHRR 305, at [24], ECHR; on access to justice and Article 6(1), A Le Sueur, 'Access to Justice in the United Kingdom' [2000] EHRLRev 457, 461 ff.

[11] See also **1.14, 2.23, 11.19; 13.28**.

[12] *Garbutt v Edwards* [2005] EWCA Civ 1206; [2006] 1 WLR 2907; costs estimates must also be disclosed to the opponent at various stages and the court will have regard to these when determining costs awards: *Tribe v Southdown Gliding Club Ltd* [2007] EWHC 90080 (Costs), considering *Leigh v Michelin Type Co plc* [2003] EWCA Civ 1766; [2004] 1 WLR 846.

[13] eg *Daniels v Commissioner for Police for the Metropolis* [2005] EWCA Civ 1312; [2006] CP Rep 9, at [32] and [35].

from vindicating their meritorious rights or presenting sound defences to bogus or exaggerated claims. The fact that court litigation is so expensive is one reason for the recent expansion of mediation (generally, see chapter 11). The 'Woolf reforms' were expected to alleviate the problem of the high cost of civil litigation (generally on the aims of those reforms, see **2.13** ff). But the situation has not improved, as Buxton LJ in the Court of Appeal admitted in 2007:[14]

'The very high costs of civil litigation in England and Wales is a matter of concern not merely to the parties in a particular case, but for the litigation system as a whole. While disputants should be given every encouragement to settle their differences without going to court, that encouragement should not include the making of litigation prohibitively costly so that litigants are deterred irrespective of the merits of their case. One element in the present high cost of litigation is undoubtedly the expectations as to annual income of the professionals who conduct it. The costs system as it at present operates cannot do anything about that, because it assesses the proper charge for work on the basis of the market rates charged by the professions, rather than attempting the no doubt difficult task of placing an objective value on the work.'

Zuckerman has argued that the only way of reducing the expense of English civil litigation is to introduce a system of fixed fees commensurate with a claim's value. He compares and approves the German system of fixed fees.[15] Andrew Cannon has also concluded, after reviewing many systems of law, that fixed costs scales, which can be recovered from the losing party by a successful party, might confer the following four benefits: first, fixed fees might increase resort to the courts; secondly, they might lower the costs actually incurred by litigants; thirdly, they might reduce unnecessary activity by lawyers and litigants during the conduct of an action; finally, they might also speed up litigation.[16] However, possible counter-arguments to wholesale adoption of fixed costs are: (i) they would exert a major inflexible bureaucratic influence upon the civil justice system; (ii) they might result in unrealistic depression of lawyers' rates, and this would lead to a weakening of legal recruitment and retention of lawyers in this important field of legal activity; (iii) litigants with large budgets will be free to pay more, because the system of 'fixed costs' operates merely as a cap on recoverable costs; such a cap does not prohibit a litigant from paying an enhanced level of remuneration to his lawyer if the case is important enough to him. **9.05**

---

[14] *Willis v Nicolson* [2007] EWCA Civ 199 at [24] (earlier, in *Knight v Beyond Properties Pty Ltd* [2006] EWHC 1242 (Ch); [2007] 1 WLR 625, Mann J cautiously acknowledged a wider jurisdiction but declared that it would be exercised only in very extreme cases).

[15] A Zuckerman, 'Lord Woolf's Access to Justice: *Plus Ça Change …*' (1996) 59 MLR 773; Zuckerman notes D Leipold, 'Limiting Costs for Better Access to Justice – the German Experience' in AAS Zuckerman and R Cranston (eds), *The Reform of Civil Procedure: Essays on 'Access to Justice'* (Oxford UP, 1995).

[16] A Cannon 'Designing Cost Policies to Provide Sufficient Access to Lower Courts' (2002) 21 CJQ 198, 219.

(2) The Cost-Shifting Rule

9.06   The main rule in England is that a victorious party ('the receiving party') should recover his 'standard basis' (see **9.12**) costs from the opponent ('the paying party').[17] This rule is rooted both in the public policy of deterring bad or spurious claims and defences[18] and in the basic fairness of indemnifying the victorious party at the conclusion of litigation. As for the element of public policy, the rule has the obvious merit of acting as a disincentive against bringing or defending claims: any litigant is aware of the risk of a huge costs liability (his own and his opponent's costs) if he has the misfortune to lose the case. As for the matter of private justice, the essential fairness of the general cost-shifting rule is that the losing party has either brought or defended a case on grounds judicially determined to be unsound. He should, therefore, be ordered to indemnify the other whose claim or defence has been vindicated. Moreover, the rule has traditionally operated efficiently on the basis of 'strict liability' (for recent qualifications, see **9.10** below). This is because the losing party is obliged to pay the victorious party irrespective of the vanquished party's fault, reasonableness or motive. The 'loser must pay' rule is analogous to the result following a 'penalty shoot out': winning is all, and the rest of the game forgotten.

(3) Protective Costs Orders

9.07   In special cases, so far confined to 'public interest' litigation, the courts have discretion to protect a claimant or a defendant[19] against potential liability for costs. The leading cases establish the following criteria:[20] (i) whether the issues raised are of general public importance; (ii) whether the public interest requires

---

[17] CPR 44.3(2) states the following 'general' rule: that the unsuccessful party will be ordered to pay the costs of the successful party; but the court may make a different order; for discussion in the context of discontinuance by a claimant, *Wylde v Culver* [2006] EWHC 1313 (Ch); [2006] 1 WLR 2674; where the issues have concerned both the question of liability and quantum, and a different party has been 'successful' under these respective heads, an 'issues-based costs order' is appropriate: *McGlinn v Waltham Contractors Ltd* [2007] EWHC 698 (TCC).

[18] Neil Andrews, *English Civil Procedure* (Oxford UP, 2003) 6.31; a classic statement is by Sir Thomas Bingham in *Roache v News Group Newspapers Limited The Times*, 23 November 1992, CA, who observed that the principle that costs normally follow the event is 'of fundamental importance in deterring plaintiffs from bringing and defendants from defending actions which they are likely to lose.'

[19] *R (Ministry of Defence) v Wiltshire and Swindon Coroner* [2005] EWHC 889 (Admin); [2006] 1 WLR 134, at [34] ff, per Collins J.

[20] *R (Corner House Research) v Secretary of State for Trade and Industry* [2005] EWCA Civ 192; [2005] 1 WLR 2600; *R (Burkett) v Hammersmith LBC* [2004] EWCA Civ 1342; *R (England) v Tower Hamlets LBC* [2006] EWCA Civ 1742.

that those issues be resolved; (iii) whether the applicant has any private interest in the matter;[21] (iv) whether the order will be fair when account is taken of the parties' respective resources and the amount of costs likely to be incurred; (iv) whether the claim will be discontinued without the order.

(4) Costs Capping

The courts can impose an *ex ante* 'cap' on the 'capped' party's capacity to re-   **9.08** cover costs from the opponent, at least in the context of defamation actions brought under conditional fee agreements without 'after-the-event' legal expenses insurance (on such fee arrangements, see **9.19** below).[22] It should be noted that the cap is a limit upon recoverable costs; it does not prohibit the capped party from in fact incurring costs above that cap; but in the latter situation, such excess costs will not be recoverable, because they will lie above the cap. So far the courts have been reluctant to expand this 'costs capping' jurisdiction beyond that special context. In fact, the Court of Appeal has recently suggested that imposition of costs caps in the context of personal injury litigation is so complex a task that the matter should be resolved by the Rule Committee, rather than by the courts.[23] In the absence of a general regime of costs capping, the courts will try to control excessive costs by use of case management powers (see **3.14**) and *ex post facto* costs decisions (see **9.11**).[24]

(5) Discretionary Adjustment of Costs

Costs decisions are discretionary. This discretion can be exercised in one or   **9.09** more of the following respects: whether to order one party to pay the other's costs; the amount of those costs; for what period costs are to be paid; when costs are to be paid; and questions of interest upon these payments.[25] Lord Woolf MR in *AEI Rediffusion Music Ltd v Phonographic Performance Ltd* (1999) attempted to temper the perceived rigidity of the 'winner takes all' ap-

---

[21] cf *Weir v Secretary of State for Transport* [2005] EWHC 24 (Ch) (claimant making private claim as well as other disinterested claims).

[22] *King v Telegraph Group Ltd* [2004] EWCA Civ 613; [2005] 1 WLR 2282, esp at [101].

[23] *Willis v Nicolson* [2007] EWCA Civ 199 at [24] (earlier, in *Knight v Beyond Properties Pty Ltd* [2006] EWHC 1242 (Ch); [2007] 1 WLR 625, Mann J cautiously acknowledged a wider jurisdiction but declared that it would be exercised only in very extreme cases).

[24] *Knight v Beyond Properties Pty Ltd*, ibid.

[25] CPR 44.3(1); P Hurst, '… Costs including conditional fees in England and Wales' (2005) 10 ZZP 39, 40.

proach (see **9.06** above). He said: 'too robust an application of the "follow the event principle" encourages litigants to increase the costs of litigation'; and he suggested 'if you recover all your costs as long as you win, you are encouraged to leave no stone unturned in your effort to do so.'[26]

9.10   The courts apply the following criteria when determining whether costs were unreasonably incurred or whether they are unreasonable in amount:[27] the parties' conduct before and during the proceedings, including efforts made to resolve the dispute; the amount or value of the case, its importance to the parties, and its complexity, difficulty, or novelty; the skill, effort, specialised knowledge and responsibility involved; time spent on the case; the circumstances in which the work was done.

9.11   Costs decisions are made by the trial judge or by the court hearing the pre-trial matter or appeal. Assessment of costs can be: by summary assessment (on the spot and often rough-and-ready costs determinations);[28] by detailed assessment (before costs judges);[29] in accordance with fixed costs rules (in specific situations);[30] or in accordance with the parties' agreement.[31] In some situations, the only court proceedings concern costs.[32] These are 'costs only' proceedings (see **9.25** for examples).

---

[26] [1999] 1 WLR 1507, 1522–3, CA.

[27] CPR 44.5(3); for rejection of an exorbitant costs claim, *Henry Boot Construction Ltd v Alstom Combined Cycles Ltd* [2005] EWCA Civ 814; [2005] 1 WLR 3850, CA, at [87] to [90] (costs claim was 'breathtaking'); for an example of the court reducing a party's costs award because of his failure to establish more than one fifth of the damages claimed, *Jackson v Ministry of Defence* [2006] EWCA Civ 46 (examined **10.29**); similarly, for an award of only a percentage of costs claimed, to reflect merely partial success on the points raised, see *Kew v Bettamix Ltd* [2006] EWCA Civ 1535; *The Times* 4 December 2006; on the question of dishonest aspects of a party's conduct of the case, *Ultraframe (UK) Ltd v Fielding* [2006] EWCA Civ 1660; [2007] 2 All ER 983; for adverse costs decisions to reflect failure to comply with pre-action protocols, *Straker v Tudor Rose (A Firm)* [2007] EWCA Civ 368 (where the court held that the first instance judge had over-reacted and made too severe a costs reduction); costs estimates must also be disclosed to the opponent at various stages and the court will have regard to these when determining costs awards: *Tribe v Southdown Gliding Club Ltd* [2007] EWHC 90080 (Costs), considering *Leigh v Michelin Type Co plc* [2003] EWCA Civ 1766; [2004] 1 WLR 846.

[28] CPR 44.7.

[29] ibid; and CPR Part 47.

[30] CPR Part 45.

[31] CPR 48.3.

[32] CPR 44.12A ('costs-only proceedings'); applicable where 'the parties to a dispute have reached an agreement on all issues (including which party is to pay the costs) which is made or confirmed in writing; but they have failed to agree the amount of those costs; and no [substantive] proceedings have been started.' As Lord Scott explained in *Callery v Gray (Nos 1 and 2)* [2002] UKHL 28; [2002] 1 WLR 2000, at [89]: 'Rule 44.12A and Section 17 of the Costs Practice Direction relate to "costs only" proceedings. "Costs only" proceedings may be commenced where the parties, before the commencement of litigation, have agreed in writing on all issues in the case, including which party is to pay the costs, but have been unable to agree the amount of the costs (see CPR 44.12A). In effect, the court is allowing its

(6) 'Standard' and 'Indemnity' Basis Costs[33]

The normal award is for payment to the victorious party of his costs assessed   **9.12**
on the 'standard costs' basis. However, sometimes, especially where the paying party's procedural conduct has been reprehensible, costs are assessed in a
manner more generous to the 'receiving party', namely on the 'indemnity' basis. 'Indemnity costs' expose the paying party to liability for nearly all costs
incurred by the other in the relevant litigation. 'Standard costs' are calculated
less generously towards the receiving party,[34] because the costs claimed by that
party must be proportionate overall. The Court of Appeal has prescribed the
following approach to assessment of 'standard costs': 'If the costs as a whole
are not disproportionate … then all that is normally required is that each item
should have been reasonably incurred and the costs for that item should be reasonable'; and it added, 'If on the other hand the costs as a whole appear disproportionate then the court will want to be satisfied that the work in relation to
each item was necessary and, if necessary, that the cost of the item was
reasonable.'[35] By contrast, 'proportionality' does not regulate 'indemnity
costs'. Examples of awards of indemnity costs are: a defendant's unjustified

---

costs quantification procedures to be used to support an out-of-court settlement under
which one party is to pay the reasonable costs and disbursements of another party. It is implicit in such a settlement agreement (unless the contrary is expressly stated) that the costs to
be paid should be quantified on the standard basis in accordance with the Rules and Practice
Directions that would have been applicable if there had been a court order for the payment
of the costs.'

[33] The word 'indemnity' is used in the context of costs in three different senses: (i) in contrast with 'standard basis costs' (see next note); (ii) to denote the basic costs-shifting rule (see
9.06); (iii) to denote the traditional principle, that a receiving party is entitled to legal fees
only if that payment arises under a legally enforceable agreement between him and his lawyer (considered in *Garbutt v Edwards* [2005] EWCA Civ 1206; [2006] 1 WLR 2907); (iii) is
now qualified by the need to accommodate conditional fee agreements, on which, CPR
43.2(3).

[34] *Virani Ltd v Manuel Revert y Cia SA* [2003] EWCA Civ 1651; [2004] 2 Lloyd's Rep
14; on the difference between standard basis and indemnity costs, see P Hurst, *Civil Costs*
(4th edn, 2007); MJ Cook, *Cook on Costs* (2007); and Neil Andrews, *English Civil Procedure* (2003) 36.21ff; Hurst, ibid, states: 'On the standard basis the court will only allow
costs which are proportionate to the matters in issue and will resolve any doubt which it may
have as to whether the costs were reasonably incurred or reasonable and proportionate in
amount in favour of the paying party' (noting CPR 44.4(10(2)); and he comments, 'Where
costs are to be assessed on the indemnity basis the court will resolve any doubt which it may
have as to whether costs were reasonably incurred, or were reasonable in amount, in favour
of the receiving party. There is no requirement for the costs to be proportionate on the indemnity basis', noting CPR 44.4(3); see also *Three Rivers DC v The Governor & Company
of the Bank of England* [2006] EWHC 816 (Comm) at [14], per Tomlinson J; see also *Fourie
v Le Roux* [2007] UKHL 1; [2007] 1 WLR 320, at [8] to [11]; [38] to [40], [46], [49].

[35] *Home Office v Lownds* [2002] EWCA Civ 365; [2002] 1 WLR 2450, at [31], per Lord
Woolf CJ.

refusal to accept a Part 36 settlement offer (see discussion at **10.26**); hopeless litigation (or at least seriously unreasonable conduct of litigation);[36] or a party's reliance on a seriously defective report from one's own expert.[37]

(7) Costs Orders Against Non-Parties

9.13   The English courts have the following statutory power to order a non-party to pay costs:[38]

'… the costs of and incidental to all [civil] proceedings … shall be in the discretion of the court, and the court shall have power to determine *by whom* and to what extent the costs are to be paid …'.

The House of Lords in *Aiden Shipping Ltd v Interbulk Ltd* (1986) held that the words 'by whom' should be interpreted widely to justify costs orders against non-parties.[39] Since that decision, three categories of 'non-party' have emerged: (1) so-called 'pure' (that is, non-commercial) funders; (2) commercial funders; (3) other non-parties having a special interest in the case's result. We will deal with these in turn.

9.14   As for category (1), non-party costs orders will not normally be made against 'pure' funders. These are non-parties whose financial contribution to litigation has been actuated by feelings of friendship, natural affection, or political allegiance. The leading illustration is *Hamilton v Al Fayed (No 2)* (2002).[40] In this case the Court of Appeal refused to make an order for costs

---

[36]   *EQ Projects v Alavi* [2006] EWHC 29 (TCC), at [38]; *Waites Construction Limited v HGP Greentree Alchurch Evans Limited* [2005] EWHC 2174 (TCC); *Three Rivers DC v Bank of England* [2006] EWHC 816 (Comm); see the test formulated in *National Westminster Bank Plc v Rabobank Nederland* [2007] EWHC 1742 (Comm) at [28] and [47]; at [47] he said: 'did [the losing party's conduct of the case], taken as a whole, cross the frontier between a party trying as well as professionally it could to find a sustainable basis for a claim when confronted by complex evidence which was often contradictory, but making errors of judgment and changes of position and presentation, possibly understandable but in all the circumstances objectively unreasonable or unsatisfactory, and a party conducting the litigation overall in a manner so unreasonable or so unsatisfactory as to justify an indemnity costs order?'

[37]   *Re Colt Telecom Group plc* [2002] EWHC 2815 (Ch) at [80] and [110], per Jacob J.

[38]   Supreme Court Act 1981, s 53(1); and similarly s 53(3); a non-party costs order can be made following an orginal application for such (the more common situation) or as a variation of a costs order initially made against a party to the litigation; in the latter situation, the court will require proof of a material change of circumstance or an earlier misrepresentation concerning the paying party's financial position, *Latimer Management Consultants Ltd v Ellingham Investments Ltd* [2006] EWHC 3662 (Ch); [2007] 3 All ER 485 at [30] and [40].

[39]   [1986] AC 965, HL.

[40]   [2002] EWCA Civ 665; [2003] QB 1175; for comment on Australian discussion of maintenance and champerty, see D Capper (2007) 26 CJQ 288, considering *Campbell Cash and Carry Pty Ltd v Fostif Pty Ltd* [2006] HCA 41 (High Court of Australia).

against non-commercial funders who had generously supported a defamation action brought by Neil Hamilton, a former Member of Parliament, against Mr Al Fayed, a successful businessman.[41] Hamilton's supporters were a cohort of friends and political well-wishers. Hamilton lost the case, but lacked the funds to satisfy the victorious party's very large costs order (c £1.3 million). The court held that a prospective litigant's interest in obtaining access to justice should be given priority over the victorious litigant's private interest in obtaining practical enforcement of his interest in recovering his costs. However, although unanimous, the decision was not straightforward. One member of the three-judge Court of Appeal, Hale LJ (who now sits in the House of Lords), admitted that she felt 'reluctantly persuaded to agree' with this approach.[42] She added:[43]

'There must, however, be exceptional cases where it would be quite unjust not to make an order [for costs against a 'pure' funder]: principally where the litigation was oppressive or malicious or pursued for some other ulterior motive. The fact that it was quite unmeritorious would be powerful evidence of ulterior motive but neither a necessary nor a sufficient criterion in itself.'

It is submitted that the *Hamilton* case's general refusal to award costs against   **9.15** non-commercial funders might be reconsidered in a future case by the House of Lords.[44] With respect, that decision fails to reflect properly the fact that the 'pure' funders in this case were exercising a clear choice to support Hamilton's litigation. Of course, as the Court of Appeal emphasised, it is better that a litigant in High Court proceedings should receive legal representation rather than be compelled to conduct his case without such assistance. Furthermore, it is plain that potential private or 'pure' funders will be disinclined to support a claim if (contrary to the *Hamilton* case's ruling) they face potential liability to pay the other side's costs. But such non-parties act as free agents. Furthermore, their support is not an expression of 'natural love and affection' towards their kith and kin. On the facts of the *Hamilton* case, the non-parties' motivation was predominantly ideological or political (although in some instances it might have been based on unalloyed friendship). It is suggested that non-party

---

[41] Owner of Harrods; father of the late Princess Diana's boy-friend, Dodi, (both died in the Paris car-crash in 1997): on the father, http://en.wikipedia.org/wiki/Mohammed_Al-Fayed.

[42] ibid, at [73] and [87].

[43] ibid, at [86].

[44] See the doubts of Hale LJ in the *Hamilton* case, ibid, at [73], [86], [87]; and the comment in *Arkin v Borchard Lines* Ltd [2005] EWCA Civ 655; [2005] 1 WLR 3055, at [44], where the court hinted that the result in cases similar to the *Hamilton* case (discussed above) might be reconsidered in a later decision: 'While we have confined our comments to professional funders, it does not follow that it will never be appropriate to order that those who, for motive other than profit, have contributed to the costs of unsuccessful litigation, should contribute to the successful party's costs on a similar basis'; the *Hamilton* decision was approved in a dictum in *Dymocks Franchise Systems (NSW) Pty Ltd v Todd* [2004] UKPC 39; [2004] 1 WLR 2807, at [25], per Lord Brown.

funders should not be immune from liability to pay costs in these circumstances. The principle of access to justice must be counter-balanced against the principle that bad or spurious claims should be deterred and the victorious party's reasonable expectation that he will be ordinarily indemnified for the costs he has incurred in achieving his victory (see **9.06** above for both the public policy and private fairness aspects of the costs-shifting rule). The *Hamilton* decision is unconvincing.

9.16   Category (2) (see **9.13**) concerns commercial funders. The Court of Appeal in the *Arkin* case (2005) decided that such a non-party funder might be liable for costs, to the extent of his financial contribution to the defeated party's litigation.[45] The court said: 'if the funding is provided on a contingency basis of recovery, the funder will require, as the price of the funding, a greater share of the recovery should the claim succeed' but this is preferable to denying defendants a 'right to recover any costs from a professional funder whose intervention has permitted the continuation of a claim which has ultimately proved to be without merit.'[46]

9.17   Category (3) (see **9.13**) is wide and might even cover 'myriad forms'.[47] Thus, costs can be awarded against a non-party if he has a specific interest in the outcome of the litigation and has taken steps to influence its conduct; or he is the real party interested in the case's outcome (or at least 'the real party in ... very important and critical respects');[48] or he has behaved in some other way that makes it just and reasonable to make an order.[49] Thus solicitors acting for claimants under a conditional fee agreement have been ordered to pay the costs of the victorious party.[50] These costs were incurred in litigation aimed at determining whether the conditional fee agreement was valid. On the facts of the

---

[45] *Arkin v Borchard Lines* Ltd [2005] EWCA Civ 655; [2005] 1 WLR 3055, at [40]: a non-party 'commercial funder' of litigation brought by A was found liable to pay the victorious party B's costs to the extent that the non-party provided finance in that litigation; funding agreement was not champertous.

[46] ibid, at [41]; see also [42] and [43].

[47] *Goodwood Recoveries Ltd v Breen* [2005] EWCA Civ 414; [2006] 1 WLR 2723, at [74].

[48] *Myatt v NCB (No 2)* [2007] EWCA Civ 307; [2007] 1 WLR 1559, at [7] ff.

[49] *Dymocks Franchise Systems (NSW) Pty Ltd v Todd* [2004] UKPC 39; [2004] 1 WLR 2807, at [25], per Lord Brown; *Goodwood Recoveries Ltd v Breen* [2005] EWCA Civ 414; [2006] 1 WLR 2723 (director or shareholder controlling litigation; no need for dishonesty or bad faith; causal test; for a similar situation, *Latimer Management Consultants Ltd v Ellingham Investments Ltd* [2006] EWHC 3662 (Ch); [2007] 3 All ER 485, the latter decision containing a good analysis of the evolving principles, at [32] to [37] and [52] and [53]; *Barndeal Ltd v London Borough of Richmond Upon Thames* [2005] EWHC 1377 (QB); *CIBC Mellon Trust Co v Stolzenberg* [2005] EWCA Civ 628; [2005] CP Rep 45 at [25]; *Chantrey Vellacott v The Convergence Group* [2007] EWHC 1774, Rimer J (where the order against a non-party company director was on an idemnity basis).

[50] *Myatt v NCB (No 2)* [2007] EWCA Civ 307; [2007] 1 WLR 1559, at [7] ff.

case, the solicitors had a substantial economic interest in establishing the validity of these fee arrangements. The court ordered the solicitors to contribute half of the costs to be paid to the victorious party.

(8) 'Wasted Costs' Orders Against Lawyers and Experts

A lawyer might be ordered to pay costs to an opposing party as a result of the **9.18** lawyer's improper conduct of the case, or the lawyer might be prevented from recovering costs from his client because of such misconduct. 'Wasted costs' orders are made in respect of 'costs incurred by a party (a) as a result of any improper, unreasonable or negligent act or omission on the part of any legal or other representative or any employee of such a representative; or (b) which, in the light of any such act or omission occurring after they were incurred, the court considers it is unreasonable to expect that party to pay.'[51] A court can make a wasted costs order against a solicitor or barrister in respect of a hearing. Such an order might also be made in connection with out-of-court legal assistance, such as the lawyer's settling of pleadings ('statements of case', **3.08**) or other documents immediately relevant to the exercise of a right of audience.[52] But judges must be wary of making wasted costs orders where the relevant lawyer's client is unwilling to waive legal advice privilege.[53] The courts will try to prevent wasted costs proceedings becoming a protracted form of 'satellite litigation'.[54] Attention is also drawn to **7.38** where it was noted that the courts can award wasted costs against a party-appointed *expert* whose 'gross dereliction' of his duty to the court has resulted in the opposing party incurring avoidable costs.

(9) Conditional Fee Agreements[55]

This is the English 'no win, no fee' system. This type of legal funding agree-   **9.19** ment gives a lawyer a reward for 'success' in the litigation. The Courts and Legal Services Act 1990 introduced conditional fees. This system was greatly

---

[51] Supreme Court Act 1981, s 51(6)(7)(13), inserted by Courts and Legal Services Act 1990, s 4.

[52] *Medcalf v Mardell (No 2)* [2002] UKHL 72; [2003] 1 AC 120 (substantially endorsing *Ridehalgh v Horsefield* [1994] Ch 205, CA); in *Gray v Going Places Leisure Travel Ltd* [2005] EWCA Civ 189, at [11] to [15] guidance was given on the timing of wasted costs applications and hearings; *Regent Leisuretime Ltd v Skerett* [2006] EWCA Civ 1032; [2006] CP Rep 42 illustrates the high threshold for making such an order.

[53] *Medcalf* case, ibid.

[54] ibid.

[55] MJ Cook, *Cook on Costs* (2007); M Harvey, *Guide to Conditional Fee Agreements* (2nd edn, 2006); Neil Andrews, *English Civil Procedure* (Oxford UP, 2003) ch 35.

expanded in 1998 by delegated legislation. It now embraces all civil litigation or arbitration, other than certain family law matters.[56] This legislation over-rides the traditional opposition (see **9.23**) of the English Common Law to liti-gation lawyers having any form of financial interest in the case's outcome (see **9.24**). But the legislation legitimises conditional fee agreements only if they comply with the statutory scheme of recognition (see **9.25**). There is some in-terest in the possibility that English law might ultimately adopt the US system of contingency fees. The American attorney's prize for success on the plain-tiff's behalf is a percentage return of the damages awarded at judgment or agreed during settlement (see **9.27**). The author's opinion (for elaboration of this view, see **9.30** ff) is that the English CFA system is, on balance, an accept-able means of 'privatising' access to justice, reducing public expenditure on legal aid, and accelerating funding decisions. However, it is necessary to be vigilant to protect this system against abuse. This is because CFAs can signifi-cantly increase the overall expense of the civil process. This increased burden is now borne by the class of potential defendants who pay for liability insur-ance. The same system can also tempt lawyers to conduct cases for their own financial benefit rather than solely for their client's interests.

9.20   An English conditional fee agreement concerns the provision of advocacy or litigation services. It stipulates that the client's 'fees and expenses, or any part of them' shall be 'payable only in specified circumstances'.[57] The agreement usually specifies that the lawyer can receive a 'success fee', as well as his ordi-nary fee.[58] The success element is a 'percentage increase'.[59] This bonus cannot exceed 100 per cent of the normal fee.[60] Lord Bingham in the House of Lords in *Callery v Gray* (2002) said that the three aims of the CFA system are (see also **9.30** ff on the benefits and problematic features of CFAs): to control and reduce public expenditure on civil justice funding, allowing it to be refocused on needy cases; secondly, to improve access to justice for meritorious claims; thirdly, to deter weak cases and enable defendants to recover costs from poor claimants by encouraging such claimants to purchase 'after-the-event' insur-ance cover (on this last aspect, see the next paragraph).[61]

---

[56] Main provisions: Courts and Legal Services Act 1990, ss 58, 58A (substituted by Access to Justice Act 1999, s 27); Supreme Court Act 1981, s 51(2) (as amended by Access to Justice Act 1981, s 31); Conditional Fee Agreements Order 1998 (SI 1998, No 1860); Conditional Fee Agreements (Revocation) Regulations 2005 (SI 2005/2305); CPR 43.2(1)(a), (l), (m), (o) 44.3A, 44.3B, 44.5, 44.15, 44.16, 48.9; PD (48) 55.

[57] Courts and Legal Services Act 1990, s 58(1) (as substituted by Access to Justice Act 1999, s 27); for the limits of 'advocacy or litigation services', *Gaynor v Central West London Buses Ltd* [2006] EWCA Civ 1120; [2007] 1 WLR 1045.

[58] CPR 48.9(2).

[59] ibid.

[60] Conditional Fee Agreements Order 1998 (SI 1998, No 1860), Art 4.

[61] *Callery v Gray (Nos 1 and 2)* [2002] UKHL 28; [2002] 1 WLR 2000, at [2], per Lord Bingham.

If a claimant wins under a CFA funded action, the defendant will be liable **9.21** for each of the following three items: the claimant's ordinary costs; secondly, the claimant's lawyer's 'success fee'; thirdly, the claimant's 'after-the-event' ('ATE') insurance premiums for legal services. ATE cover is important to cover the claimant's risk that he will normally become liable to pay the defendant's costs if he loses the action.[62] Lord Woolf CJ in the Court of Appeal in *Callery v Gray (No 1)* (2001)[63] noted that it is an inevitable feature of Government policy in this field that unsuccessful defendants are subjected to an additional costs burden. Although a defendant might also enter a conditional fee agreement, this is less common. The system of conditional fees has raised the stakes of contesting liability, to the prejudice of defendants.[64] Lord Hope spoke frankly of this in *Callery v Gray* (2002):[65]

'The new regime is not beyond criticism ... The burden of meeting the cost of access to justice now falls on liability insurers. It thus falls indirectly on their policy holders, who are likely to have to face increased premiums. Furthermore, unless the new regime is controlled very carefully, its effect may be to benefit ATE insurance providers unreasonably and to place a disproportionate burden on liability insurers. It may lead to a culture of incurring additional costs which lacks any incentive on claimants to keep costs down.'

As a result, defendants will be even more inclined to settle cases. If they are prudent, they will settle a case more readily than they were wont to do before the CFA system was introduced. It is apparent that the legislature has favoured access to justice by claimants and disfavoured defendants in their attempt to resist claims.

There has been extensive litigation (indeed a 'costs war': see **9.25** below) **9.22** concerning appropriate levels of both success fees[66] and insurance premiums.[67] Furthermore, in the core areas of tort litigation, specific rules govern reasonable success fees in claims concerning road traffic accidents and employers'

---

[62] Access to Justice Act 1999, s 29.

[63] *Callery v Gray (No 1)* [2001] EWCA Civ 1117; [2001] 1 WLR 2112, CA, [60] to [64], per Lord Woolf CJ.

[64] Of course most 'defendants' are in substance insurance companies who are defending the case in the name of the insured under the principle of subrogation: the appearance of the defendant's name in the case's title is deceptive, masking forensic reality.

[65] *Callery v Gray (Nos 1 and 2)* [2002] UKHL 28; [2002] 1 WLR 2000, at [54].

[66] *Callery v Gray (Nos 1 and 2)* [2002] UKHL 28; [2002] 1 WLR 2000; *Halloran v Delaney* [2002] EWCA Civ 1258; [2003] 1 WLR 28; *Claims Direct Test Cases* [2003] EWCA Civ 136; [2003] 4 All ER 508; *Atack v Lee* [2005] EWCA Civ 1712; [2005] 1 WLR 2643.

[67] *Callery v Gray* [2001] EWCA Civ 1117; [2001] 1 WLR 2112, at [54]; *Callery v Gray (Nos 1 and 2)* [2002] UKHL 28; [2002] 1 WLR 2000; *Sarwar v Alam* [2001] EWCA Civ 1401; [2002] 1 WLR 125 (relationship between 'before-the-event' and 'after-the-event' legal expenses insurance cover); *Rogers v Merthyr Tydfil County BC* [2006] EWCA Civ 1134; [2007] 1 WLR 808 (validity of staged ATE premium).

liability.[68] The Court of Appeal has recently held that the rules governing success fees in the road traffic and employment liability contexts are mandatory,[69] that is, the courts have no discretion to reduce the 100 per cent bonus prescribed in the CPR.

9.23   As explained at **9.19**, Parliament introduced a conditional fee agreement system in 1990 and expanded it in 1998. Legislation was necessary because the Common Law (that is the long line of earlier judicial precedents on this topic) is opposed to lawyers having a financial stake in the outcome of their clients' litigation or arbitration. This traditional objection is based on two related factors. First, the Common Law is concerned to protect the integrity of the lawyer-client relationship. It is dangerous for the lawyer to assume a financial interest in the outcome of litigation. The fear is that the prospect of gain might destroy professional objectivity. The lawyer's advice might become slanted towards securing his financial 'stake', rather than focused solely upon the client's interests. Secondly, it is necessary to safeguard the integrity of the civil process. Courts rely on the honesty and disinterested professionalism of the parties' advocates and other legal advisors. But financial inducements to win the case might seduce lawyers into perverting the course of justice. They might be tempted to tailor or suppress evidence, over-influence experts, present half-truths to the court, and engage in other forms of trickery or bad faith (see also **9.33**).[70]

9.24   We have noted that, although legislation has validated conditional fee agreements (subject to compliance with the statutory scheme), the Common Law

---

[68] CPR 45.15 to 45.22 (pre-trial conclusion of case: 12.5 per cent success fee for road traffic accident claims; 25 per cent if a claim against employer for personal injury): *Nizami v Butt* [2006] EWHC 159 (QB); [2006] 1 WLR 3307; for the position concerning cases conluding at trial, see the next note.

[69] *Lamont v Burton* [2007] EWCA Civ 429; [2007] 3 All ER 173: '[1] CPR 45.16(a) provides that the percentage increase which is to be allowed in relation to solicitors' fees in road traffic accident claims to which Section III of Part 45 applies is "100% where the claim *concludes at trial*" ... The issue ... is whether the 100% increase is mandatory in all cases or whether, as the defendant submits, there is a discretion to vary it ... The point is of some importance ... .[It] has equal relevance to employers' liability claims which are the subject of Sections IV and V of Part 45 ...'; '[26] Section III of Part 45 contains a carefully balanced scheme for the award of success fees in road traffic accident cases. [Its] object ... is to provide certainty and avoid litigation over the amount of success fees to be allowed to successful parties ... It is inherent in the scheme that in some individual cases, the success fee will be unreasonably high and in others unreasonably low. But that is the price that has to be paid for achieving certainty and avoiding litigation over the amount of success fees. [The court's general discretion with regard to costs, contained in CPR Part 44, on which see **9.09**] cannot be invoked to circumvent the careful structure of rule 45 and to undermine its objective of achieving certainty.'

[70] A Walters (2000) 116 LQR 371, 372; on maintenance and champerty, *R (Factortame Ltd) v Secretary of State for the Environment, Transport and the Regions (No 8)* [2002] EWCA Civ 932; [2003] QB 381, at [31] to [44]; earlier, *Thai Trading Co v Taylor* [1998] QB 781, 785–8, CA, cited in *Awwad v Geraghty & Co* [2001] QB 570, 578, CA.

has consistently opposed litigation lawyers acquiring a financial 'stake' in the outcome of their client's litigation. Now it is necessary to consider the three main forms that such potential financial interest might take: (1) success fees payable to the victorious party's lawyer; (2) the normal fee might be reduced[71] or waived[72] (the 'speculative fee' system); (3) the USA 'contingency fee system',[73] that is, the successful claimant's lawyer might recover a percentage of his client's monetary award (or settlement). The American 'contingency fee' remains unlawful in English law (on American contingency fees, see **9.27** below).[74] But (1) and (2) above are now lawful in England if, as will now be explained, the lawyer complies with the statutory scheme.[75]

Because of the position at Common Law (see the preceding paragraph), an **9.25** English CFA is valid only if it complies with the statutory regime. In 2005 Parliament revoked complicated regulations prescribing formalities for valid CFAs.[76] Defeated defendants' insurers had seized upon even the most trifling failure by the client's lawyer to satisfy such formalities. In this way, insurers tried to escape costs liability for success fees and insurance premiums. This was ironic because these formalities were originally intended as a form of consumer protection to protect the party undertaking a CFA claim or defence, and not as a means of exonerating defendant insurers from liability to pay costs. Such challenges became an intense 'costs-war'.[77] Since 2005, however,

---

[71] eg *Aratra Potato Co Ltd v Taylor Joynson Garrett* [1995] 4 All ER 695, Garland J (20 per cent reduction in fee if claim lost; agreement unlawful at common law because 'champertous', viz lawyer having stake in outcome of action; such a fee arrangement is now lawful under Courts and Legal Services Act 1990, s 58(2)(a), as substituted by Access to Justice Act 1999, s 27(1)).

[72] eg *Thai Trading Co v Taylor* [1998] QB 781, CA (noted Neil Andrews [1998] CLJ 469); for comment, 'The Ethics of Conditional Fee Arrangements' (Society for Advanced Legal Studies, 2001) 2.9.2.

[73] A Cannon, 'Designing Cost Policies to Provide Sufficient Access to Lower Courts' (2002) 21 CJQ 198, at 226; M Zander, 'Where are We Heading with the Funding of Civil Litigation' (2003) 22 CJQ 23; M Zander, 'Will the Revolution in the Funding of Civil Litigation in England Eventually Lead to Contingency Fees?' (2003) 52 DePaul LR 259; 'The Ethics of Conditional Fee Arrangements' (Society for Advanced Legal Studies, 2001); for discussion of the US perspective, T Rowe, 'Shift Happens: Pressure on Foreign Attorney-Fee Paradigms from Class Actions' (2003) 13 Duke J Comp & Int L 125; JG Fleming, *The Contingent Fee and its Effect on American Tort Law* (1988); Michael Horowitz, 'Making Ethics Real, Making Ethics Work: A Proposal for Contingency Fee Reform' (1995) 44 Emory LJ 173.

[74] *Callery v Gray* [2001] EWCA Civ 1117; [2001] 1 WLR 2112, 2115, at [6], CA.

[75] 1990 Act, ss 58 and 58A (as amended).

[76] Conditional Fee Agreements (Revocation) Regulations 2005 (SI 2005/2305): revoking, notably, Conditional Fee Agreements Regulations 2000 (SI 2000/692).

[77] On this overall 'war', see, eg, *Claims Direct Test Cases* [2003] EWCA Civ 136; [2003] 4 All ER 508, at [226]; 'battles' include *Garbutt v Edwards* [2005] EWCA Civ 1206; [2006] 1 WLR 2907; *Garrett v Halton BC* [2006] EWCA Civ 1017; [2007] 1 WLR 554; *Nizami v Butt* [2006] EWHC 159 (QB); [2006] 1 WLR 3307; *Myatt v NCB (No 2)* [2007] EWCA Civ 307; [2007] 1 WLR 1559.

there has been a relaxation of these formalities. Now it is enough that, before entering a CFA agreement, the solicitor should explain [to the prospective client]: 'the circumstances in which the client may be liable for their own costs and for the other party's costs; the client's right to assessment of costs, wherever the solicitor intends to seek payment of any or all of their costs from the client; and any interest the solicitor may have in recommending a particular policy or other funding.'[78]

9.26   In *Campbell v MGN (No 2)* (2005) the House of Lords considered the interplay of the conditional fee system and the human right of 'freedom of expression' protected by Article 10 of the European Convention on Human Rights.[79] This litigation concerned a claim by the 'super-model', Naomi Campbell, against the defendant newspaper publisher. This action was for breach of confidentiality and 'privacy' (see also cases cited in chapter 6 at n 108). The trial judge awarded her damages of £ 3,500, and her costs. The Court of Appeal reversed both aspects. Campbell gained permission to appeal to the House of Lords (surprisingly, given the House's statement in 2002 that it felt ill-equipped to fathom the CFA system: see **8.13**).[80] It was only at this third stage of the litigation that Campbell and her lawyers entered a conditional fee agreement. The House of Lords restored the trial judge's order for damages and his costs order. The claimant claimed from the defendant costs of over £ 1 million, which included £ 279,981 in respect of the success fees. The defendant challenged the claimant's right to obtain the success fee element. The basis of this challenge was that the prospect of paying such a bonus would have a 'chilling' effect on newspapers' freedom of expression, and so constitute a 'disproportionate' constraint under Article 10 of the European Convention on Human Rights (incorporated into English law by the Human Rights Act 1998). The House of Lords rejected the defendant's challenge concerning this bonus. It held that the CFA legislation embodied clear public policy. By this series of enactments (see the note at **9.19**), Parliament had decided to secure access to

---

[78] The Solicitors' Practice (Client Care) Amendment Rule (2005) amending the Law Society's 'Solicitors' Costs Information and Client Care Code' (1999); receiving party's lawyer's failure to give receiving party a costs estimate does not relieve paying party of liability for costs, *Garbutt* case, ibid.

[79] [2005] UKHL 61; [2005] 1WLR 3394.

[80] *Callery v Gray (Nos 1 and 2)* [2002] UKHL 28; [2002] 1 WLR 2000, at [8], per Lord Bingham, referring to the conditional fee context: '... responsibility for monitoring and controlling the developing practice in a field such as this lies with the Court of Appeal and not the House, which should ordinarily be slow to intervene. The House cannot respond to changes in practice with the speed and sensitivity of the Court of Appeal, before which a number of cases are likely over time to come ...'; and, ibid, at [17], per Lord Hoffmann: 'The Court of Appeal is traditionally and rightly responsible for supervising the administration of civil procedure. This is an area in which your Lordships have in the past seldom intervened and, it must be said, the few exceptions to this policy of self-restraint have usually tended to confirm the wisdom of the general practice.'

justice for litigants who would be otherwise unable to afford to pay for legal representation, including claims against the media. In its view, this attractive public policy does not infringe Article 10 of the Convention. The House of Lords also rejected the further argument that because Campbell was notoriously wealthy she did not need to finance her litigation on a 'no win no fee' basis. On this point, the court took the pragmatic view that it would be inappropriate for solicitors to be required to 'means test' clients before entering such a fee agreement. One can sympathise with the House of Lords' wish not to complicate or impede resort to the legislative CFA scheme. But the case is a disturbing example of a litigant's cynical use of such fee agreements to increase the costs 'leverage' against defendants.

(10) English Conditional Fee Agreements and American Contingency Fees[81]

Zander has presented various arguments in support of the contention that England should go further and adopt the US system of contingency fees (USA COFs).[82] First, he observes that USACOFs are simpler to explain to clients than English CFAs (but perhaps English clients are more attentive). Secondly, he notes that the percentage of the attorney's USACOF remuneration is necessarily 'proportionate' to the value of the client's damages. Thirdly, the US attorney's 'bonus' for success is tied to the amount of the judgment or out-of-court settlement. And so USACOFs provide an incentive for the attorney to maximise damages recovery. Zander's fourth argument, however, is less convincing. He suggests that USACOFs are less likely to spawn satellite litigation (that is, litigation not concerned with the main issues in the case; for the English 'costs war' in this respect, see **9.25**). However, the reason for this is that American civil procedure does not recognise the basic costs-shifting rule. As we have seen (**9.06**), that rule is at the core of the English costs system, and provides the starting point for any assessment of costs in a particular case.

9.27

Finally, Zander contends that the American contingency fee system does not provide an economic incentive for attorneys to run up hourly costs. And he contrasts this with the English CFA system, under which the bonus is reckoned by the hours worked in winning the case. This last point is arguably Zander's

9.28

---

[81] T Rowe, 'Shift Happens: Pressure on Foreign Attorney-Fee Paradigms from Class Actions' (2003) 13 Duke J Comp & Int L 125; JG Fleming, *The Contingent Fee and its Effect on American Tort Law* (1988); Michael Horowitz, 'Making Ethics Real, Making Ethics Work: A Proposal for Contingency Fee Reform' (1995) 44 Emory LJ 173.

[82] M Zander, 'Where are We Heading with the Funding of Civil Litigation?' (2003) 22 CJQ 23; M Zander, 'Will the Revolution in the Funding of Civil Litigation in England Eventually Lead to Contingency Fees?' (2003) DePaul LR 39.

best challenge to the English system of CFAs. The English practice of billing by the court enables CFA-sponsoring law firms to generate quite disproportionate amounts of costs. This is because the firm is not restrained by the need to justify a costs bill to its client. *Ex post facto* costs assessments are an expensive and uncertain check upon such CFA fee 'churning';[83] and 'costs-capping' has yet to become a general feature of English practice (**9.08**). Furthermore, the courts might not become aware of the size of the problem, because cases are often settled without a costs challenge by the defendant.

9.29   However, not all the arguments are in favour of the US system of remunerating the successful lawyer. Zander must concede that the US contingency fee is paid to the attorney from the plaintiff's damages. Is it right that the lawyer should subtract a large slice of the client's damages award? Moreover, anticipating that attorneys will take such a slice, there is a pressure within the US damages system for judges and juries to make generous awards. Furthermore, within the United Kingdom, there is widespread anxiety that to import USA-COFs would stimulate aggressively 'entrepreneurial' activity by prospective claimants' lawyers (see **10.12**).

(11) Assessment of the English Conditional Fee System

9.30   The CFA system is a bold legislative break with the Common Law's traditional hostility towards such fee arrangements. However, the new system seems, on balance, justified. Its foremost benefit is that it has unlocked the door to civil litigation, enabling poor, middle-income individuals, and small businesses to go to court. Before this system, civil litigation had become the tri-opoly of large businesses, millionaires, and indigent and perhaps jobless litigants-in-person. Secondly, because the conditional fee system offers privatised economic access to justice, it avoids public expense on legal aid.[84] Thirdly, the CFA system avoids the bureaucratic delay of obtaining a legal aid decision. Finally, this same system acts as a sieve which excludes unmeritorious claims. Claimant solicitors do this sifting, because they will take agree to a CFA only if reasonably assured of its eventual success. A practical problem for solicitors

---

[83] 'Churning': this expression is used pejoratively to denote 'inventive' costs claims, intended to 'milk' the eventual payor: see further **9.31**.

[84] An often neglected aspect of the civil legal aid system is that it operated often as merely a 'loan' towards legal expenses, the legal aid board having rights to recoup this expenditure by having a 'first charge' on damages or property recovered (or retained); however, not all the state money spent in funding claims would be recouped by the legal aid fund from the damages obtained; this is because some claimants lost their actions; or their claims yielded sums smaller less than the amount of legally aided costs; or because the claim was not for damages or recovery of property, for example, it concerned divorce or other family issues; or the legally aided party was a defendant.

is that they can continue to offer after-the-event insurance only if they maintain a reasonable record of successful claims. Insurance companies will be chary of solicitors who consistently mis-judge the cogency of claims taken on a CFA basis. Insurers can thus exert an important commercial restraint upon pursuit of unusually risky cases.[85]

Against this list of benefits, it must be admitted that the CFA system presents dangers and difficulties. There is the problem of 'over-charging' by lawyers and insurance companies and an overall increase in the cost of the legal process. As Lord Bingham has noted:[86]   **9.31**

'One possible abuse [created by the new CFA system is] that lawyers would be willing to act for claimants on a conditional fee basis but would charge excessive fees for their basic costs, knowing that their own client would not have to pay them and that the burden would in all probability fall on the defendant or his liability insurers. With this expectation the claimant's lawyers would have no incentive to moderate their charges.'

He continued:

'Another possible abuse was that lawyers would be willing to act for claimants on a conditional fee basis but would contract for a success uplift grossly disproportionate to any fair assessment of the risks of failure in the litigation, again knowing that the burden of paying this uplifted fee would never fall on their client but would be borne by the defendant or his insurers.'

He added:

'A third possible abuse was that claimants, although able to obtain after the event insurance, would be able to do so only at an unreasonably high price, the after the event insurers having no incentive to moderate a premium which would be paid by the defendant or his insurers and which might be grossly disproportionate to the risk which the insurer was underwriting.'

And he summarised the advantageous position of CFA funded claimants:

'Under the [CFA] regime, a claimant who makes appropriate arrangements can litigate without any risk of ever having personally to pay costs either to those acting for him or to the other side and without any risk of ever having to pay an after the event insurance premium whatever the outcome: the practical result is to transfer the entire cost of funding this kind of litigation to the liability insurers of unsuccessful defendants (and defendants who settle the claims made against them) and thus, indirectly, to the wider public who pay premiums to insure themselves against liability to pay compensation for causing personal injury.'

We can agree with Lord Bingham's analysis (see preceding paragraph), that conditional fee agreements provide an economic incentive to lawyers to maximise the hours allocated to a claim (or defence) conducted on such a basis,   **9.32**

---

[85] On this emerging insurance market, see 'The Ethics of Conditional Fee Arrangements' (Society for Advanced Legal Studies, London, 2001), paras 2.59 to 2.70.

[86] *Callery v Gray (Nos 1 and 2)* [2002] UKHL 28; [2002] 1 WLR 2000, at [5].

provided victory is reasonably in prospect.[87] More hours mean a larger victory bonus. The client does not have to pay for this. The other side, if defeated, will instead pay. The courts have noted that conditional fees agreements remove from claimants and their lawyers the incentive to control costs.[88] Another source of inflation under the CFA system is the level of the premium for 'ATE' legal expenses insurance. This premium can be recovered from the losing party. The House of Lords in *Callery v Gray* (2002) has suggested that costs judges must provide the lead in providing a ratchet against 'receiving parties' recovering unreasonable levels of insurance premiums.[89] But this is easier said than done: there are problems in establishing standard or average rates of premium for different types of 'ATE' cover;[90] and perhaps a judge cannot be expected to assess the reasonableness of insurance risks.[91] The courts, notably costs judges, must be vigilant to prevent abuse.

9.33   A second problem engendered by the CFA system concerns conflicts of interest and duty (see also **9.23**):[92] a lawyer's wish to secure a conditional fee might seduce him into placing his interests ahead of both his client's interest and the wider demands of justice. Some judges have tried to play down this factor.[93] In 1998 Millett LJ said in the *Thai Trading* case: ' ... the fear that lawyers may be tempted by having a financial incentive in the outcome of litigation to act improperly is exaggerated, and there is a countervailing public policy in making justice accessible to persons of modest means.'[94] But, in a 1998 lecture, Sir Gavin Lightman (a judge in the Chancery Division of the High Court) expressed grave anxiety whether policy-makers have taken seriously enough the conflicts of interest engendered by the CFA system.[95] A third problem, noted

---

[87] For analysis of professional rules governing solicitors and barristers in this regard, 'The Ethics of Conditional Fee Arrangements' (Society for Advanced Legal Studies, London, 2001) chs 3, 4.

[88] *Callery v Gray* [2001] EWCA Civ 1117; [2001] 1 WLR 2112, at [95]; similar comments were made in *Callery v Gray (Nos 1 and 2)* [2002] UKHL 28; [2002] 1 WLR 2000.

[89] *Callery v Gray (Nos 1 and 2)* [2002] UKHL 28; [2002] 1 WLR 2000, especially the speeches of Lords Hoffmann and Scott.

[90] *Callery v Gray* [2001] EWCA Civ 1117; [2001] 1 WLR 2112, at [14] and [71]; affirmed by *Callery v Gray (Nos 1 and 2)* [2002] UKHL 28; [2002] 1 WLR 2000.

[91] *Callery v Gray* [2001] EWCA Civ 1117; [2001] 1 WLR 2112, at [16].

[92] For analysis of professional rules governing solicitors and barristers in this regard, see 'The Ethics of Conditional Fee Arrangements' (Society for Advanced Legal Studies, London, 2001) chs 3, 4 and P Kunzlik, 'Conditional Fees-the Ethical and Organisational Impact on the Bar' (1999) 62 MLR 850.

[93] Neil Andrews (case note) [1998] CLJ 469–71.

[94] *Thai Trading Co v Taylor* [1998] QB 781, 790, CA; although this decision was rejected in *Awwad v Geraghty & Co* [2001] QB 570, CA, Millett LJ's comment in the *Thai* case, just cited, remains of interest.

[95] Mr Justice Lightman, 'Civil Litigation in the Twenty-First Century' (1998) 17 CJQ 373, 381, proposing a standing committee to deal with professional conflicts of interests arising from conditional fee agreements.

above at **9.26**, is the occasionally cynical use of a CFA by very wealthy claimants to exert increased financial pressure upon defendants.

Certainly all custodians of civil justice – the courts, Law Society, the Bar,   **9.34** the Ministry of Justice, and others – should remain alert to these perils. But conditional fees offer the great benefit of access to justice for those who otherwise would be denied the opportunity to go to law. The CFA system is a pragmatic response to a social and political crisis: exclusion of ordinary people from civil justice. The system is not unproblematic. But perhaps the risks are worth taking.

Part III

Alternative Civil Justice

Chapter 10

Settlement[1]

Contents

(1) Introduction

'A "culture of negotiation" is already in place ... assertion of legal rights
through litigation is very much a matter of last resort.'[2]

'Settlement ... is typically the culmination of a bruising process ...
during which one party's representatives have successfully worn
down the other ...' (*Simon Roberts*)[3]

The following propositions will be discussed. First, the settlement process is a **10.01**
manifestation of two 'freedoms': the parties' freedom of contract and of litigants' freedom to delineate claims and defences and dispose of their action on
agreed terms. Secondly, settlement is the most common way in which civil disputes are concluded in England. Without such a high level of settlement, it
would be necessary for there to be a large expansion of formal adjudication by
courts, tribunals, ombudsmen, and arbitrators. Thirdly, it is official policy that
there should be a culture of settlement. For example, the high level of settlement is sustained by pre-action protocols and greater resort to mediation (on
the latter see chapter 11). Fourthly, costs incentives increase the pressure to accept settlement offers. Finally, the English courts hardly ever actively broker

---

[1] Besides the literature cited in this chapter, see the large bibliography on 'ADR' at
11.65.

[2] S Roberts, 'Alternative Dispute Resolution and Civil Justice ...' (1993) 56 MLR 452
454–5.

[3] S Roberts, 'Settlement as Civil Justice' (2000) 63 MLR 739, 743.

settlement by suggesting the terms of possible settlement. The exception is 'early neutral evaluation' by a Commercial Court judge. But this can be offered only with the parties' consent. It is very little used. One topic concerning settlement is discussed in a different chapter: the reader is referred to **11.49** for discussion of 'privilege' in the context of settlement negotiations ('without prejudice' privilege).[4]

(2) Freedom of Contract and Freedom to Settle

10.02   The principle of 'freedom of contract' embraces the following liberties:[5] first, parties have a general freedom to enter into transactions which are intended (explicitly or otherwise) to create legal obligations; this freedom includes the power to formulate individual terms within such a transaction, or to acquiesce in 'default' terms 'implied' by statute or common law; secondly, parties to a transaction can stipulate that it will not be legally binding; thirdly, freedom to contract includes liberty to compromise a legal dispute, or to waive legal liability; or a contract of compromise, provided very clear wording is used, can exclude liability that might arise in the future.[6] Exercise of these interrelated freedoms is subject to the overarching limitations of (i) personal capacity,[7] (ii)

---

[4]   Neil Andrews, *English Civil Procedure* (Oxford UP, 2003) ch 25; Brown and Marriott, *ADR Principles and Practice* (2nd edition, 1999) 22–050 ff; *Cross and Tapper on Evidence* (11th edn, 2007) 507–8; D Foskett, *The Law and Practice of Compromise* (6th edn, 2005) ch 27; C Hollander, *Documentary Evidence* (9th edn, 2006) ch 16; M Iller, *Civil Evidence: The Essential Guide* (Sweet & Maxwell, 2006) 8–88 to 8–104; C Passmore, *Privilege* (2nd edn, 2006) ch 10; *Phipson on Evidence* (16th edn, 2005) 24–14 ff; B Thanki (ed), *The Law of Privilege* (2006) ch 7; *Zuckerman on Civil Procedure* (2nd edn, 2006) ch 16; see also J McEwan, '"Without Prejudice": Negotiating the Minefield' (1994) 13 CJQ 133.

[5]   *Chitty on Contracts* (29th edn, 2004) 1–010 ff; PS Atiyah, *The Rise and Fall of Freedom of Contract* (Oxford UP, 1979); *Atiyah's Introduction to the Law of Contract* (6th edn, 2006, Oxford UP) (by S Smith) (index at 432); R Brownsword, *Contract Law: Themes for the Twentieth-First Century* (2000) ch 2; HG Collins, *The Law of Contract* (4th edn, Cambridge UP, 2003) (index at 438); C Fried, *Contract as Promise: A Theory of Contractual Obligation* (Harvard UP, 1981); J Gordley, *The Philosophical Origins of Modern Contract Doctrine* (Oxford UP, 1991); D Kimel, *From Promise to Contract* (Hart, Oxford, 2005) ch 5; DJ Ibbetson, *A Historical Introduction to the Law of Obligations* (Oxford UP, 1999) chs 7, 11, 12, 13; SA Smith, *Contract Theory* (Oxford UP, 2004) (see index at 448).

[6]   The House of Lords has held that an employer had failed to spell out with sufficient clarity in a contract of compromise its wish to stifle possible claims arising in the future, including claims only subsequently recognised at law, following case-law development: *BCCI v Ali* [2001] UKHL 8; [2002] 1 AC 251, HL, [19], [21] [35], [86]; cf dissent at [73] per Lord Hoffmann; the decision is considered in details at Neil Andrews, *English Civil Procedure* (Oxford UP, 2003) 23.65 to 23.77.

[7]   viz, the parties, if natural persons, should be over 17 and sane; or properly constituted 'legal persons', for example, validly formed companies.

public policy, (iii) the parties' inability to exclude liability for fraud at Common Law,[8] and (iv) statutory regulation of adhesion clauses.[9]

The freedoms just listed concern 'substantive' control of parties' transac- **10.03** tional rights. In addition, litigants possess various powers to define or terminate civil actions (see **10.06**). First, the parties and their legal representatives control, by unilateral pleading and joint arrangements, the metes and bounds of the action (for the same approach in Germany see **10.04**). Secondly, litigants' freedom to reach settlements is a leading principle of modern English civil procedure.[10] However, before giving judgment, an English court can act of its own motion to raise a point of public policy, including a matter of human rights. Thus in *C v P plc* (2006), the first instance judge took the initiative to enlist the assistance of various counsel, including an '*amicus curiae*', to debate before the court the impact of the Human Rights Act 1998 on a particular aspect of civil procedure.[11]

In German law, the parties' control of the scope of proceedings rests upon **10.04** major principle. As Peter Murray and Rolf Stürner explain:[12]

'The principle that the parties have control over the nature and scope of civil litigation (*Dispositionsmaxime*) is a fundamental guiding principle of German civil justice and finds expression in statutes and court rules as well as in tradition and practice (also referred to as *Parteiprinzip*). Most civil cases can only be initiated by a complaint of a private party. The scope of the proceeding in terms of the issues presented and relief requested is governed by the formal claims for relief (*Anträge*) of the parties. The parties have the right to withdraw proceedings, to vary their form by agreement, and to terminate them by settlement.'

The American Law Institute/UNIDROIT project on 'transnational principles **10.05** of civil procedure' (2006) recognises as fundamental the parties' (especially the plaintiff's) power to prescribe the scope of civil proceedings[13] and a party's unilateral power to determine the scope of the matters to be contested.[14] These powers will now be elaborated in the English context.

---

[8] *HIH Casualty and General Insurance Ltd v Chase Manhattan* [2003] 1 All ER (Comm) 349; [2003] 2 Lloyd's Rep 61, HL.

[9] 'Exclusion clauses', even between business parties, are regulated by reference to a test of 'reasonableness' (see the Unfair Contract Terms Act 1977); consumers are protected against unfair terms in standard form contracts (the Unfair Terms in Consumer Contracts Regulations 1999).

[10] Neil Andrews, *English Civil Procedure* (Oxford UP, 2003) 6.76 ff.

[11] Evans-Lombe J in *C plc v P* [2006] EWHC 1226 (Ch); [2006] Ch 549, noted Neil Andrews [2007] CLJ 47; the Court of Appeal decided the case on a different basis: see **6.26**.

[12] *German Civil Justice* (Durham, North Carolina, 2004) 156–7.

[13] ALI/UNIDROIT's *Principles of Transational Civil Procedure* (Cambridge UP, 2006) principle 10.5, at page 29.

[14] ibid; also, ibid, principle 10.3, 'The scope of the proceedings is determined by the claims and defences of the parties in the pleadings, including amendments.'

10.06   In English law the parties can agree a settlement of a pending dispute before judgment is given on the merits of the case,[15] or they can agree to vary or extinguish judgment. A settlement need not be in writing. The Court of Appeal has upheld a settlement reached by telephone between the parties' solicitors.[16] A claimant can throw away bad or good cards at will. Thus he can elect to plead part of a potential claim, discarding the rest;[17] or he can withdraw a claim or discontinue an action; or he might decide not to enforce a judgment, perhaps as an act of clemency, perhaps out of a sense of futility. Similarly, a defendant can refrain from pleading a defence to a claim (or choose not to plead all arguable defences);[18] or allow judgment to be entered in default of a defence; or decide not to resist enforcement of a judgment, even though there are arguable grounds for appealing or otherwise challenging the judgment or mode of enforcement.

---

[15] Once the court has indicated its decision in a draft judgment, with reasons yet to be supplied, the parties cannot necessarily settle the dispute; instead the court at that point has a discretion whether to perfect judgment by giving reasons, or to withhold judgment in deference to the parties' wish to settle: *Prudential Assurance Co Ltd v McBains Cooper* [2000] 1 WLR 2000, 2005–10, CA; also noting at 2009 that the House of Lords in *Grovit v Doctor* [1997] 1 WLR 640, 647 E-F, refused to accept the appellant's application to withdraw the appeal; the courts are reluctant to hear appeals on matters which have become moot or hypothetical because of the parties' settlement or concession of defeat, *Prudential Assurance Co Ltd* case, ibid, at 2005–6, and authorities cited at Neil Andrews, *English Civil Procedure* (Oxford UP, 2003) 6.80 n 158, also noting US authority.

[16] *Littlefair, Williamson, & Beardall v Vinamul* [2006] EWCA Civ 31, at [34] (no need for this to be followed by written confirmation).

[17] A famous example is the liquidator's partial claim on the facts of *Central London Property Trust Ltd v High Trees House Ltd* [1947] 1 KB 130, Denning J (at common law, landlord entitled to unpaid rent for years 1941 to 1945; but landlord's liquidator modifying claim to arrears for very recent months, ibid at 131; judge addressing, in a dictum, the question whether Equity would prevent landlord claiming all the arrears).

[18] eg, *Dann v Hamilton* [1939] 1 KB 509, 512, Asquith J, noting that counsel for the defendant raised the defence of volenti non fit injuria but not common law contributory negligence (whether passenger's awareness of defendant driver's drunkenness amounted to the volenti defence); the defence of limitation under the Limitation Act 1980 is sometimes waived by a defendant (3.09).

(3) The Importance of Settlement[19]

A very high percentage of English civil actions do not proceed to trial[20] (the **10.07** decline of civil trials in the USA has also attracted comment, see also **11.26**).[21] This is because most English actions culminate not in judgment on the merits following examination of witnesses and documents, but in an agreement of compromise or settlement between the parties. Settlement can arise with or without commencement of formal proceedings[22] and with or without ('unassisted settlement').[23] In England, pre-action protocols regulate the process of bargaining towards a settlement before commencement of formal proceedings.[24] There are other forms of termination without judgment at trial: withdrawal or discontinuance of the claim, judgment by default (where no defence is offered, **5.31**), or summary judgment (where the claim or defence has no 'real prospect of success', **5.18**) or striking out (this is possible if the type of claim is legally unrecognised, or the proceedings involve an abuse of process,[25]

---

[19] Neil Andrews, *English Civil Procedure* (Oxford UP, 2003) chs 23, 24, 25; H Genn, 'Understanding Civil Justice' (1997) 48 CLP 155, 177 ff; S Roberts, 'Settlement as Civil Justice' (2000) 63 MLR 739–47 (and earlier 'Alternative Dispute Resolution and Civil Justice ...' (1993) 56 MLR 452; 'The Paths of Negotiation' (1996) 49 CLP 97–109; for his study of 'ADR', M Palmer and S Roberts, *Dispute Processes* (1998)), and M Galanter and M Cahill, 'Most Cases Settle: Judicial Promotion and Regulation of Settlements' (1994) 46 Stanford L Rev 1329 (on the USA practice); a highly detailed practitioner manual is D Foskett, *The Law and Practice of Compromise* (6th edn, 2005); for a much shorter account by Foskett, *Settlement under the Civil Procedure Rules* (1999).

[20] For example, Sir Leonard Hoffmann, 'Changing Perspectives on Civil Litigation' (1993) 56 MLR 297, noting the increasing resort to pre-trial summary procedures, pre-action disclosure, witness statements, and provisional and protective relief; since 1998, to this list must be added, 'pre-action protocols', expansion of pre-action disclosure orders, the CPR's imposition of case-management, and judicial stays and costs orders to promote mediation.

[21] eg M Galanter, 'The Vanishing Trial ... in Federal and State Courts' (2004) 1 J Empirical Legal Studies 451; J Resnik, 'For Owen M Fiss: Some Reflections on the Triumph and Death of Adjudication' (2003) 58 Miami U L Rev 173; J Resnik, 'Whither and Whether Adjudication' (2006) 86 Boston ULRev 1101, 1123 ff; J Resnik, 'Uncovering, Discovering and Disclosing How the Public Dimensions of Court-Based Processes are at Risk' (2006) 81 Chicago-Kent LR 521 and J Resnik and DE Curtis, 'From "Rites" to "Rights" of Audience: The Utilities and Contingencies of the Public's Role in Court Business' in A Masson and K O'Connor (eds), *Representation of Justice* (Brussels, 2007); A Miller, 'The Pre-trial Rush to Judgment: Are the "Litigation Explosion", "Liability Crisis", and Efficiency Cliches Eroding our Day in Court and Jury Commitments?'(2003) 78 NYULRev 982.

[22] For differentiation between pure settlements, consent judgments, and agreed dismissal of cases, and the question of res judicata, Neil Andrews, *English Civil Procedure* (Oxford UP, 2003) 23.33 to 23.45.

[23] The leading work is D Foskett, ibid, (6th edn, 2005); on CPR Part 36, see **10.25**.

[24] See also **2.27, 3.01, 6.07, 10.10, 11.09**; and Neil Andrews, *English Civil Procedure* (Oxford UP, 2003) 3.13 to 3.18, 23.07, 26.63 to 26.66.

[25] Generally on abuse of process, Neil Andrews, *English Civil Procedure* (Oxford UP, 2003) ch 16.

or there has been serious procedural default: **5.23**, including failure to comply
with an 'unless' order, **2.19**)

10.08   Furthermore, since the CPR was introduced in 1999, there has been a general decline of circa nine per cent in civil litigation. In particular, there has
been a significant reduction in medium-sized or large cases taken to the High
Court (see the figures cited in the footnote and summarised in the table
below;[26] and see the preceding paragraph for similar American experience).
Proceedings in the High Court have ceased to be the main response to a problematic business or civil dispute, even if it involves a significant sum.[27] London practitioners report difficulty in 'selling' High Court litigation to their
clients.[28]

Decline in English Civil Litigation 1999–2005 (Claims Commenced)

(1)	County Courts			
	(1999)	2,000,337	(2005)	1,870,374
(2)	Chancery Division (High Court)			
	(1999)	37,281	(2005)	34,125
(3)	Queen's Bench Division		(High Court, excluding next two courts)	
	(1999)	72,161	(2005)	15,317[29]

---

[26] *Judicial Statistics*, annual reports, for the years 1999 and 2005: available on line:
http://www.dca.gov.uk/dept/depstrat.htm). These record the following: county court claims
commenced in 1999, 2,000,337 (source 1999 report, p 39) and in 2005, 1,870,374 claims
(source 2005 report, p 46; of these 2005 claims, 48 per cent were for less than £500); Chancery Division claims (High Court) commenced in 1999, 37,281 (source 1999 report, p 21)
and 34,125 in 2005 (source 2005 report, p 27); Queen's Bench Division (High Court) claims
commenced in 1999, 72,161 (source 1999 report, p 27), and in 2006 15317 (source 2005
report, p 37); Commercial Court (High Court) claims commenced 1999, 1205 (source 1999
report, p 35), and 981 in 2005 (source 2005 report, p 41); Technology and Construction
Court (High Court) claims commenced in 1999, 483 (source 1999 report, p 35) and 340 in
2005 (source 2005 report, p 50); 'Civil Court Fees' (Court Service, September 2002), at
paras 3.7 ff (between 1998 and 2001 there was a 22.5 per cent reduction in the number of
county court claims and, during the same period, a 76 per cent fall in High Court claims).
[27] The creation of a Supreme Court under the Constitutional Reform Act 2005 will
strengthen the tendency for the highest echelon of judges to devote a high percentage of their
time to public law, human rights, and constitutional matters, rather than private law and
commercial disputes. It is easily predicted that media attention to these high-profile cases
will distract attention from the important business of providing adjudication of matters relevant to commerce: I am grateful to Professor Shetreet, Hebrew University, Jerusalem, for
observations on this topic: seminar University of Cambridge, 2006.
[28] Comments to the author by a London practitioner; 'The Lawyer' 7 May 2007, p 1,
reports that Sir David Steel, in charge of the Commercial Court list, asked law firms to consider sending cases to the court for arbitration, especially cases raising points of pure law;
the newspaper inferred a shortfall of work for that court, and quoted some lawyers in support; but Steel J told this newspaper that the court's overall volume of work had increased by
30 per cent in 2006.
[29] Mostly, it appears, this reduction was due to the fact that the more attractive High

(4) Commercial Court (High Court)
(1999)   1,205   (2005)   981

(5) Technology etc Court (High Court)
(1999)   483   (2005)   340

(6) Totals
(1999)   2,111,467   (2005)   1,921,137
(a reduction of c 9 per cent)

(4) Official Support for Settlement

As Roberts has commented, 'the courts present themselves not just as agencies **10.09** offering judgment but as sponsors of negotiated agreement.'[30] For many years, influential English judges have shouted 'three cheers' for this consensual means of resolving civil disputes.[31] Lord Donaldson said (1987):

'... the procedure of the court must be, and is, intended to achieve the resolution of disputes by a variety of methods, of which a resolution by judgment is but one, and probably the least desirable. Accordingly, anything which enables the parties to appreciate the true strength and weakness of their positions at the earliest possible moment and at the same time enables them to enter into fully informed and realistic discussions designed to achieve a consensual resolution of the dispute is very much in the public interest.'[32]

Lord Woolf said in his first report (1995): 'the philosophy of litigation should be primarily to encourage early settlement of disputes.'[33] In these judges' opinion, it is better to conclude a settlement, even one based on imperfect knowledge and perhaps slightly skewed by economic or other factors, rather than submit to the long and ultimately public process of hearing witnesses, experts, and presenting submissions of law.[34]

Court enforcement procedures for executing default judgments ceased to be available for relatively modest claims; but other factors are probably in play: K Williams, 'State of Fear: Britain's "Compensation Culture" Reviewed' (2005) 25 LS 499, 503 n 25.

[30] S Roberts, 'Settlement as Civil Justice' (2000) 63 MLR 739.

[31] See the quotations collected in Neil Andrews, *English Civil Procedure* (Oxford UP, 2003) 9.25.

[32] *Naylor v Preston Area Health Authority* [1987] 1 WLR 958, 967–8, CA, per Sir John Donaldson MR (later Lord Donaldson MR).

[33] *Access to Justice: Interim Report* (Stationery Office, 1995) ch 7, para 7(a).

[34] For comment (and further references to literature) on disparities and uncertainties in the settlement process, see H Genn, 'Understanding Civil Justice' (1997) 50 CLP 155, 178 ff; see also H Genn, *Hard Bargaining: Out of Court Settlement in Personal Injury Actions* (Oxford UP, 1987) (reviewed Neil Andrews [1989] CLJ 506, 507, describing this book as 'a powerful antidote to complacency').

10.10   The Practice Direction on '[Pre-Action] Protocols' emphasises the duty of prospective parties and their legal advisors to consider ADR:[35] 'The courts increasingly take the view that litigation should be a last resort, and that claims
should not be issued prematurely when a settlement is still likely.' The Law Society for England and Wales issued in 2005 a 'practice advice' recommending
that solicitors should routinely consider whether their clients' disputes are suitable for ADR.[36] The European Commission has also embraced mediation and
proposed a directive on the topic.[37]

10.11   The CPR (1998) also emphasises the need to encourage settlement. ADR,
'Alternative dispute resolution', is an important aspect of that important goal
(see chapter 11 on mediation). Thus, the court's obligations of 'active case-
management' include the duty to help the parties to settle the whole or part of
the case.[38] The court must also encourage and facilitate use of ADR, if this
seems appropriate.[39] One judge has neatly suggested that ordinary civil litigation is now itself the 'alternative dispute resolution' system.[40]

10.12   It is also noteworthy that the Compensation Act 2006 aims to control the
stimulation of unmeritorious claims by claims handlers.[41] The NHS Redress

---

[35] 'Practice Direction, Protocols' 4.7; see also text of 'The Pre-Action Protocol for Construction and Engineering Disputes' (April 2007) 5.4 for emphasis on ADR as an alternative
to litigation in that context: http://www.dca.gov.uk/civil/procrules_fin/contents/frontmat-
ter/notes44_advance.htm.

[36] Law Society Gazette (2005) (16 June) pp 38–9; S Roberts, 'Settlement as Civil Justice'
(2000) 63 MLR 739, 741 and 'Alternative Dispute Resolution and Civil Justice ...' (1993) 56
MLR 452, 460–1, traces enthusiasm for ADR in the mainstream of civil litigation to Sir Roy
Beldam's 'Report of the Committee on Alternative Dispute Resolution' (Bar Council, October 1991).

[37] COM (2004) 718 final, Brussels dated 22.10.2004 (draft directive on 'certain aspects
of mediation in civil and commercial matters') http://europa.eu.int/eur-lex/en/com/pdf/
2004/com2004_0718en01.pdf; for the European Code of Conduct for Mediators: http://
europa.eu.int/comm/justice_home/ejn/adr/adr_ec_code_conduct_en.htm.

[38] CPR 1.4(2)(f).

[39] CPR 1.4(2)(e).

[40] Senior Master Robert Turner, cited K Mackie, D Miles, W Marsh, T Allen, *The ADR
Practice Guide* (2007), 5; Twining has emphasised this point in a sophisticated survey of
theoretical literature, 'Alternatives to What? ...' (1993) 56 MLR 380.

[41] Part 2 of the Compensation Act 2006 regulates the activities of claims managers: s
4(2)(b) states '"claims management services" means advice or other services in relation to
the making of a claim'; and s 4(2)(c) states '"claim" means a claim for compensation,
restitution, repayment or any other remedy or relief in respect of loss or damage or in respect
of an obligation'; and see the (draft) Compensation (Regulated Claims Management Services) Order 2006; this reflects anxiety concerning the practice of 'claims-farming'. In 2004,
the Government said: '... we strongly oppose any culture where people believe that if there is
an injury there must inevitably be someone else to blame, and someone else to pay. And we
oppose people being encouraged to believe it is always worth "having a go", however [un-
meritorious] the claim. This creates false expectations that there is easy money just waiting
to be had. Some personal injury advertising does just this.' *www.dca.gov.uk/majrep/bet-
tertaskforce/better-task-force.pdf*; see also the House of Commons Constitutional Affairs

Act 2006 creates mechanisms for out-of-court disposal of claims or complaints relating to health provision, including monetary redress. This relief is intended to be a voluntary substitute for legal proceedings.[42]

(5) Attractions and Problems of the 'Culture of Settlement'

Attractions

There are many reasons why settlement, including mediation, has received **10.13** such strong support, both from private and official sources. First, settlement can be more flexible than final judgment before the courts.[43] It can confer an element of 'success' for both parties. By contrast, judgment normally creates only a single winner[44] and the court is restricted to the standard private or public law remedies.[45] An example of mediation's flexibility concerns a group litigation action brought by parents of deceased children against a children's hospital trust (Alder Hey Hospital, Liverpool). The hospital had removed organs from dead children without their parents' permission. The claim for damages proceeded for some time. The procedural judge (Senior Master Robert Turner) then successfully recommended mediation before an outsider. A settlement was agreed, consisting of five elements: a very modest amount of compensation; a grant by the hospital towards relevant research; an undertaking by the Government to issue better guidelines for hospitals; a memorial to the children; a public apology by the doctors concerned.[46]

Committee, 'Compensation Culture' (2006, HC 754–1: *www.publications.parliament.uk/ pa/cm200506/cmselect/cmconst/754/754i.pdf* (which includes discussion of conditional fee agreements)' cf also this measured individual remark, by the Lord Chancellor, 'As strongly as we resist spurious claims, we should also robustly defend the rights of people to make genuine claims. Rights and responsibilities would be meaningless if they could not ultimately be enforced' (Lord Falconer, 10 November 2004. Compensation Culture. Speech to the Insurance Times Conference, quoted at *http://www.monbiot.com/archives/2004/ 11/16/the-myth-of-compensation-culture/* taken from *The Guardian* 16 November, 2004; for background, K Williams, 'State of Fear: Britain's "Compensation Culture" Reviewed' (2005) 25 LS 499.

[42] s 6(5), Compensation Act 2006: 'A scheme [introduced under the 2006 Act] must provide for a settlement agreement under the scheme to include a waiver of the right to bring civil proceedings in respect of the liability to which the settlement relates'; s 6(6): 'A scheme must provide for the termination of proceedings under the scheme if the liability to which the proceedings relate becomes the subject of civil proceedings.'

[43] K Mackie, D Miles, W Marsh, T Allen, *The ADR Practice Guide* (2007) 3.4.1.

[44] Unless there is a finding of contributory negligence against the claimant, or there is a successful cross-claim or set-off defence made by the defendant.

[45] For comment on the range of outcomes in fact desired by disputants, H Genn, 'Understanding Civil Justice' (1997) 50 CLP 155, 174 ff.

[46] Details explained by this judge at a seminar, Cambridge, 23 January 2006.

10.14   Secondly, settlement will be valuable when the parties have a continuing relationship, for example, joint ventures, employment relationships, or former spouses with young children. In the *Shirayama* case (2004) a dispute arose between the long-term tenants of a major property in Central London (the former 'County Hall').[47] Relations had become seriously strained. However, many of the issues were relatively small. The High Court judge held that mediation by a non-court neutral was appropriate.

10.15   Thirdly, the system of enforcement can ensure that satisfaction of a settlement is not left solely to the parties' sense of honour. It can be clothed as a binding arrangement and enforced by the legal process.[48] First, a monetary settlement can be enforced as a debt claim (**8.28** ff). Secondly, settlements (of money or other types of claim) agreed after commencement of formal proceedings can be entered as a 'consent order'.[49] One form of consent order attractively preserves confidentiality in the precise terms of the settlement. Its terms are not open to public inspection (a so-called 'Tomlin Order').[50]

10.16   Fourthly, the process of reaching settlement is nearly always much cheaper than taking the case to trial. Billing by the hour provides an economic incentive to litigation lawyers to increase the intensity and complexity of proceedings.[51] Does it not make economic sense to avoid this, where there is a reasonable chance of a compromise?

10.17   Finally, settlement is a veiled process. This can be attractive to disputants. By contrast, adjudication in the ordinary courts involves full publicity.[52]

---

[47] *Shirayama Shokusan Co Ltd v Danovo Ltd* [2004] 1 WLR 2985, Blackburne J.

[48] K Mackie, D Miles, W Marsh, T Allen, *The ADR Practice Guide* (2000) 12.2.

[49] D Foskett, *The Law and Practice of Compromise* (6th edn, 2005) 9.09 ff.

[50] K Mackie, et al, ibid, Appendix F, at 351, for model 'Tomlin order' agreements; D Foskett, ibid, 9.21 ff, and 10.31; for an example of such a 'Tomlin Order', *McKennit v Ash* [2006] EWCA Civ 1714; [2007] 3 WLR 194 at [76].

[51] Generally on the costs system, see the specialist works: M Cook, *Cook on Costs* (2007); P Hurst, *Civil Costs* (4th edn, 2007); and see, in the present work, **9.01** ff.

[52] The general rule is that a hearing must be in public: CPR 39.2(1); CPR 39.2(3) and PD (39) 1.5 set out exceptions; the primary source is s 67, Supreme Court Act 1981; the requirement of publicity is also contained in Article 6(1) of the European Convention on Human Rights (incorporated in Sch 1, Human Rights Act 1998); the relevant part of Art 6(1) reads: 'Judgment shall be pronounced publicly but the press and public may be excluded from all or part of the trial in the interests of morals, public order or national security in a democratic society, where the interests of juveniles or the protection of the life of the parties so require, or to the extent strictly necessary in the opinion of the court in special circumstances where publicity would prejudice the interests of justice.'

Problems

However, some might criticise this rush to privatised justice. A vigorous oppo- **10.18**
nent is Owen Fiss (Yale Law School). In his polemic, 'Against Settlement'
(1984), he wrote:[53] 'Settlement is for me the civil analogue of plea bargaining:
consent is often coerced; the bargain may be struck by someone without authority ... Although dockets are trimmed, justice may not be done.' He added:
'Like plea bargaining, settlement is a capitulation to the condition of mass society and should be neither encouraged nor praised.' These matters are further
addressed at **11.24**.

Certainly, the process of settlement is not perfect. Possible objections to **10.19**
settlement (including mediated settlements) are:[54] parties to settlement might
not fully understand their respective positions; (2) the parties might be unequal in various ways; (3) a party might have procured the settlement by underhand dealing; (4) a party's full civil entitlement should not be reduced by
compromise;[55] (5) assessment of the 'merits' must be measured, precise, and
exacting;[56] (6) the public search-light at trial should be shone upon serious
wrongdoing.

As for factors (1) to (5), Hazel Genn, a leading British authority on the pro- **10.20**
cess of settlement, has said:'

... studies highlight ... the ways in which power influences the outcome of settlement
negotiations ... Factors which are important are: legal intelligence – getting the right
lawyers and experts; financial resources-paying for the [same]; and having the psycho-
logical, social, and economic ability to endure litigation.'[57]

---

[53] (1984) Yale LJ 1073 (re-printed in D Galligan (ed) *Procedure* (Dartmouth, 1992) ch
16); see also O Fiss, *The Law As It Could Be* (New York, 2003). For references to the debate
which Fiss's 1984 article engendered in the US, O Fiss and J Resnik, *Adjudication and Its
Alternatives* (Foundation Press, New York, 2003) 481, 488; and see J Resnik, 'For Owen M
Fiss: Some Reflections on the Triumph and Death of Adjudication' (2003) 58 Miami U L Rev
173.

[54] For a convenient collection of literature addressing these points, H Genn, 'Understanding Civil Justice' (1997) 50 CLP 155, 186–7; for an example of an aggrieved party to a
compromise 'throwing the contractual book' at the opponent, in an attempt to overturn the
compromise, *Halpern v Halpern (No 2)* [2007] EWCA Civ 291(distribution of estate among
family members; allegation that not all relevant assets were revealed and that the compromise
should be regarded as vitiated on numerous suggested grounds; the report at [2007] 3 All ER
478 concerns a specific aspect of the case; consult the online version at [1] ff for the numerous
contractual challenges).

[55] One of Jeremy Bentham's anxieties: S Roberts, 'Settlement as Civil Justice' (2000) 63
MLR 739, 743 n 11, W Twining, 'Alternatives to What? ...' (1993) 56 MLR 380, 384 (examining various theorists' accounts of the civil process, notably, Bentham, Llewellyn, Fuller,
and Damaska).

[56] For a stimulating account of accuracy and legality, JA Jolowicz, 'The dilemmas of civil
litigation' in *On Civil Procedure* (Cambridge UP, 2000) ch 4.

[57] H Genn, 'Understanding Civil Justice' (1997) 50 CLP 155, 179; see also H Genn,
Hard Bargaining: Out of Court Settlement in Personal Injury Actions (Oxford UP, 1987)

As for the sixth of these considerations, the openness of civil trial, an American commentator, Paul Carrington, has said: '... what people bring to court is the refuse of our national and community life. Mendacity, greed, brutality, sloth, and neglect are the materials with which we work ...'[58]

10.21   Sir Jack Jacob, writing in 1985, before the ADR movement had made a serious impact in mainstream English civil justice, endorsed the ideal of open access to courts for the widest range of disputes:[59] 'It should be a fundamental aim of civil justice to open wide the gates of the Halls of Justice and to provide adequate and effective methods and measures, practices and procedures, reliefs and remedies, to deal with all justiciable claims and complaints.' He added: 'Such an aim would produce greater harmony and concord in society and increase the understanding and respect of the community for law and the system of civil justice.' But now this judgment-centric view seems debatable. England has not adopted Jacob's aim.

10.22   It is certainly desirable that some types of disputes should not be conveniently swept under the carpet by a last-minute settlement designed to avoid adverse publicity. Examples taken from contemporary British life might be: a senior female police-woman complains that her rise within the hierarchy has been obstructed by sexual discrimination;[60] a family wishes to complain that their son's suicide within the British armed forces was the result of bullying by

---

(reviewed Neil Andrews [1989] CLJ 506 and other studies cited Genn (1997) ibid; see also H Genn, *The Paths to Justice: What People Do and Think About Going to Law* (Hart, Oxford, 1999); H Genn, 'Court-Based ADR Initiatives for Non-Family Civil Disputes: The Commercial Court and the Court of Appeal' (Department for Constitutional Affairs Research Reports 1/2002, 2002): *www.hmcourts-service.gov.uk/docs/adr_initiatives. pdf.*

   [58] Paul D Carrington, 'Teaching Civil Procedure: A Retrospective View' (1999) 49 Jo of Leg Educ 311–32, at 328.

   [59] JIH Jacob, 'Justice Between Man and Man' (1984) 34 Jo of Legal Education 268 (cited H Genn, 'Understanding Civil Justice' (1997) 50 CLP 155, 185–6; Genn suggests that 'our future prosperity has more to do with what is going on in offices and factories in the Far East than with whether Lord Woolf's fast track will achieve its objectives.' cf also Jacob's statement in 'Access to Justice in England', by the same author, *The Reform of Civil Procedural Law* (1982) 125, 126–7: 'In a civilised society, there should be no room for barriers to justice, no second-class access to justice, just as there should be no second-class justice' (reprinting of his contribution to M Cappelletti and B Garth, *Access to Justice, a World Survey* (Guiffree and Sijthoff, Italy, 1978) vol 1, bk 1); and Jacob's later statement in *The Fabric of English Civil Justice* (1987) 277, '... there should be, not only equality before the law, but equality of access to the law and legal services ... alike for rich and poor and those of moderate means, and that such access should extend to all civil claims and defences at all levels of the judicial process, without regard to the nature of the dispute or complaint or the relief or remedy claimed.'

   [60] See the 'Halford' affair, July 1992, discussed Neil Andrews, *Principles of Civil Procedure* (1994) 26.

fellow soldiers;[61] a car-dealer's standard-term warranty for repair of new vehicles is mischievously declared to have been 'forfeited' for a reason which is no longer tenable under competition law;[62] a tenant has failed for many years to induce his landlord, a large charity, to satisfy its repair obligations, and it appears that there have been similar complaints by other tenants against this landlord.[63]

Assessment of the Debate

Admittedly, settlement is not a perfect process, nor is the outcome necessarily   **10.23** reasonable or fair. But it is hard to assess the 'intrinsic quality' of the terms of particular settlements because these agreements are nearly always confidential (the *fact* that there has been a settlement – as distinct form its terms – cannot be kept 'privileged'; although even the *fact* that settlement has occurred might be confidential; on the privilege/confidence distinction, see **6.27**, and on the scope of privilege in this context **11.58**). The substantive fairness of settlement agreements is really a matter of surmise, illuminated only by the feeble glow of anecdote. No doubt, many claimants (especially potential claimants) end up accepting a very poor, even derisory, compromise.[64] Conversely, it is possible for the other side to be induced to pay a sum, by way of compromise, which was unmerited by the objective features of the claim. But it is not really possible to advance beyond these generalities.

It is submitted that objections to settlement cannot justify curtailing this   **10.24** crucial practice. The wise policy is to encourage settlement. Adjudication on the merits of the case in formal court proceedings should remain a residual mechanism. It is appropriate only for disputes in five main situations: (i) where there is no real element of factual difference between the parties (open and

---

[61] Such complaints have received publicity in recent years: for Parliamentary comment in 2006 on a QC's report into one set of incidents, http://www.publications.parliament.uk/pa/ld199900/ldhansrd/pdvn/lds06/text/60329–05.htm.

[62] Typically, customer's garage failing to fit replacement mechanical part bearing manufacturer's 'logo', even though part in fact fitted has same objective specification as the manufacturer's named part; facts told to the author: for the legal background to this, see the Office of Fair Trading's comments at http://www.oft.gov.uk/News/Press+releases/2003/PN+170–03.htm.

[63] Examples must be legion; eg, *English Churches Housing Group v Shine* [2004] EWCA Civ 434.

[64] The House of Lords has held that an employer had failed to spell out with sufficient clarity in a contract of compromise its wish to stifle possible claims arising in the future, including claims only subsequently recognised at law as a result of case-law development: *BCCI v Ali* [2001] UKHL 8; [2002] 1 AC 251, HL, at [19], [21] [35], [86]; cf dissent, ibid, at [73], per Lord Hoffmann; the decision is considered in detail in Neil Andrews, *English Civil Procedure* (Oxford UP, 2003) 23.65 to 23.77.

shut cases where the defendant is merely playing for time; often these can be disposed of judicially on the merits by use of summary judgment or striking out proceedings, **5.18, 5.23**); or (ii) where attempts at settlement and mediation have failed and fresh attempts are unlikely to succeed; or (iii) where mediation is bound to fail because of a party's obstinacy; (iv) where the cost of mediation might exceed that of stream-lined public adjudication; (v) where there is a real value in exposing heinous or reprehensible misconduct to public view (**10.22**) as distinct from the common fare of 'mendacity, greed, brutality, sloth, and neglect' (**10.20**).

(6) Settlement Offers and Costs Incentives to Compromise

10.25   The English rules (CPR Part 36) allow a claimant or defendant to make a settlement offer[65] (defendants need no longer make payments into court: an offer to pay is enough).[66] A prospective party can also make a settlement offer.[67] The settlement offer, unless cancelled, will be open to acceptance by the other party ('offeree') within a specified period (normally 21 days).[68]

10.26   If the offeree decides not to accept the settlement offer, he will take a 'costs risk'.[69] Consider the first type of costs risk. This concerns the situation where *the claimant rejects* the defendant's settlement offer. If the claimant at trial 'fails to obtain a judgment more advantageous than a defendant's Part 36 offer', then, 'unless [the court] considers it unjust to do so', claimant must pay the

---

[65] CPR Part 36 has recently been amended (April 2007); the following works must be read with caution because they are based on the pre-April 2007 rules: D Foskett, *The Law and Practice of Compromise* (6th edn, 2005) chs 14 to 26; Neil Andrews, *English Civil Procedure* (Oxford UP, 2003) ch 24; *Zuckerman on Civil Procedure* (2006) ch 25.

[66] New text of CPR Part 36.4, effective April 2007; the impetus had been supplied by cases which had allowed public authorities or insured parties to make settlement offers: *Crouch v King's Healthcare NHS Trust* [2004] EWCA Civ 1332; [2005] 1 WLR 2105; *Stokes Pension Fund v Western Power Distribution plc* [2005] EWCA Civ 854; [2005] 1 WLR 3595, at [24] ff; developments considered in 'Part 36 of the CPR: Offers to Settle and Payments into Court: Responses to Consultation' (August 2006): *www.dca.gov.uk/civil-proc36/response0206.pdf*; for the text of the April 2007 rules, see http://www.justice.gov.uk/civil/procrules_fin/index.htm.

[67] CPR 36.3(2); eg in the *Straker* case, noted at n 69 below.

[68] Acceptance by the claimant of the offer entitles him to standard basis costs: CPR 36.10(3); *Lahey v Pirelli Tyres Ltd* [2007] EWCA Civ 91; [2007] 1 WLR 998 (offeree entitled to all such costs, as assessed on that basis; considering parallel pre-April 2007 rule); noted J Sorabi (2007) 26 CJQ 284.

[69] CPR 36.14; see *Straker v Tudor Rose (A Firm)* [2007] EWCA Civ 368 (where the court emphasised that the claimant's failure to beat the defendant's settlement offer should normally entitle the defendant to his costs; allowance can be made for the defendant's unreasonable failure to negotiate pre-action; but, in this last respect, the first instance judge had over-reacted and made too severe a costs reduction).

defendant's costs incurred after the date when the claimant should have accepted the settlement offer. The defendant will only be liable for the claimant's costs incurred before that date. The second costs risk arises where *the defendant rejects* the claimant's settlement offer. If 'judgment against the defendant is at least as advantageous to the claimant as the proposals contained in a claimant's Part 36 offer', then, 'unless [the court] considers it unjust to do so', the defendant will be liable to pay the claimant not just the ordinary measure of costs ('standard' costs) but an aggravated measure (so-called 'indemnity costs', on which see **9.12**), with the further possibility of a high level of interest on those costs.

Because of the high level of costs in English civil litigation, these 'costs risks' **10.27** provide a powerful incentive to accept terms of proposed settlement. A model 'transnational' civil procedural code, the American Law Institute/UNIDROIT project, endorses Canadian and English use of such settlement leverage.[70]

Narrow Defeats and Hollow Victories

A claimant might only narrowly 'beat' a settlement offer. In that situation, the **10.28** defeated party might legitimately complain that the claim was exaggerated in its size or that an excessive number of issues were raised. In the face of this, the court has a broad discretion to adjust its costs decision (generally on the court's costs discretion, **9.09**). By this means, the court can register disapproval of a claimant's overall conduct during the case.

For example, in *Jackson v Ministry of Defence* (2006), the claimant had **10.29** been injured while participating in military training.[71] The claim was for roughly £ 1 million. A large component of this involved an allegation that the

---

[70] ALI/UNIDROIT's *Principles of Transational Civil Procedure* (Cambridge UP, 2006), rule 16.6 at pages 118, 120.

[71] [2006] EWCA Civ 46; similarly, but in the converse case of a *claimant's settlement offer*, rejected by the defendant, *Jones MP v Associated Newspapers Ltd* [2007] EWHC 1489 (QB), Eady J considered the application of CPR Part 36 to a defamation judgment in favour of a claimant; the jury awarded £ 5,000; the claimant's settlement offer, rejected by the defendant newspaper, had been for £ 4, 999 *plus a public apology*; although the judgment was for £1 more than the rejected settlement offer, Eady J said at [22], 'I am unable to conclude that the offer made last year was "at least as advantageous" as the ultimate outcome and, therefore, I do not consider that Part 36.14 applies in this particular instance'; the claimant had not achieved a real victory on these facts; accordingly, the victorious claimant was not entitled to indemnity costs but merely standard basis costs; adopting the test formulated by Sir Thomas Bingham MR in *Roache v News Group Newspapers Ltd* [1998] EMLR 161, CA: 'who, as a matter of substance and reality, has won? Has the plaintiff won anything of value which he could not have won without fighting the action through to a finish? Has the defendant substantially denied the plaintiff the prize which the plaintiff fought the action to win?'

claimant had suffered permanent disability. But the defendant's settlement offer was for only £ 150,000. At trial, the claimant obtained damages of £ 155,000. But he failed to establish permanent disability. The trial judge emphasised that the claimant had only narrowly beaten the settlement offer, so that the victory was rather hollow. In fact the claimant had lost on the main issue of 'permanent disability'. In light of this, the judge reduced the claimant's costs by 25 per cent. This costs decision was made in exercise of the broad discretion to consider (among other things) the unreasonable or exaggerated nature of the claim. The Court of Appeal acquiesced in the judge's assessment, but suggested that the reduction might have been greater.

(7) The Court's Role in Achieving a Settlement

General Position in England

10.30   Subject to the two special cases examined below (settlements affecting children, etc, and 'ENE' in the Commercial Court), the English courts do not actively suggest to the parties possible terms of settlement.[72] Instead judges prefer to procure settlement indirectly by suggesting mediation, where appropriate (see **11.35 ff**). The courts can impose a stay on proceedings to ensure that this process is at least considered by the parties. The court can also impose costs sanctions where a litigant has unreasonably refused a suggestion, whether made by the court or the other party, that mediation might be usefully employed (on 'stays' and costs sanctions in this context, see **11.38** and **11.40**).

---

[72] S Roberts, 'Settlement as Civil Justice' (2000) 63 MLR 739, 741, contrasting some US practices, M Galanter, 'The Emergence of the Judge as Mediator in Civil Cases' (1986) 69 Judicature 257 and M Galanter and M Cahill, 'Most Cases Settle: Judicial Promotion and Regulation of Settlements' (1994) 46 Stanford L Rev 1329; see also, for more detail, S Roberts, 'Settlement as Civil Justice' (2000) 63 MLR 739, 741 and 'Alternative Dispute Resolution and Civil Justice ...' (1993) 56 MLR 452, 458 ff, 469–70 (noting the anxiety, first, that judicial integrity will be compromised by such direct involvement and, secondly, that judicial suggestions will become an unregulated and impure form of hybrid law).

Court Ratifying Settlements Affecting Children or Mentally Infirm Litigants

The English court must approve proposed compromises of claims affecting the **10.31** interests of children (those under 18) or of mental patients[73] (for details, see the specialist work).[74] Even in this context, however, the court's role is initially reactive, in the sense that the court does not propose the initial terms of settlement. However, it can influence the outcome.

Early Neutral Evaluation ('ENE') in the Commercial Court

This settlement procedure is peculiar to the Commercial Court. It has been **10.32** slow to gather momentum.[75] The gist of ENE is that a judge can make a non-binding evaluation of the case's merits. He must be neutral for the purpose of this discrete task: someone other than the judge conducting the pre-trial case-management and other than (if different) the trial judge. 'ENE' cannot be thrust upon the parties. It appears that a judge can suggest ENE.[76] However, both parties must assent to that suggestion.

Other legal systems have experimented with similar schemes. There is a **10.33** system of judicial mediation in the Delaware Court of Chancery (USA).[77] This involves a judge, other than the eventual trial judge, making 'evaluative' comments on the relevant dispute with a view to procuring settlement. Leo Strine Jr, Vice-Chancellor of that court, explains its attraction to litigants:

'The involvement of a business judge is important because it is the closest thing to the "horse's mouth" that parties to litigation can get ... Judicial mediators are scrupulous about honoring their obligation not to talk to the assigned trial judge about the mediation ... The judicial mediator is expected to and does provide his own views of the merits and of the risks that the mediating parties face. This affords the parties the maximal opportunity to make a reasoned judgment regarding how the litigation might culminate at judgment.'[78]

---

[73] CPR 21.10, adopting old RSC Ord 80 procedure; until the court's approval, the claimant is not entitled to interest on a sum paid into court, *Brennan v ECO Composting Ltd* [2006] EWHC 3153 (QB); [2007] 3 All ER 67, Silber J, at [30].

[74] D Foskett, *The Law and Practice of Compromise* (6th edn, 2005) ch 35.

[75] A Colman, *Commercial Court* (5th edn, 2000) 21 (noting only two instances in the first five years of the ENE system), see also ibid at 74; S Sugar and R Wilson (eds), *Commercial and Mercantile Courts Litigation Practice* (2004).

[76] 'The Admiralty and Commercial Court Guide' (7th edn, 2006) section G2.

[77] Leo Strine Jr, '"Mediation Only Filings" in the Delaware Court of Chancery ...' (2003) 53 Duke LJ 585, 591–3; available on-line: *www.law.duke.edu/journals/dlj/articles/dlj53p585.htm*.

[78] ibid, at 592.

(8) Concluding Remarks

10.34   The main points can be summarised as follows.

First, settlement is taking firmer hold as the optimal form of concluding a dispute (it is tendentious to describe this as 'dispute resolution'). The rules and practices reflect, more pointedly than ever before, settlement's central position within the English system of civil justice.

Secondly, many factors can increase the chances that parties (including potential litigants) might reach a settlement. In England these matters include: (i) the rise of pre-action protocols (**2.27** ff; **3.01** ff; **6.07** ff); (ii) the high cost of litigation (**9.03** ff); (iii) the costs-shifting rule (**9.06** ff); (iv) settlement offers and the accompanying costs incentives to accept such offers (**10.25** ff); (v) the privilege attaching to confidential settlement negotiations (see **11.49** for this and for privilege in the context of mediation discussions); (vi) in recent times, the greater readiness of practitioners and judges at all stages to advise or recommend negotiation or mediation rather than litigious dog-fighting (**10.09** ff).

Thirdly, settlement avoids various forensic inconveniences. It can relieve the disputants from a long, fraught, expensive, and not wholly predictable, legal process. That process can involve judgment, successive appeals, and enforcement (on this 'end-game', see chapter 8). It is little wonder that most litigants, like Helen of Troy, would prefer settlement to prolonged war. Nor is it remarkable that (as we have seen) the policy of the English system is to foster the conditions for termination by accord rather than judgment.

Finally, trial of the merits by oral examination of witnesses has ceased to be the starting-point for procedural discussion. Advocates and litigants learn their lines and hire their costumes for a play which is seldom heard.[79] In outward form modern litigation remains preparation for a final hearing. Thus the system of case management, and the expensive pre-trial phase, presuppose that trial will occur. However, the reality is that, for most litigants, trial and appeal are beyond the horizon. Nor should this be a matter for regret. In 2006, a sorely tested judge, his judicial assistant, and two phalanxes of counsel and solicitors, were starting 'day 256' in court among the 'lever-arch' files when the exit door from Hades was unlocked: the claimants had abandoned the claim.[80] Rational English disputants would prefer to settle rather than have

---

[79] For example, Sir Leonard Hoffmann, 'Changing Perspectives on Civil Litigation' (1993) 56 MLR 297, noting the increasing resort to pre-trial summary procedures, pre-action disclosure, witness statements, and provisional and protective relief; since 1998, to this list must be added, 'pre-action protocols', expansion of pre-action disclosure orders, the CPR's imposition of case-management, and judicial stays and costs orders to promote mediation.

[80] *Three Rivers DC v The Governor and Company of the Bank of England* [2006] EWHC 816 (Comm) (12 April 2006), Tomlinson J at [1]: 'On 2 November 2005, Day 256 of the trial, the English liquidators of Bank of Credit and Commerce International SA, the

even one 'day in court'. The newly invigorated 'culture of settlement' recognises that preference. And this private wish chimes with the general[81] public interest in reducing the rate of cases fought to trial.

Claimants, finally abandoned their attempt to prove that in its supervisory regulation of the activities of BCCI SA in the United Kingdom between 1980 and 1991 the Bank of England acted in a knowingly unlawful and wholly dishonest manner.'

[81] See **10.24** for the categories of dispute where judgment is desirable, even necessary.

Chapter 11

Mediation

Contents

(1) Introduction

11.01 Mediation has become popular in England. This 'alternative' form of 'civil justice' can operate as a complete substitute for civil litigation, or it can supplement that formal process after court proceedings have begun, and even after judgment has been given but an appeal is pending (on this last situation, **11.42**). The main points will be:

(1) the process of mediation and the outcome of that process – a mediated settlement – can be superior to adjudication of the dispute by a court;

(2) mediation is possible only if both parties are willing to discuss their dispute, to examine the merits of their position in good faith, and ultimately to consider making concessions, whether tactical or magnanimous (however, a court might sometimes be justified in suggesting mediation even if both parties seem initially opposed to this, **11.39**);

(3) the court system encourages pursuit of mediation; the courts can direct litigants in pending actions or appeals to pursue mediation if the parties, or one of them, requests, or if the court itself suggests; leverage to pursue mediation takes the form of a 'stay' upon current proceedings or the threat of an adverse costs order;

(4) an English court will enforce a mediation agreement by ordering a stay of litigation brought in violation of that agreement;

(5) Government has a strong interest in promoting ADR because it is less expensive than civil litigation;

(6) civil proceedings before the courts are becoming a system of last resort to be pursued only when more civilised and 'proportionate' techniques have failed or could never be made to work;

(7) but traditional court litigation will continue because it offers a strong form of dispute-resolution; the court's coercive powers are indispensable in some contexts, especially in claims against fraudulent or uncooperative persons (on this theme see also **13.19**);

(8) court litigation also embodies many values, notably the principle of publicly accessible proceedings and reasoned decisions;

(9) confidential communications during mediation are privileged against compulsory production in legal proceedings;

(10) it is not yet settled in English law whether there is a general and distinct doctrine of 'mediation privilege'; for the author's concluding submissions on this point, see **11.61**.

(2) Varieties of Dispute Resolution and the Spectrum of ADR

The three main 'alternatives' to civil litigation before the English courts are: (i) *party-to-party negotiation leading to settlement*: this is the most common way in which a dispute or claim is terminated (see chapter 10); (ii) *mediation or conciliation:* these will be discussed in this chapter; (iii) *arbitration* (see chapter 11)[1]: this tends to be a rather formal style of proceeding; commercial arbitration conducted in England can replicate many aspects of High Court commercial litigation, although this tendency is regrettable, has been lamented (**12.35**), and should be resisted. **11.02**

In addition to settlement, mediation and arbitration, just mentioned, four other styles of dispute-resolution should be mentioned: (a) *stream-lined adjudication outside the ordinary court system:* 'ombudsmen'[2] administer justice, often on a 'documents-only' basis, in a range of specific fields, for example, pensions or investments disputes; (b) *'expert determination'*: this concerns a refer- **11.03**

---

[1] On the combination of mediation and arbitration, see **12.12** ff; see also D Plant 'ADR and Arbitration' in LW Newman and RD Hill (eds), *The Leading Arbitrators' Guide to International Arbitration* (Juris publishers, Bern, 2004) 245 ff; K Mackie, D Miles, W Marsh, T Allen, *The ADR Practice Guide* (2007) 3.3.2.6 ('med-arb').

[2] For references, see Neil Andrews, *English Civil Procedure* (Oxford UP, 2003) 9.27 n 31; on the rise of informal litigation regimes governing disputes in the banking, building societies, investment, insurance, and pensions industries, E Ferran, 'Dispute Resolution Mechanisms in the UK Financial Sector' (2002) 21 CJQ 135; R Nobles, 'Access to Justice through Ombudsmen: the Courts' Response to the Pensions Ombudsman' (2002) 21 CJQ 94; Lord Woolf, *Access to Justice: Interim Report* (1995) 111 at [40].

ence to an impartial third party of a technical problem, for example, a request to make a valuation of company assets or commercial property; statute also allows experts to make swift decisions if disputes arise during the course of a building project; these decisions are initially provisional; they become binding if, within a short period, neither party seeks to re-open the determination (by litigation or arbitration);[3] (c) *'early neutral evaluation'*:[4] this involves a neutral third party, often a lawyer, providing a non-binding verdict on the merits of the dispute; in the English Commercial Court, the parties can consent to a High Court judge providing such an 'early neutral evaluation'(see also **10.30**);[5] (d) *mini-trial*: this is an adjunct to mediation; as leading commentators have said: 'in essence lawyers or other advisors for each party present a "mini" version of their case to a panel consisting of a senior executive of their client and of the other party ... The procedure may take place without a neutral's involvement but will usually be more effective if a capable neutral chairs the presentation stage;'[6] a 'mini-trial' can create a 'stronger feeling of having had a day in court than mediation', and 'a better opportunity to assess the performance of key witnesses'.[7]

11.04   A third party neutral can intervene in various ways. He might act as:

(1) *shuttle-cock messenger:* he will then be a 'go-between', passing messages between parties who cannot any longer communicate directly with each other; or

(2) *facilitator*: the mediator might endeavour to act as a mutual confidant to the parties, for the purpose of brokering a settlement, without commenting on the merits of the parties' respective positions; or

(3) *evaluator*: the mediator might make a non-binding, perhaps persuasive, evaluation of one or more of the parties' claims or position (whether at the request of the parties, or of his own accord); as Stitt has commented, 'a facilitative mediator tries to enable the disputants to reach consensus on what they think is a fair outcome, while an evaluative mediator tries to lead [them] to his ... own assessment of what is fair';[8] or

---

[3] *Pegram Shopfitters Ltd v Tally Weijl* [2003] EWCA Civ 1750; [2004] 1 WLR 2082, CA, especially at [1] to [10], on accelerated resolution of construction disputes (so-called 'adjudication') under Part II, Housing Grants, Construction and Regeneration Act 1996, and the Scheme for Construction Contracts (England and Wales) Regulations 1998 (SI 1998/649); generally on mediation and experts, L Blom-Cooper (ed), *Experts in Civil Courts* (Oxford UP, 2006) ch 10.

[4] K Mackie, D Miles, W Marsh, T Allen, (2007) 3.2.2.3.

[5] Admiralty and Commercial Courts Guide (7th edn, 2006), section G2; for comment, Neil Andrews, *English Civil Justice and Remedies: Progress and Challenges: Nagoya Lectures* (Shinzan Sha Publishers, Tokyo, 2007) 3.23.

[6] K Mackie, D Miles, W Marsh, T Allen, *The ADR Practice Guide* (2000) 13.1 (not reproduced in 2007 edition).

[7] ibid at 13.2.

[8] AJ Stitt, *Mediation: A Practical Guide* (2004) 1.4; see also D Spencer and M Brogan, *Mediation: Law and Practice* (Cambridge UP, 2006) 104–7.

(4) *exhortation to settle on suggested terms*: here the neutral applies pressure, (perhaps by virtue of his office), to the parties with the aim of inducing them to accept a settlement on specified or suggested terms; or

(5) *imposing binding decision*: here the neutral acts plainly as an arbitrator appointed, by agreement, to decide a specific dispute by issuing a binding award, and clothed with full statutory powers under the Arbitration Act 1996;[9] on this topic see chapter 12.

In this chapter we are concerned with matters falling within (1) to (4) of this spectrum. The mediator's role is to act as an independent and disinterested third party and encourage the parties to talk and to move towards a possible agreed settlement. This role is normally covered by section (2), but he might make an evaluative intervention (see (3) above).

Paul Newman has suggested that a truly effective mediator should display the following six qualities:[10] (1) 'empathy – the ability to get on with the parties, understand their position, even if he does not agree with them, and the ability to deflect parties from their fixed views'; (2) 'patience – the ability to wait for the parties to make movements in their own time'; (3) 'self-assurance – the ability to inspire confidence in the parties, with a game plan of what is to be achieved without obviously leading the parties'; (4) 'clarity of thought – the ability to ask questions which are intelligent and result in new information and perspectives'; (5) 'ingenuity – the capacity to bring in new ideas when the discussion appears to be flagging or on the point of failing, including the power to think laterally and propose novel solutions for the parties to think about and promote as their own ideas'; (6) 'stamina – the mediation sessions may take place over an extended period of time, and there may be less scope for breaks as momentum increases towards possible agreement.' **11.05**

The practice of conducting mediation sessions is fully explained in specialist manuals (or rather suggested methods, since this is a flexible art).[11] It is usual for a mediator to be paid jointly by the parties to the dispute. Free-lance mediators do not enjoy security of tenure. Many UK mediators are 'accredited', having received professional training from various private organisations.[12] There is no need for the mediator to have a legal training or qualification. However, in England many commercial mediators are 'lawyers': former bar- **11.06**

---

[9] See eg *Russell on Arbitration* (23rd edn, by D StJ Sutton and J Gill, 2007); M Mustill and S Boyd, *Commercial Arbitration* (2nd edn, 1989, and companion volume, 2002).

[10] P Newman, in M Liebmann (ed), *Mediation In Context* (2000, London and Philadelphia) 183–4.

[11] K Mackie, D Miles, W Marsh, T Allen, *The ADR Practice Guide* (2007) especially ch's 11 ff; AJ Stitt, *Mediation: A Practical Guide* (2004); M Liebmann (ed), *Mediation In Context* (2000, London and Philadelphia); D Spencer and M Brogan, *Mediation: Law and Practice* (Cambridge UP, 2006) especially ch 2.

[12] eg, from 'CEDR'.

risters, solicitors, or judges, or current lawyers. Mediation is not yet a feature of most law degrees. Nor is it an aspect of professional training as a lawyer.

11.07   It seems inevitable that the UK government and European law will require mediation to be a fully regulated and professionally accountable service. The European Commission has proposed a directive on mediation and has issued a Code of Conduct for Mediators.[13]

(3) Mediation as the Handmaiden of Settlement

11.08   Mediation is best considered as a means of procuring a settlement, that is, consensual conclusion of a dispute by the parties without submission to a binding decision by a third party neutral (generally on settlement, see chapter 10). Leading English judges have embraced the public policy aim that settlement should be promoted at all stages in the life of a civil dispute, including after commencement of formal proceedings. As a result of greater levels of settlement, fewer cases will proceed to trial. As Lord Donaldson said (1987):

> '... the procedure of the court must be, and is, intended to achieve the resolution of disputes by a variety of methods, of which a resolution by judgment is but one, and probably the least desirable. Accordingly, anything which enables the parties to appreciate the true strength and weakness of their positions at the earliest possible moment and at the same time enables them to enter into fully informed and realistic discussions designed to achieve a consensual resolution of the dispute is very much in the public interest.'[14]

Similarly, Lord Woolf said in his interim report (1995): 'the philosophy of litigation should be primarily to encourage early settlement of disputes.'[15]

11.09   Mediation might be the avenue leading to a settlement, or settlement can be achieved without mediation. In fact settlements can arise in four main ways. The first two concern settlements reached without the intervention of mediators. First, non-mediated settlements can be reached without commencement of formal proceedings. This is by far the most common type of settlement. In England, pre-action protocols now regulate the process of bargaining towards a settlement before commencement of formal proceedings (see also **3.01, 6.07**).[16] These are a means of avoiding formal proceedings. Such protocols

---

[13] COM (2004) 718 final, Brussels dated 22.10.2004 (draft directive on 'certain aspects of mediation in civil and commercial matters'): http://europa.eu.int/eur-lex/en/com/pdf/2004/com2004_0718en01.pdf; for the European Code of Conduct for Mediators: http://europa.eu.int/comm/justice_home/ejn/adr/adr_ec_code_conduct_en.htm.

[14] *Naylor v Preston Area Health Authority* [1987] 1 WLR 958, 967–8, CA, per Sir John Donaldson MR (as he then was).

[15] *Access to Justice: Interim Report* (1995) ch 7, para 7(a).

[16] Neil Andrews, *English Civil Procedure* (Oxford UP, 2003) 3.13 to 3.18, 23.07, 26.63 to 26.66; and see the author's General Report (comparing almost 20 jurisdictions) on the

now apply to various types of proceeding. One of their aims is to enable each side to gain access to important information held by the other side, for example, hospital records. Secondly, a non-mediated settlement might be agreed after commencement of formal proceedings. Most formal civil proceedings culminate not in judgment on the merits, but in an agreement of settlement. Thirdly, the parties might agree a mediated settlement without a formal court action having been commenced. Finally, mediated settlements can be agreed after formal proceedings have been issued, or even after trial has begun or concluded.

There has been a remarkable increase in the popularity and importance of mediation. Although some disputants perceive mediation as a sign of 'weakness', this prejudice is waning. Litigation is becoming a process of last resort (**11.29**, **11.32**; see also chapter 1). Mediation clauses are now common in commercial agreements (see **11.46** below). **11.10**

(4) Mediation's Advantages over Litigation

The five main advantages of mediation, when compared with litigation, are as follows.[17] First, the parties can select the mediator: in litigation, they cannot choose which judge will adjudicate in a particular case. Secondly, the mediation process is confidential: the litigation process is public, notably trial and other hearings. Thirdly, mediation offers scope for fashioning flexible remedies or solutions. By contrast, the array of remedies in formal court proceedings is restricted. Judgment in favour of the claimant normally results in outright victory for that party. Fourthly, parties to a successful mediation might even achieve an amicable outcome: few litigants leave the court as friends, unless judgment has been entered by consent and in a spirit of good will. Finally, mediation can save time and expense, compared to many forms of court proceedings.[18] These beneficial aspects will now be elaborated. At **11.24** below, however, we will note various problems associated with mediation. **11.11**

'Pre-action Phase' for the world congress of the International Association of Procedural Law, Brazil 2007, forthcoming.

[17] See also **13.13** for discussion of the perceived problems of court proceedings, arranged under the headings: 'publicity', 'hassle or distress', 'unpredictable outcomes', 'remedial inflexibility'.

[18] AJ Stitt, *Mediation: A Practical Guide* (2004) ch 2; D Spencer and M Brogan, *Mediation: Law and Practice* (Cambridge UP, 2006), 84 ff consider the 'five philosophies' or precepts of 'confidentiality', 'voluntariness' (see esp ch 8, at pp 306 chronicling Australian mediation orders by courts), 'empowerment' (viz parties can negotiate for themselves), 'neutrality' and 'unique solution' (viz creativity, not being bound by prescribed norms and legal remedies).

Choice of Neutral Third Party

11.12   Mediators are not (normally)[19] appointed or selected by the State. Instead the parties choose them on an ad hoc basis. By contrast, litigation involves selection of a judge by the court. Furthermore, the judge is a lawyer, university-educated, and with many years of practical experience of legal practice. It is certainly a bonus if the judge happens to possess specialist experience outside the law.

Confidentiality and Privilege

11.13   Mediation is a private and confidential process (**11.49** below), although the fact that the parties have reached a settlement is not privileged.[20] By contrast, nearly all hearings in civil proceedings are in public.[21]

Participation by the Parties' Key Players

11.14   Mediation is more likely to succeed if the persons participating in this process are senior representatives of the relevant company or organisation. They should also enjoy full authority to settle the matter by a binding agreement. By contrast, senior company officials often choose to remain aloof from a civil case's development and opportunities for settlement or pressure of work prevents them attending closely to civil proceedings (for example, the Governor of the Bank of England, excusably, did not attend all 256 days of England's lon-

---

[19] 'Conciliators' employed by the Government's 'ACAS' service in the field of labour disputes are an exception to this proposition: eg, s 18(7) Employment Tribunals Act 1996 (as re-styled by s 1(2) Employment Rights (Dispute Resolution) Act 1998); there has been a pilot scheme for use of High Court judges in the Technology and Construction court to sit as mediators, with the parties' consent, but this has not attracted significant use: 'The Lawyer' 25 June 2007;

[20] On the non-privileged status of the *fact* that there has been a settlement, *Tomlin v Standard Telephones & Cables Ltd* [1969] 1 WLR 1378, CA; applied in *Brown v Rice* [2007] EWHC 625 (Ch) Stuart Isaacs QC, on which see **11.50** ff below.

[21] The general rule is that a hearing must be in public: CPR 39.2(1); CPR 39.2(3) and PD (39) 1.5 set out exceptions; the primary source is s 67, Supreme Court Act 1981; the requirement of publicity is also contained in Article 6(1) of the European Convention on Human Rights (incorporated in Sch 1, Human Rights Act 1998); the relevant part of Art 6(1) reads: 'Judgment shall be pronounced publicly but the press and public may be excluded from all or part of the trial in the interests of morals, public order or national security in a democratic society, where the interests of juveniles or the protection of the life of the parties so require, or to the extent strictly necessary in the opinion of the court in special circumstances where publicity would prejudice the interests of justice'; J Jaconelli, *Open Justice* (Oxford UP, 2002); J Jacob, *Civil Justice in the Age of Human Rights* (Aldershot, 2007) ch 2.

gest trial: but he did embrace warmly Nicholas Stadlen and Bankim Thanki, both QC, and other counsel, at the end of their successful defence of this marathon case, see **5.28** for references to this case).

Mediation is Non-adversarial

Mediation is intended to enable the parties to establish common ground. By contrast, court proceedings notoriously encourage rival parties to stake out rigid points of difference.[22]   **11.15**

Multiple Parties

Mediation is not restricted to bipartite disputes, but can extend to cases where there are several parties. Traditional adjudication can accommodate such complex configurations, but only at the price of greater delay, expense, and inconvenience (on multi-party litigation, see chapter 14).   **11.16**

Speed

The parties can agree the timetable for the mediation process and specific dates. The intense 'face-to-face' stage can be as short as a few hours, and need not exceed one or two days. Litigants under the CPR system enjoy much less control over timetabling of hearings and trial than parties to mediation (on case management **3.13** ff).   **11.17**

Success Rate

One estimate suggests 75 to 90 per cent of commercial mediations result in settlement.[23] By contrast, mediations monitored within three English county courts produced a much lower rate of settlement: from 60 per cent to 30 per cent.[24] However, even if no settlement is reached, the process of mediation can   **11.18**

---

[22] Lord Woolf in his 1995 and 1996 *'Access to Justice'* reports, and the reforms of 1999, tried to end this aggressive style of litigation; there has been an improvement, but his reforms have not eliminated this problem.

[23] K Mackie, D Miles, W Marsh, T Allen, *The ADR Practice Guide* (2000) 11.11 suggest that 80 per cent of commercial mediations result in a settlement, and, ibid at 16.6, 90 per cent in the context of personal injury claims; in 2007 edition, a 'Substantial majority'.

[24] H Genn, 'Twisted Arms: Court Referred and Court Linked Mediation under Judicial Pressure' (Department of Constitutional Affairs, 2007) 202–3 (including cross references to

remove the sharp 'sting' of the dispute, or at least enhance each party's understanding of the opponent's position and motivation. But these benefits might not be apprehend by the parties, who are likely to resent money and time spent on abortive mediations.

Costs and Expense

11.19 There is much scope for each party to incur a large legal expenses bill in litigation (**9.03** ff). But, according to the data cited at **11.18** above, a large majority of voluntary 'commercial' mediations produce a settlement. The mediation process is relatively cheap. The UK Government is also promoting a 'free' ADR service for small claims.[25]

Co-operation

11.20 If mediation is to succeed, both sides must be willing to discuss their dispute and examine the merits of their position in good faith, and ultimately to consider making concessions, whether tactical or magnanimous[26] ((however, a court might sometimes be justified in suggesting mediation even if both parties seem initially opposed to this, **11.39**). Not everyone will exhibit such flexibility. Some are fraudsters or persistent non-payers who cannot be softened by even the most skilful mediator.[27] The English courts have refrained from compelling[28] unwilling parties to engage in mediation, as distinct from requiring

---

other on-line studies): see 'research' at http://www.justice.gov.uk/publications/research. htm.

[25] http://www.justice.gov.uk/whatwedo/alternativedisputeresolution.htm.

[26] On this cardinal contribution to the success of mediation, H Genn, 'Twisted Arms: Court Referred and Court Linked Mediation under Judicial Pressure' (Department of Constitutional Affairs, 2007) (report on a 'pilot scheme', concerning automatic referral to mediation at the Central London County Court): at pp 202–3, and citing Dutch support for this view: see 'research' at http://www.justice.gov.uk/publications/research.htm.

[27] But, even in this context, the courts are prepared to keep an open mind; in a case involving serious allegations that a person had benefited under a forged will, the Court of Appeal stated that the context 'cried out for ADR': *Couwenbergh v Valkova* [2004] EWCA Civ 676; noted by Tony Allen at www.cedr.co.uk/index.php?location=/library/articles/Mediating_fraud_cases.htm.

[28] However, in May 2007 Hazel Genn, UCL, London, presented a report on a 'pilot scheme', concerning automatic referral to mediation at the Central London County Court (with the right to 'opt-out' exercised in a large number of cases'), 'Twisted Arms: Court Referred and Court Linked Mediation under Judicial Pressure' (Department of Constitutional Affairs, 2007) (report on a 'pilot scheme', concerning automatic referral to mediation at the Central London County Court): see 'research' at http://www.justice.gov.uk/publications/research.htm.

them to consider ADR or to select a mediator from an agreed list or exchanged lists. If a party fails to consider ADR as a serious option when it has been recommended or it is appropriate, the available 'sanctions' are: the relevant party might have his case placed 'on hold' (technically a 'stay' of proceedings), or adverse costs orders can be made in the parallel civil proceedings (as explained at **11.40** ff below).

Flexible Outcomes

Settlements resulting from mediation can be more flexible or nuanced than final judgment before the courts.[29] In particular, a settlement can confer an element of 'success' or at least 'face-saving' for both parties. By contrast, a court normally makes a decision solely in favour of one party.[30] The court is also restricted to the standard remedies: payment of debt, damages, or the award of injunctions, declarations, orders for return of property, or (a fairly recent innovation) an 'apology' in defamation proceedings.[31] In *Dunnett v Railtrack plc* (2002), Brooke LJ, a member of the Court of Appeal, underlined the benefits of ADR and its potential for imaginative and flexible solutions:[32] 'Skilled mediators are now able to achieve results satisfactory to both parties in many cases which are quite beyond the powers of lawyers and courts to achieve … .' **11.21**

Continuing Relationships

A mediated settlement will be especially valuable when the parties are not merely casually connected by a relatively short and 'one-off' transaction, but have a continuing relationship, for example, joint ventures, employment relationships, or former spouses with young children.[33] **11.22**

---

[29] K Mackie, D Miles, W Marsh, T Allen, *The ADR Practice Guide* (2007) 1.2.

[30] Unless there is a finding of contributory negligence against the claimant, or there is a successful cross-claim or set-off defence made by the defendant.

[31] For comment on the range of outcomes in fact desired by disputants, see H Genn, 'Understanding Civil Justice' (1997) 50 CLP 155, 174 ff.

[32] [2002] 1 WLR 2434, CA, esp at [14].

[33] In *Shirayama Shokusan Co Ltd v Danovo Ltd* [2004] 1 WLR 2985 (Blackburne J), a dispute arose between the long-term tenants of a major property in Central London (the former 'County Hall'). Relations had become seriously strained. However, many of the issues were relatively small. The High Court judge held that ADR was appropriate.

Enforcement[34]

11.23 A mediated monetary settlement can be enforced as a debt claim (on the various forms of enforcement, see **8.28** ff). Sometimes the settlement might be more formally clothed as a 'consent order', although this presupposes that formal proceedings have been brought. One special type of consent order preserves confidentiality in the precise terms of the settlement. These terms are not open to public inspection (a so-called *'Tomlin Order'*).[35]

(5) Anxieties Concerning Mediation

11.24 As mentioned above (**11.08**), mediation is a 'handmaiden of settlement'. It follows, therefore, that attacks on privatised settlement (or the retreat of public adjudication) are also attacks upon mediation. The author refers the reader to more detailed discussion of the attacks on settlement at **10.18** ff. But here it should be noted that the most notable attack is Owen Fiss's 'Against Settlement' (1984).[36] His main contention is that settlement is open to suspicion. This is because the parties might have an imperfect understanding of their respective positions, or the parties might be unequal in various ways, or a party might have procured the settlement by underhand dealing.[37] Furthermore, trial permits public examination of unlawful or reprehensible conduct. In particular, public safety or financial scandals should not be swept under the ADR carpet.

11.25 But another aspect to this debate concerns the status and conduct of mediators in particular and the contrast with the judicial role. In England most mediators are not public servants. Professionally they live or die according to the demands of the market place. By contrast, there are strong, indeed hallowed, constraints upon judges, exercising their traditional adjudicative function. Judges enjoy independence and they must remain impartial.[38] They are ex-

---

[34] K Mackie, D Miles, W Marsh, T Allen, *The ADR Practice Guide* (2007) 7.7.

[35] ibid, Appendix B, at 317, for model *'Tomlin* order' agreements; surprisingly, in *Brown v Rice* [2007] EWHC 625 (Ch) Stuart Isaacs QC held that a settlement agreement reached after commencement of proceedings is void for uncertainty unless it specifies the precise mode of effecting the compromise (by consent judgment or by a *Tomlin* order).

[36] (1984) Yale LJ 1073; for references to the debate which this engendered in the US, see O Fiss and J Resnik, *Adjudication and Its Alternatives* (Foundation Press, New York, 2003) 481, 488; for further references, see **10.18** n 53.

[37] On the equality issue, D Spencer and M Brogan, *Mediation: Law and Practice* (Cambridge UP, 2006), 111 ff, and ch 7; on allegations of impropriety during negotiations resulting in a compromise, see *Halpern v Halpern (No 2)* [2007] EWCA Civ 291 at [1] ff (distribution of estate among family members; allegation that not all relevant assets were revealed and that the compromise should be regarded as vitiated on numerous suggested grounds).

[38] For detailed examination of the numerous constitutional and human rights con-

pected to reach decisions based upon cogent evaluation of the case's merits. Important judicial decisions can have a wider impact than the immediate dispute by adding to the body of precedent (see **2.08**). Even when merely illustrative, judicial decisions can provide useful information by indicating consistent application of various rules or principles and exercise of open-ended discretionary powers.[39] There are high expectations: that public adjudication will be measured, precise, and scrupulous rather than (as mediators freely acknowledge) approximate and paying scant attention to substantive rights. If judgments fail to deliver such high-quality of justice, the appeal system can rectify the defect (**8.12** ff). Ultimately judges might be disciplined for sloppy or corrupt performance of their responsibility.

American commentators have also observed (see also **10.07**)[40] that many US civil actions settle, some as a result of out-of-court private mediation. One concern is that this unregulated 'privatised' mediation service relies economically on preserving a fee stream.[41] This lack of economic independence might induce mediators to procure settlements in favour of 'repeat-players'.   **11.26**

As for the broader points made by Fiss, the author's view is that this root-and-branch attack on settlement is unpersuasive, indeed exaggerated (see **11.24** above and **10.18**).[42] In my opinion, senior English judges have been right to extol settlement (for example, Lords Donaldson and Woolf, quoted above at **11.08**). Their opinion is that, on balance, it is nearly always better to conclude a settlement, even one based on imperfect knowledge and perhaps slightly   **11.27**

---

straints on the public system of adjudication, Neil Andrews, *English Civil Procedure* (Oxford UP, 2003) ch's 4, 5, 7.

[39] R Cranston, 'Complex Litigation: the Commercial Court' (2007) 26 CJQ 190, 194: 'in deciding cases courts enunciate and replenish the law. Judgments are not only a reasoned explanation for the parties' benefit ... but a statement for the commercial community of the law for the present day ... At the very least they provide a guide to ... commercial parties, enabling cases to be settled without the occasion of litigation. Even where the [court] applies existing precedents that at least enables the public to know that cases can be settled along existing lines.'

[40] eg M Galanter, 'The Vanishing Trial ... in Federal and State Courts' (2004) 1 J Empirical Legal Studies 451; J Resnik, 'For Owen M Fiss: Some Reflections on the Triumph and Death of Adjudication' (2003) 58 Miami U L Rev 173; J Resnik, 'Whither and Whether Adjudication' (2006) 86 Boston ULRev 1101, 1123 ff; J Resnik, 'Uncovering, Discovering and Disclosing How the Public Dimensions of Court-Based Processes are at Risk' (2006) 81 Chicago-Kent LR 521 and J Resnik and DE Curtis, 'From "Rites" to "Rights" of Audience: The Utilities and Contingencies of the Public's Role in Court Business' in A Masson and K O'Connor (eds), *Representation of Justice* (Brussels, 2007); A Miller 'The Pre-trial Rush to Judgment: Are the "Litigation Explosion", "Liability Crisis", and Efficiency Cliches Eroding our Day in Court and Jury Commitments?'(2003) 78 NYULRev 982.

[41] D Spencer and M Brogan, *Mediation: Law and Practice* (Cambridge UP, 2006), 157 ff, and ch 6.

[42] (1984) Yale LJ 1073; for references to the debate which this engendered in the US, see O Fiss and J Resnik, *Adjudication and Its Alternatives* (Foundation Press, New York, 2003) 481, 488; for further references, see **10.18** n 53.

skewed by economic or other factors, rather than submit to the long and ultimately public process of hearing witnesses, experts, and presenting submissions of law.[43]

11.28   In any event, there is no 'either-or' choice to be made between settlement (and mediation) and civil trial.[44] The formal adjudicative process, including trial, will survive (see also **13.19** and **13.20**). Indeed this formal process is constitutionally guaranteed and its various features protected under human rights legislation (**2.11**). The wise policy is to encourage settlement and mediation. Court proceedings are appropriate only for disputes where: there is no real element of factual difference between the parties (open and shut cases, or ones where the defendant is merely playing for time); or where attempts at settlement and mediation have failed; or where mediation is bound to fail because of the adamantine intransigence of at least one party.[45] Conversely, mediation is likely to be suitable where the parties share an interest in one or more of the following: secrecy; quickness of result; economy in achieving that result; maintaining a lasting relationship.[46]

---

[43] For comment (and further references to literature) on disparities and uncertainties in the settlement process, see H Genn, 'Understanding Civil Justice' (1997) 50 CLP 155, 178 ff.

[44] A point attractively made by C Menkel-Meadow, 'Whose Dispute It Anyway: A Philosophical and Democratic Defense of Settlement (In Some Cases)' (1995) 83 Geo LJ 2663.

[45] P Newman, in M Liebmann (ed), *Mediation In Context* (2000, London and Philadelphia), 180–1, adds to the list just mentioned 'the parties have come to understand that mediation may provide them with the best option to have their day in court [a phrase used metaphorically here to denote face-to-face presence before a third party neutral!] a form of catharsis'; and 'both parties have learnt the value of mediation and the drawbacks of litigation' and 'there may be problems with witness availability or quality and the full intensity of a possible trial is best avoided'.

[46] P Newman, in M Liebmann (ed), ibid, 181, has crisply suggested that mediation is unlikely to work in the following situations: (1) the dispute concerns more a question of law than fact and established and clear law manifestly favours one party; (2) one party wishes to delay the resolution of the dispute for as long as possible; (3) one or both parties are not acting in good faith; (4) one party believes that litigation will be a complete vindication of his position; (5) there is [significant] inequality of bargaining power between the parties; (6) one of the parties lacks the resources to satisfy its obligations under a contract; (7) 'the dispute is one where the creation of legal precedent is desirable' [presumably, this refers to the situation where a strong and 'repeat player' party wishes to obtain general clarification of the law].

(6) Mediation's Growth in England[47]

Senior Master Robert Turner, a most experienced civil judge, has suggested **11.29** that twenty-first century English court litigation has become the 'alternative dispute resolution' system.[48] Similarly, the pre-action protocols state:[49] 'litigation should be a last resort, and claims should not be issued prematurely when a settlement is still likely ...'[50] Furthermore, the Law Society for England and Wales in 2005 issued a 'practice advice' recommending that solicitors should routinely consider whether their clients' disputes are suitable for ADR.[51] The European Commission has also embraced mediation and proposed a directive on the topic.[52]

One reason for this rise in ADR is that the mediation process is now better **11.30** understood, especially within the commercial sector. Secondly, litigation remains an expensive and problematic means of resolving many types of civil dispute. Thirdly, Government recognises that ADR permits disputes to be resolved less expensively than civil litigation.[53] Fourthly, the court system directly encourages litigants to pursue mediation in appropriate cases (for exceptional judicial involvement in procuring settlement, the reader is referred to **10.30**). We now turn to the judicial policy in England of encouraging resort to out-of-court mediation.

---

[47] Useful general surveys include: D Gladwell, 'Alternative Dispute Resolution and the Courts', Butterworths' Civil Court News in June 2004; M Partington, 'Alternative Dispute Resolution Developments: Future Challenges' (2004) 23 CJQ 99; M Nesic, 'Mediation – on the Rise in the United Kingdom' (2001) 13 Bond Law Review, issue 2, December: all three articles are available on-line at www.adr.civiljusticecouncil.gov.uk.

[48] Senior Master Robert Turner, Queen's Bench Division, (who retired from that post in 2007, after 20 years), cited K Mackie, D Miles, W Marsh, T Allen, *The ADR Practice Guide* (2007) 5.

[49] Neil Andrews, *English Civil Procedure* (Oxford UP, 2003) 3.13 to 3.18, 23.07, 26.63 to 26.66; for an empirical study, T Goriely, R Moorhead and P Abrams, *More Civil Justice? The Impact of the Woolf Reforms on Pre-Action Behaviour* (Law Society and Civil Justice Council, 2001).

[50] Practice Direction-Protocols, para 4.7.

[51] L Soc Gaz (2005) (16 June) 38–9.

[52] COM (2004) 718 final, Brussels dated 22.10.2004 (draft directive on 'certain aspects of mediation in civil and commercial matters'): http://europa.eu.int/eur-lex/en/com/pdf/2004/com2004_0718en01.pdf; for the European Code of Conduct for Mediators: http://europa.eu.int/comm/justice_home/ejn/adr/adr_ec_code_conduct_en.htm.

[53] Admittedly, there is a competing fiscal interest in receiving court fees payable upon commencement of proceedings; cf 'Civil Court Fees' (Court Service, September 2002), paras 3.7 ff: a consultation paper on fee changes, noting that between 1998 and 2001 there was a 22.5 per cent reduction in the number of county court claims and, during the same period, a 76 per cent fall in High Court claims; this resulted in large shortfalls in court fee income.

(7) Mediation and the English Procedural Framework[54]

Mediation Recommended

11.31 The idea that litigants might usefully proceed to mediation is not left to chance. Judicial encouragement to mediate is instead a pervasive feature of the modern civil justice system: the courts can 'stay proceedings' to accommodate mediation; and they can award costs sanctions if a party unreasonably fails to mediate. By 'staying an action', the court can require the parties to take steps to agree on a mediator and 'report back' on failure so to agree (for details, see **11.38** below).

Pre-Action Duty of Parties to Consider ADR

11.32 The CPR states that:

> 'the courts increasingly take the view that litigation should be a last resort, and that claims should not be issued prematurely when a settlement is still likely. Therefore, the parties should consider whether some form of alternative dispute settlement would be more suitable than litigation, and if so, endeavour to agree which form to adopt.'[55]

Prospective or Actual Party's Unreasonable Refusal to Consider Opponent's Suggestion that Dispute Should be Mediated

11.33 A party, or prospective litigant, can ask the opponent to consider mediation on a 'without prejudice save as to costs' basis. If the other party accedes to this proposal, the court can later take into account the content of these negotiations when determining any costs question in the later stages of this dispute. Thus the parties will have waived privilege for the purpose of determining any subsequent costs issue arising from the breakdown of the mediation. But that is the extent of the waiver: the court must not consider these discussions with regard to any other matter.[56]

---

[54] For a valuable typology of court-assisted modes of ADR, see WD Brazil and J Smith, 'Choice of Structures ...' (1999) 6 Dispute Resolution Magazine 8, cited in O Fiss and J Resnik, *Adjudication and Its Alternatives* (Foundation Press, New York, 2003) 467, at 468: court employs full-time in-house neutrals; or contracts with non-profit making organisations for such a programme; or directly pays firms to serve as neutrals; or orchestrates voluntary mediations; or refers parties to neutrals (whether selected by the court or by the parties) who charge; this last is the general English model, and furthermore, the parties select the neutral.

[55] 'Practice Direction-Protocols' 4.7.

[56] *Reed Executive plc v Reed Business Information Ltd* [2004] EWCA Civ 887; [2004] 1 WLR 3026 CA, at [35] per Jacob LJ (dictum).

When making costs decisions, the courts are prepared to take a critical view of a party's unwillingness to accede to the opponent's suggestion that the case might be referred to mediation (see **11.40** below for detail on this costs discretion). The courts are increasingly sceptical of the defensive retort that certain types of dispute are not appropriate for mediation. For example, the Court of Appeal has declared that mediation is useful in both building disputes[57] and work-related 'stress' claims.[58]   **11.34**

Judicial Duty to Consider Suggesting ADR or Ordering a 'Stay of Proceedings' to Accommodate ADR

The procedural code (the 'CPR') states that the court's overall responsibility includes 'helping the parties to settle the whole or part of the case'[59] and 'encouraging the parties to use an alternative dispute resolution procedure if the court considers that appropriate.'[60] The English position involves selective judicial recommendation of mediation.   **11.35**

This can be contrasted with the position in the Canadian province of Ontario, which has introduced mandatory mediation. However, a study reveals some possible pitfalls: that in many cases this can involve an unnecessary financial burden; that the mediation stage might be premature; that the pool of mediators might be inadequate; and that there can be significant variations in the practice from locality to locality even within the same jurisdiction.[61]   **11.36**

Commercial Court 'ADR Order': Duty of Parties to Give Reasons for Not Pursuing ADR

The (English) Commercial Court's so-called 'ADR order' is something of a misnomer. It does not compel the parties to engage in ADR, but at most to take 'such serious steps as they may be advised to resolve their disputes by ADR procedures ...' The parties must 'inform the court ... what steps towards ADR have been taken and (without prejudice to matters of privilege) why such steps   **11.37**

---

[57] *Burchell v Bullard* [2005] EWCA Civ 358.

[58] eg *Vahidi v Fairstead House School Ltd* [2005] EWCA Civ 765 at [27], per Longmore LJ; the Court of Appeal heard an appeal in an employment dispute in which a teacher had alleged that her employer's negligence had caused a psychiatric problem; the court suggested that work-related 'stress' claims are especially suited to mediation.

[59] CPR 1.4(2)(f).

[60] CPR 1.4(2)(e); Chancery Guide (2005) ch 17; Admiralty and Commercial Courts Guide (2006), section G and appendix 7.

[61] S Prince, 'Mandatory Mediation: The Ontario Experience' (2007) 26 CJQ 79.

have failed.'[62] A party cannot be sanctioned for his allegedly negative or bad faith contribution to discussions at the ADR meeting. These discussions are privileged. The topic of 'mediation privilege' is discussed below (**11.49 ff**).

Staying Proceedings

11.38   A court can direct that the proceedings be stayed for a month at a time[63] while the parties pursue ADR or other settlement negotiations.[64] A 'stay' places the pending civil action in suspense. Proceedings can be resumed when this becomes appropriate. The stay can be issued either at the parties' request or on the initiative of the court. However, there is no necessity to order a stay. For example, the Commercial Court can make a so-called 'ADR order', even without a stay (see **11.37**).[65]

11.39   In *Shirayama Shokusan Co Ltd v Danovo Ltd* (2004) Blackburne J held that, even though one party is opposed to ADR, a court can order a stay of proceedings to accommodate ADR, or at least make a recommendation that there should be ADR.[66] The judgment records another judge's dictum that the court could take this active step in the teeth of both parties' opposition.[67] It is submitted that a judge should feel free to recommend ADR even if both parties are not keen. Furthermore, the judge might even order a stay to enable them to reflect on this possibility (at **11.20** it has been admitted, however, that if the parties prove, or one of them remains, entirely resistant to mediation discussions, the attempt is bound to fail). A stay merely places the proceedings in a state of suspense. It does not compel the parties actually to engage in mediation, which would be as vain an order as attempting to compel a horse to drink water.

Costs Sanctions for Unreasonable Refusal to Mediate

11.40   The court, when exercising its broad discretion to make appropriate costs orders, will look askance at a party's unconvincing reasons for not engaging in ADR.[68] Two such sanctions have so far emerged: denial of costs in favour of a

---

[62] Admiralty and Commercial Courts Guide (2006), section G and (draft order) appendix 7.

[63] CPR 26.4(3).

[64] CPR 3.1(2)(f); CPR 26.4(1)(2).

[65] K Mackie, D Miles, W Marsh, T Allen, *The ADR Practice Guide* (2007) 5.2.

[66] [2004] 1 WLR 2985, Blackburne J.

[67] ibid at [19], citing *Cable & Wireless v IBM United Kingdom Ltd* [2002] 2 All ER (Comm) 1041, Colman J.

[68] Michael J Cook, *Cook on Costs* (2006) 113–6 (summary of cases); K Mackie, et al, op cit n 65 above, chapter 6.

victorious party; or an order of aggravated costs (known as 'indemnity costs', **9.12**) against a defeated party. These will be explained in turn.

Where the party who has refused mediation is victorious in the relevant liti- **11.41** gation, general principle ('the costs-shifting rule', see **9.06**) requires that he should normally be entitled to recover his costs from the opponent. But the court can reverse this usual approach an instead declare that the victorious party should not receive his costs, in view of his rejection of the chance to mediate,[69] at least if it was unreasonable for him to reject the other party's suggestion[70] (the losing party bearing the burden of proof in this respect, **11.45**), or if the victorious party had the temerity to reject the court's recommendation.

An example of the latter type of rejection occurred in *Dunnett v Railtrack* **11.42** *plc* (2002).[71] The defendant had been victorious both at trial and on appeal. But that party had rejected a judicial suggestion that the pending appeal might be mediated. This case arose from these facts. The claimant alleged that, as a result of the defendant company's negligence, her three horses had escaped from their field onto the defendant's track and had then been killed by an express train. However, at trial the claimant lost. A Lord Justice had given the defeated claimant permission to appeal, but this judge wrote to both parties suggesting that mediation was appropriate. In response to this suggestion, it appears that the claimant had expressed some willingness to pursue this path. This is not surprising because she had already lost at first instance, had no legal representation, and would be liable for extensive legal costs if she lost a second time, on appeal. But the defendant company flatly rejected this judicial suggestion, considering (adopting an objective and forensic perspective) that the formal legal merits of the dispute were clearly in its favour. Although that company was successful in the appeal, the Court of Appeal considered that the railway company's decision to resist ADR had been unjustified.[72] The court held that it should be denied its costs (it appears that this denial was confined to the costs of the appeal).

---

[69] Besides the *Dunnett* case [2002] 1 WLR 2434, CA, see *Royal Bank of Canada Trust Corpn v Secretary of State for Defence* [2003] EWHC 1479 (Ch) [2004] 1 P & CR 448; in probate litigation, where the costs shifting rule (**9.06**) is in any case applied more flexibly (*Wylde v Culver* [2006] EWHC 1313 (Ch), [2006] 1WLR 2674), costs were denied against a party, in view of his refusal to accede to the opponent's suggestion that the case might be mediated, *Jarrom v Sellars* [2007] EWHC 1366 (Ch) at [21], [28], [29].

[70] *Hurst v Leeming* [2002] EWHC 1051 (Ch); [2003] 1 Lloyd's Rep 379 (refusal to mediate not unreasonable because mediation had no reasonable prospect of success); *Société Internationale de Télécommunications Aéronautiques SC v Wyatt Co (UK) Ltd (Maxwell Batley, Part 20 defendants)* [2002] EWHC 2401 (Ch); (2003) 147 Sol Jo LB 27.

[71] [2002] 1 WLR 2434, CA, at [13] ff.

[72] ibid, at [16], per Brooke LJ (in exercise of the broad discretion concerning costs contained in CPR Part 44); for a similar decision, see *McMillan Williams v Range* [2004] EWCA Civ 294.

11.43   It will be more common to apply a costs sanction against a party who not only refused to consider mediation but lost the substantive case (or appeal). This type of *refusenik* might be ordered to pay the other side's costs on an 'indemnity basis' rather than 'standard basis' (**9.12**).[73]

Criteria for Determining Unreasonableness of a Party's Refusal to Pursue Mediation

11.44   The Court of Appeal in *Halsey v Milton Keynes General NHA Trust* (2004) listed the following criteria:[74]

'... factors which may be relevant to the question whether a party has unreasonably refused ADR will include (but are not limited to): the nature of the dispute; the merits of the case; the extent to which other settlement methods have been attempted; whether the costs of the ADR would be disproportionately high; whether any delay in setting up and attending the ADR would be prejudicial; whether the ADR had a reasonable prospect of success.'

11.45   As for this last factor, the court added that where party A, who has succeeded in the litigation, had earlier refused to participate in mediation, despite party B's suggestion or willingness, B bears the burden of showing (on the balance of probabilities) that the mediation would have had a reasonable prospect of success, assuming A had participated in a co-operative fashion.[75]

(8) Mediation Agreements[76]

11.46   It is highly desirable that commercial agreements should include a mediation clause.[77]

---

[73] *Virani Ltd v Manuel Revert y Cia SA* [2003] EWCA Civ 1651; [2004] 2 Lloyd's Rep 14; on the difference between standard basis and indemnity costs, see **9.12**.

[74] [2004] 1 WLR 3002, CA, at [16] ff; [2004] EWCA Civ 576 CA (on which S Fielding (2004) NLJ 1394; D Pliener (2004) NLJ 879); for a strong application of this costs regime, in which the *Halsey* criteria were fully considered, *P4 Ltd v Unite Integrated Solutions Plc* [2006] EWHC 2924 (TCC), Ramsey J.

[75] [2004] 1 WLR 3002, CA, at [16] ff; [2004] EWCA Civ 576, at [28].

[76] D Joseph, *Jurisdiction and Arbitration Agreements and their Enforcement* (2005) Part III; K Mackie, D Miles, W Marsh, T Allen, *The ADR Practice Guide* (2007) ch 9; see also Centre for Effective Dispute Resolution at: *www.cedr.co.uk/library/documents/contract_clauses.pdf*; D Spencer and M Brogan, *Mediation: Law and Practice* (Cambridge UP, 2006) ch 12 for Australian material.

[77] eg K Mackie, D Miles, W Marsh, T Allen, ibid, 9.2.

Such a clause was considered in *Cable & Wireless v IBM United Kingdom*   **11.47**
Ltd (2002) (on the case's importance for dispute resolution clauses requiring
mediation before *arbitration* see **12.12**).[78] The relevant clause was a so-called
'tiered' provision. It initially required the parties to endeavour to negotiate a
resolution by considering the relevant dispute within their own organisations. The clause stated that mediation would be obligatory if these negotiations collapsed.[79] Thereafter, if the dispute were still unresolved, 'proceedings' before a court might take place. After negotiation had failed, one party
decided to by-pass the stipulated stage of mediation, and brought a claim before the English High Court. The other party challenged this. Colman J in
the Commercial Court held that the mediation clause was valid.[80] He construed the dispute resolution clause (clause 41, paragraphs 1 and 2 had been
slightly confusingly drafted) as imposing a contractual duty not to proceed
to litigation until the mediation process had been employed. Colman J found
that there had been a breach of the dispute resolution agreement because a
party had 'jumped' the mediation stage and proceeded straight to litigation:
'… there can be no doubt that C&W has declined to participate in any ADR
exercise. As such it is in breach of clause 41.2. IBM is thus at least prima
facie, entitled to the enforcement of the ADR agreement.' In response to this
breach, Colman J placed a 'stay' (**11.38**) upon formal proceedings which one
party had begun in defiance of this mediation agreement. But he acknowledged that a 'stay' would not be automatic in all cases:

'However, given the discretionary nature of the remedy it is important to consider
what factors might also be relevant to the way in which the court's discretion should
be exercised … Strong cause would have to be shown before a court could be justified in declining to enforce such an agreement. For example, there may be cases
where a reference to ADR would be obviously futile and where the likelihood of a
productive mediation taking place would be so slight as not to justify enforcing the
agreement. Even in such circumstances ADR would have to be a completely hopeless exercise.'

The interplay of 'arbitration and mediation' is further examined elsewhere (see
12.12 ff).   **11.48**

---

[78] *Cable & Wireless plc v IBM UK* [2002] 2 All ER (Comm) 1041, Colman J.
[79] Generally, K Mackie, D Miles, W Marsh, T Allen, *The ADR Practice Guide* (2007)
9.6.4.
[80] A Colman, 'ADR: An Irreversible Tide?' (2003) 19 Arbitration International 303.

(9) Privileged Mediation Discussion[81]

11.49   It has long[82] been recognised that non-mediated settlement negotiations can
be privileged. This is known as 'without prejudice' privilege.[83] The parties
normally adopt such protection by express agreement, but sometimes privilege
rests merely upon implicit consensus.[84]

11.50   What of the present context, when the settlement negotiations occur during
mediation? The following seven propositions are clear:

(i) privilege applies broadly in the context of mediation discussions;[85] it will
cover oral confidential statements made during the mediation process by all

---

[81] Literature concerning privilege in the context of mediation or conciliation: Neil Andrews, *English Civil Procedure* (2003) 25.45 to 25.48; Brown and Marriott *ADR Principles
and Practice* (2nd edition, 1999) 22–079 to 22–097; *Cross and Tapper on Evidence* (10th
edn, 2004) 501–2; K Mackie, D Miles, W Marsh, T Allen, *The ADR Practice Guide* (2007)
7.2 ff; P Matthews and H Malek, *Disclosure* (2nd edn, 2000) 9–118 to 9–120; B Thanki
(ed), *The Law of Privilege* (2006) 7.24, 7.38 to 7.39; for USA and Australian sources, P
Newman, in M Liebmann (ed), *Mediation In Context* (2000, London and Philadelphia)
188; see also D Spencer and M Brogan, *Mediation: Law and Practice* (Cambridge UP, 2006)
ch 9, noting esp at 329, Australian legislation on this topic; for general comment, Scottish Law
Commission's Report, 'Evidence: Protection of Family Mediation [1992] SLC 136 (Report)
(June 1992) (containing notes on the draft Bill); the Civil Evidence (Family Mediation)
(Scotland) Act 1995; see also comments from various sources collected by Brown and Mar-
riott, ibid (2nd edition, 1999) 22–089 to 22–091, and the symposium in (1988) 12(1) Seton
Hall Legis J.

[82] On the development of this privilege, D Vaver, '"Without Prejudice" communications-
their admissibility and effect' (1974) Univ Brit Col L Rev 85 (cited by Robert Walker LJ in
Unilever plc v The Proctor & Gamble Co [2000] 1 WLR 2436, 2445, CA).

[83] Neil Andrews, *English Civil Procedure* (2003) ch 25; Brown and Marriott, *ADR
Principles and Practice* (2nd edition, 1999) 22–050 ff; *Cross and Tapper on Evidence* (11th
edn, 2007) 502 ff; D Foskett *The Law and Practice of Compromise* (6th edn, 2005) ch 27; C
Hollander, *Documentary Evidence* (9th edn, 2006) ch 16; M Iller, *Civil Evidence: The Es-
sential Guide* (Sweet & Maxwell, 2006), 8–88 to 8–104; *Phipson on Evidence* (16th edn,
2005) 24–14 ff; C Passmore, *Privilege* (2nd edn, 2006) ch 10; B Thanki (ed), *The Law of
Privilege* (2006) ch 7; *Zuckerman on Civil Procedure* (2nd edn, 2006) ch 16; see also J Mc-
Ewan, '"Without Prejudice": Negotiating the Minefield' (1994) 13 CJQ 133.

[84] *Reed Executive plc v Reed Business Information Ltd* [2004] EWCA Civ 887; [2004] 1
WLR 3026; *Aird v Prime Meridian Ltd* [2006] EWCA Civ 1866; there must be a sufficient
indication of a dispute, and therefore an open admission of liability cannot give rise to privilege, *Bradford & Bingley plc v Rashid* [2006] UKHL 37; [2006] 1 WLR 2066; the relevant
negotiations might ante-date litigation by quite a long interval; the test formulated in *Fram-
lington Group Ltd v Barnetson* [2007] EWCA Civ 502, at [34], per Auld LJ, is: 'whether in
the course of negotiations the parties contemplated or might reasonably have contemplated
litigation if they could not agree' and rejecting the view that negotiations should have occurred 'in the course of, or after threat of litigation on it, or by reference to some time limit
set close before litigation'; the rejected view would 'not ... fully serve the public policy interest underlying it of discouraging recourse to litigation and encouraging genuine attempts to
settle whenever made.' Now reported as *Barnetson* etc [2007] 1 WLR 2443.

[85] *Instance v Denny Bros Printing Ltd* [2000] FSR 869, at 881–2, where Lloyd J noted
that Robert Walker LJ in the *Unilever* case [2000] 1 WLR 2436, 2446, 2448 H-2449, had

the participants, including the mediator's input, as well as documents prepared for or created during the same process;

(ii) (unless both parties agree) neither party should divulge to non-parties what he told the opponent or the mediator, or what the opponent or the mediator told that party;

(iii) (unless both parties agree) the mediator cannot divulge to non-parties what he heard from either party, or indeed from both parties, or what he said or did during the process (on the question whether the mediator might be *compellable* to give evidence, see **11.54** below);

(iv) protecting confidentiality in this context must include the power (exercisable by either party) to obtain an injunction[86] against the other party, mediator, or non-parties; the injunction can prevent use of the information in legal proceedings (English or foreign);[87] or disclosure to non-parties;

(v) neither party (unless both parties agree) is compellable to give evidence of what he told the other party or the mediator, or what he was told by the other party or by the mediator;

---

preferred the view that 'without prejudice' privilege is not confined to admissions in the strict sense (doubting Hoffmann LJ's analysis in *Muller v Linsley & Mortimer* [1996] PNLR 74, 79–80); Robert Walker LJ in the *Unilever* case [2000] 1 WLR 2436, 2443–4, also persuasively contended that the same privilege should not require that the parties 'must constantly monitor every sentence, with lawyers or patent agents sitting at their shoulders as minders'; on this question see also B Thanki (ed), *The Law of Privilege* (Oxford UP, 2006) 7.13, also noting that in *Hodgkinson and Corby v Wards Mobility Services* [1997] FSR 178, 190, Neuberger J emphasised that Hoffmann LJ's 'admissions' restriction applies only in the unusual situation where the sole basis of 'without prejudice' is public policy, as distinct from an implied contract; this will happen when 'without prejudice' is binding upon non-parties (as on the facts of *Rush & Tompkins Ltd v Greater London Council* [1989] AC 1280, HL); but in the ordinary two-party situation, the implied contract basis of privilege will provide comprehensive protection of confidential discussion; in *Somatra Ltd v Sinclair Roche & Temperley* [2000] 1 WLR 2453, at [22] Clarke LJ said that in this context 'the concept of admissions must be given a wide meaning in this context so as in effect to include all matters disclosed or discussed in the without prejudice discussions concerned': viz admissions should not be confined to statements against interest; other cases have sustained this retreat from Hoffmann LJ's suggestion: *Wilkinson v West Coast Capital* [2005] EWHC 1016 (Ch), at [16] per Mann J; the matter was further discussed in *Bradford & Bingley plc v Rashid* [2006] UKHL 37; [2006] 1 WLR 2066.

[86] Injunction to prevent use of privileged discussion was granted by Lloyd J in *Instance v Denny Bros Printing Ltd* [2000] FSR 869, where the proposed use would be in US proceedings, and the information was privileged both as 'without prejudice' communication and under the terms of a mediation agreement: B Thanki (ed), *The Law of Privilege* (Oxford UP, 2006) 7.24; the *Instance* case was approved in *Prudential Insurance Company of America v Prudential Assurance Company Ltd* [2003] EWCA Civ 1154; injunctive relief in respect of privileged discussion at a mediation session was also granted in *Venture Investment Placement v Hall* [2005] EWHC 1227 (Ch).

[87] For this last possibility, *Instance v Denny Bros Printing Ltd* [2000] FSR 869, where the proposed use would be in US proceedings, (intended use in US proceedings of privileged discussion relating to earlier English proceedings; injunction granted by English High Court to prevent use in US proceedings).

(vi) *Brown v Rice* (2007) confirms that a party to a mediated settlement, no less than an unmediated settlement, can adduce the contents of settlement negotiations to prove whether a settlement was reached and to ascertain its terms;[88] the court will apply contractual principles to determine whether a binding settlement agreement has arisen during mediation;

(vii) mediation agreements, as in *Brown v Rice*, often prescribe that a binding settlement must be reduced to writing and signed by the parties, or by their authorised representatives; such a formality clause also governs acceptance of an offer made during the conclusion of the mediation meeting(s) but expressed to be open for acceptance within a specified period after the meeting has ended (unless the need for writing and signature has been varied, waived or consensually overridden by another provision).

11.51   But two uncertainties remain. First, is the privilege attaching to this context the same as that applicable to non-mediated settlement discussion? Secondly, is the mediator compellable to give evidence even if both parties to the mediation agree that he should be permitted to give evidence? On both points *Brown v Rice* (2007) is inconclusive.[89]

11.52   It is disappointing that *Brown v Rice* (2007) and recent Court of Appeal decisions do not address Sir Thomas Bingham MR's clear series of propositions (as summarised by the author of this note) in *Re D* (1993).[90] First, he noted that there is an independent head of privilege, 'a new category of privilege' (viz 'conciliation', as now seems preferable, 'mediation' privilege) applicable when a neutral third party is attempting to assist disputants to reach an understanding or compromise.[91] At any rate, this head of privilege is recognised in the context of conciliation of matrimonial disputes, notably matters concerning children.[92] Secondly, Sir Thomas Bingham MR said: 'we can see no reason why rules which have developed in relation to "without prejudice" privilege should necessarily apply to the other [head of privilege]'.[93] Thirdly, he suggested that this independent head of privilege does not yield merely because one party later asserts that the other did not show a 'genuine willingness to compromise'.[94] Finally, Sir Thomas Bingham MR denied that evidence can be

---

[88] *Brown v Rice* [2007] EWHC 625 (Ch) Stuart Isaacs QC.

[89] ibid.

[90] *Re D* [1993] Fam 231, 237–241, CA (giving the court's judgment)

[91] ibid, at 238; despite the Law Reform Committee's statement in 1967 that no such independent privilege needed to be crystallised, at least in legislation: 16th Report on 'Privilege in Civil Proceedings' (1967, Cmnd 3472), noted C Tapper (1968) 31 MLR 198, 202 (observing that the case law privilege should remain open to waiver by both parties).

[92] Adding, at [1993] Fam 231, 241, that other contexts might 'have to be decided in the light of their own special circumstances'; the decision was later noted and to an extent codified in *Practice Direction (Family Proceedings: Financial Dispute Resolution)* [1997] 1 WLR 1069.

[93] *Re D* [1993] Fam 231, 238, CA.

[94] ibid.

given 'of threats, even credible threats, made by parties in the course of attempted conciliation'. On this point he added, 'where deep human emotions are engaged, as they often are in disputes concerning children, such threats are commonplace ... unless parties can speak freely and uninhibitedly, without worries about weakening their position in contested litigation if that becomes necessary, the conciliation will be doomed to fail.'[95]

The possible distinction between party-to-party privileged negotiations and mediated discussions would have practical importance only if (a) there were some difference in their underlying basis; and/or (b) some difference in the scope of exceptions applicable to these privileges. These points will be considered in turn. **11.53**

Is the Privilege Shared by the Mediator (Does He Have 'Autonomous' Privilege)?

This is perhaps the most vexed question. One view is that the mediator lacks 'autonomous' privilege: in other words, mediation or conciliation privilege is solely the joint 'property' of the disputants, as distinct from the mediator. According to that view, the parties' joint decision to waive privilege is decisive;[96] no protection is left thereafter; and the mediator has no power to veto this process of party waiver. Consistent with this analysis, there are four streams of British and Commonwealth support: (i) there is clear English authority that, in the family context, conciliation privilege exists only for the benefit of spouses and not for marriage counsellors or other neutral advisors;[97] (ii) the statute governing conciliation of labour disputes in England provides for waiver by **11.54**

---

[95] ibid, at 238–9.

[96] Waiver by 'mutual conduct' occurred in *Hall v Pertemps Group Ltd* [2005] EWHC 3110 (Ch); *The Times* 23 December 2005, Lewison J (allegation of threats made during mediation; held at [16] that threats are in general covered by the privilege and that no exception applies; but also holding at [16] that the parties had mutually waived privilege, at least in respect of that incident, by entering pleadings in satellite litigation concerning the alleged threats); but implied waiver will not be readily inferred, because this would undermine the salutary protection of privilege, notably in the context of mediation: *Smiths Group plc v George Weiss* [2002] EWHC 582 (Roger Kaye QC, sitting as a High Court judge): p 23 of transcript; available at www.cedr.co.uk/library/edr_law/Smith_Grp_v_Weiss.pdf.

[97] *Pais v Pais* [1971] P 119, Sir George Baker: third party priest resisting a witness subpoena; husband alleging that wife had waived privilege; if wife had indeed waived, the judge acknowledged that the door would be open to subpoena the conciliator/priest, because the latter has no protection other than under the parties' umbrella; analysis supported by Cohen and Denning LJJ's remarks in *McTaggart v McTaggart* [1949] P 94, 96 (spouses had waived privilege by each giving evidence of conciliation session; conciliator thereafter became a compellable witness); in the *Pais* case, Baker J also referred to *Cross on Evidence* (3rd edn 1967) 249 for acceptance of this analysis.

the parties alone;[98] (iii) the Scottish family mediation privilege permits the parties alone to waive privilege;[99] (iv) the major Australian evidence statute is similarly framed.[100] But the converse view, favoured by mediation practitioners and their organisations, is that a mediator should enjoy privilege even if both parties waive their rights to confidentiality.[101] This analysis underlies the European draft Directive (see Article 6 (3)) which contemplates that privilege under that Article can be waived only by the agreement of both the parties and the mediator.[102]

11.55   It is submitted there are two reasons why mediation privilege should not protect the mediator once both parties have waived it (arguments against 'autonomous' mediation privilege). First, analysis in terms of exclusive party-control is consistent with the true nature of mediation: confidential exchange of views and representations presided over by a disinterested neutral with the aim of agreeing a resolution of the dispute. The mediator is not empowered in the manner of a judge or arbitrator to make binding determinations (judges enjoy substantive immunity; and arbitrators under English law have a qualified immunity from civil liability).[103] Secondly, to afford an autonomous form of mediation privilege would indirectly shield mediators from substantive liability

---

[98] In the field of labour disputes, a statutory head of 'conciliation privilege' protects communications made by employees, or former employees, and by employers to 'Conciliation Officers' (members of the Advisory, Conciliation and Arbitration Service, 'ACAS', an organisation funded by government); conciliation officers try to promote out-of-tribunal settlement of individual complaints lodged before Employment Tribunals, for example, unfair dismissal claims under the employment legislation; statute provides: 'Anything said to a conciliation officer in connection with the performance of his functions under this section shall not be admissible in evidence in any proceedings before an [Employment Tribunal] except with the permission of the person who communicated it to that officer: s 18(7) Employment Tribunals Act 1996 (as re-styled by s 1(2) Employment Rights (Dispute Resolution) Act 1998).

[99] s 2(1)(c), Civil Evidence (Family Mediation) (Scotland) Act 1995; for general comment, Scottish Law Commission's Report, 'Evidence: Protection of Family Mediation [1992] SLC 136 (Report) (June 1992); the Scottish Law Commission, ibid, commented at 3.55: 'In our view protection of mediation information should be restricted to the minimum necessary to promote an efficient family mediation service. On this ground we do not think conferring a separate and independent power on mediators to withhold evidence can be justified. We appreciate the concern felt by mediators about having to give evidence in court, but it is a duty which many other professionals have to carry out when called to do so. Furthermore, we imagine that mediators would only rarely be called to give evidence. At present the courts seek to deter the questioning of priests whom parishioners have consulted, although no legal privilege exists. This practice might well be extended to mediators.'

[100] s 131(2), Evidence Act 1995 (Cth, NSW, Tas) (Australia).

[101] K Mackie, D Miles, W Marsh, T Allen, *The ADR Practice Guide* (2007) 7.4.

[102] COM (2004) 718 final, Brussels dated 22.10.2004 (draft directive on 'certain aspects of mediation in civil and commercial matters'): *http://europa.eu.int/eur-lex/en/com/pdf/2004/com2004_0718en01.pdf*.

[103] s 29, Arbitration Act 1996 (this immunity does not extend to conduct or omissions 'in bad faith' nor to the consequences of resignation).

for misconduct during the proceedings. If such substantive immunity is to be created, its merits should be directly debated and not achieved by an evidential side-wind.[104]

It should be noted that the Scottish family mediation privilege permits evidence concerning mediation sessions to be admitted in civil proceedings against mediators for property damage or personal injury (but not defamation actions). Evidence concerning mediation discussion is also admissible if the mediator is subject to Scottish criminal or disciplinary proceedings.[105] **11.56**

Furthermore, autonomous privilege for mediators might be otiose. Many mediators already insert exclusion clauses to shield them from liability for tortious wrongdoing or breaches of contract or confidence (sometimes limited to non-fraudulent misconduct).[106] **11.57**

Uncertainty concerning Exceptions to Privilege

This is the second vexed uncertainty concerning privilege in the context of mediation discussions. The case law is unclear whether the exceptions applicable to 'without prejudice' privilege in respect of 'unassisted' settlement negotiations should apply in identical form to mediation discussions. Let us first note the established canon of exceptions applicable to 'without prejudice' privilege. In the leading authority, Robert Walker LJ presented the following (non-exhaustive)[107] list of exceptions, in the *Unilever* case (2000):[108] (i) to deter- **11.58**

---

[104] Brown and Marriott, *ADR Principles and Practice* (2nd edition, 1999) 22–092 to 22–094: in the absence of substantive immunity for a mediator, a unilateral decision by a party to sue a mediator for breach of confidence, negligence, breach of contract, or some other wrong, would encounter these difficulties: (i) the need for the other party to waive privilege in the mediation discussions (refusal to waive is likely to obstruct access to crucial evidence) and (ii) the courts' power to strike out as an abuse of process a collateral challenge upon a civil judgment, on this doctrine see Neil Andrews, *English Civil Procedure* (Oxford UP, 2003) 40.87 to 40.89, and the other authorities discussed at Neil Andrews, *Principles of Civil Procedure* (1994) 17–012 (obviously, (ii) will not apply unless the case ended either in a consent judgment or, where there was no settlement, the action concluded in judgment).

[105] s 2(1)(d)(v), (vi), Civil Evidence (Family Mediation) (Scotland) Act 1995; see comments in Scottish Law Commission's Report, 'Evidence: Protection of Family Mediation [1992] SLC 136 (Report) (June 1992) 3.58, 3.66.

[106] Brown and Marriott, *ADR Principles and Practice* (2nd edition, 1999) 22–093.

[107] *Unilever plc v The Proctor & Gamble Co* [2000] 1 WLR 2436, 2445, CA, where Robert Walker LJ said that this summary 'is far from exhaustive': see, eg, discussion of *Gnitrow Ltd v Cape plc* [2000] 1 WLR 2327, CA in Neil Andrews, *English Civil Procedure* (Oxford UP, 2003) 25.19 to 25.22.

[108] *Unilever* case [2000] 1 WLR 2436, 2444–5, CA; Robert Walker LJ added: '(8) the 'hybrid' and possibly 'distinct' species of privilege relevant to conciliation or mediation discussions'; but B Thanki (ed), *The Law of Privilege* (Oxford UP, 2006) 7.26 contends that this is not really an exception, but perhaps a free-standing species of privilege.

mine whether a settlement agreement has arisen; (ii) whether that agreement was procured by misrepresentation, fraud or undue influence; (iii) estoppel: to prove that a clear statement made during settlement discussions has induced reliance by the other party;[109] (iv) 'unambiguous impropriety';[110] it is arguable that this exception might be usefully sub-divided since it covers a miscellany of objectionable circumstances where the courts have exercised a value-judgement to exclude privilege (see **11.59** and **11.60**); (v) 'to explain delay or apparent acquiescence';[111] (vi) to show some fact other than the truth of the relevant statement, for example, that a party has acted reasonably to attempt to mitigate loss;[112] (vii) the settlement negotiations have been expressly rendered 'without prejudice save as to costs'.[113]

11.59   *Brown v Rice* (2007) is clear authority that exceptions (i) and (ii), as mentioned just above, apply in the context of mediation privilege.[114] Nor would it appear that any sensible objection can be made against applying exceptions (iii), (v), (vi) and (vii) to confidential mediation discussion. The real problem concerns exception (iv) (embracing threats, evidence of past wrongdoing, abuse of a privileged occasion, and the like). In the context of mediation proceedings the courts recognise the need for a modified approach.[115] The case law indicates that robust tactics and hard-hitting words will be tolerated. But in ex-

---

[109] Robert Walker LJ, *Unilever* case, [2000] 1 WLR 2436, 2444, CA, citing *Hodgkinson and Corby v Wards Mobility Services* [1997] FSR 178, 191–2, per Neuberger J (on the facts of the 1997 case, no clear and unequivocal representation was found); a party was held not to have become estopped from relying on 'without prejudice' privilege on the facts of *Smiths Group plc v George Weiss* [2002] EWHC 582 (Roger Kaye QC, sitting as a High Court judge): p 37 for conclusion: transcript available at www.cedr.co.uk/library/edr_law/Smith_Grp_v_Weiss.pdf.

[110] Robert Walker LJ, *Unilever* case, [2000] 1 WLR 2436, 2444, CA, explaining that 'exclusion of the evidence would act as a cloak for perjury, blackmail, or some other "unambiguous impropriety"'; see the review in *Savings & Investment Bank Ltd v Fincken* [2003] EWCA Civ 1630; [2004] 1 WLR 667 at [40] ff, per Rix LJ; the emerging notion of 'abuse of a privileged occasion' is illustrated by *Brunel University v Vaseghi* [2006] UKEAT 0307_06_1610 (16 October 2006) (employee alleging victimisation by employer in connexion with racial discrimination complaint against latter; EAT at [24] concluding that settlement privilege should yield because employee's claim would be unfairly hampered); see also Neil Andrews, *English Civil Procedure* (Oxford UP, 2003) ch 25, esp 25.33, 25.43; D Foskett, *The Law and Practice of Compromise* (6th edn, 2005) 27.28 ff C Passmore, *Privilege* (2nd edn, 2006) 10.059 ff ; B Thanki (ed), *The Law of Privilege* (Oxford UP, 2006) 7–26 to 7–29.

[111] B Thanki (ed), ibid, 7.34.

[112] *Muller v Linsley & Mortimer* [1996] PNLR 74, CA, per Hoffmann LJ; that case is rationalised as a discrete exception both by Robert Walker LJ in the *Unilever* case [2000] 1 WLR 2436, 2445, CA and in B Thanki (ed), ibid, 7.21, 7.33.

[113] Robert Walker LJ, *Unilever* case, [2000] 1 WLR 2436, 2445, CA, referring to authorities.

[114] *Brown v Rice* [2007] EWHC 625 (Ch) Stuart Isaacs QC.

[115] *Cross and Tapper on Evidence* (11th edn, 2007) 507–8.

treme cases, the courts are prepared to admit an exception if the mediator or a disputant has received evidence of serious wrongdoing by the other (whether committed or contemplated).

The scope of the 'unambiguous impropriety' exception has yet to be fixed in the context of mediation privilege. Three mediation[116] cases have been reported, the first in the context of protecting children, the other two in commercial contexts. First, the Court of Appeal in *Re D* (1993) held that an exception to privilege arises when, during conciliation of a family dispute, a father allegedly made a confidential statement to a conciliator 'clearly indicating that the maker has in the past caused or is likely in the future to cause serious harm to the well-being of a child'.[117] The court can investigate the facts.[118] On investigation by the court, the facts did not justify application of this exception. In *Venture Investment Placement v Hall* (2005) the parties acknowledged, and the judge accepted, that there would be no breach of mediation privilege if a party to such a discussion had made (presumably in good faith) a complaint to the Police regarding the other party's alleged misconduct (whether this be misconduct admitted during the mediation or actually occurring during such a process).[119] That case would seem to support, therefore, an exception for criminal wrongdoing. However, in *Hall v Pertemps Group Ltd* (2005) Lewison J said that, in general, the veil of privilege will not be lifted just because one party alleges that the opponent made 'threats' during a mediation discussion.[120] This robust approach seems sensible. Threats can vary considerably in their potency and heinousness. **11.60**

The Future of Mediation Privilege

In 1993 Sir Thomas Bingham declared that the common law now recognised a new species of privilege.[121] At the time of writing (2007), following an explosion of interest in mediation beyond the context of family disputes, there has **11.61**

---

[116] cf the strong decision in *RE EC (Disclosure of Material* [1996] 2 FLR 123 (during care proceedings (viz not mediation) an admission of child-killing was made; the court held that it should not be released to the Police); noted Brown & Marriott, *ADR Principles and Practice* (2nd edition, 1999) 22–068.

[117] *Re D (Minors)* [1993] Fam 231, 241, CA.

[118] Such investigation might have to be postponed until trial, rather than carried out during a pre-trial application for an interim injunction: see *Venture Investment Placement v Hall* [2005] EWHC 1227 (Ch) at [14].

[119] *Venture* case, ibid, at [14].

[120] *Hall v Pertemps Group Ltd* [2005] EWHC 3110 (Ch); *The Times* 23 December 2005, Lewison J (allegation of threats made during mediation; Lewison J holding at [16] that threats are in general covered by the privilege and that no exception applies; but also holding at [16] that the parties had mutually waived privilege, at least in respect of that incident, by entering pleadings in satellite litigation concerning the alleged threats).

[121] *Re D (Minors)* [1993] Fam 231, 236, CA.

been no sharp judicial analysis of the bounds of 'conciliation' or 'mediation' privilege, nor English legislation.[122] Unless a case is taken to the Court of Appeal, but preferably to the House of Lords, within the next year or so, Parliament might need to clarify the scope of privilege in the context of mediated discussions. It is submitted, however, that: (i) a mediator should not enjoy 'autonomous' privilege (as defined at **11.54**) if the parties have jointly waived privilege in mediation discussions (even if the mediator did not consent to this waiver, or even directly opposed it); (ii) case law should continue to clarify the extent to which 'threats' during mediation should justify withdrawing privilege, as against the party who has issued the threats; not every threat should have this effect; (iii) in view of (ii), it would be better for the matter to be left to judicial development rather than legislation.

(10) Conclusion

11.62　Mediation is a valuable substitute for civil proceedings, or at least a possible exit from such proceedings. The rise of mediation, not just in England, is largely attributable to the perception that litigation is hazardous and expensive, that there is only one winner in a law-suit, that the adjudicative process (and extensive preparation for the final hearing) involves a heavy-handed fight for justice, and that litigation offers little scope for direct participation by the parties, as distinct from outside legal representatives and in-house lawyers.

11.63　Even so, civil litigation, especially trial, involves important attributes of 'public' justice: an accessible demonstration of forensic integrity and rigour, and the opportunity for wrongdoers to be held publicly accountable.[123]

---

[122] *Brown v Rice* [2007] EWHC 625 (Ch), at [20]: 'It may be in the future that the existence of a distinct mediation privilege will require to be considered by either the legislature or the courts but that is not something which arises for decision now ...'; *Reed Executive plc v Reed Business Information Ltd* [2004] EWCA Civ 887; [2004] 1 WLR 3026, at [30], per Jacob LJ: 'I can think of no rational reason why party-to-party negotiations should not be treated on the same basis. Indeed sometimes the line between a third-party assisted ADR and party-to-party negotiations may be fuzzy. Just because there is a mediator is no reason for the parties not to talk to each other if that is found to be helpful at some point in the process ...'; *Aird v Prime Meridian Ltd* [2006] EWCA Civ 1866 at [5], per May LJ: 'It is well-known and uncontentious in this case that mediation takes the form of assisted "without prejudice" negotiation and that, with some exceptions not relevant to this appeal, what goes on in the course of mediation is privileged, so that it cannot be referred to or relied on in subsequent court proceedings if the mediation is unsuccessful ...'

[123] For comment (and further references to literature) on the 'public' dimensions of the civil court process, see H Genn, 'Understanding Civil Justice' (1997) 50 CLP 155, 186–7.

Furthermore, as even committed mediators must concede, the formal civil **11.64**
process is important, even indispensable, in some contexts, for example:[124]
'establishing a legal precedent; making a public statement on the importance
of an industry practice; achieving summary [disposal of both claims or de-
fences]; enforcing judgments or awards; compelling disclosure of documents
and examining witnesses; obtaining injunctive relief; forcing a party into judgment.' Civil litigation can deal effectively with types of dispute which are not
amenable to the necessarily co-operative style of mediation. This is because
State-supported litigation is subject to strong sanctions. The courts can compel witnesses to attend, punish perjury, enforce judgments, and apply their
contempt of court power if injunctions are flouted (**8.35**). The court system has
ample means of protecting parties against the other's non-compliance or bad
faith. This includes protective measures such as freezing injunctions, civil
search orders, and orders of security for costs (on all of these, see chapter 4).

(11) Bibliography

The literature on this topic, which is enormous, includes the following:[125] **11.65**

(1) Texts and practical guides

RL Abel, *The Politics of Informal Justice* (New York, 1986);
Jerold S Auerbach, *Justice Without Law* (New York and Oxford, OUP, 1983);
C Buhring-Uhle, *Arbitration and Mediation in International Business* (The Hague, 1996);
L Bulle and M Nesic, *Mediation: Principles, Process, Practice* (2001);
H Brown and A Marriott, *ADR: Principles and Practice* (2nd edn, 1999);
R Caller (ed), *ADR and Commercial Disputes* (2002);
Civil Procedure ('White Book'), vol 1 at 1.4.11;
E Carroll and K Mackie, *International Mediation* (2nd edn, 2006);
JG Collier and V Lowe, *The Settlement of Disputes in International Law* (Oxford UP, 1999);
O Fiss and J Resnik, *Adjudication and Its Alternatives* (Foundation Press, New York, 2003), chs 4 and 6;

---

[124] K Mackie, D Miles, W Marsh, T Allen, *The ADR Practice Guide* (2007) 3.4.1.

[125] For further references see the bibliographies in S Roberts and M Palmer, *Dispute Processes* (Cambridge UP, 2006), Neil Andrews, *English Civil Procedure* (Oxford UP, 2003) at 23.12, and O Fiss and J Resnik, *Adjudication and Its Alternatives* (Foundation Press, New York, 2003) ch 4, notably p 495; O Chase, *The Rise of ADR in Cultural Context, in Law, Culture, and Ritual: Disputing Systems in Cross-Cultural Context* (NYU Press, 2005) ch 6 (citing extensive and recent US literature); AJ Stitt, *Mediation: A Practical Guide* (2004) at 143 ff (also citing extensive North American literature); D Spencer and M Brogan, *Mediation: Law and Practice* (Cambridge UP, 2006) 494 ff.

D Foskett, *The Law and Practice of Compromise* (6th edn, 2005), ch 43 ('Settlement through ADR');

H Genn, *Mediation in Action* (London: Calouste Gulbenkian Foundation, 1999);

P Hibberd and P Newman, *ADR and Adjudication in Construction Disputes* (Blackwell, Oxford, 1999);

Int Bureau, Permanent Ct of Arbitration, *International ADR* (The Hague, 2000);

M Liebmann (ed), *Mediation In Context* (2000, London and Philadelphia);

K Mackie, D Miles, W Marsh, T Allen, *The ADR Practice Guide* (2007);

R Merkin, *Arbitration Law* (Lloyd's of London, 2004 update of 1991 text), ch 6 (on 'ADR'); (Informa Business Publishing, London, 2006)

C Newmark and A Monaghan, *Butterworths' Mediators on Mediation* (2005)

S Roberts and M Palmer, *Dispute Processes* (Cambridge UP, 2006);

D Spencer and M Brogan, *Mediation: Law and Practice* (Cambridge UP, 2006);

AJ Stitt, *Mediation: A Practical Guide* (2004);

V Varano (ed), *L'Altra Giustizia* (Milano, 2007);

S York, *Practical ADR* (2nd edn, 1999)

(2) Comment

P Brooker and A Lavers, 'Issues in the Development of ADR for Commercial and Construction Disputes' (2000) 19 CJQ 353 and 'Commercial and Construction ADR: Lawyers' Attitudes and Experience' (2001) 20 CJQ 327;

Oscar Chase, 'ADR and the Culture of Litigation: the Example of the United States of America' in L Cadiet, T Gray and E Jeuland (eds), *Mediation et arbitrage: Alternative a la justice ou justice alternative? Perspective comparatives* (Lexis SA, Paris, 2005), 135–151; and in O Chase, *Law, Culture, and Ritual: Disputing Systems in Cross-Cultural Context* (New York UP, 2005), ch 6 (a rich examination of various factors underlying the ADR movement in the US; also copiously citing US literature);

B Clark and C Dawson, 'ADR and Scottish Commercial Litigators' (2007) 26 CJQ 228;

A Colman (Sir Anthony Colman, a former Commercial Court judge), 'ADR: An Irreversible Tide?' (2003) 19 Arbitration International 303;

E Ferran, 'Dispute Resolution Mechanisms in the UK Financial Sector' (2002) 21 CJQ 135;

O Fiss, 'Against Settlement' (1984) Yale LJ 1073;

Lon Fuller, 'Mediation: Forms and Limits' (1970–1) 44 S Cal LR 305;

Lon Fuller, 'The Forms and Limits of Adjudication' (1979) 92 Harvard L Rev 353;

H Genn, 'Understanding Civil Justice' (1997) 50 CLP 155;

DR Hensler, 'Out Courts, Ourselves: How the ADR Movement is Reshaping our Legal System' (2003) 108 Penn State L Rev 165;

Burkhard Hess (Univ of Heidelberg), 'Mediation and ADR in German and the European Union-Current Developments and Trends' (paper delivered to conference before the Supreme Peoples' Court, Beijing, September 2002);

R Ingleby, 'Court Sponsored Mediation ...' (1993) 56 MLR 441;

C Menkel-Meadow, 'Whose Dispute It Anyway: A Philosophical and Democratic Defense of Settlement (In Some Cases)' (1995) 83 Geo LJ 2663, extracted O Fiss and J Resnik, *Adjudication and Its Alternatives* (Foundation Press, New York, 2003) 488 ff;

R Nazzini, 'Transnational Litigation and ADR: The Philosophy of the CPR' in M Andenas, N Andrews, and R Nazzini (eds), *The Future of Transational Civil Litigation* (British Institute of International and Comparative Law, London, 2006);

F Neate, 'Mediation: a Constructive Approach to Dispute Resolution' in *Global Reflections on International Law, Commerce and Dispute Resolution (liber amicorum in honour of Robert Briner)* (ICC, Paris, 2005) 557 ff;

M Nesic, 'Mediation – on the rise in the United Kingdom' (2001) 13 Bond Law Review, issue 2, December;

R Nobles, 'Access to Justice through Ombudsmen: the Courts' Response to the Pensions Ombudsman' (2002) 21 CJQ 94;

M Partington, 'Alternative Dispute Resolution Developments: Future Challenges' (2004) 23 CJQ 99;

D Plant, 'ADR and Arbitration' in LW Newman and RD Hill (eds), *The Leading Arbitrators' Guide to International Arbitration* (Juris, Bern, 2004) 245 ff;

S Prince, 'Mediating Small Claims: Are we on the Right Track?' (2007) 26 CJQ 328;

Judith Resnik, 'Many Doors? Closing Doors? Alternative Dispute Resolution and Adjudication' (1995) 10 Ohio State Journal on Dispute Resolution 211;

S Roberts, 'Settlement as Civil Justice' (2000) MLR 739;

Steve Subrin, 'A Traditionalist Looks at Mediation' (2003) 3 Nevada LJ 196;

Various authors:

ADR Supplements (2004) New LJ 1391–1402 and (2005) New LJ 725–34;

Symposium in (1993) 56 MLR (No 3, May), especially articles by Cyril Glasser and S Roberts (277),

M Cappelletti (282); C Menkel-Meadow (361); W Twining (380); R Ingleby (441); S Roberts (452);

(3) Government research

Hazel Genn, ' Court-Based ADR Initiatives for Non-Family Civil Disputes: the Commercial Court and the Court of Appeal' at www.dca.gov.uk/research/2002/1-02es.htm.

Hazel Genn, 'Twisted Arms: Court Referred and Court Linked Mediation under Judicial Pressure' (Department of Constitutional Affairs, 2007) (report on a 'pilot scheme', concerning automatic referral to mediation at the Central London County Court): see 'research' at http://www.justice.gov.uk/publications/research.htm.

Sue Prince and Sophie Belcher, 'An Evaluation of the Effectiveness of Court-based Mediation Processes in Non-Family Civil Proceedings at Exeter and Guildford County Courts' (December 2006): see 'publications' at *www.dca.gov.uk/civil/adr/*.

Lisa Webley, Pamela Abrams and Sylvie Bacquet, 'Evaluation of the Birmingham court-based Civil (non-family) mediation scheme' (December 2006): see 'publications' at *www.dca.gov.uk/civil/adr/* see the same web-site for other research.

(4) Web-sites and ADR providers

The CPR, Practice Directions, Pre-Action Protocols and Court Guides: http://www.
justice.gov.uk/civil/procrules_fin/menus/rules.htm
Ministry of Justice (now supporting the former Department of Constitutional Affairs' web-site on ADR: *www.dca.gov.uk/civil/adr/* this site also contains a library of publications).
ADRGroup: *www.adrgroup.co.uk*
CEDR (Centre for Effective Dispute Resolution, London): *www.cedr.co.uk/*
National Mediation Helpline: *www.nationalmediationhelpline.com/*
Other ADR providers: see the list at (2005) New LJ 733.

Chapter 12

The Framework of English Arbitration[1]

Contents

---

[1] There is a massive literature concerning international arbitration, including under English rules:

General Works on Commercial Arbitration (place of publication London, unless otherwise stated): J Tackaberry and A Marriott (eds), *Bernstein's Handbook of Arbitration and Dispute Resolution Practice* (4th edn, 2003); Buhring-Uhle, *Arbitration and Mediation in International Business* (Kluwer, The Hague, 1996); JG Collier and V Lowe, *The Settlement of Disputes in International Law* (Oxford UP, 1999); WL Craig, WW Park, J Paulsson, *International Chamber of Commerce Arbitration* (3rd edn, 2000, Oceana/ICC Publishing); D Joseph, *Jurisdiction and Arbitration Agreements and their Enforcement* (2005); JDM Lew (ed), *Contemporary Problems in International Arbitration* (Kluwer, The Hague, 1987); R Merkin, *Arbitration Law* (Informa Business Publishing, 2006); M Mustill and S Boyd, *Commercial Arbitration: Companion Volume* (2001); LW Newman and RD Hill (eds), *The Leading Arbitrators' Guide to International Arbitration* (Juris Publishers, Bern, Switzerland, 2004); WW Park, *Arbitration of International Business Disputes: Studies in Law and Practice* (Oxford UP, 2006); J-F Poudret and S Besson, *Comparative Law of International Arbitration* (2nd edn, 2007); A Redfern and M Hunter, *The Law and Practice of International Commercial Arbitration* (3rd edn, 1999); and student edition (2003); *Russell on Arbitration* (23rd edn, 2007); A Tweeddale and K Tweeddale, *Arbitration of Commercial Disputes: International and English Law and Practice* (Oxford UP, 2005); also important is *Dicey, Morris, and Collins on the Conflict of Laws* (14th edn, 2006), ch 16 (and referring to other literature) .

Abbreviations: MB (2nd edn, 1989): Mustill and Boyd, *Commercial Arbitration* (2nd edn, 1989); **MB (2001)**: Mustill and Boyd, *Commercial Arbitration: Companion Volume* (2001); **AA:** Arbitration Act 1996 (reproduced with commentary in MB (2001) Part III); **DAC 1996**: Departmental Advisory Committee of Arbitration Law Report on the Arbitration Bill (in MB (2001), appendix 1); **DAC 1997**: Departmental Advisory Committee of Arbitration Law Supplementary Report on the Arbitration Bill (in MB (2001), appendix 2);

(1) Introduction

12.01 In this chapter we will consider the framework and the main themes of the English arbitration system. The Arbitration Act 1996 is a sophisticated code. Arguably, its leading features are (the main provisions are cited in the Appendix at **12.47**):

(i) shared responsibility between parties and the arbitrator to render the process speedy, fair, and efficient (**12.29, 12.30**);

(ii) recognising the parties' scope to agree modifications of particular processes (**12.09, 12.30, 12.47** citing sections 1 and 4 of the 1996 Act); and the parties' scope to agree upon the applicable substantive norms against which the dispute is to be adjudicated (**12.08, 12.23**);

(iii) on application by a party, the courts retain the ultimate power to determine whether the arbitrator or panel has been validly constituted (questions of validity, jurisdiction, and appointment), whether the arbitrator has complied with basic standards of procedural justice, and whether the substantive rules governing the dispute have been accurately applied (**12.30, 12.32**);

(iv) empowering the arbitrator to conduct the process in a speedy, efficient and accurate fashion (**12.30, 12.33**).

(2) The Nature of Arbitration

12.02 Arbitration is a means by which two or more parties can refer a dispute to a neutral decision-maker for a final decision (an 'award'). The award is binding on the parties (see further **12.05**). It can be recognised and enforced within the English or foreign legal systems under the New York Convention 1958 to which many nations are party.[2] An arbitration tribunal's power to reach a binding decision on the merits is to be contrasted with mediation (or conciliation) (generally, see chapter 11). As explained at **11.04**, a mediator, although neutral, is not empowered or expected to give a binding decision. A mediator is instead mandated to facilitate a consensual resolution of the parties' dispute.

12.03 The arbitrator must respect the parties' right to present points of claim, defence, to adduce evidence, and to make submissions concerning substantive

---

NYC 1958: New York Convention on the Recognition and Enforcement of Foreign Arbitral Awards 1958 (in MB (2001), appendix 3); **UML**: UNCITRAL Model Law on International Commercial Arbitration (in MB (2001), appendix 4).

There are many on-line bibliographies, including the following: *http://www.uncitral. org/uncitral/en/uncitral_texts/arbitration_biblio.html*; *http://libpweb1.nus.edu.sg/llb/pu bns/arbitrn.html*; *http://www.peacemakers.ca/bibliography/bib10arbitration.html*; http: //www2.lib.uchicago.edu/~llou/intlarb.html.

[2] New York Convention on the Recognition and Enforcement of Foreign Arbitral Awards 1958 (in **MB (2001)**, appendix 3).

norms.[3] The process displays the triangular configuration of a *'lis'*, that is a juridical dispute between at least two persons. There will be a claim, defence, and factual or legal arguments within the framework of those outline contentions. Supporting material will be marshalled, opposed, and tested. The parties must enjoy an equal opportunity to present their cases. The tendency is for the matter to be considered in an intense and focused way. The neutral arbiter must preserve his appearance of impartiality. He should not become enthusiastic in pursuing his initial perception of the case's merits before all the relevant material is assembled. The arbitrator must examine the dispute judiciously and reach a decision (an 'award').

Arbitration shares with court adjudication two core procedural values or principles: impartiality of the arbitrator, and a duty to hear the other's case.[4] However, arbitration does not embody the principle of publicity (for the confidential nature of arbitration proceedings, see **12.07** and **12.27**).[5] The arbitrator should give reasons in support of his award,[6] unless the parties have 'contracted out' of this requirement.[7] In fact most awards are reasoned. There is a (heavily qualified) power to challenge the award before the court on the basis of an error of law (see, for suggested improvement, **12.46**).[8]   **12.04**

The arbitral award on the merits becomes *res judicata*. And so it is binding on the parties and their successors in title (on this doctrine, see also **8.22** ff).[9] The award can be made a judgment and enforced within the English judicial system of enforcement (on which see **8.28** ff). Alternatively, the award can be enforced outside England under the New York Convention 1958 to which many nations are party.[10]   **12.05**

---

[3] The singular 'arbitrator' is used throughout, rather than 'tribunal'; although English arbitration is accustomed to arbitration panels consisting of two or more (normally, nowadays, an uneven number), most references are heard by a single arbitrator.

[4] For detailed examination of these fundamental procedural principles, Neil Andrews, *English Civil Procedure* (Oxford UP, 2003) 4.28 ff, 5.01 ff.

[5] On this principle, in the context of English civil court proceedings, Neil Andrews, ibid, 4.49 ff.

[6] On this principle, in the context of English civil court proceedings, ibid, 5.39 ff.

[7] s 69 **AA**; if 'reasons' are dispensed with, by agreement, there is no such right of appeal: s 69(1) AA: 'An agreement to dispense with reasons for the tribunal's award shall be considered an agreement to exclude *the court*'s jurisdiction under this section ...'; and s 45(1) **AA**.

[8] s 69 AA 1996; on which **12.32** below.

[9] s 58(1) **AA**.

[10] New York Convention on the Recognition and Enforcement of Foreign Arbitral Awards 1958 (in **MB (2001)**, appendix 3); for the process in England of recognition and enforcement of a New York Convention award, s 101 **AA**; for an example, *Svenska Petroleum Exploration AB v Government of the Republic of Lithuania (No 2)* [2006] EWCA Civ 1529; [2007] 2 WLR 876.

(3) Arbitration's Attractiveness to Disputants

12.06   There are many reasons why parties are attracted to arbitration rather than court proceedings. The School of International Arbitration, Queen Mary, University of London reported in 2005 that companies gave the following reasons for preferring international commercial arbitration to court proceedings:[11] flexibility of procedure, ready enforcement of awards (including enforcement in foreign jurisdictions, applying the New York Convention, 1958),[12] the privacy afforded by the process, and the opportunity for parties to select arbitrators.' These points will now be elaborated.

12.07   Arbitration is a confidential process (on the distinction between rights of 'confidentiality' and 'evidential privileges', see **6.26** and **6.27**). The English Arbitration Act 1996 does not codify this aspect. Instead it was considered preferable to allow this topic to evolve through case law development. The exceptions to confidentiality in the context of arbitration are examined at **12.27**.[13]

12.08   Secondly, the parties can control the process in many respects. In particular, they can agree upon who is to sit as arbitrator or members of the panel. Arbitrators need not be lawyers. They can be selected on the basis of specialist knowledge and experience.[14] The English legislation also enables the parties to agree whether the substance of the dispute will be subject to (i) English law or (ii) a foreign system of law (the latter can apply even if the 'seat' of the arbitration is in England) or (iii) norms drawn from general principles of equity or religious law.[15]

---

[11] Available on-line at: *http://www.pwc.com/Extweb/pwcpublications.nsf/docid/0B3 FD76A8551573E85257168005122C8*. I am grateful to Stephen York for this reference.

[12] New York Convention on the Recognition and Enforcement of Foreign Arbitral Awards 1958 (in **MB (2001)**, appendix 3).

[13] **MB (2001)** 112–3; **DAC 1996** [10] to [17].

[14] On the system of experts in English court proceedings, **7.01** of the present work; specifically on expertise and arbitration, L Blom-Cooper (ed), *Experts in Civil Courts* (Oxford UP, 2006) ch 10.

[15] (i) and (ii) are covered by the reference to 'the law chosen by the parties as applicable to the substance of the dispute' in s 46 (1)(a) **AA**; (iii) is admitted by the reference in s 46(1) (b) **AA** to 'such other considerations as are agreed by them or determined by the tribunal'; **MB (2001)** 326–8 (and 124–127). The point at (iii) (non-English and non-foreign state law) renders arbitration practice under English rules more flexible that other contractual choices of law (see remainder of this note). Thus the Contracts (Applicable Law) Act 1990 (incorporating in Sch 1, the Rome Convention 1981 'on the law applicable to contractual obligations') does not apply to 'arbitration agreements', see Sch 1, 1990 Act, at Article 1(2) (d); it has been said in the Court of Appeal, *Halpern v Halpern* [2007] EWCA Civ 291, at [24], that the Rome Convention does not apply to 'the true construction of an agreement to arbitrate' and that 'it was appreciated that such agreements are excepted from the Rome Convention [see Article 1(2)(d) and *Dicey, Morris, and Collins on the Conflict of Laws* (14th edn, 2006) 16–015].' But where the Rome Convention does apply (viz other than to an 'arbitration agreement'), it has been held that a chosen law must be a national law:

Thirdly, the procedure adopted in individual arbitration references can be   **12.09**
tailor-made to suit the dispute's specific features. Where necessary, 'every case
demands its own procedure'.[16]

Fourthly, parties to arbitration also hope that the process will be swifter   **12.10**
and cheaper, but no less accurate than, court litigation. The 1996 Act injects
the discipline of time-management and cost-effectiveness into the arbitral process, while respecting the parties' interest in gaining a fair result: 'The tribunal
shall ... adopt procedures suitable to the circumstance of the particular case,
avoiding unnecessary delay or expense, so as to provide a fair means for the
resolution of the matters falling to be determined.'[17]

Fifthly, money awards are readily enforceable under the terms of the New   **12.11**
York Convention 1958.[18]

Halpern v Halpern [2007] EWCA Civ 291 at [21] ff, citing *Dicey, Morris, and Collins on
the Conflict of Laws* (14th edn, 2006) 32–081, which notes the authority of *Shamil Bank
of Bahrain EC v Beximco Pharmaceuticals* [2004] EWCA Civ 19; [2004] 1 WLR 1784,
CA, at [40] ('Sharia law' not a national law). The passage in *Dicey, Morris, and Collins*,
32–081, states: 'Article 1(1) of the Rome Convention makes it clear that the reference to
the parties' choice of "the law" to govern a contract is a reference to the law of a country
["a choice between the laws of different countries"]. It does not sanction the choice or application of a non-national system of law, such as the lex mercatoria or general principles
of law ... . It is suggested that a choice of lex mercatoria or general principles of law is not
an express choice of law under the Rome Convention. So also in *Shamil Bank of Bahrain
EC v Beximico Pharmaceuticals Ltd* [see reference above] the Court of Appeal held that a
choice of the principles of Sharia law was not a choice of law of a country for the purposes
of the Rome Convention.' Similarly, 'Jewish law', although recognised worldwide by Or-
thodox Jews, is not the law of a specific legal system: *Halpern v Halpern* [2007] EWCA
Civ 291.

[16] The need for arbitrators not simply 'to copy the CPR' (or Commercial Court Guide) is
echoed in a recent report on the operation of the Arbitration Act 'Report (2006) on the Arbitration Act 1996', at [43] to [45]; report prepared for the Commercial Court Users' Committee, the British Maritime Law Association, the London Shipping Law Centre, and other
bodies; accessible at *www.idrc.co.uk/aa96survey/Report_on_Arbitration_Act_1996.pdf*.
See too **MB (2001)** 197; but at 186, Mustill and Boyd balance this with the comment, '... the
Act should not encourage arbitrators to approach every arbitration completely afresh ... It is
generally good practice to consider whether to give the parties the kind of procedure which
they have come to expect.' The report acknowledges the contribution of Sir Mark Saville,
now Lord Saville, to the framing of the 1996 Act.

[17] s 33(1)(b) **AA**.

[18] New York Convention on the Recognition and Enforcement of Foreign Arbitral
Awards 1958 (in **MB (2001)**, appendix 3); for the process in England of recognition and enforcement of a New York Convention award, s 101 **AA**; for an example, *Svenska Petroleum
Exploration AB v Government of the Republic of Lithuania (No 2)* [2006] EWCA Civ
1529; [2007] 2 WLR 8.

(4) Links between Mediation and Arbitration

Mediation As a Mandatory Prelude to Arbitration

12.12 Many corporations now prefer to use international arbitration in combination with ADR mechanisms. Such a combination of techniques will be specified in a 'multi-tiered' dispute resolution clause.[19] Such a clause was considered in an English decision, *Cable & Wireless v IBM United Kingdom Ltd* (2002)[20] (see **11.47**). In that case, the parties had stipulated that mediation should be a mandatory prelude to *court proceedings*. But other dispute resolution clauses might stipulate that mediation should be the compulsory stage before commencement of *arbitration proceedings*. Arbitration and court proceedings are alternative ways in which the dispute can be determined, in the absence of a settlement or mediated settlement. The *Cable & Wireless* case demonstrates that the contractual commitment to mediate is legally enforceable. If a party, in breach of the resolution clause, fails to pursue mediation, and instead prematurely commences arbitration or court proceedings, the remedy is to halt the relevant premature adjudicative process. This involves a judicial order. It might involve either (i) an 'anti-suit injunction' aimed at halting, by an *in personam* order, the offending party's continuation of premature arbitration proceedings, or (ii) premature foreign civil proceedings or (iii) a 'stay' of premature English civil proceedings (a 'stay' is an order prohibiting further activity in the action; this bar remains effective until lifted by the court: see **11.31**, **11.38**). Within the 'Brussels' system of jurisdiction, however, the use of anti-suit injunctions mentioned at (ii) has become problematic. In (July) 2007 the question of the grant of anti-suit injunctions to enforce arbitration agreements by enjoining litigants from continuing *court proceedings* remains the subject of a pending reference to the European Court of Justice made by the House of Lords, discussed at **12.21**). A different question, however, arises if English courts are asked to award an anti-suit injunction, if necessary, to stop *arbitral proceedings* from proceeding in breach of a party's agreement to mediate. No interference with the jurisdiction of the *courts* of member States is involved in this latter context. For this reason, it would appear to be axiomatic that, even in the context of civil proceedings falling with the 'Brussels' system of jurisdiction, anti-suit injunctions can prevent a party to *arbitral proceedings* from proceeding in breach of a party's agreement to mediate.

---

[19] The School of International Arbitration, Queen Mary, University of London, report (2005), available on-line at: *http://www.pwc.com/Extweb/pwcpublications.nsf/docid/0B 3FD76A8551573E85257168005122C8*. I am grateful to Stephen York for this reference.

[20] *Cable & Wireless plc v IBM UK* [2002] 2 All ER (Comm) 1041, Colman J.

Arbitration if Mediation Fails

So-called 'Med-Arb' 'recognises that mediation may not resolve all the issues   **12.13**
... If no agreement, or only partial agreement, is reached, the mediator changes
roles and becomes an arbitrator empowered to impose a binding decision on
them.'[21] However, this interesting hybrid has not been much used in the UK.
There are problems. First, there is the question whether the switch to arbitration might not be premature. Secondly, the spectre of supervening arbitration
might have a 'chilling' effect on mediation sessions. Furthermore, the third
party might try to avoid arbitration and coerce the parties into accepting a
settlement.[22]

Mediation during Arbitration

The Model Law produced by UNCITRAL contains no provision for this.   **12.14**
However, the Japanese *arbitration legislation* does allow consensual mediation.[23] One problem arises if the arbitrator himself acts as mediator but fails to
achieve a conciliated settlement. There is then a question whether he is inca-
pacitated from continuing to act. Perhaps the parties' express or implied agreement should be taken to pre-empt subsequent objection by one party on this
basis. Another question is whether a mediated settlement in this context will
be recognised under the New York Convention (1958).[24] It might be argued
that a 'consent award' is not the same as an arbitral tribunal's imposed 'award'.
If so, the settlement reached in the arbitration will need to make specific reference to the question of its enforcement in foreign jurisdictions.

(5) The Volume of Arbitration Business

Arbitration business is reported to be booming. The London Chartered Insti-   **12.15**
tute of Arbitration comments:[25] 'Increasingly, commercial parties have been
resorting to arbitration. ... Most of the disputes involve foreign parties who

---

[21] P Newman, in M Liebman (ed), *Mediation in Context* (2000, London and Philadelphia) 185–6; DC Elliott, 'Med/Arb: Fraught with Danger or Ripe with Opportunity' (1996)
62 Jo of Chartered Inst of Arbitrators 175–83; D Spencer and M Brogan, *Mediation: Law
and Practice* (Cambridge UP, 2006), 471 ff.
[22] ibid at 186.
[23] Y Sato and H Kobayashi, 'Combination of Arbitration and Conciliation' (distributed
by K Matsaura at Nagoya February 2007 symposium).
[24] New York Convention on the Recognition and Enforcement of Foreign Arbitral
Awards 1958 (in **MB (2001)**, appendix 3).
[25] http://www.arbitrators.org/Institute/PR_international_dispute.asp.

have chosen to arbitrate in England and Wales as opposed to elsewhere.' How-ever, it is difficult to discover precise figures. Unlike court proceedings, there is no comprehensive and official register of the incidence of arbitration in differ-ent jurisdictions. It is widely accepted that English arbitration is an important form of modern dispute resolution and of revenue for lawyers. The English re-port of 2006 on the Arbitration Act 1996 suggests tentatively that between 5,000 and 10,000 arbitration references are made under that legislation each year.[26]

12.16   The number of English arbitration proceedings just cited might be an over-estimate. Although statistics concerning cases administered by arbitral institu-tions[27] show a clear and general upward trend, they also reveal a more modest level of activity: (i) the LCIA[28] (formerly known as the London Court of Inter-national Arbitration) had 37 cases in 1996 and over 120 in 2006; (ii) cases or-ganised by other institutions, probably raise the total number to around 300 cases per annum in London;[29] (iii) as for Paris, the case-load of the ICC (Inter-national Court of Arbitration)[30] has risen from under 300 in 1980 to nearly 600 in 2006.

12.17   But traditions and customs can vary. Thus a Japanese professor has sug-gested that there are no more than ten arbitrations in Japan each year.[31] This should be contrasted with the volume of arbitral business in England.

---

[26] 'Report (2006) on the Arbitration Act 1996', at [19]; report prepared for the Commer-cial Court Users' Committee, the British Maritime Law Association, the London Shipping Law Centre, and other bodies (the authors were various barristers, solicitors, and other ar-bitration specialists – see Appendix A of report for details); for the text, see: www.idrc.co.uk/aa96survey/Report_on_Arbitration_Act_1996.pdf.

[27] A summary table can be found in the statistics page of the HKIAC website: *http://www.hkiac.org/HKIAC/HKIAC_English/main.html*. I am grateful to Stephen York for these references.

[28] *http://www.lcia-arbitration.com*.

[29] A recent report by IFSL quotes that number based on research among law firms in 2002: *http://www.ifsl.org.uk/uploads/PB_Dispute_Resolution_2006.pdf*. The main centre used by international parties in London (the IDRC in Fleet Street) reports that it holds between 250–300 arbitrations each year which take 5 days on average, and a similar number of mediations.

[30] *http://www.iccwbo.org/court/* (the ICC ICA was established in Paris in 1923 and the most popular nationalities of arbitrators appointed by the ICC are still French and Swiss).

[31] Professor Takeshi Kojima, Dean of Toin University, Yokohama; Emeritus Professor of Law, Chuo University, Tokyo, private communication, February 2007.

(6) Arbitration Clauses[32]

The English Arbitration Act 1996 requires the arbitration agreement to be in writing.[33] Arbitration agreements concern agreements 'to submit to arbitration present or future disputes', which include 'differences'.[34] There can be two main types of dispute arising from a purported arbitration agreement. The first is the question whether the arbitration clause is legally binding (the question of the arbitration clause's validity). The English High Court has declared itself competent to determine that question, in exercise of its inherent jurisdiction.[35] Secondly, assuming the arbitration clause's validity, there might be an issue whether that clause embraces a dispute concerning the validity of the main transaction. In this second situation, the modern tendency is to construe arbitration clauses liberally. This confers a wide, but note entirely unlimited, field of competence to arbitrators to determine the main transaction's validity. This ensures 'one-stop' arbitration, that is, avoidance of the preliminary determination by a court of the question whether the main transaction is vitiated or invalid. In this connection, the Court of Appeal has declared that a line is to be drawn between (a) cases where there is plainly 'no contract', that is, the purported main transaction has no existence in any sense (typically because of a failure of 'offer and acceptance'), and (b) agreements which are defective ('voidable' for misrepresentation, duress, etc) or which are rendered invalid. Matters falling within category (b) are within the scope of an arbitration clause concerning disputes 'arising out of the contract'.[36]

12.18

---

[32] D Joseph, *Jurisdiction and Arbitration Agreements and their Enforcement* (2005); and other works cited at n 1 above; an agreement to arbitrate is subject to the traditional analysis of repudiatory breach and 'acceptance' by the innocent party: J Levy (2007) NLJ 1036, noting *Bea Hotels NV v Bellway LLC* [2007] EWHC 1363 (Comm), Cooke J and *Downing v Al Tameer Establishment* [2002] EWCA Civ 721, at [21], [25], [26], also noting the seminal 'contractual' analysis of arbitration agreements in *Bremer Vulcan v South India Shipping Corporation Limited* [1981] AC 909, HL; *The Hannah Blumenthal* [1983] 1 AC 854, HL; *The Splendid Sun* [1981] QB 694, CA and *The Leonidas D* [1985] 1 WLR 925, CA (on this stream of authority, **MB (2001)** 503 ff).

[33] s 3, **AA**; **MB (2001)** 16, 258 ff; for an important discussion of arbitration clauses affecting sovereign states, *Svenska Petroleum Exploration AB v Government of the Republic of Lithuania (No 2)* [2006] EWCA Civ 1529; [2007] 2 WLR 876, considering s 9(1), State Immunity Act 1978.

[34] ss 6(1), 82(1) **AA**; **MB (2001)** 22–23, suggesting that there is no discernible difference between these terms; noting, to the same effect, *Hayter v Nelson and Home Insurance* [1990] 2 Lloyd's Rep 265.

[35] *Albon etc v Naza Motor Trading SDN BHD (No 3)* [2007] EWHC 665 (Ch); [2007] 2 All ER 1075, Colman J.

[36] *Fiona Trust & Holding Corporation & Ors v Yuri Privalov & Ors* [2007] EWCA Civ 20, at [18] to [21]: '... "arising out of the contract" should cover "every dispute except a dispute as to whether there was ever a contract at all"', see Mustill and Boyd, *Commercial Arbitration*, 2nd ed at 120: 'It is not to be expected that any commercial man would knowingly

Jurisdiction Wrangling and Imposition of a Mediation Order

12.19   In *C v RHL* (2005) an application was made to a Commercial Court judge, Colman J, in London, for an anti-suit injunction to prevent litigation from proceeding in the Russian courts.[37] The Russian litigation concerned a share purchase agreement and a group of companies. The agreement contained an arbitration clause in which the parties had nominated London as the 'seat' for arbitral proceedings. The decision's novel feature is that Colman J did not issue an injunction to permit arbitration to take place in England. This would have been the expected order. Instead he issued an order, modelled on the English Commercial Court's 'ADR order' (see **11.37**), requiring the parties to pursue mediation. The salient parts of his order are cited in this note.[38]

12.20   This decision demonstrates the English judiciary's desire to embrace ADR as an adjunct to commercial dispute resolution even when the parties' chosen mode of dispute-resolution is arbitration. The case is unusual because the Russian litigation had involved extensive jurisdictional wrangling between the parties. It is doubtful whether the High Court will generally order ADR in a straightforward case where the parties are pursuing English arbitration.

---

create a system which required that the court should first decide whether the contract should be rectified or avoided or rescinded (as the case might be) and then, if the contract is held to be valid, required the arbitrator to resolve the issues that have arisen ... We would, therefore, conclude that a dispute whether the contract can be set aside or rescinded for alleged bribery does fall within the arbitration clause on its true construction. The case is different from a dispute "as to whether there were ever a contract at all", in the Mustill and Boyd sense.'

[37] *C v RHL* [2005] EWHC 873 (Comm), Colman J.

[38] ibid, at [8] '... I have no doubt that the overall interests of all parties, including RHL's associated companies and beneficial owners, would be best served if the whole group of disputes between C and RHL was referred to mediation before any further substantial costs are incurred either in pursuing or defending satellite litigation such as this application ... In many respects this series of disputes with its particular commercial background is the paradigm of a case which is likely to be settled by mediation. That procedure provides scope for the kind of commercial solution to these disputes which is beyond the power of this court or of the ICC arbitrators to engender ...' [10] '... the parties should be given 28 days to appoint a mediator or panel of mediators and to conclude their mediation meetings.' [11] '... an ADR order should be prepared which expressly provides for the selection of the neutral or neutrals, expressly requires the parties, including their fully authorised decision-takers to attend such meetings as the neutral(s) may appoint and to provide to the neutral(s) such evidence as may be required.'

Arbitration Clauses and the European Jurisdiction Regulation

The House of Lords in the *West Tankers* case (2007)[39] held that the High **12.21** Court has power to issue an anti-suit injunction to restrain a party, in breach of an arbitration clause, from commencing or pursuing court proceedings in a Member State which is subject to the European Jurisdictional regime.[40] Lord Hoffmann explained why anti-suit injunctions are legitimate in this context:[41]

I: 'Arbitration ... is altogether excluded from the scope of the Jurisdiction Regulation by article 1(2)(d).'

II: 'As Professor Dr Peter Schlosser points out in an illuminating article,[42] an exclusive jurisdiction clause [nominating a particular *court*] is in this respect quite different [from an arbitration clause]. [The former] takes effect within the Regulation under article 23 and its enforcement must therefore be in accordance with the terms of the Regulation; in particular, article 21. But an arbitration clause takes effect outside the Regulation and its enforcement is not subject to its terms.'

III: 'People engaged in commerce choose arbitration in order to be outside the procedures of any national court' [viz, as far the *substance* of the dispute is concerned].

IV: '... Arbitration cannot be self-sustaining. It needs the support of the courts ... [I]t is important for the commercial interests of the European Community that it should give such support.'

V: 'The Courts of the United Kingdom have for many years exercised the [anti-suit injunctive] jurisdiction to restrain foreign court proceedings ... [The anti-suit injunction] is generally regarded as an important and valuable weapon in the hands of a court exercising supervisory jurisdiction over the arbitration. It promotes legal certainty and reduces the possibility of conflict between the arbitration award and the judgment of a national court.'

However, it is unclear whether the European Court of Justice, a zealous protector of the European Jurisdictional regime, will tolerate an anti-suit injunction to restrain a party, in breach of an *arbitration clause*, from commencing or pursuing court proceedings in a Member State subject to the European Jurisdictional regime. This point is not yet covered by clear Luxembourg authority. And so, the House of Lords in the *West Tankers* case referred to the European Court of Justice (Luxembourg) the following question: 'Is it consistent with EC Regulation 44/2001 for a court of a Member State to make an order to restrain a person from commencing or continuing proceedings in another Member State on the ground that such proceedings are in breach of an arbitra-

---

[39] *West Tankers Inc v RAS Riunione Adriatica di Sicurta SpA* [2007] UKHL 4.

[40] The Brussels Jurisdiction Regulation (Council Regulation 44/2001 of 22 December 2001 on 'jurisdiction and the recognition and enforcement of judgments in civil and commercial matters'.

[41] *West Tankers Inc v RAS Riunione Adriatica di Sicurta SpA* [2007] UKHL 4 at [12] to [19].

[42] P Schlosser, 'Anti-suit injunctions zur Unterstützung von internationalen Schiedsverfahren' (2006) RIW 486.

tion agreement?' It is to be hoped that the answer given to this by the European Court of Justice will be 'yes'.[43] Until then, the position is unclear. By contrast, the European Court of Justice is clearly opposed to anti-suit injunctions aimed at ensuring compliance with an exclusive jurisdiction clause allocating competence *to the courts* of a Member State. In that context an anti-suit injunction would be incompatible with the European Jurisdictional regime: see **2.11**).[44]

Hybrid Arbitration and Jurisdiction Clauses

12.22   The English High Court has upheld so-called 'hybrid' dispute-resolution clauses. These enable one party to opt out of court proceedings in England by taking the case to arbitration or, conversely, enable a party to opt out of arbitration and instead bring proceedings before an English court.[45] Although such 'hybrid' clauses have been accepted under English law, other legal systems might take a different view.

(7) Scope of the English Arbitration Act 1996

12.23   The Act covers both domestic and international arbitration references intended for hearing within England (or Northern Ireland). This locus is referred to as the 'seat' of the arbitration. The English statue is not confined to commercial arbitration, unlike the UNCITRAL Model Law.[46] The English Act affects ar-

---

[43] For an argument that anti-suit injunctions should not be granted in this context, B Steinbrück (2007) 26 CJQ 358.

[44] *Gasser GmbH v MISAT Srl (Case C-116/02)* [2003] ECR I-14693 (a Member State's court, on which exclusive jurisdiction has been conferred pursuant to article 23 of the 2001 Regulation, cannot assume jurisdiction until the court of another Member State, first seised of the dispute, has relinquished jurisdiction; see also summaries of ECJ case law at **ch 2 n 36**); and for the ECJ's rejection of common law anti-suit injunctions within the European jurisdictional system, to restrain an abuse of process, *Turner v Grovit (Case C-159/02)* [2005] 1 AC 101); for comment, Neil Andrews, 'Abuse of process and obstructive tactics under the Brussels jurisdictional system ...' (2005) European Community Private L Rev 8–15 (this journal is also entitled Zeitschrift für Gemeinschaftsprivatrecht and Revue de droit privé international).

[45] *NB Three Shipping Ltd v Harebell Shipping Ltd* [2004] EWHC 2001(Comm) [2005] 1 All ER (Comm) 200; [2005] 1 Lloyd's Rep 509, Morison J; *Law Debenture Trust Corp plc v Elektrim Finance BV and others* [2005] EWHC 1412 (Ch); [2005] 2 All ER (Comm) 476; [2005] 2 Lloyd's Rep 755, Mann J; on these developments, S Nesbitt and H Quinlan, 'The Status and Operation of Unilateral or Optional Arbitration Clauses' (2006) 22 Arbitration International 133; D Joseph, *Jurisdiction and Arbitration Agreements and their Enforcement* (2005) 4–29 and discussion in R Merkin, *Arbitration Law* (Informa Business Publishing, 2006).

[46] **MB (2001)** 22.

bitration proceedings (irrespective of the date when the agreement was made) commenced at the start of 1997.[47] In most 'English' arbitration English substantive rules will determine the outcome of the dispute. But the arbitration agreement might provide that a foreign system of law should be applied during the 'English arbitration' process, or even norms drawn from general principles of Equity or religious law.[48]

Even where the arbitration is to take place outside England (and Northern Ireland), the 1996 Act empowers the English courts to support such foreign arbitration in various ways: by the grant of stays of English civil proceedings commenced in breach of an arbitration clause;[49] by issuing protective relief, such as freezing injunctions[50] (for the English High Court's powers to grant 'freezing' relief, see **4.03**); or by recognising and enforcing a final award given in the foreign arbitration.[51]   **12.24**

The Act reflects the UNCITRAL Model Law, but does not adopt it in unmodified form.[52] The English legislation covers many more facets of arbitration than that Model Law.[53] Nevertheless, the structure of the English legislation reflects the sequence of the Model Law. The English independent approach is to be contrasted with Scotland, where the Model Law has been incorporated.[54]   **12.25**

---

[47] Art 3, Arbitration Act (Commencement No 1) Order (SI 1996, 3146); s 84 **AA** 1996; **MB (2001)**, 19.

[48] See detailed discussion of these points at n 15 above.

[49] ss 2(2)(a), 9(4) **AA**.

[50] s 44 **AA**, see also s 2(3)(a).

[51] ss 2(2), 66 **AA**.

[52] UNCITRAL's web-site records that the following have produced arbitration codes 'based on' the Model Law: 'Australia, Austria, Azerbaijan, Bahrain, Bangladesh, Belarus, Bermuda, Bulgaria, Cambodia, Canada, Chile, in China: Hong Kong Special Administrative Region, Macau Special Administrative Region; Croatia, Cyprus, Denmark, Egypt, Germany, Greece, Guatemala, Hungary, India, Iran, Republic of Ireland, Japan, Jordan, Kenya, Lithuania, Madagascar, Malta, Mexico, New Zealand, Nicaragua, Nigeria, Norway, Oman, Paraguay, Peru, the Philippines, Poland, Republic of Korea, Russian Federation, Scotland, Singapore, Spain, Sri Lanka, Thailand, Tunisia, Turkey, Ukraine; within the United States of America: California, Connecticut, Illinois, Louisiana, Oregon and Texas; Zambia, and Zimbabwe.' See: http://www.uncitral.org/uncitral/en/uncitral_texts/arbitration/1985Model_arbitration.html.

[53] **MB (2001)** 14–15; ibid, 7–9 for discussion of the decision not to adopt the Model Law in England, Wales and Northern Ireland, but instead to combine some of the UNCITRAL Model Law's main ideas and produce a more detailed national arbitration statute. For details of the position in other common law jurisdictions, with regard to the Model law, see K Uff, 'Common Law Arbitration-An Overview' (2004) IDR (Jo of Int Dispute Resolution) 10, 11.

[54] **MB (2001)** 8 n 15, citing the Law Reform (Miscellaneous Provisions) Act 1990, s 66, Sch 7.

12.26   Four topics are not covered by the English Act: the question of 'arbitrability',[55] confidentiality,[56] oral agreements to arbitration,[57] and the effect of illegality upon the arbitral process and award.[58] These remain governed by judicial law.

12.27   As for 'confidentiality', a 2006 report concluded that legislation on confidentiality would be 'virtually impossible' to draft.[59] The leading judicial statement identifies three established exceptions to arbitral confidentiality, and a fourth and nascent exception:[60]

(1) '... where disclosure is made with the express or implied consent of the party who originally produced the material';

(2) where disclosure is ordered by the court: 'an obvious example of which is an order for disclosure of documents generated by an arbitration for the purposes of a later court action';

(3) where disclosure is permitted with the court's permission: the Court of Appeal here commented that such permission will be granted 'when, and to the extent to which, it is reasonably necessary for ... the establishment or protection of an arbitrating party's legal rights vis-a-vis a third party'; in this context 'the Court should not require the parties seeking disclosure to prove necessity regardless of difficulty or expense. It should approach the matter in the round ...'

(4) The Court of Appeal noted that 'in at least one decision[61] ... the English court has tentatively recognised a further exception'; in the interests of justice 'a party to court proceedings was entitled to call for the proof of an expert witness in a previous arbitration in a situation where it appeared that the views expressed by him in that proof were at odds with his views as expressed in the court proceedings'; this can be rationalised as founded on 'the importance of a judicial decision being reached upon the basis of the truthful or accurate evidence of the witnesses concerned.'

---

[55] s 81(1)(a) **AA**; cf **NYC** 1958 Art V.2(a); **MB** (2001) 70–6.

[56] **MB** (2001) 112–3; DAC 1996 [10] to [17]; for background, Brown and Marriott, *ADR Principles and Practice* (2nd edition, 1999) 22–005 to 22–007; A Redfern and M Hunter, *The Law and Practice of International Commercial Arbitration* (3rd edn, 1999); and student edition (2003), 1–43 to 1–48.

[57] s 81(1)(b) **AA**; **MB** (2001) 21, 371; P Neill, 'Confidentiality in Arbitration' (1996) 12 Arb Int 3 (and other lit cited **MB** (2001) n 12): *Ali Shipping Corpn v Shipyard Trogir* [1997] EWCA Civ 3054; [1999] 1 WLR 314, CA (Potter LJ's judgment referring, in particular, to the English decisions in *Dolling-Baker v Merrett* [1990] 1 WLR 1205, CA; *Hassneh Insurance Co v Stewart J Mew* [1993] Lloyd's Rep 243, Colman J; *Insurance Co v Lloyd's Syndicate* [1995] Lloyd's Rep 272, Colman J; *London & Leeds Estates Ltd v Paribas (No 2)* [1995] 2 EG 134, Mance J; and to the High Court of Australia in *Esso Australia Resources Ltd and Others v Plowman (Minister for Energy and Minerals)* (1995) 183 CLR 10).

[58] **MB** (2001) 15, 70 ff.

[59] 'Report (2006) on the Arbitration Act 1996', at [65]; report prepared for the Commercial Court Users' Committee, the British Maritime Law Association, the London Shipping Law Centre, and other bodies; accessible at www.idrc.co.uk/aa96survey/Report_on_Arbitration_Act_1996.pdf.

[60] All the quotations are from Potter LJ in *Ali Shipping Corpn v Shipyard Trogir* [1997] EWCA Civ 3054; [1999] 1 WLR 314, 326–8.

[61] Potter LJ in the *Ali Shipping* case, 327, noting *London & Leeds Estates Ltd v Paribas (No 2)* [1995] 2 EG 134, Mance J.

(8) Main Principles of the Arbitration Act 1996

The 2006 'Report on the Arbitration Act 1996' reveals that the English legisla-   **12.28**
tion is perceived as effective.[62] No changes were recommended.

The 1996 Act imposes duties upon both the arbitrator and the parties to   **12.29**
ensure fairness, efficiency, and an appropriate degree of speediness.[63]

The statute also attractively sets out the following overarching features[64]   **12.30**
(the Appendix at **12.47** reproduces the Act's main provisions). First, the court
retains supervisory powers. These are intended to ensure that the arbitrator or
panel has been validly constituted (questions of validity, jurisdiction, and appointment), that the arbitrator has complied with basic standards of procedural justice, and that the substantive rules governing the dispute are accurately applied (see **12.31**). Secondly, the Act's 'mandatory' provisions include
the fundamental values of impartiality and a reasonable opportunity to participate in the proceedings (*audi alteram partem*).[65] Such core elements of protection ensure that the parties are recipients of civilised justice. Furthermore,
an award will be enforceable transnationally only if basic standards of procedural fairness have been respected.[66] Thirdly, the parties' consensual auto-
nomy ('freedom of contract') is another leading feature of the Act (generally on
that freedom see **10.02**). This freedom enables them to determine, or at least
influence, how the repertoire of procedural measures should be applied in their
particular case. Parties to arbitration can shape their 'alternative' to ordinary
court procedure.[67] Fourthly, the 1996 Act obliges arbitrators to promote a
speedy and economical resolution of the dispute. This is subject to the constraints of fairness and party-agreement: 'The tribunal shall ... adopt procedures suitable to the circumstance of the particular case, *avoiding unnecessary delay or expense, so as to provide a fair means* for the resolution of the
matters falling to be determined.'[68] Fifthly, each party is obliged to 'do all
things necessary for the proper and expeditious conduct of the arbitral proceedings'.[69] This makes clear that each party cannot refuse to co-operate in the

---

[62] 'Report (2006) on the Arbitration Act 1996'; report prepared for the Commercial
Court Users' Committee, the British Maritime Law Association, the London Shipping Law
Centre, and other bodies (the authors were various barristers, solicitors, and other arbitration specialists – see Appendix A of report for details); for the text, see www.idrc.co.uk/
aa96survey/Report_on_Arbitration_Act_1996.pdf.

[63] **MB (2001)** 30–37 discussing respectively ss 33, 40 **AA**.

[64] **MB (2001)** 24–30.

[65] For detailed examination of these fundamental procedural principles, Neil Andrews,
English Civil Procedure (Oxford UP, 2003) 4.02 ff, 5.01 ff.

[66] **NYC 1958** Art V.1(b).

[67] That the parties' agreement takes priority over the arbitrator's regulation of the proceedings is emphasised, and elaborated, by **DAC 1996**, at [154] to [162], [173] to [175].

[68] s 33(1)(b) **AA**.

[69] s 40(1) **AA**.

resolution of the dispute. The parties must help the arbitrator to reach an accurate decision after employing a fair, efficient, and speedy process.

Court's Diminished Role

12.31   One of the main aims of the English Arbitration Act 1996 is that the courts should not interfere excessively in the conduct of the arbitration process. The Act thus restricts a party's power to obtain judicial control of the process or to challenge an award.[70] However, the court retains the power to control the arbitral process in the following ways:

(i) to ensure that the arbitration has been (or remains) validly constituted (questions of validity, jurisdiction, appointment);[71]

(ii) to ensure that the process does not deviate severely from acceptable standards of fair conduct ('serious irregularity');[72] a recent report considered that the English courts' approach to this matter is 'just about right';[73]

(iii) to ensure that questions of English law are correctly applied[74] (there can be no appeal on a point of foreign law,[75] nor if the substantive norms are extra-legal, such as matters of Equity etc).[76]

12.32   As for (iii) at **12.31**, the 2006 report on the 1996 Act states that a majority of respondents considered that appeals on points of English law should be retained.[77] The report also rejected the proposition that the restrictive criteria for permission to appeal (criteria specified at section 69 of the 1996 Act)[78]

---

[70] s 1 (at para 'c'); s 18(2); s 19; s 24; s 27(3); s 32; ss 42–45; s 50; s 56(2)-(8); s 63(4); s 64(2); ss 66–71; s 77; s 79 **AA**; on the background to these, see **MB (2001)** 28–30; 46–50; 52.

[71] Principally, ss 18(2), 24, 32, 67 **AA**.

[72] Principally, s 68 **AA**.

[73] 'Report (2006) on the Arbitration Act 1996', at [84] to [88]; accessible at www.idrc. co.uk/aa96survey/Report_on_Arbitration_Act_1996.pdf.

[74] s 69 **AA**; if 'reasons' are dispensed with, by agreement, there is no such right of appeal: s 45(1) **AA**.

[75] s 46(1) **AA**.

[76] s 46(2) **AA**; **MB (2001)** 45, 50–1; the declaration that such an 'equity' or similar clause will not invalidate an arbitration agreement is an important aspect of the 1996 Act; for background discussion of such extra-legal norms, see **MB (2nd edn, 1989)** 74 to 86 and see detailed discussion of these points at n 15 above.

[77] 'Report (2006) on the Arbitration Act 1996', at [66] to [69]. The report is accessible at www.idrc.co.uk/aa96survey/Report_on_Arbitration_Act_1996.pdf.

[78] s 69 **AA** 1996 states: '(1) Unless otherwise agreed by the parties, a party to *arbitral proceedings* may (upon notice to the other parties and to the tribunal) appeal to *the court* on a question of law arising out of an award made in the proceedings. An agreement to dispense with reasons for the tribunal's award shall be considered an agreement to exclude *the court*'s jurisdiction under this section. (2) An appeal shall not be brought under this section except – (a) with the agreement of all the other parties to the proceedings, or (b) with the leave of *the court*. The right to appeal is also subject to the restrictions in *section 70*(2) and (3). (3)

might be 'starving English Contract Law of nourishment' and 'hindering its development.'[79] The question whether the arbitration agreement has validly excluded recourse to the court on a point of law is itself a preliminary point of law. The court can accordingly pronounce on this matter.[80]

Procedural Fluidity

The arbitrator has considerable freedom to organise the proceedings to ensure fairness, efficiency and speediness. Subject to the parties' contrary agreement, the arbitrator can fix the nature of the proceedings in a wide range of respects.[81] He can determine: its place, language, use of witness statements; disclosure of documents; examination of parties; whether to apply formal rules of evidence on questions of admissibility, relevance and weight; whether to take 'the initiative in ascertaining the facts and the law'; use of oral or written evidence as submissions; as well as issuing 'directions' concerning matters of timing for all these steps and measures.[82] **12.33**

There are three ways in which the procedure be drawn up for a particular arbitration. The parties might have chosen arbitration which will conform to a procedure prescribed (i) by a trade association; or (ii) by an arbitration association or institute (in cross-border arbitration this is a common arrangement); (iii) (by default) the arbitrator will himself select the appropriate procedure. **12.34**

As for this last possibility, the architects of the Act exhorted arbitrators to take the initiative, where appropriate, to suggest or adopt a process to suit the particular case.[83] They should not slavishly mimic the settled procedures of High Court litigation.[84] For the most part, these items of ordinary civil pro- **12.35**

Leave to appeal shall be given only if *the court* is satisfied – (a) that the determination of the question will substantially affect the rights of one or more of the parties, (b) that the question is one which the tribunal was asked to determine, (c) that, on the basis of the findings of fact in the award – (i) the decision of the tribunal on the question is obviously wrong, or (ii) the question is one of general public importance and the decision of the tribunal is at least open to serious doubt, and (d) that, despite the agreement of the parties to resolve the matter by arbitration, it is just and proper in all the circumstances for *the court* to determine the question.' Appeal from the High Court to the Court of Appeal is further restricted by s 69(8); for discussion of s 69, *The Republic of Kazakhstan v Istil Group Ltd* [2007] EWCA Civ 471.

[79] 'Report (2006) on the Arbitration Act 1996', ibid, at [70] to [75].

[80] *Sumukan Ltd v Commonwealth Secretariat* [2007] EWCA Civ 243; [2007] 3 All ER 342 (also considering, at [53] ff, the compatibility with Art 6(1) of the European Convention of such an exclusion clause).

[81] s 34(2),(3) **AA**.

[82] ibid.

[83] **DAC 1996** [151], [153], [166].

[84] 'Report (2006) on the Arbitration Act 1996', at [43] to [45]; report prepared for the Commercial Court Users' Committee, the British Maritime Law Association, the London

cedure are 'on the menu' for the parties to select, or for the arbitrator to suggest or adopt. But for arbitrators to plagiarise wholesale the High Court procedural rules[85] would be excessive, disproportionate, unnecessarily time-consuming, and certainly unimaginative. It would also probably defeat the expectations of the parties themselves.

(9) Arbitrators' Powers under the 1996 Act

Protective, Provisional and Interim Relief

12.36   The arbitrator cannot grant freezing relief, nor can he issue a civil search order (for the English High Court's powers in these respects, see **4.03** and **4.26**).[86] A report in 2006 did not recommend that this should be changed.[87]

12.37   The Act empowers the arbitrator to issue orders for security for costs (for the English courts' powers in these respects, see **4.35**).[88] This power was previously only available by court order. The arbitrator can dismiss the proceedings if the claimant resists a peremptory order for payment of security for costs.[89]

12.38   The arbitrator cannot make an interim order (pecuniary or injunctive) unless the parties have expressly clothed him with this power[90] (for the English courts' powers in these respects, see **5.05** and **5.08**). However, he can make non-overlapping and sequential final awards, known as a 'partial awards'.[91] These take effect prior to the main award. This introduces some flexibility. The effect is that some matters can be determined before the final award.

Shipping Law Centre, and other bodies; accessible at www.idrc.co.uk/aa96survey/Report_on_Arbitration_Act_1996.pdf.

[85] eg, to deploy 'The Admiralty and Commercial Courts Guide' (7th edn, 2006); A Colman, *Commercial Court* (5th edn, 2000); S Sugar and R Wilson (eds), *Commercial and Mercantile Courts Litigation Practice* (2004).

[86] s 39(1) **AA** precludes the arbitrator from granting a 'provisional' order if it is of a type which cannot be granted as final relief by the arbitrator; the court has a power to issue a freezing injunction under s 44(3) **AA** in cases of 'urgency', on the application of a party or 'proposed' party; in the absence of 'urgency' the court can grant freezing relief only if the parties or arbitrator requests: s 44(4) AA.

[87] 'Report (2006) on the Arbitration Act 1996', at [49] to [54]. The report is accessible at www.idrc.co.uk/aa96survey/Report_on_Arbitration_Act_1996.pdf.

[88] s 38(3) **AA; DAC 1996** , at [190] to [198].

[89] s 8(3) **AA**.

[90] s 39 **AA**.

[91] s 47(1), (2)(a) and (b), **AA; DAC 1996** [226] to [231].

Collection of Evidence[92]

The arbitrator can receive sworn evidence from parties or witnesses. For this   **12.39**
purpose the arbitrator can administer the oath or affirmation (the perjury legislation will then apply).[93] But to compel prospective witnesses to appear before the arbitrator or to produce other evidence, a party must ultimately invoke the court's coercive machinery. For this purpose, the 1996 Act enables a
party, with the arbitrator's permission, to 'use the same court procedures as
are available in relation to legal proceedings to secure the attendance before
the [arbitral] tribunal of a witness.'[94]

Procedural Directions and Sanctions

Unlike the English court, an arbitrator has no power to punish a party for con-   **12.40**
tempt of court (generally on that punitive jurisdiction, see **8.35**). But arbitrators' directions or orders are not entirely 'toothless'. If not complied with, they
can be intensified so as to become 'peremptory orders'.[95] In the event of further
non-compliance, first recourse is to 'any available arbitral process in respect of
failure to comply'.[96] That refers to the various internal 'sanctions' available to
the arbitrator: (i) to prevent a party from relying upon 'any allegation or material which was the subject matter of the order'; (ii) drawing 'adverse inferences from the act of non-compliance';[97] (iii) 'proceeding to an award on the
basis of such materials as have been properly provided to' the arbitrator; (iv)
making orders in respect of the costs incurred as a result of the non-compliance.[98]

---

[92] For observations on the arbitral tribunal's approach to admissibility of evidence, see
'Report (2006) on the Arbitration Act 1996', at [46] to [48]. The report is accessible at
www.idrc.co.uk/aa96survey/Report_on_Arbitration_Act_1996.pdf.

[93] s 38(5) **AA**.

[94] ss 43, 44(2)(a) **AA** contain the court's supplementary and coercive powers in these respects.

[95] s 41(5) **AA**.

[96] s 42(3) **AA**.

[97] Civil law systems are especially familiar with the option of drawing 'adverse inferences' because their civil judges often lack a contempt of court power.

[98] s 41(7) **AA**.

Compound Interest

12.41   Arbitrators can award compound interest (or simple interest).[99] The addition
of a power to order compound interest was a striking innovation within the
Arbitration Act 1996 because it gave greater power to arbitrators than the
courts then possessed (until July 2007, compound interest was not generally
available to *English courts* for breaches of contract or tort, for non-payment of
a debt, or in respect of restitutionary claims).[100]

(10) Refining the Practice of International Arbitration

12.42   In his Cambridge lecture (2007), Stephen York, drawing upon his experience
of English and international arbitration, suggested that the following four topics require imaginative solutions.[101] I am grateful to him for permission to
summarise his contentions.

12.43   First, he suggests that steps should be taken to ensure prompt appointment
of arbitrators. It is common for the selection process by party-appointment to
take several months. This is a source of delay and expense. The position is unsatisfactory.

12.44   The second topic is the arbitrators' power to issue injunctions and other in-
terim remedies, both on an *ex parte* and *inter partes* basis.[102] On this, Stephen
York notes:[103] 'While there is some debate, the better view is that the New
York Convention[104] does not assist in the enforcement of such orders. UNCI-

---

[99]   s 49(3) **AA; DAC 1996** [235] to [238].

[100]   The courts have now acquired power to award compound interest in various situations, following the lengthy (and rather convoluted) decision in *Sempra Metals Ltd v Inland Revenue Commissioners* [2007] UKHL 34; [2007] 3 WLR 354 esp [26], [50] (Lord
Hope); [112], [113] (Lord Nicholls); [151] (Lord Scott); [165], [184] (Lord Walker); [215]
to [217], [240] (Lord Mance); the majority decision (Lords Hope, Nicholls and Walker) is
that there is a common law power to order compound interest in respect of a claim in contract (including a debt claim), tort or restitution; this decision, the impulse for which was
European Union case law, (*Metallgesellschaft Ltd v IRC* (Joined Cases C-397 and 410/98)
[2001] ECR I-1727; [2001] Ch 620, ECJ), has overtaken the English Law Commission's
recommendations for change in 'Report on Pre-Judgment Interest on Debts and Damages' (L Com No 287; 2004) (and its earlier 'Compound Interest', L Com CP No 167
(2002).

[101]   Paper delivered to the Civil Justice class, University of Cambridge, February 2007.

[102]   For the English *High Court's* powers to grant 'freezing' relief, see **4.03**; and for the
statutory power in England for *arbitrators* to award security for costs, see **12.37**.

[103]   See also A Baykitch and J Truong, 'Innovations in International Commercial Arbitration: Interim Measures a Way Forward or Back to the Future' (2005) 25 The Arbitrator and
Mediator 95.

[104]   New York Convention on the Recognition and Enforcement of Foreign Arbitral
Awards 1958 (in **MB (2001)**, appendix 3).

TRAL's Working Group has been considering changes to the Model Law.[105] *Ex parte* orders excite vigorous opposition from some commentators.'[106]

Thirdly, Stephen York observes that in both England and the USA it is common for arbitrators to permit extensive discovery of documents and disclosure of evidence. This runs counter to the approach commonly adopted in international arbitration. For the position concerning disclosure of documents during court proceedings in England, see chapter 6, especially at **6.21**.   **12.45**

Finally, in the interest of quality control, Stephen York suggests that the main bodies administering international arbitration might devise a review procedure. This would be similar to appeal, but would not involve the courts (whether at the seat of arbitration or at the place of enforcement). Very large sums and important issues, even the survival of a company, can be determined by the arbitration. For this reason, parties will want to be assured of the highest quality of decision-making and procedural regularity. He suggests that it is inadequate to provide merely limited rights of appeal under the law of 'the seat' of arbitration. That system of attenuated appeal is not intended to provide an extensive review of arbitrators' examination of the evidence and of their application of substantive law.   **12.46**

(11) Appendix: Main Provisions of the Arbitration Act

The four leading provisions are: **12.47**

Section 1: General principles:
'The provisions of [Part 1 of the Act] are founded on the following principles, and shall be construed accordingly – (a) the object of arbitration is to obtain the fair resolution of disputes by an impartial tribunal without unnecessary delay or expense; (b) the parties should be free to agree how their disputes are resolved, subject only to such safeguards as are necessary in the public interest; (c) in matters covered by [Part 1 of the Act] the court should not intervene except as provided by [Part 1].'

Section 4: Mandatory and non-mandatory provisions:
(1) 'The mandatory provision of [Part 1 of the Act] are listed in Schedule 1 and have effect notwithstanding any agreement to the contrary. [For this list see the text below]
(2) The other provisions of this Part (the 'non-mandatory provisions') allow the parties to make their own arrangement by agreement [which must be in writing] but pro-

---

[105] Papers and reports available on-line at: *http://www.uncitral.org/uncitral/en/commission/working_groups/2Arbitration.html*; see especially 44th session January 2006 on new chapter IV bis dealing with revised law concerning interim measures: *A/CN.9/WGII/WP.141 – Settlement of Commercial disputes – Interim measures of protection*. On 2 November 2006 the General Assembly of UNCITRAL approved these proposals for revision of the Model Law.

[106] H van Houtte, 'Ten Reasons Against a Proposal for Ex Parte Interim Measures of Protection in Arbitration' (2004) 20 Arbitration International 85.

vide rules which apply in the absence of such agreement.' [sub-sections (3) to (5) omitted here]

Schedule 1 specifies the relevant 'mandatory' provisions.[107] At first sight, these mandatory provisions might appear to be completely miscellaneous. However, they can be largely grouped under six headings, namely provisions which:

(i) enable the English courts to enforce arbitration agreements;[108] or

(ii) concern matters of timing;[109] or

(iii) enable the court to protect the arbitral process' integrity;[110] or

(iv) enable the court to provide support for that process;[111] or

(v) prescribe the core responsibilities of the arbitral participants;[112] or

(vi) confer immunity upon arbitrators, or otherwise protect the arbitrator from unfairness.[113]

Section 33: General duty of the tribunal:
(1) 'The tribunal shall – (a) act fairly and impartially as between the parties, giving each party reasonable opportunity of putting his case and dealing with that of his opponent; (b) adopt procedures suitable to the circumstance of the particular case, avoiding unnecessary delay or expense, so as to provide a fair means for the resolution of the matters falling to be determined.
(2) The tribunal shall comply with that general duty in conducting the arbitral proceedings, in its decisions on matters of procedure and evidence, and in the exercise of all other powers conferred on it.'

---

[107] ss 9 to 11 **AA** (stay of legal proceedings); s 12 (power of court to extend agreed time limits); s 13 (application of Limitation Acts); s 24 (power of court to remove arbitrator); s 26(1) (effect of death of arbitrator); s 28 (liability of parties for fees and expenses of arbitrators); s 29 (immunity of arbitrator); s 31 (objection to substantive jurisdiction of tribunal); s 33 (general duty of tribunal); s 37(2) (items to be treated as expenses of arbitrators); s 40 (general duty of parties); s 43 (securing the attendance of witnesses); s 56 (power to withhold award in case of non-payment); s 60 (effectiveness of agreement for payment of costs in any event); s 66 (enforcement of award); ss 67 and 68 (challenging the award: substantive jurisdiction and serious irregularity), and ss 70 and 71 (supplementary provisions; effect of order of court) so far as relating to those sections; s 72 (saving for rights of person who takes no part in proceedings); s 73 (loss of right to object); s 74 (immunity of arbitral institutions, etc); s 75 (charge to secure payment of solicitors' costs).

[108] ss 9–11**AA** – stay of legal proceedings.

[109] s 12 **AA** – 'Limitation' under general law; s 13 – time limits otherwise imposed.

[110] s 24 **AA** – power of court to remove arbitrator; s 31 – objection to substantive jurisdiction of tribunal; ss 67 and 68 – challenging the award: substantive jurisdiction and serious irregularity.

[111] s 43 **AA** – securing the attendance of witnesses; s 66 – enforcement of awards.

[112] ss 33, 40 **AA**: cited in full in Appendix below.

[113] s 26(1) **AA** – effect of death of arbitrator; s 28 – liability of parties for fees and expenses of arbitrators; s 29 – immunity of arbitrator; s 37(2) – items to be treated as expenses of arbitrators; s 56 – power to withhold award in case of non-payment; s 74 – immunity of arbitral institutions, etc.

Section 40: General duty of the parties:

(1) 'The parties shall do all things necessary for the proper and expeditious conduct of the arbitral proceedings.

(2) This includes – (a) complying without delay with any determination of the tribunal as to procedural or evidential matters, or with any order or directions of the tribunal, and (b) where appropriate, taking without delay any necessary steps to obtain a decision of the court on a preliminary question of jurisdiction or law (see section 32 and 45).'

Part IV

The Transnational Context

Chapter 13

English Civil Justice
in the Global Market

Contents

(1) Introduction[1]

In this chapter I will offer some views on both English civil justice's internal **13.01**
change and its links with the wider world of transnational dispute resolution.[2]
As first mentioned in chapter 1, and as developed in the succeeding chapters,
English civil justice has been evolving rapidly. There are three reasons why
these changes in England are interesting: they are a response by a major commercial legal system to modern needs; secondly, English procedure is arguably
an important half-way house between the USA and European systems; thirdly,
they are part of a wider, indeed global, context.

There have been important changes within both English and transnational **13.02**
'civil justice' during the last decade. First, over a dozen years have passed since
Lord Woolf published his interim report on 'Access to Justice' (1995) (see
2.13).[3] This provided the framework for the new procedural code, the CPR,

---

[1] I am grateful to Sir Derek Oulton, Fellow, Magdalene College, Cambridge, and Sir
Henry Brooke, former Lord Justice of Appeal, for helpful comments on a draft version of
this paper.

[2] I use the term 'civil justice' to embrace traditional litigation before the courts, arbitration, and other forms of dispute resolution such as mediation: see also chapters 1, 10 to 12.

[3] Lord Woolf *Access to Justice, Interim Report* (1995) and *Access to Justice, Final Report* (1996); on which Neil Andrews, *English Civil Procedure* (Oxford UP, 2003) ch 2;
among the responses to these reports were: S Flanders, 'Case Management: Failure in America? Success in England and Wales?' (1998) 17 CJQ 308; JA Jolowicz, 'The Woolf Report and

governing civil litigation in England and Wales. That code took effect in April 1999.[4] The English courts received significant managerial powers, and party control of proceedings was reduced (**2.17** ff).[5] Secondly, it is also ten years since the English Arbitration Act 1996 was enacted (see chapter 12).[6] This statute contains many innovations. Thirdly, during the last decade, British companies and lawyers have used mediation as another way in which disputes might be resolved, without resorting to formal civil proceedings or at least without going to trial (see chapter 11). Fourthly, there has been a steady stream of European initiatives in promoting greater co-operation between the courts of Member States and in finding common procedural tools (see the Appendix at **13.32** below). Finally, in 2006 Cambridge University Press published American Law Institute/UNIDROIT's *'Principles of Transnational Civil Procedure'*.[7] This model law presents a global vision of civil justice. It is likely to inspire developments within court procedure and arbitration.

(2) The English Tradition of Judicial Control and Influence

13.03 Judges in England have strongly influenced the development of civil procedure and, more broadly, of civil justice. The reasons are historical, institutional, and intellectual. Furthermore, under the CPR system, English judges now exercise many more procedural powers during the pre-trial stages of litigation than they have done for centuries (see, notably, **2.15** to **2.20**).

13.04 In 1994 the (then) Lord Chancellor, Lord Mackay, entrusted the daunting task of proposing reform of the civil procedure to a single man, Lord Woolf. It was a bold and brilliant act of delegation. Lord Woolf recognised the need for radical change.[8] He drew upon the experience and ideas of other jurisdictions.

---

the Adversary System' (1996) 15 CJQ 198; M Zander, 'The Government's Plans on Civil Justice' (1998) 61 MLR 383 and 'The Woolf Report: Forwards or Backwards for the New Lord Chancellor?' (1997) 16 CJQ 208; AAS Zuckerman and R Cranston (eds), *Reform of Civil Procedure: Essays on 'Access to Justice'* (Oxford UP, 1995) (essays by various authors); AAS Zuckerman, 'The Woolf Report on Access to Justice' (1997) 2 ZZPInt 31 ff.

[4] SI 1998/3132, with subsequent amendments: accessible at: http://www.justice.gov.uk/civil/procrules_fin/menus/rules.htm.

[5] On the new system from the perspective of the traditional adversarial principle, Neil Andrews, 'A New Civil Procedural Code for England: Party-Control "Going, Going, Gone"' (2000) 19 CJQ 19.

[6] For a bibliography on arbitration, see n 1 at **12.01**; on the Arbitration Act 1996, see especially, Departmental Advisory Committee of Arbitration Law Report on the Arbitration Bill; Departmental Advisory Committee of Arbitration Law Supplementary Report on the Arbitration Bill; both reports are reproduced as appendices in M Mustill and S Boyd, *Commercial Arbitration* (2nd edn, 1989, and companion volume, 2001).

[7] Accessible at: http://www.unidroit.org/english/principles/civilprocedure/main.htm.

[8] Lord Woolf, *Access to Justice, Interim Report* (1995) and *Access to Justice, Final Report* (1996); on which Neil Andrews, *English Civil Procedure* (Oxford UP, 2003) ch 2.

His plan was accepted and implemented by an efficient team. Senior judges rallied to his call and took the initiative in ensuring that the ideas were reflected in the leading decisions on the new code.[9] This was a classic example of lawyers taking charge of reforming their own system.

Part One of the CPR, the so-called 'Overriding Objective', requires the courts to accord equal respect and opportunity to each party, tailor the procedure to reflect the importance or value of the case, maintain time-discipline, and concentrate the court's and parties' energies on the central features of the case.[10] Lawyers no longer control the pace of pre-trial preparation. Instead they are required to co-operate with the court in a joint enterprise of dealing with cases justly.[11] At trial, judges make decisions sitting alone, without the assistance of fellow judges or jurors. Permission to appeal from judgments is required (**8.12** ff).[12]   **13.05**

The Civil Procedure Act 1997 gives prominence to senior judges in the moulding of procedural changes.[13] It prescribes membership of the Rule Committee.[14] The Civil Justice Council and its sub-committees can recommend procedural changes.[15] Judges are also prominent within these committees, which include practitioners, some academics, and court-users. Overall responsibility for the civil justice system rests with the Lord Chancellor, in his capacity as a Secretary of State for Justice, assisted by civil servants within the Ministry of Justice (created in 2007).[16]   **13.06**

Besides their influence on formal rules of procedure, senior English judges have also exercised their common law power of decision-making (**2.08** and **2.11**) to fashion new forms of procedure. A good example is the introduction in the 1970s of 'freezing injunctions'. This successful judicial venture was rati-   **13.07**

---

[9] Early case law illuminating the new process included: *GKR Karate (UK) Ltd v Yorkshire Post Newspapers Ltd* [2000] 1 WLR 2571, 2576–7, CA, (court taking preliminary issue); *Biguzzi v Rank Leisure plc* [1999] 1 WLR 1926, CA (range of court's disciplinary powers), on which **3.14**; *Securum Finance Ltd v Ashton* [2001] Ch 291, CA (delay; court's power to terminate litigation); *Swain v Hillman* [2000] 1 All ER 91, 92, CA (summary judgment), on which **5.20**; *Daniels v Walker* [2000] 1 WLR 1382 CA (single, joint experts) on which **7.13**; there have been many important decisions since, in which the Court of Appeal has developed and applied the general managerial tenets of the new rules.

[10] The 'Overriding Objective' is defined in CPR 1.1 (for the text, see **2.14**).

[11] CPR 1.3 states: 'The parties are required to help the court to further the overriding objective.'

[12] CPR 52.3(1); there are exceptions concerning matters affecting personal liberty.

[13] ss 2 to 4, Civil Procedure Act 1997, the full title of the committee is the Civil Procedure Rule Committee.

[14] s 2, ibid, provides for automatic membership of certain judges, including the Master of the Rolls; the power and influence of such senior judges cannot be doubted in the workings of this committee.

[15] http://www.civiljusticecouncil.gov.uk/.

[16] http://www.justice.gov.uk/.

fied by the legislature (**4.03 ff**).[17] The courts have also acted to end undesirable practices. For example, the Court of Appeal in 1966 which decisively resisted use of juries in ordinary civil trials.[18] More generally, judges have also interpreted the written rules in a purposive and creative manner.[19]

13.08   In other complementary spheres of civil justice, judges have also been active. Lord Mustill became the leading authority on the practice of commercial arbitration while he was still a full-time judge.[20] Other judges have more recently encouraged the spread of mediation (see **11.33 ff**).[21]

(3) 'Beyond the Temple':[22] New Influences upon Civil Justice

13.09   Long-term factors seem likely to weaken judicial grasp upon procedural development. In part this is because court-centred dispute resolution is in decline, and in part because judges are losing their position of pre-eminence within both the English and transnational array of dispute-resolution techniques.

Is Judicial Promotion the Height of Human Felicity?

13.10   First, the centrality of the High Court Bench is threatened. The quality of modern appointments remains high. But not all highly successful barristers now regard High Court appointment as the pinnacle of their career. Is this a problem? The author has been told that 'recent lists of highly approved candidates for High Court appointment seem as good as ever'.[23] In 2005 the Lord

---

[17] Formerly known as *Mareva* injunctions; CPR 25.1(1)(f) renames the injunction; s 37(3), Supreme Court Act 1981 acknowledged their validity; the leading work is S Gee, *Commercial Injunctions* (5th edn, 2004); see also N Andrews, *English Civil Procedure* (Oxford UP, 2003) paras 17.01 to 17.105.

[18] For brief details of the leading cases which 'killed off' civil jury trial (other than for the special categories of claim-defamation, malicious prosecution, false imprisonment, or fraud – for these, s 69, Supreme Court Act 1981), Neil Andrews, *English Civil Procedure* (Oxford UP, 2003) 34.09 n 18 and generally 34.06 to 34.10, especially noting *Ward v James* [1966] 1 QB 273, CA.

[19] For an appreciation of eight fundamental judicial innovations in civil procedure, Neil Andrews, 'Development in English Civil Procedure' (1997) ZZPInt 2, at 7 ff.

[20] M Mustill and S Boyd, *Commercial Arbitration* (2nd edn, London, 1989, and companion volume, 2001).

[21] eg, A Colman (Sir Anthony Colman, a former Commercial Court judge), 'ADR: An Irreversible Tide?' (2003) 19 Arbitration International 303.

[22] In London, 'the Temple' has been the traditional strong-hold of Barristers; of course, not all London-based barristers have chambers there; and there are many provincial chambers.

[23] Comment on draft by a member of the Court of Appeal.

Chancellor's senior official stated that 'the Lord Chancellor has a pool of strong candidates ... to inform his decisions on forthcoming High Court appointments'. In the same document, it was reported that on 35 occasions QCs had rejected offers of appointment to the Bench during the period 1991 to 2004.[24] But there has been a change. The new appointments procedure requires an application from a candidate. Because barristers will no longer have the chance to reject official invitations, it will cease to be possible to determine how many senior lawyers have decided not to aim for the High Court. Furthermore, as a former leading civil servant has observed, the need for a positive application will deter some applicants, who might fear rejection.[25]

Only a handful of judges in each decade make truly seminal contributions **13.11** to the law's development, as distinct from routine application or interpretation of relatively settled law, or minor adjustment to doctrine. It is crucial, therefore, that leading practitioners should continue to be attracted to join the Bench. Of course, there are economic reasons why highly paid lawyers might choose not to become judges, but continue in practice.

Disputants 'Voting With Their Feet'

Another reason for the relative decline in court-centred adjudication is that **13.12** there has been a significant reduction in medium-sized or large cases taken to the English courts[26] (and there has been a reduction in civil trials in the USA).[27] Issuing proceedings in the High Court has ceased to be the main response to a problematic business or civil dispute, even if it involves a significant sum.[28] In

---

[24] 'Department Evidence to the Senior Salaries Review Body' (June 2005): *www.dca. gov.uk/judicial/judgepay.pdf* at 16 and at 28.

[25] Sir Derek Oulton, Fellow, Magdalene College, Cambridge, comment to the author.

[26] For recent figures, see **10.08**; the decline is traceable to the CPR's introduction: in 'Civil Court Fees' (Court Service, September 2002), at 3.7 ff (between 1998 and 2001 there was a 22.5 per cent reduction in the number of county court claims and, during the same period, a 76 per cent fall in High Court claims.

[27] Oscar Chase, *The Rise of ADR in Cultural Context, in Law, Culture, and Ritual: Disputing Systems in Cross-Cultural Context* (New York UP, 2005) ch 6; M Galanter, 'The Vanishing Trial ... in Federal and State Courts' (2004) 1 J Empirical Legal Studies 451; J Resnik, 'For Owen M Fiss: Some Reflections on the Triumph and Death of Adjudication' (2003) 58 Miami U L Rev 173; J Resnik, 'Whither and Whether Adjudication' (2006) 86 Boston ULRev 1101, 1123 ff; J Resnik, 'Uncovering, Discovering and Disclosing How the Public Dimensions of Court-Based Processes are at Risk' (2006) 81 Chicago-Kent LR 521 and J Resnik and DE Curtis, 'From "Rites" to "Rights" of Audience: The Utilities and Contingencies of the Public's Role in Court Business' in A Masson and K O'Connor (eds), *Representation of Justice* (Brussels, 2007); A Miller, 'The Pre-trial Rush to Judgment: Are the "Litigation Explosion", "Liability Crisis", and Efficiency Clichés Eroding our Day in Court and Jury Commitments?'(2003) 78 NYULRev 982.

[28] Creation of a Supreme Court under the Constitutional Reform Act 2005 will

part this reduction in use of the High Court was caused by a jurisdictional change effected during the CPR reforms: the more attractive High Court enforcement procedures (execution by more assertive 'sheriffs', rather than county court bailiffs) for executing default judgments ceased to be available for relatively modest claims (generally on enforcement, see **8.28 ff**).

13.13   It seems unlikely that this decline in court litigation is the result of a fall in the number of disputes or legal defaults. It is more likely attributable to choices by disputants and prospective disputants. The courts have no monopoly on dispute-resolution. Their system is in competition with other forms of dispute-resolution. And there are several respects in which prospective litigants might regard litigation before the ordinary courts as problematic. This is because there are various problems intrinsic to public adjudication, however efficient or fair the court system might be:

(i) *publicity*: the hearing must take place with full publicity;[29]

(ii) *hassle or distress*: the entire civil process involves an intrusion by lawyers and the court into the ordinary affairs of private life and business; such disruption and intrusion are powerful disincentives to begin, defend, or continue medium- or long-term litigation;

(iii) *unpredictability*: uncertainty of outcome is a source of anxiety for prospective litigants on both sides; few cases of moderate complexity are 'open and shut', especially if they concern disputable matters of fact or expert opinion;

(iv) *remedial inflexibility*: if the claim succeeds, the courts cannot perform miracles; instead they can only award standard remedies which have been administered in countless similar cases; these are the mundane remedies of damages, debt, declarations, injunctions, redelivery of property; indeed, according to substantive law, these remedies accurately reflect what the claimant is owed; the claimant (and defendant) acquiesce in this remedial focus of the 'contest', even though this form of 'relief' often fails to reflect the nuances of their dis-

---

strengthen the tendency for the highest echelon of judges to devote a high percentage of their time to public law, human rights, and constitutional matters, rather than private law and commercial disputes. It is easily predicted that media attention to these high-profile cases will distract attention from the important business of providing adjudication of matters relevant to commerce: I am grateful to Professor Shetreet, Hebrew University, Jerusalem, for observations on this topic: seminar University of Cambridge, 2006.

[29] The general rule is that a hearing must be in public: CPR 39.2(1); CPR 39.2(3) and PD (39) 1.5 set out exceptions; the primary source is s 67, Supreme Court Act 1981; the requirement of publicity is also contained in Article 6(1) of the European Convention on Human Rights (incorporated in Sch 1, Human Rights Act 1998); the relevant part of Art 6(1) reads: 'Judgment shall be pronounced publicly but the press and public may be excluded from all or part of the trial in the interests of morals, public order or national security in a democratic society, where the interests of juveniles or the protection of the life of the parties so require, or to the extent strictly necessary in the opinion of the court in special circumstances where publicity would prejudice the interests of justice'; J Jaconelli, *Open Justice* (Oxford UP, 2002); J Jacob, *Civil Justice in the Age of Human Rights* (Aldershot, 2007) ch 2.

pute; as mediators are quick to observe, often the parties would prefer to have access to a more flexible portfolio of outcomes.

In response to these anticipated limitations of the court-based system of procedure, prospective disputants can pick and choose between different forms of dispute-resolution. For example, freedom of contract allows them to agree that their disputes will proceed to arbitration (see chapter 12), whether within or outside England and Wales. The parties can also choose mediation (at least as a 'first step') rather than arbitration or court-based litigation. Potential disputants' freedom of contract reaches its apogee in the 'multi-tiered' dispute-resolution agreement. This allows them to set themselves a series of steps: in-house negotiation, external mediation, and finally arbitration or a nominated court (**11.47**).[30]   **13.14**

The Age of the International Legal Practice

It is also obvious that the solicitor branch of the profession is now challenging the barrister/judicial professional axis (generally on these branches of the legal profession, **2.05** to **2.07**). Large firms offer large salaries (or partnership earnings) and (relative) security of employment. They are major recruiters of legal talent.[31] Many solicitors are leading figures within the field of international commercial dispute resolution. London law firms often have offices worldwide. They can also hire in-house barristers.[32] Many non-barrister lawyers have a 'revolving' practice as client advisors, mediators, arbitrators, and part-time judges. 'Solicitor advocates' are now a formally recognised hybrid within the English legal profession. They have the 'right of audience' in the higher courts of first instance and on appeal (**2.07**).   **13.15**

This changing scene presents an acute dilemma for some law students. It is true that very talented people are still drawn to the English Bar. As one recent member of the Court of Appeal has said: 'the intelligence of the top echelons of the young Bar is absolutely frightening'; and 'the independence of a barrister in private practice is still greatly sought after.'[33] But the risk of failure must be considered. Legal recruitment has become competitive and dynamic. There are remarkable opportunities for solicitors, whether hired by English or foreign   **13.16**

---

[30] *Cable & Wireless plc v IBM UK* [2002] 2 All ER (Comm) 1041, Colman J.

[31] However, the long hours worked in City of London commercial practices is having a debilitating effect on lawyers; some move 'side-ways' to less pressurised legal employment: *The Financial Times* 5 June, 2006, pp 1–2.

[32] For example, one of the leading law firms in London has an 'advocacy unit' to which it has recently attracted two QCs, an interesting development: http://www.herbertsmith.com/People/MurrayRosenQC.htm.

[33] Comment on draft version of this paper.

firms, and whether based in London or elsewhere, to engage in innovative work (on transactions or disputes, or both) in more than one continent.

European Law

13.17   The European Commission is another source of non-judicial influence (see the Appendix at **13.32**). It continues to expand its regulation of Member States' systems of civil justice. English judges have no direct control over this. Even the British Government has merely diplomatic influence upon these pan-European initiatives. Furthermore, decisions of the European Court of Justice and of the European Court of Human Rights are another source of external influence upon development of English civil justice (**2.11**).

Civil Justice and the Law Schools

13.18   Finally, scholarship is beginning to provide an intellectual framework for English civil justice. Traditionally, there has been no significant university influence upon the system of English civil procedure. Instead procedural luminaries on the Bench have plugged this intellectual gap.[34] However, scholars are now contributing analytical or fundamental work.[35] As the subject assumes a 'transnational' perspective, such scholarly writing and activity will become especially important (see, in particular, American Law Institute/UNIDROIT's *'Principles of Transnational Civil Procedure'*).[36] *Civil Justice Quarterly* is an important national and international forum for analysis.[37]

---

[34] Sir Jack Jacob, *The Fabric of English Civil Justice* (1987) (a classic distillation of the pre-CPR (1998) system, its traditions and values, presented as the Hamlyn Lectures for 1986); T Bingham, *The Business of Judging* (Oxford UP, 2000); M Cook, *Cook on Costs* (2007); P Hurst, *Civil Costs* (4th edn, 2007); and the judicial contributions to *Civil Procedure* (the White Book) and *The Civil Court Practice* (the Green Book).

[35] JA Jolowicz, *On Civil Procedure* (Cambridge UP, 2000); AAS Zuckerman and Ross Cranston (eds), *The Reform of Civil Procedure* (Oxford UP, 1995); AAS Zuckerman (ed), *Civil Justice in Crisis: Comparative Perspectives of Civil Procedure* (Oxford UP, 1999); *Zuckerman on Civil Procedure* (2006); R Cranston, *How Law Works: The Machinery and Impact of Civil Justice* (Oxford UP, 2006); and the various writings of the present author, including Neil Andrews, *English Civil Procedure* (Oxford UP, 2003); and earlier, on the pre-CPR system, Neil Andrews, *Principles of Civil Procedure* (1994); and note, for example, the impressive list of predominantly British academic lawyers assembled by Professors Sherr and Zander at the 'WG Hart Workshop 2007 on "Access to Justice"' in London. Foreign scholars have also shown interest, for example, the following remarkable study: A De Luca, *L'Accesso alla Giustizia in Inghilterra: fra Stato e Mercato* (Torino, 2007).

[36] (Cambridge UP, 2006); accessible at: http://www.unidroit.org/english/principles/civil procedure/main.htm.

[37] Currently edited by Adrian Zuckerman.

(4) Continuing Role of the Court System and Judicial Sanctions

As just examined, entrenched factors seem likely to undermine the centrality **13.19** of the court-system. However, it would be wrong to expect traditional litigation before the ordinary courts to disappear. The civil legal system, no less than the criminal system, provides protection and redress against disorder and unlawful conduct. After the Defence of the Realm against external aggression, the State's next most important function is to provide protection for the Queen's subjects against unlawful violence, fraud, and various forms of misconduct. Mediaeval monarchs entrusted this function to the judges.[38]

In short, a state-administered and well-sanctioned civil process is the ap- **13.20** propriate forum for dealing with various types of dispute, notably: claims to ensure payment of debts which cannot be reasonably disputed; applications to settle a multitude of family disputes; claims to obtain compensation for various civil wrongs; or to obtain injunctions against outrageous neighbours or businesses; or applications to regulate complex wills or trusts; or to provide judicial review of decisions made by Government Ministers, public authorities or municipal government.

The Common Law is remarkable in entrusting powerful remedies to the **13.21** courts and the judicial system: contempt of court supporting various injunctions; writs of possession; seizure orders; witness summonses, etc (see, notably, **8.23** to **8.35**, especially **8.33**). Furthermore, in accordance with the principle of 'comity between nations', and consistent with the United Kingdom's international treaty obligations and the requirements of European Union law, English law empowers the courts to provide orders to assist the foreign civil process (for example, the provision of 'protective relief', on which see chapter 4). Such assistance can also be offered to active or prospective foreign litigants or judgment creditors (**4.24**) either pre-judgment, when the relevant foreign proceedings are contemplated or pending, or to enforce a foreign judgment.[39]

The courts also support the system of arbitration (see chapter 12). Arbitra- **13.22** tion agreements cannot be circumvented by resort to court proceedings con-

---

[38] A relic of the mediaeval monarch's 'quasi-parental' powers (his duty to act as *parens patriae*), is the administration of funds paid into court as compensation payable to minors; this jurisdiction has long since vested in the Queen's Remembrancer and Senior Master (of the Queen's Bench); in effect the judge, acting through his court staff, acts as trustee of these funds until the former claimant reaches 18; a similar jurisdiction existed with respect to compensation paid into court for the relief of widows (whose husbands had died following the defendant's negligence); this was intended to protect 'compensation rich' widows from the cynical advances of money-grabbing suitors; new cases under this second jurisdiction ceased in the early 1960s; I am grateful to former Senior Master Robert Turner for information on these matters.

[39] For details, see the various works on private international law, notably *Dicey, Morris and Collins on the Conflicts of Laws* (14th edn, 2006).

cerning the substance of the dispute (see **12.21**). Arbitrators lack power to punish people for acts of 'contempt of court' (on which **8.33** ff). And so the arbitrator must ultimately turn to the High Court for support. Recalcitrant witnesses must be ordered to attend the arbitration hearing by judicial sanction (**12.39**). If not spontaneously honoured, arbitration awards must be enforced by use of the court-system's methods of enforcement (see **8.28** ff). In these and many other ways, the internal law of arbitration must be supplemented and reinforced by the relevant national system of controlled and legitimate force.

13.23   Mediators also require the support and co-operation of the courts in various ways (see further chapter 11). First, the mediation agreement might require the court system's recognition and enforcement (by the issue of a stay or an anti-suit injunction, **11.47**). Secondly, the mediated settlement might need to be enforced by recourse to court-based systems of enforcement (**8.28** ff). Thirdly, mediation also relies upon indirect judicial support or co-operation, for example, by the courts respecting the confidentiality of the mediation process (**11.49** ff). Finally, it should be noted that there is pressure from European authorities to have a pan-European system for accrediting mediators by central or officially regulated authority.[40]

(5) Competition between National Systems

13.24   National civil procedural systems will endure. But there are many significant differences between them. In the face of such diversity, the issue of forum-selection arises, especially when a dispute involves parties situated in different jurisdictions. One or both parties might contemplate a choice of appropriate forum. Or one party might wish to challenge his opponent's tactical decision to commence proceedings in a particular jurisdiction. Indeed sometimes the cynical choice has already been made to litigate in one State, say by seeking a negative declaration in the courts of Torpidia or Lethargia, precisely because those States' court-systems are so slow that the matter is unlikely to come to judgment for many years. Under the *lis alibi pendens* rules, other States are likely to be precluded from receiving the same dispute in parallel proceedings.[41]

---

[40] Proposal for a Directive of the European Parliament and the Council on 'certain aspects of mediation in civil and commercial matters': 22 October, 2004, 2004/0251 (COD)) (supplemented by a Commission Staff Working Paper 'Annex', of same date, SEC (2004) 1314); there is already in operation a Code of Practice; the position is evolving rapidly; the reader is referred to the web-site of the Civil Justice Mediation Council (http://www.adr. civiljusticecouncil.gov.uk).

[41] This has produced difficult and controversial decisions of the European Court of Justice: see *Turner v Grovit* (Case C-159/02) [2005] 1 AC 101; *Erich Gasser GmbH v MISAT Srl* (Case C-116/02) [2005] 1 QB 1; *Owusu v Jackson* (Case C-281/02) [2005] QB 801; on

The transnational market-place for dispute-resolution is flexible. Litigation **13.25**
advisors are aware that their national court system might not provide an adequate forum. They might prefer cross-border systems of arbitration, mediation
or quasi-judicial rules. There is a commercial incentive to devise such alternatives. Innovation does not require enactment by sovereign states of a formal
code of procedure.[42] Indeed the most powerful engine for procedural inven-
tion is not the mind of the solitary reformer, nor even an expert team's working group or colloquium, but the transnational and internal market-places for
civil dispute-resolution.

Competition between national procedural systems is both inevitable and **13.26**
desirable. It is inevitable because, even if the leading economic nations were to
unite and adopt the same set of procedural rules and institutions, there would
be differences in the efficiency and fairness with which these rules were applied. Such competition is also desirable because no one knows which is the
best procedural code or the optimal mix of particular procedural institutions
and methods. So it is necessary to experiment, compare and contrast.[43]

How does English justice stand in this competitive system? London lawyers **13.27**
(and the English courts) know that they are in competition with foreign lawyers and systems to win a larger slice of the transnational cake. England offers
a superb opportunity to receive professional litigation assistance from specialist lawyers, with excellent modern technical support. Specialist judges can
hear the case (for example, in the Commercial Court, **2.04** and **3.19** ff).[44] Unlike some civil trials in the USA, nearly all English civil judgments are reached
and sums fixed without the uncertainty of jury deliberation (for the vestigial
presence of jury trial in English civil actions, **8.02**).[45] In England, there are
ample opportunities to seek protective, interim or summary relief (chapters 4
and 5). 'Protective relief' includes support for civil 'proceedings commenced or

---

the first two of this triad, Neil Andrews, 'Abuse of Process and Obstructive Tactics under
the Brussels Jurisdictional System: Unresolved problems for the European Authorities'
(2005) European Community Private L Rev 8 (this journal is also entitled Zeitschrift für
Gemeinschaftsprivatrecht and Revue de droit privé international) .

[42] eg in large international construction projects, 'fast track' adjudication is often agreed
by parties, who refer disputes to 'dispute review boards'; the World Bank has a standard
bidding document in this matter: see http://*www.freshfields.com/publications/pdfs/2006/
15119/pdf* for details.

[43] AAS Zuckerman, 'Conference on "The ALI-UNIDROIT Principles and Rules of Transnational Civil Procedure"' (2002) CJQ 322.

[44] Specifically on the English Commercial Court, see Neil Andrews, *English Civil Justice
and Remedies: Progress and Challenges: Nagoya Lectures* (Shinzan Sha Publishers, Tokyo,
2007) ch 3.

[45] Jury trial is confined to serious criminal cases (for example, murder, rape, armed robbery) and civil actions for defamation or misconduct by the police (the torts of defamation,
malicious prosecution, and false imprisonment): Neil Andrews, *English Civil Procedure*
(Oxford UP, 2003) 34–06 ff.

to be commenced' anywhere in the world (**4.24** and **4.25**). The courts emphasise the importance of granting freezing injunctions to assist other jurisdictions, particularly in the struggle against large and sophisticated fraud.[46] The system of disclosure of documents provides the key to unlock the opponent's database or folders (**6.21**).[47] The court can receive expert evidence from hand-picked specialists (generally, see chapter 7). Each party will have abundant opportunity to present its version of events and its legal contentions. Trial by ambush has been prohibited (**6.02**).[48] Specialist advocates appear at hearings (**2.07**). Civil appeals are not automatic, but require judicial permission (**8.12**ff).[49] The system of enforcement is efficient and potent (**8.28** ff). Delay in the disposal of court litigation has been reduced, partly because there are fewer cases clogging the courts (**2.22**), especially at trial, and partly because case-management prevents litigation from meandering without time-tabling or other control (**3.13** ff). But large cases can become prolonged (**3.19** ff).[50]

13.28   However, there is the enduring problem of cost, sometimes exacerbated by procedural complexity. Billing by the hour provides an economic incentive to lawyers to increase the intensity and complexity of proceedings (**9.03**).[51]

(6) Innovative Thinking on Civil Justice

13.29 It is sometimes clear that one system is superior to another in some respect. Examples of such manifest defects are: judges who are corrupt, or who lack the understanding to cope with difficult issues; processes which take many years even in relatively straightforward instances; discovery operations which produce massive fees but little understanding of the case's real merits; appeal procedures which take a further age to be exhausted; wholly inefficient en-

---

[46] *Crédit Suisse Fides Trust SA v Cuoghi* [1998] QB 818, CA; *Ryan v Friction Dynamics Ltd* (2 June 2000, Neuberger J); on this line of cases, see A Johnson in M Andenas, N Andrews, R Nazzini (eds), *The Future of Transnational Commercial Litigation: English responses to the ALI/UNIDROIT Draft Principles and Rules of Transnational Civil Procedure* (British Institute of Comparative and International Law, London, 2006).

[47] See also Neil Andrews, *English Civil Procedure* (Oxford UP, 2003) ch 26.

[48] PD (39) 3.2 provides that trial bundles, exchanged by the parties and delivered to the court, should include: the claim form and statements of case; a case summary; witness statements 'to be relied on as evidence' and witness summaries; plans, photographs etc; expert reports.

[49] CPR 52.3(1); there are exceptions concerning matters affecting personal liberty: see **8.12**.

[50] On the collapse of BCCI trial, the longest civil trial in English history, *The Times* 13 April 2006 52–3, 57; for the House of Lords' pre-trial decision not to strike out this claim, see *Three Rivers DC v Bank of England (No 3)* [2001] 2 All ER 513, HL) which the author criticised, see Neil Andrews, *English Civil Procedure* (Oxford UP, 2003) 20.17 to 20.19.

[51] Generally on the costs system, see chapter 9; and the specialist works: M Cook, *Cook on Costs* (2007); P Hurst, *Civil Costs* (4th edn, 2007).

forcement rules; systematic failure to respect or respond efficiently to other systems' requests for legitimate support in matters of evidence or protective relief, or requests for enforcement of awards or judgments.

The Working Group's Rome deliberation in the years 2000 to 2003 pro-   **13.30**
duced American Law Institute/UNIDROIT's *'Principles of Transnational
Civil Procedure'*[52] (they were preceded by the 'Storme' project in Europe,
which was the first attempt at recognising a transnational set of common
principles).[53] The American Law Institute/UNIDROIT project was an interesting experiment in selecting some of the better ideas from this global mix of
procedural institutions and practices. This exercise was not an attempt to
eliminate national differences and prevent competition between rival systems.
Instead it was a quest for similarities between civilised systems and traditions.
In general, the American Law Institute/UNIDROIT *'Principles'*, properly implemented and administered, might support an efficient, just and modern
system of adjudication and (with some modification) arbitration.[54] They will
serve as a powerful catalyst for procedural discussion[55] and as a 'model law'
enabling reformers and dispute-resolution technicians to rise above national
difference. On some matters it was necessary for the Working Party to compromise, or leave things to be decided later by the relevant national or supra-
national organization. For example, the comment on principle 22.4, concern-

---

[52] Published in 2006 by Cambridge UP as *Principles of Transnational Civil Procedure*; the working group's membership was as follows: Neil Andrews, Clare College, Cambridge, UK; Professor Frédérique Ferrand, Lyon, France; Professor Pierre Lalive, University of Geneva and practice as an arbitrator, Switzerland; Professor Masanori Kawano, Nagoya University, Japan; Madame Justice Aida Kemelmajer de Carlucci, Supreme Court, Mendoza, Argentina; Professor Geoffrey Hazard, USA; Professor Ronald Nhlapo, formerly of the Law Commis-sion, South Africa; Professor Dr iur Rolf Stürner, University of Freiburg, Germany. The two General Reporters for the UNIDROIT project were Professors Hazard and Stürner; the two reporters for the ALI project were Professors Hazard and Taruffo (University of Pavia, Italy).

[53] M Storme (ed, et al), *Approximation of Judiciary Law in the European Union* (Gent, 1994) (Professor Marcel Storme is the long-serving President of the International Associa-tion of Procedural Law).

[54] For comments on the project, see the bibliographies in *ALI/UNIDROIT: Principles of Transnational Civil Procedure* (Cambridge UP, 2006); see especially the special issue of the Uniform Law Review (2002) Vol VI, for many articles discussing this project; G Hazard Jr et al, 'Principles and Rules of Transnational Civil Procedure' 33 NYU J Int L and Pol 769; R Stürner, 'Some European Remarks on a New Joint Project of the American Law Institute and UNIDROIT' (2000) 34 Int L 1071.

[55] For example, M Andenas, N Andrews, R Nazzini (eds), *The Future of Transnational Commercial Litigation: English responses to the ALI/UNIDROIT Draft Principles and Rules of Transnational Civil Procedure* (British Institute of Comparative and International Law, London, 2006); and P Fouchard (ed), *Vers un Proces Civil Universel? Les Règles Trans-nationales de Procédure Civile de L'American Law Institute* (Paris, 2001); Stephen Gold-stein, 'Revisiting Preliminary Relief in Light of the ALI/UNIDROIT Principles and the New Israeli Rules' in *Studia in honorem: Pelayia Yessiou*-Faltsi (Athens, 2007) 273–96.

ing use of court-appointed or party-appointed experts states (see further **7.19**):

'Use of experts is common in complex litigation. Court appointment of a neutral expert is the practice in most civil-law systems and in some common-law systems. However, party-appointed experts can provide valuable assistance in the analysis of difficult factual issues. Fear that party appointment of experts will devolve into a "battle of experts" and thereby obscure the issues is generally misplaced. In any event, this risk is offset by the value of such evidence. Expert testimony may be received on issues of foreign law.'

(7) Conclusion

13.31   There have been six main points.

The Changing Face of Civil Justice in the Global Age

(1) Global businesses, serviced by large law firms, expect to choose the optimal system of dispute-resolution, whether that might be litigation, arbitration, or mediation.

(2) Within the major trading nations, including England, the influence of the judiciary is likely to diminish because of this powerful privatised justice movement.

The Enduring Need for Civil Courts and State Systems of Enforcement

(3) However, the state system of court-based litigation and sanctions will not disappear; not only are there certain types of dispute which are especially suitable for court litigation, or only capable of just resolution before such a strong and public tribunal; but the state system also supports non-judicial systems by providing protective relief, compelling evidence to be adduced, and enforcing arbitration awards or settlement agreements.

Common Procedural Principles among Nations

(4) National judicial systems should co-operate in formal ways. Civilised nations should also work towards establishing common procedural standards. However, harmonisation of procedure on all points of detail is a remote possibility.

(5) Competition between national civil justice systems will continue and is also desirable.

Innovation

(6) The power of new procedural thinking should not be resisted for chauvinistic reasons.[56] Procedural experts should keep their minds open to two possibilities: that there are better ways of doing similar things; and that from time to time exciting ways of doing quite new things will emerge.[57]

(8) Appendix: The European Union and Civil Justice

The major sources of information on this topic are: 13.32

---

[56] John H Langbein, 'Cultural Chauvinism in Comparative Law' (1997) 5 Cardozo J of Int & Comp L 41.

[57] Recent examples: D Asser et al, 'A summary of the interim report on Fundamental Review of the Dutch Law of Civil Procedure' (2003) 8 ZZPInt 329–87; US law, G Hazard and M Taruffo, *American Civil Procedure* (Yale UP, New Haven, 1993); Oscar Chase, *The Rise of ADR in Cultural Context, in Law, Culture, and Ritual: Disputing Systems in Cross-Cultural Context* (New York Univ Press, 2005); J Resnik, *Processes of the Law* (Foundation Press, New York, 2004); S Subrin and M Woo, *Litigating in America* (Aspen, New York, 2006); and on German law, PL Murray and R Stürner, *German Civil Justice* (Durham, USA, 2004); and on a large range of systems, various authors in: W Rechberger and Klicka (eds), *Procedural Law on the Threshold of a New Millenium, XI. World Congress of Procedural Law*, (Center for Legal Competence, Vienna 2002); M Storme (ed), *Approximation of Judiciary Law in the EU* (Dordrecht, 1994); M Storme (ed), *Procedural Laws in Europe – Towards Harmonization*, (Maklu, Antwerpen/Apeldoorn, 2003); M Storme and B Hess (eds), *Discretionary Power of the Judge: Limits and Control* (Kluwer, Dordrecht, 2003); R van Rhee, *European Traditions in Civil Procedure* (Intersentia and Hart, Oxford, 2005); L Cadiet, T Clay, E Jeuland (eds), *Médiation et arbitrage –Alternative dispute resolution – Alternative à la justice ou justice alternative? Perspectives comparatives* (Lexis Nexis Litec, Paris, 2005); N Trocker and V Varano (eds), *The Reforms of Civil Procedure in Comparative Perspective* (Torino, 2005); Oscar Chase, Helen Hershkoff, Linda Silberman, Vincenzo Varano, Yasuhei Taniguchi, Adrian Zuckerman, *Civil Procedure in Comparative Context* (Thomson West, 2007); the 2007 World Congress, Brazil, for which see n 73 at **2.26**; A Uzelac and C van Rhee (eds) *Public and Private Justice* (Antwerp, 2007); V Varano (ed), *L'Altro Giustizia* (Milano, 2007); on 'transnational principles', ALI/UNIDROIT's *Principles of Transnational Civil Procedure* (Cambridge UP, 2006); on this project, H Kronke (ed), special issue of the Uniform Law Review (2002) Vol VI; M Andenas, N Andrews, R Nazzini (eds), *The Future of Transnational Commercial Litigation: English responses to the ALI/UNIDROIT Draft Principles and Rules of Transnational Civil Procedure* (British Institute of Comparative and International Law, London, 2006); and P Fouchard (ed), *Vers un Proces Civil Universel? Les Règles Transnationales de Procédure Civile de L'American Law Institute* (Paris, 2001).

the European Judicial Network's website (in many languages): http://ec.europa.eu/civiljustice/

on the whole range of matters, A Layton and H Mercer, *European Civil Practice* (2nd edn, 2004); on jurisdiction and enforcement of foreign judgments, the leading works on private international law, *Dicey, Morris, and Collins on the Conflict of Laws* (14th edn, 2006) and A Briggs and P Rees, *Civil Jurisdiction and Judgments* (4th edn, 2005).

Topics covered by existing EU rules are:

Jurisdiction and Enforcement of Judgments:

The revised 'Brussels Convention': Council Regulation 44/2001 of 22 December 2001 on 'jurisdiction and the recognition and enforcement of judgments in civil and commercial matters'; on which see the report by B Hess, T Pfeiffer and P Schlosser, 2007;

Related Regulations: Regulation (EC) No 805/2004 of the European Parliament and of the Council, 21 April 2004, creating a 'European Enforcement Order' for uncontested claims and Council Regulation 2201/2003/EC of 27 November 2003 concerning 'jurisdiction and the recognition and enforcement of judgments in matrimonial matters and the matters of parental responsibility', repealing Regulation (EC) No 1347/2000.

Judicial Co-operation:

Council Decision 2001/470 EC, 28 May 2001, establishing a European Judicial Network in civil and commercial matters;

Council Regulation 743/2002, 25 April 2002, establishing a general Community framework of activities to facilitate the implementation of judicial co-operation in civil matters.

Service of Process:

Council Regulation 1348/2000, 29 May 2000, on the service in Member States of judicial and extra-judicial documents in civil or commercial Matters [as between EU Member States, this Regulation supersedes the Hague Convention on the Service Abroad of Judicial and Extra-judicial Documents in Civil or Commercial Matters (15 November 1965)];

See also the Report of the European Commission, 1 October 2004 (COM (2004) 603 final) on the application of this Regulation; and see the proposal for amendment of this Regulation, 11 July 2005: COM (2205) 305 final/2; 2005/0126 (COD).

Evidence:

Council Regulation 1206/2001, 28 May 2001, on 'co-operation between the courts of the Member States in the taking of evidence in civil or commercial matters' (supported by a 'Practice Guide for the Application of the Regulation on the Taking of Evidence').

Injunctions in support of consumer protection:

Directive 98/27 EC, 19 May 1998, on 'injunctions for the protection of consumers' interests'.

Insolvency Proceedings:

Council Regulation 1346/2000.

Mediation: European Code of Practice

Already in operation: http://ec.europa.eu/civiljustice/adr/adr_ec_code_conduct_en. htm.

Proposals:

Proposed Directive on Mediation

Proposal for a Directive of the European Parliament and the Council on 'certain aspects of mediation in civil and commercial matters': 22 October, 2004, 2004/0251 (COD)) (supplemented by a Commission Staff Working Paper 'Annex', of same date, SEC (2004) 1314); there is already in operation a Code of Practice (see above).

Order for Payment Procedure

Proposal for a Regulation of the European Parliament and of the Council creating a 'European payment' order (streamlined process for payment of debts where no defence is raised): COM/2004/0173 final/3; COD 2004/0055.

Small Claims Proceedings

Proposal for a Regulation of the European Parliament and the Council establishing a 'European Small Claims Procedure': 15 March, 2005, COM 2005/0087 final; COD 2005/0020.

Competition Proceedings

A Green Paper recommending a complex set of procedural steps to facilitate greater access to justice and private claims-making by those affected by anti-competitive practice within the EU: 'Damages Actions for breach of EC antitrust rules': 19 December 2005: COM (2005) 672; on which C Hodges, 'Competition enforcement, regulation and civil justice: what is the case?' (2006) 43 CMLR 1; see also Hodges, 'The Europeanisation of Civil Justice: Trends and Issues' (2007) CJQ 96, which includes reference to the Department of Trade and Industry's (UK) July 2006 consultation of a UK Representative Actions mechanism: http://www.dti.gov.uk/consultations/page30259.html.

Part V

Special Proceedings
for Complex Claims

Chapter 14

Multi-Party Litigation[1]

Contents

(1) Introduction

'Multi-party' litigation occurs when there are many claimants and defendants, **14.01** or even large numbers on both sides of the action. Accommodating such large litigation is a challenge. There is an enormous literature on this topic, concerning both English law[2] and other systems.[3] In England 'multi-party' litigation can take one of three forms: representative proceedings;[4] mass claims under a

---

[1] See also the longer treatment of this topic in the author's contribution to the Duke Law School colloquium in Geneva (co-ordinated by T Rowe) (2000), N Andrews, 'Multi-Party Proceedings in England: Representative and Group Actions' (2001) Duke J Com Int L 249–67, and in his 2003 textbook: Neil Andrews, *English Civil Procedure* (Oxford UP, 2003) ch 41.

[2] Besides the author's discussion (see n 1 above), see: C Hodges, *Multi-Party Actions* (Oxford UP, 2001); C Hodges, 'The Europeanisation of Civil Justice: Trends and Issues' (2007) 26 CJQ 96; M Mildred, 'Group Actions' in GG Howells (ed) *The Law of Product Liability* (2001); R Mulheron, *The Class Action in Common Law Systems: A Comparative Perspective* (Hart, Oxford, 2004); R Mulheron, 'Some Difficulties with Group Litigation Orders – And Why a Class Action is Superior' (2005) 24 CJQ 40; R Mulheron, 'From Representative Rule to Class Action: Steps rather than Leaps' (2005) 24 CJQ 424; Jillaine Seymour, 'Representative Proceedings and the Future of Multi-Party Actions' (1999) 62 MLR 564–84; and 'Judicial Response to the Representative Parties Rule in England and Australia' (D Phil thesis, Oxford Univ, 2001); Lord Woolf, 'Access to Justice: Final Report' (June 1996) 223–248; *Zuckerman on Civil Procedure* (2006) 12.20 ff.

[3] The voluminous 'foreign material' is presented in a bibliography in the final footnote, n 60, at the end of this chapter.

[4] CPR 19, Section II; Neil Andrews, *English Civil Procedure* (Oxford UP, 2003) 41.57 ff; N Andrews, 'Multi-Party Proceedings in England: Representative and Group Actions' (2001) Duke J Com Int L 249, 250–7.

'group litigation order';[5] or consolidated litigation (procedurally a rather straightforward type of litigation, which will not be further discussed).[6] These large actions should be contrasted with run-of-the-mill procedural joinder of small numbers of parties. Thus where two claimants or two defendants are involved, the matter is a mere question of joinder of parties.[7] Similarly, when a defendant seeks a contribution from a third party, the latter being annexed to the main action, this is a well-regulated and largely unproblematic matter of ordinary procedure.[8] Instead this chapter concerns litigation where the relevant 'parties' often run into the tens, hundreds, even thousands. As we shall see, a person whose legal interests can be directly affected by the outcome of civil litigation (other than merely as a result of a change in the law, a 'new precedent', achieved during the litigation) can be a 'party' in a true sense to the litigation, or he might be subject to the litigation as a 'represented' person. In this situation, only the 'representative' is a 'party' in the full sense (see, **14.08** for details).[9]

(2) Representative Proceedings

14.02 Representative proceedings are relatively uncommon in England.[10] Mulheron has conveniently listed many procedural differences between 'class actions' (as adopted, with variations, in the USA, Australia and Canada – British Colum-

---

[5] CPR 19, Section III; and Practice Direction 19B; Neil Andrews, *English Civil Procedure* (Oxford UP, 2003) 41.10 ff.

[6] N Andrews, 'Multi-Party Proceedings in England: Representative and Group Actions' (2001) Duke J Com Int L 249, 257; noting CPR 3.1(2)(g); 19.1; 19.2(3); ordinary joinder of co-claimants in *Lubbe v Cape plc* [2000] 1 WLR 1545, HL, resulted in over 3,000 claimants seeking personal injury damages against a multi-national company concerning its manufacturing activities in South Africa.

[7] CPR 19.1 to 19.4, 19.5

[8] CPR 20.5.

[9] On the same point, see further Neil Andrews, *English Civil Procedure* (Oxford UP, 2003), 41.62 ff.

[10] On the position in European countries, C Hodges, 'The Europeanisation of Civil Justice: Trends and Issues' (2007) 26 CJQ 96, 114 ff; as for the position elsewhere in the common law world, R Mulheron, *The Class Action in Common Law Systems: A Comparative Perspective* (Hart, Oxford, 2004); for literature on the US class action, see the final note in this chapter; for possible English changes in the context of consumer claims for compensation, see the Department of Trade and Industry's 'Representative Actions in Consumer Legislation', consultation paper, 2006; on line at *www.dti.gov.uk/consultations/page30259.html* (contemplating representative proceedings by designated bodies to obtain damages on behalf of named individuals, rather than a class of consumers in general).

bia and Ontario) and English representative proceedings.[11] The current English rule provides:[12]

(1) Where more than one person has the same interest in a claim – *a.* the claim may be begun; or *b.* the court may order that the claim be continued, by or against any one or more of the persons who have the same interest as representatives of any other persons who have that interest.
(2) The court may direct that a person may not act as a representative.
(3) Any party may apply to the court for an order under paragraph (2).
(4) Unless the court otherwise directs any judgment or order given in a claim in which a party is acting as a representative under this rule – (a). is binding on all persons represented in the claim; but (b). may only be enforced by or against a person who is not a party to the claim with the permission of the court.

Representative proceedings can provide an efficient means of gaining 'closure' of a dispute affecting a host of persons. A good example is the *Equitable Life* case, where a defendant life insurance company sponsored a representative action. Ultimately, the House of Lords issued a declaration in this action.[13] That declaration established the true interpretation of a clause in the defendant company's life assurance policy. Ninety thousand policy-holders were bound by this decision. The representative mechanism can also be used for effective injunctive relief against a disruptive unincorporated association (a 'protest group').[14]   **14.03**

However, representative proceedings remain distinctly marginal in England. There are two reasons for this. First, the courts have interpreted the main rule, cited at **14.02**, in a restrictive way. This has severely reduced the opportunity to use this type of action as a means of obtaining compensation on behalf of individual members of the represented class (see further **14.05** to **14.07**). Secondly, there is an economic deterrent to the bringing of such proceedings. This concerns the claimant's personal 'costs risk'. As we shall see, even if the claim is won, the claimant might be unable to recover costs from the members of the class. The costs risk is, however, even more acute if he loses the case, because then he will be personally liable for the opponent's costs (on the   **14.04**

---

[11] R Mulheron, 'From Representative Rule to Class Action: Steps rather than Leaps' (2005) 24 CJQ 424, 445–6, notably judicial control of settlement; aggregated assessment of damages; payments of pecuniary recovery into a fund; cy-pres distribution of the fund; protection of the representative party's right to recoup costs from this fund; judicial monitoring of lawyers' remuneration, etc.

[12] CPR 19.6; on CPR 19.6(4), see *Huntingdon Life Sciences Group plc v Stop Huntingdon Animal Cruelty (SHAC)* [2007] EWHC 522 (QB); see also J Seymour [2007] CLJ 605.

[13] *Equitable Life Assurance Society v Hyman* [2002] 1 AC 408, HL; on which, Neil Andrews, *English Civil Procedure* (Oxford UP, 2003) 41.83.

[14] *Oxford University v Webb* [2006] EWHC 2490 (QB), Irwin J applying CPR 19.6, and considering, at [56] ff, *M Michael's (Furrier's) Limited v Askew* (CA, unreported, 23 June 1983) and other authorities; see also *Huntingdon Life Sciences Group plc v Stop Huntingdon Animal Cruelty (SHAC)* [2007] EWHC 522 (QB).

'costs risk' see further **14.08**). These two factors, the questions of damages and costs, will now be explained.

14.05   It is extremely rare for English representative proceedings to culminate in a damages award in favour of the represented class. Damages have been awarded in this context only if: (i) the global amount owing to the represented class is known, and the individuals' shares are readily ascertainable;[15] or (ii) the members of the class are content for their damages to be worked out in a post-judgment 'inquiry' and then to be paid to a special fund.[16]

14.06   Why is this? Before the CPR, the stumbling-block was the courts' literal and narrow interpretation of the leading statutory phrase, *'where more than one person has the same interest in a claim'*.[17] It had been held not to be enough that the suggested class of claimants is suing in respect of the same cause of action (for example, in contract or in the tort of negligence); nor that their claims raise strikingly similar factual issues, perhaps arising from the same incident. The presence, or even the possible presence, of different defences (for example, individual contractual clauses imposing limitations upon liability or, in the case of negligence claims in tort, the possible presence of different degrees of contributory negligence), would preclude a representative claim. Typical of the English courts' unwillingness to accede to damages claims in this context was the Court of Appeal's (majority) analysis in *Markt & Co Ltd v Knight SS Co Ltd* (1910)[18] (the rather convoluted reasoning of the three judges is summarised in the note below).[19] Judicial crafting in 1981 of a two-stage procedure – (I)

---

[15] As in the claim for economic loss resulting from a maritime collision (the claimants' total loss, already incurred, was ascertained at the time of the litigation): *Monarch SS Co Ltd v Greystoke Castle (Cargo Owners)* [1947] AC 265, HL; on which, Neil Andrews, *English Civil Procedure* (Oxford UP, 2003) 41.81.

[16] *EMI Records Ltd v Riley* [1981] 1 WLR 923, 926, Dillon J; on which, Neil Andrews, *English Civil Procedure* (Oxford UP, 2003) 41.82; and R Mulheron, 'From Representative Rule to Class Action: Steps rather than Leaps' (2005) 24 CJQ 424, 435.

[17] CPR 19.6(1), cited at **14.02** above.

[18] *Markt* case, [1910] 2 KB 1021, 1030, 1035, 1040, CA, on this decision, see the next note.

[19] In the *Markt* case, [1910] 2 KB 1021, the Court of Appeal stated, in terms which are technically obiter dicta (on that point, Neil Andrews, *Principles of Civil Procedure* (1994) 7–005), that the claims for compensation by 44 cargo-owners against the defendant carrier, based on alleged breach of separate contracts, could not proceed by representative proceedings; Vaughan-Williams LJ, ibid, at 1030, emphasised the possibly heterogeneous nature of the set of (contractual) bills of lading applicable between the cargo-owners and the carrier; Fletcher-Moulton LJ, ibid at 1035, took the severe view that an individual claim for damages (whether or not founded on breach of contract) is by definition not a claim for common relief, and therefore incompatible with the spirit of representative proceedings, as earlier expressed by Lord Macnaghten in *Duke of Bedford v Ellis* [1901] AC 1, 8, HL, who said: 'Given a common interest and a common grievance, a representative suit was in order if the relief sought was in its nature beneficial to all whom the plaintiff proposed to represent.' The dissentient on the representative action point in the *Markt* case, Buckley LJ, [1910] 2 KB 1021, 1048, considered that a representative action could proceed on the basis of a declara-

representative action establishing the defendant's liability towards members of the represented class, with (II) individual claims by members of that class to quantify their recoverable loss – did not stimulate significant use of representative proceedings.[20]

However, recent first instance decisions place emphasis on the notion of a **14.07** common interest, as distinct from an identical set of claims. These decisions also emphasise the wider procedural aim of promoting efficient administration of justice. In *Independiente Ltd v Music Trading On-Line (HK) Ltd* (2003) Morritt V-C said:[21]

'provisions of the civil procedure rules ... emphasise the need to interpret the phrase "the same interest" and to apply the provisions of CPR Rule 19.6 both flexibly and in conformity with the overriding objective [in CPR Part 1]. Accordingly there are three questions: do the [suggested class members] have (1) a common interest, (2) a common grievance and (3) is the relief sought by the claimants in its nature beneficial to the [class members]?'

It is possible, and certainly desirable, that a strong Court of Appeal will endorse this liberal tendency and not follow the pre-CPR decisions, such as the *Markt* case, cited at **14.06**. However, even if fresh flexibility is exhibited on the interpretation of 'same interest', it is unlikely that a torrent of litigation will ensue. This is because the costs problem (see the next paragraph) will continue to inhibit recourse to this procedure.

The costs problem arises in this way. Represented parties are not fully- **14.08** fledged 'parties' to the action. Therefore, they are not subject *as parties* to liability for costs[22] or documentary disclosure. The proceedings can be com-

---

tion of liability for breach of contract; Buckley LJ's suggestion foreshadowed Vinelott J's decision in the *Prudential* case, [1981] Ch 229, on which see the next note; see further on the 1910 case, Neil Andrews, *Principles of Civil Procedure* (1994) 7–005; and the excellent analysis of the requirement that the class of represented persons and the representative claimant should have the 'same interest', under CPR 19.6, by R Mulheron 'From Representative Rule to Class Action: Steps rather than Leaps' (2005) 24 CJQ 424, 426–431, 433–5, 437, esp 428–30.

[20] *Prudential Assurance Co Ltd v Newman Industries Ltd (No 1)* [1981] Ch 229, Vinelott J (not disturbed on this point on appeal, [1982] 1 Ch 204, 222–4, CA); on Vinelott J's 2-stage procedure, Neil Andrews, *English Civil Procedure* (Oxford UP, 2003) 41.75 ff; JA Jolowicz [1980] CLJ 237.

[21] *Independiente* case [2003] EWHC 470 (Ch), Morritt V-C at [23]; and see generally his discussion at [21] to [32]; on this decision, Mulheron (2005) 24 CJQ 424, at 426–7, and J Seymour (2005) 24 CJQ 16–22; see also *Howells v Dominion Insurance Co Ltd* [2005] EWHC 552 (QB), on which J Seymour (2005) 24 CJQ 309–315; and *Sharma v Yardley* [2005] EWHC 3076 (Ch) at [8], per Judge Norris QC.

[22] The costs point was been affirmed in *Howells v Dominion Insurance Co Ltd* [2005] EWHC 552 (QB), on which J Seymour (2005) 24 CJQ 309–315; see also Neil Andrews, *English Civil Procedure* (Oxford UP, 2003), 41.63, 41.89 noting *Price v Rhondda UDC* [1923] WN 228; (1923) 130 LT 156, Eve J; for the suggestion that these decisions should be reconsidered, see Waller J in *Bank of America National Trust and Savings Association v John Taylor* [1992] 1 Lloyd's Rep 484, 495.

menced without their consent.[23] The action can be settled without their approval.[24] It follows that the starting-point remains that a representative must bear the entire cost of such litigation if the case is lost. Even if the representative wins the case, there is the risk that he might not succeed in recovering all his costs from the losing opponent. This costs 'short-fall' might ultimately be borne by representative if he cannot persuade his fellow represented parties to share the burden equitably. For these reasons, prospective representative claimants will be apprehensive about their personal liability for costs. In short, 'costs' have a 'chilling' effect on English representative proceedings. And more cold water is poured on this procedure by the general inability to obtain damages at large on behalf of the class.

(3) Group Litigation Orders ('GLO')[25]

14.09 Such orders are the mainstay of the English system's treatment of multi-party litigation (an 'opt-in' system, see **14.12** below). A GLO is a special form of multiple joinder, by listing of claims on a group register. Its main components are:[26] (i) the court must approve a group litigation order; (ii) unlike the representative model (see **14.08** above), group litigation involves 'opting-in' by each individual; (iii) a group member enjoys both membership of the group and the general status of a fully-fledged 'party to civil proceedings'; (iv) during the progress of the GLO, the court will exercise extensive case management and

---

[23] R Mulheron, 'From Representative Rule to Class Action: Steps rather than Leaps' (2005) 24 CJQ 424, 442–3, noting *Independiente Ltd v Music Trading On-Line (HK) Ltd* [2003] EWHC 470 (Ch) at [32] and *Howells v Dominion Insurance Co Ltd* [2005] EWHC 552 (QB) at [26]; see now J Seymour [2007] CLJ 605.

[24] On the 'non-party' status of represented persons, Neil Andrews, *English Civil Procedure* (Oxford UP, 2003) 41.62 ff.

[25] R Mulheron, 'Some Difficulties with Group Litigation Orders – And Why a Class Action is Superior' (2005) 24 CJQ 40, 45 neatly lists six prerequisites for a GLO (see further **14.10** ff): (1) a number of claims; (2) common or related issues of fact or law; (3) consistency with CPR Part 1, the 'Overriding Objective'; (4) consent of the Lord Chief Justice, Vice-Chancellor or Head of Civil Justice; (5) neither consolidation nor representative proceedings would be appropriate; (6) class needs to be defined; on this last point Mulheron notes PD 19B, paras 3.2(2), (3), where the text refers, respectively, to the need to specify the 'number and nature of claims already issued' and 'the number of parties likely to be involved)'.

[26] See also the summary by Lord Walker in *Autologic Holdings plc v Commissioners of Inland Revenue* [2005] UKHL 54; [2006] 1 AC 118, at [86]: 'The key features and normal effect of any GLO are that it identifies the common issues which are a pre-condition for participation in a GLO; it provides for the establishment and maintenance of a register of GLO claims; it gives the managing court wide powers of case management, including the selection of test claims and the appointment of a lead solicitor for the claimants or the defendants, as appropriate; it provides for judgments on test claims to be binding on the other parties on the group register; and it makes special provision for costs orders.'

issue directions; (v) decisions on 'common' issues are binding on, and in favour of, the group; (vi) group members share liability for costs incurred concerning the 'common' issues. These and related points will now be explained.

First, there is the question of 'funding'. In general, apart from family dis- **14.10** putes where special social factors apply, 'economic access to justice'[27] in Eng-land is no longer promoted by public expenditure on legal aid. Instead there has been a major shift towards the 'privatised' conditional fee system ('CFA') (generally on the CFA system, see **9.19** ff).[28] The successful party's lawyer is then entitled (a) to his ordinary fee, with (b) the bonus of a percentage 'success fee' (not to exceed 100 per cent) of that fee. In accordance with the general costs-shifting rule, however, both items (a) and (b) are payable by the defeated party. If the CFA-funded party loses the case, he is not liable to pay any fee to his lawyer. But he must pay the other party's costs. However, insurance is available, as part of the CFA package, to cover this costs risk (known as 'after-the-event' insurance for legal expenses). The cost of such ATE cover is also payable by the defeated defendant, in accordance with the costs-shifting rule. The English system's adoption of 'privatised' CFA-funding, and away from public legal aid,[29] has also affected multi-party litigation. Formally, the rules and guidance permit public financial support of unusually deserving group litigation.[30] In fact public funding for group litigation is seldom granted.[31] The

---

[27] The distinction between formal and economic or 'effective' access to justice was ac-knowledged in *Hamilton v Fayed (No 2)* [2002] 3 All ER 641, CA, at [65], by Chadwick LJ, and [81], by Hale LJ; on 'access to justice' and conditional fees and the decline of legal aid, see Neil Andrews, *English Civil Procedure* (Oxford UP, 2003), ch's 9, 35; for observations in the context of multi-party proceedings, C Hodges, 'The Europeanisation of Civil Justice: Trends and Issues' (2007) 26 CJQ 96, 98 ff.

[28] Generally on conditional fee agreements, MJ Cook, *Cook on Costs: 2007* (2007); M Harvey, *Guide to Conditional Fee Agreements* (2nd edn, 2006); Neil Andrews, *English Civil Procedure* (Oxford UP, 2003) ch 35; and see *Brown v Russell Young* [2007] EWCA Civ 43; [2007] 2 All ER 453 (where the court upheld the defendant's liability to pay costs of claimants under a conditional fee arrangement, both in respect of 'generic' and 'individual' costs elements).

[29] On conditional fees and the decline of legal aid, see Neil Andrews, *English Civil Procedure* (Oxford UP, 2003) ch 35.

[30] See 'The Funding Code', Part B, at section D, issued by the Community Legal Services Commission: at http://www.legalservices.gov.uk/civil/guidance/funding_code.asp.

[31] The following comment by Dr C Hodges at the 2006 Oxford conference on multi-party actions is cited with his permission: 'The funding of large cases remains complex and controversial. The size of the funding required and the 'loser pays' rule require sophisticated arrangements to be put in place in order both to fund ongoing costs and to cover the risk of losing. There is an impasse over how complex cases should be run in future. The previous freedom with which Legal Aid was dispensed has disappeared. Public funding is restricted, made available for cases only on a prioritised basis, and subject to considerable bureaucracy. The Legal Services Commission is now very wary of funding large cases, and prefers to fund test cases. Only one case (Sabril, alleged visual field constriction, made by Sanofi-Aventis) is currently funded by the LSC: the action is proceeding with test cases.'

CFA system can be useful in this context (although the impediments to this are obvious, given the high risk of defeat in some types of multi-party litigation concerning technical matters or where the substantive law is uncertain). Otherwise, at least in principle, multi-party litigation must be funded from the following private sources: (1) 'before-the-event' legal expenses insurance,[32] (2) trade union support,[33] or (3) a 'war-chest' filled by wealthy friends or relatives.[34] However, it is unlikely that any of these three sources of private finance will assist multi-party litigation.

14.11   Secondly, there is a two-level system of official approval of a Group Litigation Order. The court must first decide to grant a GLO, normally on an application, although the court can make such an order of its own motion.[35] A senior judge must then ratify that preliminary decision.[36]

14.12   Thirdly, each claimant must elect to sue ('opt-in'). He must issue a claim before being included on the GLO register.[37] A variation upon this is where the court orders a claim, originally brought as separate proceedings, to be transferred to a GLO register.[38] This process of active commencement ('opting-in') contrasts with representative proceedings. In the latter context the represented parties do not need to take a positive decision to be represented (although they can 'opt-out', see **14.08** above).[39] If the GLO deadline has been missed, a claim can be brought separately, that is, independently of the group register procedure.[40] This of course presupposes that this claim has not already become statute-barred.[41]

---

[32] In the UK 'BTE' legal expenses insurance is 'patchy', unlike Germany (where litigation costs are more predictable and the court system is speedier).

[33] Membership of trade unions has diminished since the 1970s.

[34] eg, and most notoriously, in *Hamilton v Fayed (No 2)* [2002] 3 All ER 641, CA (Hamilton, then a Member of Parliament, was helped by political 'friends' to run a defamation action against Fayed, the owner of 'Harrods'; Hamilton's friends, as non-parties, were held not to be liable to Fayed for legal costs after Hamilton lost the action); on this case, **9.14**.

[35] PD (19B) 4.

[36] PD (19 B) 3.3: such ratification to be provided by the Lord Chief Justice or, in the case of proceedings in the Chancery Division, the Vice-Chancellor, or in county courts, the Head of Civil Justice.

[37] PD (19B), 6A.

[38] CPR 19.11(3); 19.13(f); PD (19B) 10.

[39] This opt-in/opt-out procedural dilemma is examined in detail by R Mulheron, 'Some Difficulties with Group Litigation Orders – And Why a Class Action is Superior' (2005) 24 CJQ 40, 49 ff.

[40] eg *Taylor v Nugent Care Society* [2004] EWCA Civ 51; [2004] 1 WLR 1129, at [14] to [19] (not an abuse of process justifying dismissal of this independent claim, but costs sanctions are possible); on which R Mulheron, 'Some Difficulties with Group Litigation Orders – And Why a Class Action is Superior' (2005) 24 CJQ 40, 41, and passim.

[41] Limitation Act 1980; R Mulheron, 'Some Difficulties with Group Litigation Orders – And Why a Class Action is Superior' (2005) 24 CJQ 40, 56 (noting that some non-English systems suspend the limitation period once a class action starts).

Fourthly, the court manages the case in the interests of procedural efficiency **14.13** and overall fairness and equality between all sides. The court's directions can include the following:[42] providing for one or more claims on the group register to proceed as test claims;[43] appointing the solicitor of one or more parties to be the lead solicitor for the claimants or defendants;[44] specifying the details to be included in a statement of case in order to show that the criteria for entry of the claim on the group register have been met;[45] or specifying a date after which no claim may be added to the group register unless the court gives permission (see also Senior Master Turner's summary, presented at **14.16** below).[46]

Fifthly, if the group loses the case, each group member is liable to the vic- **14.14** torious party both for that member's share of the common costs of the proceedings and for any individual costs specifically incurred with respect to his claim. 'Common costs' take three forms: 'costs incurred in relation to the GLO issues'; 'individual costs incurred in a claim which is proceeding as a test claim'; 'costs incurred by the lead solicitor in administering the group litigation.' 'Group litigants' will normally be subject to an 'order for common costs'. This order will impose 'on each group litigant several liability for an equal proportion of those common costs'.[47] If the group is victorious, the defeated party is liable to pay costs attributable both to the 'common costs' and the 'individual costs'.[48] It has been held that the defeated defendant must pay the victorious party's 'common' and 'individual' costs where the latter's claim (as part of 'group litigation') has been funded under a conditional fee agreement.[49]

Sixthly, the court's decision on a 'common' issue is binding on (and in fa- **14.15** vour of) all members of the group. A party who is adversely affected by a judgment or order can seek permission to appeal.[50] Such a 'common' issue will normally concern questions of liability or the availability of a particular head of loss. Thereafter, however, each claimant must establish that he has suffered

---

[42] For greater detail, see the list of issues described in C Hodges, *Multi-Party Actions* (Oxford UP, 2001) 5.06 and 5.07.

[43] CPR 19.13(b).

[44] ibid (c).

[45] ibid (d); on this question, see the observations of Lord Woolf in *Boake Allen Ltd v Revenue and Customs* [2007] UKHL 25 at [33].

[46] ibid (e).

[47] CPR 48.6A(3); for comment, C Hodges, *Multi-Party Actions* (Oxford UP, 2001) 8.1 and 8.11.

[48] Subtleties, including the position of (i) discontinuing or (ii) settling or (iii) dismissing individual claimants, were considered in *Sayers v Merck & SmithKline Beecham plc* [2002] 1 WLR 2274, CA; noted M Goldberg (2002) New LJ 437–8 and M Mildred (2002) 65 MLR 597.

[49] *Brown v Russell Young* [2007] EWCA Civ 43; [2007] 2 All ER 453; on conditional fee agreements generally, MJ Cook, *Cook on Costs: 2007* (2007); M Harvey, *Guide to Conditional Fee Agreements* (2nd edn, 2006); Neil Andrews, *English Civil Procedure* (Oxford UP, 2003) ch 35.

[50] CPR 19.12(2).

personal loss.[51] English law does not award damages without proof of actual loss suffered by individual claimants. Exemplary damages are not awarded for breach of contract.[52] The categories of exemplary damages for tort claims are restricted to oppressive, arbitrary or unconstitutional conduct by public servants, or wrongdoing cynically calculated to achieve a gain, or to statutory instances of punitive damages.[53]

(4) Judicial Comments on the Group Litigation System

14.16 I am grateful to the former Senior Master of the Queen's Bench Division, and Queen's Remembrancer, Robert Turner, for these remarks (given to the author, May 2007)[54] on recent group litigation.

Background to the CPR Rule on Representative Proceedings

(1) 'It was very obvious before Lord Woolf's reforms that the English civil procedure system lacked a practical means for dealing with multiple party claims. The rules for representative actions did not work and were seldom resorted to.[55] Consolidation was a heavy-handed approach to the problem. It could only really be used if the same two firms of solicitors were representing the relevant sets of claimants and defendants. Furthermore, consolidation could only be used once the litigation had commenced. A new approach was required. Introduction of the concept of the GLO was one of the brainwaves of Lord Woolf's reports and inquiry.[56] It provided access to justice for a whole range of claimants who might not otherwise have braved the prospect of litigation. The case management tools of the

---

[51] CPR 19.12(1)(a): a judgment or order made in a claim on the group register in respect of a common issue (a 'GLO issue') binds all the parties to 'other claims that are on the group register at the time the judgment is given or the order is made unless the court orders otherwise'.

[52] *Addis v Gramophone Co Ltd* [1909] AC 488, HL; *Perera v Vandiyar* [1953] 1 WLR 672, CA; *Kenny v Preen* [1963] 1 QB 499, CA; see also Lord Lloyd in *Ruxley Electronics and Construction Ltd v Forsyth* [1996] 1 AC 344, 373 E, HL; 'Aggravated, Exemplary and Restitutionary Damages', (L Com No 247, 1997) 5.71–5.73; cf *Design Progression Ltd v Thurloe Properties Ltd* [2004] EWHC 324 (Ch); [2005] 1 WLR 1, Peter Smith J (exemplary damages against a landlord for statutory wrong; and remarks ibid at [137] ff); R Cunningham, 'Should Punitive Damages be Part of the Judicial Arsenal in Contract Cases? (2006) 26 LS 369.

[53] *Kuddus v Chief Constable of Leicerstershire* [2001] UKHL 29; [2002] 2 AC 122 (noting *Rookes v Barnard* [1964] AC 1129, 1223, 1227, HL, per Lord Devlin).

[54] I should like to record my gratitude to him, and to his colleague Master John Leslie, Queen's Bench Division, for their support over many years to the Civil Procedure class, University of Cambridge.

[55] Referring to CPR 19.6's precursors in the RSC and CCR rules (pre-CPR rules for High court and county court litigation, respectively): on the representative system, which survives, but is seldom effective other than for injunctions and declaratory relief, see **14.02** ff above.

[56] Lord Woolf, 'Access to Justice: Final Report' (June 1996) 223–248.

multi-track were well suited to the challenges of the GLO. A balance was possible between the claimants and the defendants.'

(2) 'The new rule CPR 19.11 was one of the shortest and simplest Rules introduced by the CPR. It has proved easy to apply and has left scope to the judges making the Orders and managing the claims to use their initiative and imagination. However, the new system has raised some new procedural challenges. The GLO system requires a high degree of co-operation between all the participants. These are the main procedural issues raised under the new system:

  i.   How should the GLO issues be defined?
  ii. Who should be the lead solicitor for the claimants and the defendants?
  iii. How do you manage the Register?
  iv. Should you issue single claims and pay the fee or could you avoid this by issuing a single claim with a schedule of claimants etc?
  v.   How do you publicise the existence of the GLO?
  vi. How do you determine the cut off date for joining the GLO?'

The Preliminary Hearing

(3) 'This calls for real skill on the part of the judge (in the High Court in London where most such cases start – this will be either the Senior Master or the Chief Master). There can be up to 100 lawyers present representing 3,400 claimants and three defendants. There will be up to half a dozen Silks in the front row and scores of juniors and solicitors behind. All must have their say but somehow 'agreement' must be achieved as GLOs only work if the parties and especially their lawyers cooperate.'

The Draft Order

(4) 'It is essential for the parties to liaise in advance of the hearing to attempt to prepare the initial draft Order. The judge needs to have substantial experience. The Senior Master (Robert Turner) has prepared a system for provincial judges who need to get the approval of the President of the QBD or the Head of Civil Justice. Their Orders are sent to him for informal advice on their contents and their form. One of his senior managers checks through the Order with the Senior Master and, if necessary, they send it back to the provincial judge to redraft.'

The Approval Mechanism

(5) 'This was intended to deter too many of these orders being made. It has been successful. The Senior Master is not aware of any of the approval judges actually refusing to approve an order submitted to them but the need to seek their approval has limited the number of Orders made.'

The Management Role of the Judge

(6) 'The managing judges need certain qualities: patience; authority; common sense; decisiveness.'

The Range of GLOs[57]

(7) 'A Register of GLOs is kept by the Senior Master and by the Law Society. The titles of the Orders do not always do justice to the complexity or the range of the claims. The Senior Master has recently dealt with the following GLOs:

   i.   A hotel in Spain to which tour operators sent parties long after they allegedly knew of the serious risk of food poisoning that existed.

   ii.   The Alder Hey hospital organ removal litigation involving hundreds of deceased young children and their grieving families. The Senior Master sent this to mediation with huge success.

   iii. The hot drinks claims against McDonalds. These claims failed (in England).

   iv. Long distance flight thrombosis claims.[58]

   v.   Removal of indigenous inhabitants from the Chagos Islands in the Indian Ocean.[59]

   vi. The unexploded shells cases from the Army's training areas in Kenya.

   vii. Pension cases where long-serving employees were allegedly cheated out of their final salary pension entitlements.

   viii. The Buncefield disaster (explosion at oil depot; devastation of vicinity; property claims; 3,400 claimants).

   ix. Ivory Coast contamination claims, involving oil dumping.'

Success of the GLO System

(8) Senior Master Robert Turner comments: 'in the GLOs with which I have been involved we have achieved settlements or decisions in half or a third of the time that normal litigation might have taken. The parties have always gone away satisfied by the result. Demands on the Court have been greatly reduced. Many people who might otherwise have not obtained just compensation have gained a remedy which they would not have attempted to seek but for the existence of the GLO system.'

---

[57] See the list at http://www.hmcourts-service.gov.uk/cms/150.htm.

[58] *Deep Vein Thrombosis and Air Travel Group Litigation* [2005] UKHL 72; [2006] 1 AC 495.

[59] G Scanlan, 'The Chagos Islanders' Case-a Question of Limitation?' (2007) 26 CJQ 292.

Bibliography of Foreign Material

For convenience, this large body of material is cited in the final note to this chapter[60] (literature concerning *English* multi-party litigation is cited in the notes at **14.01** at the beginning of this chapter). The topic was also considered

---

[60] American Law Institute, 'Principles of the Law of Aggregate Litigation' (Discussion draft, 2007): reporter Samuel Issacharoff (New York University); associate reporters Robert H Klonoff (Missouri-Kansas Law Schools), Richard A Nagareda (Vanderbilt Univ L School), Charles Silver (University of Texas L School, Austin) – ch 1 'Definitions and General Principles', ch 2 'Aggregate Treatment of Common Issues', ch 3 'Aggregate Settlements'; this document contains substantial references to US literature); B Bresner, 'Recent Developments in Class Action Litigation in Canada' (1998) Int Jo of Insurance Law, 187; J Bronsteen and O Fiss, 'The Class Action Rule' (2006) 78 Notre Dame L R 1419; Stephen B Burbank, 'The Class Action in American Securities Regulation' (1999) 4 ZZP Int, 321 (esp at 322–6, 332–6, on the history and prospects of federal class actions in the US); Richard B Cappalli and Claudio Consolo, 'Class Actions for Continental Europe? A Preliminary Inquiry' (1992) 6 Temple Int and Comp LJ 217 (at 261 ff, Consolo considers various ways of conceptualising representative claims); the Duke Law School symposium (co-ordinated by T Rowe): 'Debates Over Group Litigation in Comparative Perspective' (Duke/Geneva symposium, 2000): (2001) 11 Duke Jo of Int & Comp Law 157–421: Jack B Weinstein (USA); Deborah H Hensler (USA); Edward H Cooper (USA); Neil Andrews (England); Garry D Watson (Canada); S Stuart Clark and Christina Harris (Australia); Christopher Hodges (Europe); Harald Koch (Germany and EU); Gerhard Walter (Germany and Switzerland); Roberth Nordh (Sweden); Michele Taruffo (Comparative Comments); H Erichson, 'Doing Good, Doing Well' (2004) 57 Vand L R 2087; A Gidi, 'Class Actions in Brazil-A Model for Civil Law Countries' (2003) 51 Am J Comp L 311; B Hay and D Rosenberg, '"Sweetheart" and "Blackmail" Settlement in Class Actions: Reality and Remedy' (2000) 75 Notre Dame L R 1377; E D Hensler, 'The New Social Policy Torts: Litigation as a Legislative Strategy ...' (2001) 51 DePaul L R 493; JA Jolowicz, 'Protection of Diffuse, Fragmented and Collective Interests', in *On Civil Procedure* (Cambridge UP, 2000) 97 (comparative discussion of various procedures for vindicating or recognizing such interests, under English, US and French law); PH Lindblom and G Watson, 'Complex Litigation – A Comparative Perspective' (1993) 12 CJQ 33 (overview of various jurisdictions' approach to complex litigation); PH Lindblom, 'Individual Litigation and Mass Justice: A Swedish Perspective and Proposal on Group Actions in Civil Procedure' (1997) 45 Amer J Comp L 805; RL Marcus, 'Reassessing the Magnetic Pull of Megacases on Procedure' (2001) 51 DePaul L Rev 457 (considering complex commercial, public law and mass tort litigation); A Miller, 'Of Frankenstein Monsters and Shining Knights: Myth, Reality and the "Class Action Problem"' (1979) 92 Harv LR 664; Pennsylvania, University of: Symposium on Class Actions and Mass Torts: Edward H Cooper, 'Aggregation and Settlement of Mass Torts' (2000) 148 U of Pennsylvania L Rev 1943; Edward R Becker and Jerome M Marcus, 'Penn Law School Mass Torts Symposium: A Response to Professor Cooper', ibid, 2001; Richard L Marcus, 'Benign Neglect Reconsidered', ibid 2009; David L Shapiro, 'Class Actions: The Class as Party and Client' (1998) 73 Notre Dame L Rev 913 (considered by Silberman, see citation in this note, below, at 210–2); J Resnik, 'From Cases to Litigation' (1991) 54 Law & Contemp Prob 5; R Phillips, 'Class Action & Joinder in Mississippi' (2001) 71 Miss LJ 447; P Schuck, *Agent Orange on Trial: Mass Toxic Disasters in Courts* (Harvard UP, 1986); E Sherman, 'Consumer Class Actions: Who Are the Real Winners?' (2004) 56 Me L Rev 223; Linda Silberman, 'The Vicissitudes of the American Class Action – With a Comparative Eye' (1999) 7 Tulane Jo of Int and Comp Law 201; Charles Silver, 'Class Actions ...' in B Bouckaert and G De Geest (eds), *Encyclopaedia*

at the World Congress in Brazil (2007), and another colloquium was held in Oxford in December 2007. For publication details of the Brazil conference see n 73 at **2.22**.

of Law and Economics, (Edward Elgar Publishing, 2000) vol V, 194 ff; SC Yeazell, *From Mediaeval Group Litigation to the Modern Class Action* (Yale UP, New Haven, 1987) (historical survey of representative proceedings in England and the US).

Index

Veröffentlichungen zum Verfahrensrecht

Herausgegeben von Rolf Stürner und Gerhard Walter

Alphabetische Übersicht

Kwaschik, Annett: Die Parteivernehmung und der Grundsatz der Waffengleichheit im Zivilprozeß. 2004. *Band 35.*

Lames, Peter: Rechtsfortbildung als Prozeßzweck. 1993. *Band 9.*

Lüke, Wolfgang: Die Beteiligung Dritter im Zivilprozeß. 1993. *Band 8.*

Marotzke, Wolfgang: Von der schutzgesetzlichen Unterlassungsklage zur Verbandsklage. 1992. *Band 6.*

McGuire, Mary-Rose: Verfahrenskoordination und Verjährungsunterbrechung im Europäischen Prozessrecht. 2004. *Band 34.*

Miras, Antonio: Die Entwicklung des spanischen Zivilprozeßrechts. 1994. *Band 12.*

Mossler, Sven F. : Beschleunigter Rechtsschutz für Zahlungsgläubiger in Europa. 2004. *Band 38.*

Müller, Henning Ernst: Behördliche Geheimhaltung und Entlastungsvorbringen des Angeklagten. 1992. *Band 7.*

Oepen, Klaus: Massefremde Masse. 1999. *Band 21.*

Otte, Karsten: Umfassende Streitentscheidung durch Beachtung von Sachzusammenhängen. 1998. *Band 19.*

Reichenbach, Sandy B.: § 1004 BGB als Grundlage von Beweisverboten. 2004. *Band 37.*

Reischl, Klaus: Die objektiven Grenzen der Rechtskraft im Zivilprozeß. 2002. *Band 28.*

Riepl, Frank: Informationelle Selbstbestimmung im Strafverfahren. 1998. *Band 17.*

Rink, Florian: Die Sicherheit von Grundpfandrechten in Deutschland und England. 2006. *Band 43.*

Ritz, Philipp: Die Geheimhaltung im Schiedsverfahren nach schweizerischem Recht. 2007. *Band 48.*

Rott, Thilo: Vereinheitlichung des Rechts der Mobiliarsicherheit. 2000. *Band 23.*

Schafft, Thomas: Selektion von Rechtsmittelverfahren durch gesetzliche Zugangsbeschränkungen. 2005. *Band 40.*

Scheuermann, Isabel: Internationales Zivilverfahrensrecht bei Verträgen im Internet. 2004. *Band 36.*

Schnabl, Daniel: Die Anhörungsrüge nach § 321a ZPO. 2007. *Band 44.*

Stadler, Astrid: Der Schutz des Unternehmensgeheimnisses im deutschen und U.S.-amerikanischen Zivilprozeß und im Rechtshilfeverfahren. 1989. *Band 3.*

Städtler, Hans Jörg: Grundpfandrechte in der Insolvenz. 1998. *Band 18.*

Stürner, Rolf: Die richterliche Aufklärung im Zivilprozeß. 1982. *Band 1.*

Timmerbeil, Sven: Witness Coaching und Adversary System. 2004. *Band 33.*

Toepel, Friedrich: Grundstrukturen des Sachverständigenbeweises im Strafprozeßrecht. 2002. *Band 27.*

Ziegert, Kathrin: Die Interventionswirkung. 2003. *Band 30.*

Einen Gesamtkatalog erhalten Sie kostenlos vom Verlag
Mohr Siebeck · Postfach 2040 · D-72010 Tübingen.
Neueste Informationen im Internet unter www.mohr.de